Reimagining Political Ecology

New Ecologies for the Twenty-First Century

SERIES EDITORS:

Arturo Escobar, University of North Carolina, Chapel Hill

Dianne Rocheleau, Clark University

Reimagining Political Ecology

Edited by Aletta Biersack and James B. Greenberg

DUKE UNIVERSITY PRESS

Durham & London 2006

Printed in the United States of America on acid-free paper ∞

Designed by Erin Kirk New

Typeset in Galliard by Tseng Information Systems, Inc.

Library of Congress Cataloging-in-Publication Data appear on the last printed
page of this book.

Duke University Press gratefully acknowledges the support of two organizations
that provided funds toward the production of this book:

NORDECO Foundation (Nordic Agency for Development and Ecology) of
Copenhagen, Denmark

Provost's Author Support Fund of the University of Arizona

For Roy A. Rappaport (1926–97)

in continuing conversation

Contents

About the Series

There is widespread agreement about the existence of a generalized ecological crisis in today's world. There is also a growing realization that the existing disciplines are not well equipped to account for this crisis, let alone furnish workable solutions; a broad consensus exists on the need for new models of thought, including more constructive engagement among the natural, social, and humanistic perspectives. At the same time, the proliferation of social movements that articulate their knowledge claims in cultural and ecological terms has become an undeniable social fact. This series is situated at the intersection of these two trends. We seek to join critical conversations in academic fields about nature, globalization, and culture with intellectual and political conversations in social movements and among other popular and expert groups about environment, place, and alternative socionatural orders. Our objectives are to construct bridges among these theoretical and political developments in the disciplines and in nonacademic arenas and to create synergies for thinking anew about the real promise of emergent ecologies. We are interested in those works that enable us to envision instances of ecological viability as well as more lasting and just ways of being-in-place and being-in-networks with a diversity of humans and other living beings and nonliving artifacts.

New Ecologies for the Twenty-First Century aims at promoting a dialogue among those engaged in transforming our understanding and practice of the relation between nature and culture. This includes revisiting new fields (such as environmental history, historical ecology, ecological economics, or political ecology), tendencies (such as the application of theories of complexity to rethinking a range of questions, from evolution to ecosystems), and epistemological concerns (e.g., constructivists' sensitivity toward scientific analyses and scientists' openness to considering the immersion of material life in meaning-giving practices). We find this situation hopeful for a real dialogue among the natural, social, and human sciences. Similarly, the knowledge produced by social movements in their struggles is becoming essential for envisioning sustainability and conservation. We hope that these trends will become a point of convergence for forward-looking theory, policy, and practical action. We seek to provide a forum for authors and readers to widen—and perhaps reconstitute—the fields of theoretical inquiry, professional practice, and social struggles that characterize the environmental arena at present.

Acknowledgments

Four of the contributions (those of Dove, Greenberg, Lansing, and Pálsson) were given in truncated and draft form on the panel that Aletta Biersack and James Greenberg organized for the 1997 annual meeting of the American Anthropological Association in honor of Roy A. Rappaport ("Culture/Power/History/Nature: Papers in Honor of Roy A. Rappaport"). The panel was the second organized session of the newly organized Anthropology and Environment section of the American Anthropological Association (see Crumley, ed., 2001, for the papers of the inaugural session, "Human Dimensions of Environmental Change: Anthropology Engages the Issues"). Alf Hornborg's paper on the 1997 panel, "Ecological Knowledge and Personhood: Rethinking Cognized Models," appears as "Ecological Knowledge and Personhood: Have We Always Been Capitalists?" in *Ecology and the Sacred*, edited by Ellen Messer and Michael Lambek (2001). Conrad Kottak's paper on this occasion appears as "The New Ecological Anthropology" in "Ecologies for Tomorrow: Reading Rappaport Today," edited by Aletta Biersack (1999:23–35). Others giving papers on the 1997 panel included Philippe Descola and Jonathan Friedman. Arturo Escobar, Maurice Godelier, and Pete Vayda served as the panel's very capable discussants. Jim Greenberg and I thank all participants for making the occasion memorable. We would like also to thank Ellen Messer and Michael Lambek for discussions in 1996 about Rappaport's work and how best to mark his passing (see their edited volume *Ecology and the Sacred* [2001]). The contributors, along with Jerry Jacka and Quent Winterhoff, prepared the artwork for this volume. Finally, Jim Greenberg and I would like to thank Skip Rappaport for encouraging the project and for his years of mentoring.

Introduction

Reimagining Political Ecology: Culture/Power/History/Nature

Aletta Biersack

The term *political ecology* was first used in its neo-Marxist sense by the anthropologist Eric R. Wolf (1972) to signify the study of how power relations mediate human–environment relations.[1] In this it marked a departure from the canonical texts of Marx and Engels, which, for all their investment in economic analysis, nonetheless ignored nature and the environment.[2] Placing power at the center of analysis, political ecology also differed from an apolitical "cultural" ecology that focused on the problematics of adaptation to the environment without attending to the structures of inequality that mediated human–nature articulations (Friedman 1974). In combining political economy with ecology, political ecology strove to rectify the deficiencies in both frameworks, a merger that geographers would announce in the 1980s (see Blaikie and Brookfield 1987:17).

Political ecology's political economy is not the political economy of Marx and Engels. Rather, it grew out of "dependency theory," associated by anglophones with the writings of Andre Gunder Frank (1969a), and the "world system theory" of Immanuel Wallerstein (1974). The latter in particular envisioned class in global terms. The workers of the world lived for the most part in "third world" nations on the "periphery" of the world system while the capitalist "owners of the means of production" resided primarily in "first world" nations in the "core" of the world system. The world system was thus as much a geography as it was a structure, a stratified geography of developed and undeveloped nations.

Beginning in the 1980s, social science would grapple with "postmodernist" critiques of the simplifications of "modernist" theories, theories that, for starters, were heavily invested in the dualistic view that nature existed outside the human realm, as a distinct, independent order (see Pálsson, this volume). Postmodernism also attacked theories that read the trajectory of history in terms of an idea of progress and that emphasized overarching, coherent, rationalized wholes (system, structures, totalities) on the grounds that such theories failed to acknowledge difference, the partiality and bias of any one perspective, fragmentation, and incoherence. Structural Marxism, of which world system theory was one exemplification—as totalizing, as grand-theoretical, as Eurocentric, as teleological, and as progress-oriented a framework as one is likely to find—together with political ecology, structural Marxism's most recent offspring, was vulnerable to the postmodernist critique.

Political ecology has engaged with these and other aspects of late twentieth-century theory, transforming itself from the neo-Marxism of world system theory to discernibly *post*-Marxist frameworks.[3] Key to today's political ecology are five provocative theoretical reorientations:

1. Earlier ecologies, including political ecology in its first generation, differentiated symbolic from material factors (in the Marxist lexicon, superstructure from base) and tended to reduce the one to the other.[4] Today's political ecology resists such reductions and focuses upon the nexus of symbolic and material factors, how each conditions the other. Moreover, and more radically, whereas reality had been defined as extrasymbolic, a matter of simple fact, political ecologists today recognize that reality, insofar as it is invested with meaning, is produced "discursively," through signifying practices of various sorts, an argument that postmodernism shares with strands of poststructuralism.[5]

2. Relatedly, today's political ecologists critique the nature/culture dualism and focus upon the reciprocal impacts of nature and culture, using such terms as *second*, *social*, or *humanized* nature to signify a nature that is the by-product of human conceptualizations, activities, and regulations—a nature, as it were, that is *after* nature (Escobar 1999).[6]

3. As noted, political ecology in its first generation wedded ecology to world system theory, a theory that envisioned the world as organized into a single class system, first-world nations owning the means of production and third-world nations supplying the labor and producing the surplus value. Ecology, meanwhile, tended to focus on the local, overlooking the global. Neither framework considered the dynamics of local–global articulations, the emphasis of political ecology today.

4. Political ecology in its first generation and the cultural ecology that pre-ceded it tended to think in terms of structures, systems, and interlocking variables and had little to say about actors and their agency. Today's political ecology inevitably engages to some degree with "practice theory" (Bour-dieu 1977; Ortner 1984), a theory that attends to the constraints of structure but also to the indeterminacies of agency and events.

5. The range of differences and social inequalities that are relevant to today's political ecology is broad. In thinking beyond the class inequalities of classi-cal Marxism (which is notoriously gender blind), political ecology has been inspired by feminism, but differences of "race" and ethnicity, among others, are also crucial in theorizing human–nature articulations.

The turn of any century is a time for taking stock. This volume looks at where political ecology has been and where it is headed, at least in the near term. *Reimagining Political Ecology* is by design vaguely oxymoronic. Politi-cal ecology is certifiably materialistic, but *imagining* and *imagination* are code words for meaning-centered approaches, and the title strives to place the ten-sions between neo- and post-Marxist perspectives at the center of our under-standing of what political ecology is and what it might be. Responding to sev-eral crosscurrents in social theory, today's political ecology is "grounded less in a coherent theory" (Peet and Watts 1996:6) than in a fluid and ambivalent space that lies among political economy, culture theory, history, and biology. The volume's title gestures toward this terrain, inviting its readers to enter the space of culture/power/history/nature. Within this space "diverse networks of scholars and other concerned groups may communicate" (Blaikie 1999:131).

The introduction begins with a discussion of one particular legacy, in equal measure fertile and problematic: the work of Roy A. Rappaport (1926–97). Rappaport was a complex "linking" figure (Brosius 1999c:278, n. 4). His *Pigs for the Ancestors* was overtly and self-consciously "ecosystemic," informed by the notion that cultural processes must be understood as adaptive devices. Yet he is remembered as much for his claim that in the human realm constraint is symbolic and not just material, a matter of meaning as much as of need. Rappa-port's work helps steer us between idealism and materialism, toward subtle and nuanced approaches to human–nature relations in all their complexity. Four of the contributors (Brosius, Greenberg, Lansing, and myself) were Rappa-port's students, and we trust he would have reveled in our various engagements with, and departures from, his teachings and writings, as well as in the choice of venue for this volume: Escobar's and Rocheleau's interdisciplinary series

"New Ecologies for the Twenty-First Century." The introduction's second section chronicles the onset of political ecology in the 1970s and 1980s. Although Wolf (1972) was the first to use the term *political ecology* in a neo-Marxist sense, neo-Marxist political ecology was developed more by geographers than by anthropologists, a story that is told, however synoptically, in the second section of this introduction. The third, fourth, fifth, and sixth sections expand upon the five shifts in premise summarized above. The penultimate section proposes a research agenda for today, and the final section briefly introduces the contributions to this volume.

Rappaport's Bridging Work

Published in 1968, Rappaport's *Pigs for the Ancestors* is a classic of modernist ecology. In its vision of nature as independent from, and prior to, culture, *Pigs for the Ancestors* pronounced science to be the epistemology of choice (see Dove, this volume). Written before the critique of anthropological writing (Clifford and Marcus, eds., 1986; Marcus and Fischer 1986), *Pigs for the Ancestors* paid considerable attention to the local worldview but favored the "operational" (or, in the language of Marvin Harris, "etic") models of science to indigenous, "cognized" (or etic) perspectives. Moreover, *Pigs'* nature is extrahuman, an "environment." It was not itself a construct of the human imagination or, indeed, an artifact of human activity—a nature that is social, human, historical, the by-product rather than the condition of human occupation.

The book concerned the Tsembaga Maring of New Guinea and how a ritual sacrifice, the *kaiko*, functioned to regulate human–nature, human–human, and even local–regional relations. The kaiko was a massive pig slaughter to honor and feed ancestral guardians and to compensate allies in time of war. As long as the ancestors were not reciprocated for their support with this prestation of pork, warfare could not continue, and so the kaiko and the extensive preparations for it marked a lull in Maring warfare. The kaiko could not occur until there was a critical mass of fattened pigs to appease the ancestors and to compensate the allies for their losses, protracting this lull. But there was a downside to this martial intermission. Maring women were responsible for feeding the pigs, and as the pigs fattened, the women's labor intensified. The pigs, meanwhile, became more and more unruly, raiding gardens for food. In this way, pressures on women and gardens mounted to a breaking point, when the pigs were finally sacrificed. Among other things, the kaiko functioned to disperse pork and protein widely throughout a regional population. Thus, the kaiko served multiple purposes: social, political, economic, nutritional, and environmental.

While Rappaport explicitly undertook to demonstrate human adaptations to a nature that stood outside the human realm, it is clear in retrospect that what he actually offered in *Pigs for the Ancestors* was an ethnography of nature, as it were: a study of the intersection of culture and nature, rooted as this intersection is in human activity, conceptualization, values, and social relations. Everything depends on how we understand the kaiko. The kaiko may indeed have resolved a number of difficulties, but it is also true that the kaiko—and the entire logic of warfare, compensation, sacrifice, and gender relations that was foundational to it—was the cause of these problems. Explaining the kaiko functionally ignores the maladies that flow from *it*. What is needed is not a functionalist explanation of the kaiko—which, in any case, will always be contradicted by the fact that the kaiko causes the very conditions it is said to relieve—but an ethnography of the entire range of human–nature interchanges of which the kaiko is but one moment—in short, an *ethnography* of nature.[7]

Rappaport borrowed from systems theory, cybernetics, and nutritional science in a way that was compelling for the time (see Dove, this volume; Dove 2001) but that drew sharp criticism in the 1970s from culturalists (Sahlins 1976) and from those influenced by the critique of positivism at the heart of the "interpretive turn" (Geertz 1973). As political economy gained ground—spurred on by such landmark texts as Wolf's *Europe and the People Without History*—the failure of *Pigs for the Ancestors* to attend to history also came under attack. It was argued that the work presumed, without demonstrating, equilibrium, self-regulation, or homeostasis; that it overlooked social actors and their choices; that it "vulgarly" ignored the social relations of production, which organized human–nature articulations; that it reduced culture to nature; that it was ahistorical and localistic, ignoring global factors.[8]

Rappaport responded to such criticism with a signature move, one that helped shift ecology away from the dichotomization of symbolic and material approaches that was endemic to the social theory of the day. He argued that humanity lives "in terms of meanings in a physical world devoid of intrinsic meaning but subject to causal law" (back cover of the paperback edition of *Ecology, Meaning, and Religion*) and that any ecology "must take account of meaning as well as cause, and of the complex dynamic of their relationship" (ibid.; see Messer and Lambek, eds., 2001).[9] Recognizing that meaning might not lead to adaptive behavior, Rappaport also countenanced, in violation of functionalism's tenets, the possibility of maladaptation. Such observations led Rappaport to elaborate a general model of adaptive systems and their "disorders" (1979, 1994a, 1994b), and in these ruminations can be found an explicit critique of "the maladies of civilization" (Hvalkof and Escobar 1998:430) as well as an implicit, albeit incipient, political ecology.

In fact, Rappaport's intellectual trajectory drew him slowly, tacitly toward political ecology (see Greenberg, this volume). His "engaged" and "repatriated" anthropology—announced in "The Anthropology of Trouble," the Distinguished Lecture in General Anthropology delivered at the annual meeting of the American Anthropological Association in 1992 (Rappaport 1993) —focused specifically on what his earlier analysis of a New Guinea society had neglected: matters of political economy. Although Rappaport's analysis is couched in terms of "the disordering of adaptive structures" (Rappaport 1994a:273), it could also be understood as a "green" indictment of the indifference of capitalism per se to ecological values and an exposure of the conflict or contradiction between two kinds of material factors, the one economic and the other biological, stemming from this indifference. Rappaport's policy-related theoretical contributions are implicitly political ecological, but with the stylish twist of an "interpretive turn," a turn to meaning. It is toward a kind of political ecology that Rappaport gestured in his discussion of a "general conception of adaptation and maladaptation" (1994b:301) in his contribution to Robert Borofsky's *Assessing Cultural Anthropology*: "The 'macroanthropological' formulation represented here seems to bear closer resemblance to political economy, to some forms of ecological anthropology, and to a good deal of theorizing in archeology" (ibid.). Indeed, in the last years of his life, Rappaport served on the editorial board of the *Journal of Political Ecology* (Greenberg, personal communication).

Enter Political Ecology

The adaptationist paradigm of cultural ecology explained culture through its adjustments to an extrahuman order, reducing culture to nature. This argument precludes a focus on human–nature relations in other than adaptationist and reductionist terms. Moreover, to the extent that nature is considered the sole causal force, all power resides therein, and power ceases to be sociohistorical and structural.

Marxism provides a tonic to these suppositions in insisting on the socio-historical character of power and the centrality of the political to any analysis. Political ecology is rooted in the twentieth-century variants of traditional Marxism dependency theory and world system theory. As noted, world system theory envisions a global class system, the owners of the means of production residing in a systemic, but also spatialized (first world), center or core, while many workers are located in an equally systemic and spatialized (third world) periphery. This system is a system of domination and exploitation, workers selling their labor at a discount on the periphery but buying core-generated commodities at a premium within a structure of dependency and underdevelopment (Frank 1969a). Whereas earlier ecologies typically concentrated upon a local population, community, society, or culture, political economy targets the complex hierarchies and cross-cutting linkages through which communities are embedded in larger political, economic, and social structures (Wolf 1982). The implication for ecology is that the local is subordinated to a global system of power relations and must be understood entirely with respect to that subjection, in terms of what is commonly referred to as capitalist penetration and its effects. Dependency theory and world system theory recast capitalism on a global scale, locating exploitation in underdeveloped or third world countries (Ragin and Chirot 1984; Wolf 1982).

The first Marxist use of the term *political ecology* appears to have been that of Eric Wolf. At the time Rappaport's colleague at the University of Michigan, Wolf published an afterword to "Dynamics of Ownership in the Alpine Context" (1972:201–05), a panel of papers presented at the annual meeting of the American Anthropological Association in 1971, and in this afterword Wolf iterated again and again what would become the mantra of political ecology in its first generation: that local-level analysis was inadequate to the task, that village ecology could be understood only if the village were set within a wider framework (see Goodman and Leatherman 1998:13; Greenberg and Park 1994; Peet and Watts 1996:4–5). This is the theme of all of Wolf's writings. Most notably, it is the theme of his magnum opus, *Europe and the People Without History*, which argued that the "insights of anthropology" must be "rethought in the light of a new, historically oriented political economy" (1982:ix), the political economy of Frank and Wallerstein (ibid.:21–23).

A year after Wolf published his afterword, Bernard Nietschmann published *Between Land and Water*, which examined the subsistence ecology of the Miskito Indians of eastern Nicaragua in political economic terms. Nietschmann taught at the University of Michigan, where he was influenced by both Wolf and Rappaport. In this study, Nietschmann focused not only on "the interrelationships of human subsistence needs and means and environmental stability within a local system" (1973:2), but also on "how forces generated from larger and more complex social and economic systems have changed, disrupted, and are destroying the ecological and social stability of the Miskito system" (ibid.). Tearing a page from *Pigs for the Ancestors*, which he specifically cited, Nietschmann described the Miskito subsistence system as "a complex system incorporating various mechanisms and characteristics for regulation and adaptation" (ibid.:231). Yet he also considered the impact of superordinate forces upon local equilibria: "Many of the Miskito's reactions and adaptations to outside systems have been and are increasingly maladaptive in that they tend to simplify and degrade ecosystems and decrease social control of access to, and distribution of resources" (ibid.:237). Even in this regard, Nietschmann drew sustenance from Rappaport. Such disequilibria evidenced "a trend toward hypercoherence, or too much coherence with outside systems" (ibid.:243) and an "overall tendency toward reducing the Miskito's general purpose system organized around subsistence for the community's population to a specific purpose system oriented toward differentiated access" (ibid.; see Greenberg, this volume). Nietschmann thus drew Rappaport's ecosystemic analysis—again, explicitly cited—onto political ecological terrain.

Nietschmann was a geographer, and leadership in the first generation of political ecology belonged within geography, where a "radical development geography" (Bryant 1998:80) argued "against neo-Malthusian notions of how best to deal with the world's growing population and ecological 'crisis' " (ibid.) and that "mainstream environmental research" had focused narrowly on demographic factors, neglecting questions of political economy and in particular the inequalities of capitalism (ibid.; see note 1). Thus, in his contribution to *Interpretations of Calamity*, Michael Watts insisted that "the relation between nature and society" (1983a:257) was grounded "in the labour/process and the irreducibly intersubjective quality of social life" (ibid.:257–58; see also Friedman 1974). These relations were ultimately not local but global—with respect to famines in Hausaland, for example, a matter of the impact of colonialism on the "social relations of production and hence the relation between nature and society" (ibid.:258). This argument was elaborated in Watts's monograph *Silent Violence*. Before capitalism, Watts argued, subsistence could be secured in "a type of moral economy" (1983b:xxii–xxiii), understood in Thompsian terms, and this moral economy had enabled peasants to withstand the ordinary risks of agricultural production (ibid.:xxii). But with market penetration and the expansion of commodity production, the moral economy was undermined and peasants became newly "vulnerable to both market crises and the climate" (ibid.:xxiii). "As a result, colonial famines were not natural, drought-induced disasters but in a real sense socially produced" (ibid.) through the commoditization of food production (ibid.) and the loss of prior safety nets.

Equally pathbreaking, *The Political Economy of Soil Erosion in Developing Countries* by Piers Blaikie (1985) powerfully and explicitly merged environmental studies with political economy. The book focused on "the ways in which the development of capitalism affects peasantries and pastoralists, and thereby the ways in which they use the environment" (ibid.:119). In particular, Blaikie argued that capitalism extracted surpluses from peasants and pastoralists, who then, in their need for money, overutilized their natural resources, "[taking] out of the soil, pastures and forests what they cannot afford to put back in" (ibid.:7). This tendency was exacerbated by land-users' "displacement and often confinement into a small land area" (ibid.) and by state taxation schemes that necessitated market participation and/or wage labor (ibid.). In this way, Blaikie attributed environmental events and environmental status to political economy, understood in terms of world system theory.

Building upon these theoretical gains, Blaikie teamed with Harold Brookfield to coedit the highly influential volume *Land Degradation and Society*, published in 1987. In their introduction, Blaikie and Brookfield argued for dialogue between the social and natural sciences. Yet the book sought "the deeper causes of land degradation" (Blaikie and Brookfield 1987a:xix) far more in the social than in the natural sciences. Soil erosion was not to be explained in terms of "characteristics of soil, geology and climate, and . . . purely physical constraints" (ibid.), for "land degradation should by definition be a social problem" (1987b:1). They called their approach a "regional political ecology" (ibid.:17, emphasis removed), the term *political ecology* referring to the combined "concerns of ecology and a broadly defined political economy. Together this encompasses the constantly shifting dialectic between society and land-based resources, and also within classes and groups within society itself" (ibid.). Acknowledging the limits of "the populist approach" (1987c:243), Blaikie and Brookfield nonetheless inserted local land managers, with their toolkit of local knowledges and practices, into this array of otherwise impersonal forces, pursuing an approach that was "highly conjunctural" (1987c:239), global but also local. These innovations—the focus on local-level decision making but within the context of "ecological 'marginality' " within a wider system (Castree and Braun 1998:12; Watts 2000:262), the conjunctural approach, the attention to local knowledge and practices—all continue to be productive today.

Geographers were by no means the only social scientists to contribute to the growing consensus that ecology was political economy or it was nothing. The anthology *Lands at Risk in the Third World: Local-Level Perspectives*, edited by the anthropologists Peter Little and Michael Horowitz, brought together various scholars keen to render ecology a social science (1987:5). The contribution of the anthropologist Marianne Schmink and the sociologist Charles Wood, "The 'Political Ecology' of Amazonia," was particularly indicative of the emerging neo-Marxist synthesis within ecology. Schmink and Wood argued that Amazonian indigenous groups tended to share "a production system oriented primarily to simple reproduction" (1987:42) and that such production systems exhibited a balance that is disrupted by the demands on production created by colonialism and capitalist penetration. But "capitalism is an inherently expanding system" (ibid.), and its "logic of expanded production is inherently degrading to land and other resources" (ibid.:43). "So long as governments do not impose their own regulatory mechanisms, the natural environment can (indeed, must) be exploited for maximum short-term gain" (ibid.), setting up the conditions of environmental degradation (see O'Connor 1998; see also Greenberg, this volume). Schmink and Wood were clear about the implications. As an extension of political economy, political ecology offered a "structural perspective, emphasizing the causal relationships between a society's economic base—the form of production and the associated class structure—and the legal institutions and administrative agencies of the state" (1987:46). This "structural perspective" differentiated powerful from weak actors—those associated with private accumulation, who owned the means of production and to whom the state tended "to cater" (ibid.:52), on the one hand, from the marginalized, poorer groups, which would be victimized by capitalism's self-interested, ruthless "rationality," on the other.

Mergers tend to create energized sites of theoretical production and synthesis, and political ecology, Marxism's green turn (see note 2), is no exception. James O'Connor's theory of capitalism's "second contradiction," published in bits and pieces in the 1980s in O'Connor's journal *Capitalism, Nature, Socialism* and in its entirety in *Natural Causes: Ecological Marxism* in 1998, is arguably the most noteworthy revision of Marxist theory that ecological Marxism has inspired. According to O'Connor, capitalism's "'first contradiction' arises from the fact that capitalist production is not only production of commodities but also production of surplus value" (1998:127). Workers do not realize this surplus value. The "exploitation of labor means simply that class struggle and economic crisis are inherent in capitalism" (ibid.), leading ultimately to a proletarian revolution and all the rest. But today capitalism devours the very resources upon which its profits depend, rendering "*the* basic contradiction of world capitalism" (ibid.:xii) the fact that "capitalist production relations . . . degrade or destroy the *conditions* of production, including and especially the environment" (ibid.:8). Environmental movements are a logical outgrowth of capitalism's second contradiction and an impediment to further capitalist accumulation (ibid.; see Greenberg, this volume; see also Escobar 1996:54–56).

Beyond Idealism/Materialism: From "First" to "Second" Nature

Political ecology arose at a time of sharp polarization between idealists (those who attributed cultures and institutions to human invention) and materialists (those who explained these in terms of physical need). This polarization precluded examining the relationship between symbols and physical constraints, a relationship that has become central to the concerns of political ecology in its second generation.

Dichotomizing the symbolic and the material presupposes distinguishing them in the first place, but the line between the two today blurs in light of the revolutionary claim of postmodernism and its close ally in this regard, poststructuralism, that signification or discourse constructs rather than reflects reality (see note 5). By implication, reality is no objective fact, existing independently of human beings, as the positivists would have it, but a language effect.[10] Reality is thus in some measure a human artifact, a claim that carries great weight in the social and human sciences today. It first gained leverage with feminism's distinction between sexual or anatomical differences, on the one hand, and gender, the conventional interpretation of those differences, on the other. At least in theory, anatomical differences were a given, a datum of nature, but gender differences were discursively constructed sociohistorical products.[11]

Constructionism challenges any sharp division between symbolic and material-political approaches. Constructing "woman" as less rational, less intelligent, and less strong than men, for example, has had, and continues to have, serious material and political consequences, consequences that are rooted in the symbolic. Moreover, if signification constructs rather than reflects reality, it is itself powerful. The question is no longer the positivist question of whether representation is accurate, copying a reality that is extrasymbolic—whether, for example, "cognized" models parallel "operationalized" models, a key problematic of older ecologies (Rappaport 1979:97–144; see also Wolf 1999b)—but what reality is being constructed, by whom, for whom, for what political purpose, and to what political effect. The constructionist argument enlarges the political sphere to include the discursive practices through which objects are invested with meaning—the way, for example, that anatomical differences are made to signify gender differences—and discourse itself.

Terms such as *second nature*, *social nature*, and *humanized nature* (see note 6) refer to that nature that is, in a sense, "after nature" (Escobar 1999a), the by-product of discourse and also activity. *Second nature* is Marx's and Engels's term, and it is the one that will be used here. First nature is original, primal, extrahuman, nature as it exists externally, independently of human activity. But second nature is nature as it has been transformed through human activity: "Nature, the nature that preceded human history, . . . is nature which today no longer exists anywhere (except perhaps on a few Australian coral islands of recent origin)" (Marx and Engels 2000:175). Second nature, in short, bears the imprint of humanity. Here I use the term *second nature* to mean something broader than Marx and Engels meant: a nature that is *humanly* produced (through conceptualization as well as activity) and that therefore partakes, but without being entirely, of the human.

If first nature belongs to the sciences, second nature is the by-product of humanity in its relation to nature and belongs as much to the study of politics, society, religion, art, and to the "soft" sciences that study them as it does to the "hard" sciences. Consequently it is possible to produce histories and ethnographies of (second) nature—accounts, that is, of the history of these articulations and the worldviews and lifeways that the environment, no longer external or prior to culture, materializes. Indeed, it could be argued that much of the cultural and new ecology of the 1950s and 1960s was directed at second rather than first nature. Carrying capacity measures the demographic capability of a particular environment given certain social arrangements and practices, for example, and is thus a datum of *second, not first*, nature (Kelly 1968; see also Friedman 1974). To the extent that this is true, modernist ecological writings of this era (see Dove and Pálsson, this volume), ostensibly scientific treatises, were all ethnographies of (second) nature.

Development, Transnational Studies, and the Concept of Place

Political ecology today more generally abandons the dualisms of the past and the reductions that binaristic thinking encouraged and focuses instead on the interchanges between nature and culture, the symbolic and the material, and (the topic of this section) the local and the global. This section uses a particular concept of place to join post-Marxist political ecology with transnational studies, and it singles out development as the topic of choice for this alliance.

The Concept of Place

Even in the heyday of neo-Marxist political ecology, the vision of capitalism as a juggernaut that transformed everything in its path and was itself impervious to noncapitalistic forces was troubling to some. The sociologist Stephen Bunker, in his *Underdeveloping the Amazon*, for example, observed that "locally dominant groups enter into world market exchanges according to their own perceived opportunities" and that "they themselves may reorganize local modes of production and extraction" (1985:54), thus functioning as a constitutive force within a larger field of intersecting regional, national, and global constraints. What necessarily attracted the analyst's eye was "the *interaction* of regional and global constraints, pressures, and opportunities" (ibid.:238; emphasis added). Similarly, in *Silent Violence*, Michael Watts questioned the "monolithic" character of "metropolitan capital" as it penetrated "Third World" formations (1983b:182), and he focused not on the alleged monolith but on its engagement with the local—that is, upon "a complex and contradictory articulation of a capitalist system with persisting noncapitalist forms of production" (ibid.). He would conclude that the "conjunction of metropolitan capital and noncapitalist social relations in northern Nigeria produced a truncated capitalism characterized by complex, varied, and hybrid forms of economic activity. European capital did not unashamedly call the shots, and what emerged was . . . a syncretic combination of the old and the new" (ibid.).

The dawn of the twenty-first century finds the Wallersteinian vision of a single, unified "world system," however still salient for some, under fire by others. Some denounce as fantastical the Wallersteinian specter of capitalism as an omnipotent totality (see Escobar 2001:153–59). In a recent critique of David Harvey's (among others') work, for example, Michael Smith argues that "Harvey invests capitalism with too much systemic coherence and capitalist class actors with too much . . . hegemonic power" (2001:46). Similarly Gibson-

Graham dismisses "Capitalism" (the discursive construction) as "a fantasy of wholeness, one that operates to obscure diversity and disunity" (1995:193; see also Gibson-Graham 1996/97). Shorn of its omnipotence, capitalism no longer supervenes but *inter*venes, engaging with the local, accommodating and negotiating with it as a condition of its own "penetration." As Stuart Hall has observed, "Globalization cannot proceed without [capitalism] learning to live with and through specificity" (1997:29); "in order to maintain its global position, capital has had to negotiate and by negotiate I mean it had to incorporate and partly reflect the differences it was trying to overcome" (ibid.:32). Mike Featherstone makes a similar point. Multinational enterprises, he says, "take into account the particularities of local cultures and adopt organizational cultural practices and modes of orientation which are flexible enough to facilitate this" (Featherstone 1993:174).[12] These arguments in effect locate the so-called global and globalizing processes within the interconnections and exchanges between the North or the West and its Other, a point to which I will soon return.

In this effort to reconceptualize globalizing processes in nonvertical terms, the word that gathers momentum is *place*.[13] While for some *place* refers to the local and all it would seem to entail,[14] for others place is *not* the local, *not* globality's Other but, rather, *the grounded site of local–global articulation and interaction*: "Places are nodes within relational fields—sites of local-global articulation" (Biersack 1999b:81). If now we ask, Where is place?, the answer is clearly both locational *and* relational. Place is "never simply local, sealed off from an outside beyond" (Moore 1998:347), and to study place is to "move from hermetically sealed sites of autonomy to relational spaces of connection and articulation" (ibid.). In fact, articulations are as crucial to defining the particularities of any place as are its "native" features. Place is defined, or rendered distinct, "precisely through the particularity of linkage to that 'outside' which is therefore itself part of what constitutes the place" (Massey 1993:67). "Individual 'places' are precisely located differentially in the global network of such relations. Further, the specificity of place also derives from the fact that each place is the focus of a distinct mixture of wider and more local social relations. . . . And, finally, all these relations interact with and take a further element of specificity from the accumulated history of a place, with that history itself conceptualized as the product of layer upon layer of different sets of linkages both local and to the wider world" (ibid.:68). Places, in short, are constructed historically in processes that spatially exceed the local and in which the extralocal is as constitutive as the local.

Turning upon the relationship between the local and the global and the dynamics of that relationship, place (as Bunker [1985] and Watts [1983a, 1983b] knew some twenty years ago) is fundamentally intermediary.[15] The concept of place is thus suitable for a political ecology that breaks with the "overdeterminations of a distinct 'global'" (Raffles 1999:350), such as is imagined in world system theory, and focuses instead on "the *trans*versal, the *trans*actional" (Ong 1999:4), the "*horizontal* and *relational*" (ibid.). The following pages use the expression "place-based approach" to signify this rotation from a vertical and binaristic to a horizontal and dialectical perspective on local–global relations.

Transnational Spaces and Place-Making

With its interest in the flow of finance capital, technology, and people and their labor across national borders, transnational studies are necessarily informed by political economy. But transnational studies also theorize the movement of images, values, and meanings within transnational circuits, and in this they depart from political economy. Political ecology today also explores the nexus of the symbolic and the material, but its relationship with transnational studies has yet to be determined. Are political ecology and transnational studies allies or overlapping domains of inquiry?

Some of the rhetoric of transnational studies would seem to preclude an alliance between the two. While we undoubtedly live under "a condition of transnationality" (Herzfeld 2001:166), imagining this condition in terms of transnational "flows" but not also their catchments, travel but not also dwelling, deterritorialization but not also transplantation, or, with respect to James Clifford's famous dichotomy, routes but not also roots (1992, 1997a) seemingly deprives ecology of any purchase within transnational studies. Ecology requires all that the root metaphor implies: concrete locations, a piece of dirt. But if we reimagine the transnational in place-based terms, transnational studies and a place-based political ecology become not only compatible but *coincident*, for the concept of place installs the local within transnational spaces even as it centers those spaces on local–global articulations and the dynamics thereof. What transnational studies and a place-based political ecology would have in common are those dynamics, as well as the related questions of how transnational spaces are created and how places are made.

Anthropologists and geographers today shift from an objectivist to a constructionist view of space. Instead of space being the container of activity, constructionists view space as the by-product of activity.[16] A garden, for example, does not so much occupy as constitute a space, through the gardening activity of its own creation. Whereas world system theory imagined geography in structural terms, as the spatialization of a mode of production that turned on the axis of first/third world nations, the constructionist perspective brings geography within the fold of practice theory and renders space historical.[17] Key questions for both place-based political ecology and transnational studies are, How are transnational spaces created, modified, or annihilated? What linkages are forged or undone, by whom, and for what purposes? What enables and disables these articulations? Are these spatializations compatible with or disruptive of other spatialization projects (see Kottak 1999; Kottak and Colson 1994)?

Neo-Marxist political ecology assumed that transnational linkages were forged from above by hegemonic Euro-American powers. But grassroots activity is equally important in understanding how the transnational spaces of capitalism and colonialism, globalization so-called, are created, reinforced, contested, or rebuffed. Several of the contributors to this volume chronicle instances of the forging *from below* of transnational ties in the context of globalization or antiglobalization projects. Hvalkof, for example, tells us that the Ashéninka gained leverage against the spatialization practices of the colonists by mobilizing World Bank support (Hvalkof, this volume). The Penan, meanwhile, have long exploited media, NGOs, and high-profile celebrities such as Sting and Al Gore to negotiate the terms of logging or ban it altogether (Brosius 1999a, 2003, this volume; see also Turner 1993b). In Robbins's account, the condition of capitalist penetration and the commodification of local resources is ironically the Maussian gift of these resources that the Urapmin of New Guinea make to foreign developers. Since the specificity of place is the specificity of linkage and since transnational spaces center on linkages, the question of how transnational spaces are created and formed is inseparable from the question of place-making whenever the linkages that give a place its specificity are transnational.[18] For Harvey (1993), space and place are not only not dichotomous, to the extent that the defining linkages of place are international, but transnational space and place *co-arise*.[19] A number of the contributions to this volume investigate the *coproduction* of place and transnational space through grassroots activity.

It has been more than a decade since Gupta and Ferguson first challenged the notion that " 'a culture' is naturally the property of a spatially localized people and that the way to study such a culture is to go 'there' ('among the so-and-so')" (1997a:3; see also Gupta and Ferguson 1997b). They would locate the

so-called local within transnational spaces, as I have done here, thus challenging the premise of a now-obsolete ethnography that " 'peoples and cultures' "
(ibid.) are geographically bounded or territorialized. To the extent that political ecology focuses on the creation of transnational space and its inevitable
corollary place-making, political ecology opens up new ethnographic vistas.
These new vistas erupt on the scale of the transnational, not the local, providing us with opportunities to respond to the critique of localistic ethnographic practices but without throwing the baby (ethnography) out with the
bathwater.

Such vistas also provide occasion for a historical anthropology that refutes
syncronic approaches and that takes practice and other contingencies seriously.
To argue that space is constructed through the activities of agents is to argue for
the historicization of both anthropological and geographical inquiry. We may
expect that historians and geographers, no less than anthropologists, would be
attracted to the new ethnographic terrain that the alliance of a place-based political ecology with transnational studies would open up, providing occasion
for interdisciplinary collaboration.

Development, Agency, and Meaning

Development frequently, if not always, involves resources, their cultivation,
and their commodification. Historically it has had a special relevance for political ecology, and it continues to have a special relevance for a place-based
post-Marxist political ecology that is in league with transnational studies.

Earlier development studies assumed a high degree of structural determinism. The rich were rich and the poor were poor because of the global structure of inequality (the capitalist mode of production) in which they both
participated. These development studies underestimated the importance of
grassroots agency and grassroots leaders as a result. Focusing on the local–
global nexus and its dynamics, a place-based approach necessarily considers
how the grass roots responds to the engines of globalization. As Gupta has
observed, any account of development must consider "its shaping by peasant
resistance and activism" (1998:13) if development's "specific trajectory" (ibid.)
at equally specific sites of local–global articulation is to be understood.

There is already a considerable literature that approaches development from
a place-based perspective, although not in so many words. Most notably, James
Scott's "resistance" names a domain of subtle "rural political agency" (Starn
1992:91): "the prosaic but constant struggle between the peasantry" [mani-

fested in] 'foot dragging, dissimulation, desertion, false compliance, pilfering, feigned ignorance, slander, arson, sabotage, and so on' [(Scott 1985:xvi)] and those who seek to extract labor, food, taxes, rents, and interests from them" (ibid.). As important as Scott's writings have been to a "broadening of academic appreciation for rural political agency" (Starn 1992:91), they arguably paint a "picture of rural people" that is unduly "quiescent," albeit "never passive" (ibid.), and fail to address "open peasant movements" (ibid.:92), "social movements" and oppositional "campaigns," and other forms of activism.[20] Such activism reasserts alterior, vernacular perspectives and lifeways in an effort to "survive the overwhelming impact of the global and transnational" (Wilson 2000:247) in "neolocal or reindigenous" (ibid.) orders.

Consider, for example, "Progress of the Victims," Hvalkof's contribution to this volume, which concerns an indigenous Peruvian group and its campaign to fend off an alien "progress" in the interest of preserving their way of life. The Ashéninka live in the Gran Pajonal (grasslands) of central Peru, and they were and still largely are dependent upon the forest for their livelihood. They compete for resources with the Andean *colonos*, a quasi-mestizo group who breed cattle and who are bent upon reclaiming the forest for cattle production. To the colonists the grasslands and cattle symbolize their "millennial dream of success, wealth, and greatness" (ibid., 203), of "civilization and progress . . . the entire modern developmentalist paradigm" (ibid.). But for the indigenous Ashéninka these same grasslands give "identity to the place and the people" (ibid.). The Ashéninka value the grasslands for their proximity to the rain forest, which "is still the soul of the Ashéninka livelihood and existence" (ibid.) and which has mythological and cosmological significance. In their environmental implications these perspectives are diametrically opposed. "Whereas the colonists terminate the forest, incessantly expanding cattle pasture" (ibid., 204), the Ashéninka "strive to regulate the balance between the grasslands and the forest" (ibid.), the dual and indispensable features of the Ashéninka world. In recovering lands, Ashéninka seek to stem the tide of progress *colonos*-style, perpetuating their way of life.

Pressure from below may be appropriative rather than oppositional, a matter of commandeering development for indigenous ends. So Sahlins has suggested. "Developman," his rendering of the Melanesian pidgin term (Tok Pisin) for development (1992, 2000:419–20, 490–91, 512–14), which refers to the hijacking of development for allodevelopmental, neotraditional purposes. The difference between development and developman is the *man* morpheme, which particularizes development by imagining it as cultural elaboration. Thus, in New Guinea, arguably the exchange/feasting/politicking capital of the world, developman stipulates "the use of foreign wealth in the expansion of feasting, politicking, subsidizing kinship" (Sahlins 2000:512) and all manner of "cultural self-realization on a material scale and in material forms never before known" (ibid.:420). The concept of progress is here relativized, rendered cultural, an argument that resonates with Hvalkof's use of the word. Similarly, in " 'But the Young Men Don't Want to Farm Any More': Political Ecology and Consumer Culture in Belize," Wilk explains in *cultural* terms the fact that the Mayan Kekchi (a.k.a. Q'eqchi') farmers of Belize intensify consumption whenever market conditions enable them to do so.

The contributions to this volume suggest that any aprioristic assumption of resistance and other oppositional politics or developman (the cultural appropriation of development) could obscure more than it reveals. Development is indeed a bandwagon upon which some indigenous populations have hopped. "The myth of modernization" (Ferguson 2000:14), with its "tropes of development and progress, emergence and advance" (ibid.:15), inspires hope and "expectations of modernity" in distant locales (see also Knauft 2002). Even Brosius, whose ethnography of the campaign of the Sarawak (Borneo) Penan against logging is arguably the best-documented case of grassroots oppositional politics in the anthropological literature (see also Turner 1993b), is ambivalent about using the word *resistance*. The most dramatic Penan antilogging demonstrations should not be viewed "exclusively as acts of resistance" (this volume, 283), he writes. Borne of "frustration" and "desperation," they are attempts "to get the government to listen" to the demonstrators and thus "simultaneously . . . efforts at *engagement*" (ibid., 283; see also 316). In essence, the Penan wish to participate in public debates, enlarging the scope of democratic processes by inserting themselves within these processes. By the same token, far from demonizing transnational corporations (cf. Taussig 1980), the Urapmin (Robbins, this volume) appear eager to enter into a Faustian pact with the transnational devil to meet what they perceive to be the condition of forming a community of mutual recognition across the color bar: the timeworn strategy of prestation.

Resistance, social movements, developman—these are varying manifestations of the local–global dynamics to which places are party. Insofar as these dynamics mediate human–nature articulations, they are central to the concerns of a place-based political ecology. They also provide occasion for exploring how symbolic and material factors are interwoven within irreducibly complex and broadly political realities. Resistance, campaigns, appropriations, and even cooptation and complicity are all motivated from within as well as from without and must be understood, at least in part, in terms of the vernacular perspectives and lifeways they tacitly or explicitly assert in the face of Northern incursions. As the contributions of Brosius, Hvalkof, Robbins, and myself make clear, grassroots agency of any sort operates "at the interface of culture and politics" (Alvarez, Dagnino, and Escobar 1998b:xi); "struggles for rights and economic and political-institutional power" are "deeply entangled" with "struggles . . . over meanings and representations" (ibid.). In bringing actors and agency within its framework, today's political ecology inevitably incorporates consciousness, ideology, and meaning and the relationship between these and material life into its study.

Difference, Feminism, and Postcolonialism

There is a final reorientation that is foundational to political ecology in its second generation, one that is enabled by the constructionist argument that reality is posterior rather than prior to discourse—in a word, constructed. Whereas political economy emphasizes class differences, today's political ecology attends to a range of differences that includes, but is not restricted to, class (Moore, Pandian, and Kosek 2003; Moore, Kosek, and Pandian, eds., 2003). For a Marxist, class difference is objective, a fact. As has already been pointed out, gender is not an objective but a discursive fact, and the same is true of race, a word that sometimes appears within quotation marks to underscore its constructed character (Gates, Jr., ed., 1985). Ethnicity, too, so the argument goes, is "invented" or "performed" into existence and is thus a discursive product. Thomas-Slayter and Rocheleau have pointed out that "access to and control of resources are inextricably linked to the positioning of people by ethnicity, race, class, and gender" (1995:7–8; see also Rocheleau, Thomas-Slayter, and Wangari 1996).[21] To the extent that these divergences make a difference in terms of "access to and control of resources," a political ecology that addresses them explores the intersection of the symbolic and the material.

For the past thirty years gender has been a constant object of contemplation and criticism across the social and human sciences. As a reading of anatomical differences, gender belongs to second nature, and early, still important writings on gender opened up a pathway into ecology. Nature is not only humanity's but humanity's other (Haraway 1989). Is nature to culture as female is to male, then?—a question Ortner raised in 1974 in her provocative think piece "Is Nature to Culture as Female Is to Male?"[22] Ortner posed this question at a time when symbolic studies distanced themselves from material studies. But gender as a symbolic construction clearly has material consequences, empowering actors differentially in terms of resource access, control, stewardship, ownership, and the division of labor. Within and without political ecology, gender is a high-profile site for exploring the nexus of the symbolic, the material, and the political. A *gendered* political ecology provides an indispensable antidote not only to the reductions of the past but to the androcentrism of earlier ecologies. It also serves to highlight the fractures and divisions within a society that is no longer conceived as "solidary" and homogeneous.[23]

The sociohistorical production of difference is no more potent or toxic than under colonial circumstances of unequal discursive and material power.[24] These cultural politics lie not outside but *within* ecology, as a historical condition of human–nature articulations. Indeed, the argument that differences are contingent, constructed, profoundly political products was most powerfully stated in *Orientalism*, Edward Said's exposé of the production of difference under the circumstances of unequal discursive and material power that lies at the heart of colonialism. A political ecology that attends to a broad spectrum of differences as well as to the production of knowledge in situations of discursive and material asymmetry is a political ecology that is drawn powerfully onto postcolonial terrain.

The place concept itself draws us there, for, in signifying the nexus of the local and global, it averts not only the structural determinism but the evolutionism, orientalism, and Eurocentrism of the familiar and racialized binaries local/global, first/third world, developed/undeveloped and, relatedly, traditional/modern (Gupta 1998:10, 172 ff.), and civilized/uncivilized. Acknowledging the impact of capitalism's outside upon the various genealogies of modernity, the place-based approach stipulates to the limitations of capitalocentric and Eurocentric analyses and reimagines the first–third world axis of "encompassment" in more horizontal, dialectical terms, as a transnational space of nonteleological (albeit constrained) engagement. Within this space power may be distributed unevenly, but it *is* distributed, engendering variabilities and heterodoxies. The place-based approach acknowledges the presence of grassroots agents and takes as an empirical question the matter of their efficacy, contributing to a postcolonial historiography that renders "subalterns" subjects of their own history (Thompson 1966). It also concentrates upon the production of transnational spaces and the inevitable corollary of that production, place-making, and in this renders subalterns *subjects of their own geography*. In these ways, a place-based political ecology necessarily partakes of and contributes to postcolonial studies, particularly in the area of development.

A Research Agenda for Today

Reviews such as this have the virtue of pointing us in what appear to be promising directions. I close this discussion with some thoughts on near-term priorities. They are tied to terms that have recurred in this introduction: second nature, agency, place and place-making, difference, postcolonial studies, and the like. Although the agenda is fundamentally interdisciplinary, anthropology does have its own purchase within it, and I begin with this purchase.

Watts has defined political ecology in terms of "the complex relations between nature and society" (2000:257), focusing on "what one might call the forms of access and control over resources and their implications for environmental health and sustainable livelihoods" (ibid.). Watts here directs us to the study of the social relations of production in all their variability, including (but not restricted to) those of capitalism. But political ecology must also attend to the *culture* of such access and control, the *culture* of production, distribution, and exchange, the *culture* of the social relations of production and other human–nature articulations. The extensive literature on social or gift exchange has taught us that exchange sometimes trumps consumption or production as the economically salient activity (this precept is all but explicit in Sahlins's developman concept and inheres in Robbins's discussion of property and prestation in this volume) and that the "social relations of production" so central to any political economy framework may actually be marginal or secondary outside capitalism. The appropriation of nature is not only historical and social (Peluso and Watts 2001:27), but also cultural. Exchange-centered and production-centered "economies" institutionalize human–nature articulations in very different ways, as participants in the formalism v. substantivism debate of several decades ago could attest (see Wilk, this volume; see also Sahlins 1972).

Escobar (1999a) has coined the phrase "nature regime" to refer to the sociohistorically variable conventions and institutionalizations of human–nature articulations, emphasizing in particular the "capitalist" and the "organic" nature regime. The latter appears to be a catchall category for conventions and institutionalizations of human–nature articulations outside Euro-American influence and requires refinement in light of anthropological data and comparisons. That said, the term *nature regime* does begin to equip a political ecology that is focused more on history and regional and cross-regional interchanges than on evolution and cultural isolates with a vocabulary for describing, first of all, ecological variability and, second, the dynamics of those interchanges. In effect, Escobar's concept of nature regime directs our attention away from the comparison of evolutionary stages of "sociocultural integration" (Steward 1955) and toward the study of globalizing processes as these unfold on the ground. Anthropology is by no means the only discipline devoted to comparison that Escobar's concept of nature regime might reinvigorate, but the concept has a special value for anthropology, a field that has long focused on the cultural variability of human–nature articulations, albeit under the guise of an *economic* rather than an ecological anthropology. In the near term, political ecology could profitably focus on comparative nature regimes, their articulations and interpenetrations, and the histories and spatializations of these articulations and interpenetrations.

In reinterpreting the cultural ecology of the 1950s, 1960s, and 1970s, as well as Rappaport's "new ecology," I used the term *ethnography of nature*. The word *nature* here refers to second rather than to first nature—to nature as it is embedded within sociohistorical realities, to a nature, then, as it is poised between biology and history (Escobar 1999a). An ethnography of nature—*Pigs for the Ancestors*, for example—examines the conventionalization or institutionalization of human–nature articulations (within modes of production, exchange, reproduction, etc.) and the actual practices that both effect and affect these articulations. It focuses, in short, on nature regime and the dynamics of interlocking nature regimes.

From its inception, political ecology has rejected the localism of earlier ecologies. In its first generation political ecology tended to be capitalocentric and viewed the local as an inflection of the global. However, this capitalocentrism was sometimes tempered by a recognition of the existence of capitalism's other or others and the space of opposition, negotiation, and/or collaboration that globalization inevitably opens up. It is upon this more nuanced understanding of the dynamics of globalization that today's political ecology must build. The ethnographies of nature that are appropriate in an era of globalizaton are quite different from Rappaport's ethnography of nature, which was limited to the locality and the immediate region, but they also deviate from a world system perspective in acknowledging the role that grassroots agency and the perceptions, motivations, and values that inform this agency play in human–environment relations. Human–nature articulations are today forged complexly within the transnational spaces of local–global articulations. Studying such articulations-within-articulations requires the "linkage" approach that Kottak and Colson have recommended (Kottak 1999; Kottak and Colson 1994), along with the "multi-sited" ethnography Marcus famously insisted upon (1995; see also Clifford 1997; Gupta and Ferguson 1997c). But they may also be studied by problematizing any one site in terms of these complexities, as the contributions to this volume demonstrate.

Much has been made here of the relationship between the local and the global, but very little has been said about the nation-state. The state's intervention in development programs is frequently "massive" (Bunker 1985:238), for the state's capitalizations of nature (Greenberg, this volume) and development policies set the stage for the local–global articulations that ethnographies of nature concern. World system theory is sometimes faulted for its inadequate theorization of the role of the state, and the same argument could be made of transnational studies, where the emphasis has been on flow across seemingly permeable national boundaries. But are these boundaries permeable, and, if they are not, how do we pursue a transnational, place-based political ecology that accommodates the state (Greenberg), the nation (Berglund), and the nation-state?

I have already indicated some of the ways in which a place-based political ecology contributes to postcolonial studies, particularly in the area of development. It remains for political ecology to decolonize the production of environmental and political ecological knowledge and to develop critical awareness of its own implication in the very dynamics it studies. The North has no monopoly on environmental knowledge, and political ecology ideally inquires into alterior bodies of practical and theoretical knowledge in the spirit of decolonizing environmental knowledge, a matter that Dove's, Pálsson's, and Lansing et al.'s contributions in particular address.[25] Also, to the extent that local decision making and environmental management are important (Blaikie and Brookfield, eds., 1987), so, too, are local knowledges and practices. Important in this regard is the issue of the gendering of environmental knowledge and practice and its history (Rocheleau, Juma, and Wamalwa-Muragori 1995).

Those issues of representation, reflexivity, and positionality that have bedeviled ethnography over the past two decades are becoming increasingly important within political ecology, the more so the greater the material stakes. How are "interpretations and representations of the environment" (Blaikie 1999:143) formed; "whose knowledge counts and why?" (ibid.); who speaks and deploys "truth" and toward what end? Moreover, where there are material stakes, political ecological *writings* have an inescapable material impact and must be approached and critiqued as such. A domain of academic representation, political ecology is implicated in the very processes the analyst seeks to study and must fall subject to reflexive, self-critical commentary, an emerging trend within political ecology that this volume helps foster.[26]

There is, finally, the need for fruitful collaboration across disciplinary lines, an interdisciplinarity that captures the scope of culture/power/history/nature.

A decided strength of political economy was its refusal to compartmentalize the various aspects of the phenomena it studied (Wolf 1982). As Clifford reminds us, Eric Wolf "defined anthropology as a 'discipline between disciplines'" (Clifford 1997:60), and the same could be said of geography and history. In the past fifteen years, geography has steadily increased its "symbolic capital" with its argument that all social phenomena are spatialized and must be studied as such. In the past ten to fifteen years anthropology has subtly but unmistakably oriented itself to geography by adopting an analytical vocabulary that is laden with terms borrowed from geography: space, landscape, geography, and place (see especially Low and Lawrence-Zúñiga, eds., 2003). As the Ipili speakers of the Papua New Guinea highlands know so well, however, there is no space apart from time and no time apart from space, and so all space-focused study is necessarily temporalized just as all historical study is necessarily spatialized. The questions are always geographical, historical, anthropological, political, economic, and sociological—all at once, a matter of culture/power/history/nature.

The constructionist position has fueled a debate, ontological and epistemological, about whether (first) nature actually exists (the realist position) or is only construction (the constructionist position), and, if it does exist, whether it can be known as such or whether every attempt to know it necessarily results in another subjective construction rather than in objective facts.[27] I dare say that the argument that there is no nature, only "nature," a construction, has little appeal for most political ecologists, for whom the stakes must be real and material if they are to be fully political. While it is undoubtedly true that "the 'forest' [that discursively, textually constructed reality] cannot preexist its construction" (Braun and Wainwright 2001:45; see Berglund, this volume), the forest remains for most political ecologists an " 'unmetaphorized' reality" (Milton 1996:215) that must be known as such. Although epistemologically and practically "it is increasingly impossible to separate nature off into its own ontological space" (Castree and Braun 1998:5), political ecology cannot afford to surrender that measure of realism that allows it to distinguish, for example, redness as symbol from redness as chemical effect with respect to Porgera's environmental issue (Biersack, this volume).

I have emphasized here the concept of second nature and even enlarged its meaning to include constructions of nature and not just the transformations of nature human activities occasion, as Marx and Engels used the term. Although second nature is "after nature," it does not supersede nature but, rather, constitutes the *interface* between (first) nature, on the one hand, and culture, power, and history, on the other. Just where the line is drawn in particular instances of second nature between, on the one hand, nature and, on the other hand, culture, power, and history will no doubt be a contentious issue, but the effort to draw this line must be made, for it is only by drawing this line that the nexus of culture/power/history/nature comes into relief and becomes an analytical object. This means that, in addition to the obvious interdisciplinarity of political ecology — the need to attend to cultural, social, historical, spatial, and political factors all at once — political ecology necessarily bridges the social/human and the natural sciences.

In a recent overview, *Anthropology: Theoretical Practice in Culture and Society*, Michael Herzfeld argues for the " 'militant middle ground' " (2001:x). This space is established at a "skeptical distance from the solipsistic extremes . . . of modern sociocultural theory: postmodernism and positivism in their more dogmatic excesses" (ibid.), and it is "strongly resistant to closure and . . . truly grounded in an open-ended appreciation of the empirical" (ibid.). Regardless of how serious political ecology's cultural or linguistic turn and its commitment to issues of power and history, the problem of the real is necessarily on the agenda of political ecology. However new its materialism (Biersack 1999c:11–12), it must also address the *material* stakes of a *material* world. Today's political ecology refuses to reduce culture to nature or nature to culture but operates productively in the space between the two — the relationship between signifying and other practices, on the one hand, and an extralinguistic material reality, on the other. Thus, Escobar places ecology "between history and biology" (1999), Peluso and Watts insist that any ecology "must seriously address the causal powers inherent in Nature itself" (2001:25), and, for all her focus on the role of culture in human–nature relations, Milton is clear about the limits of constructionism, insisting on the need to acknowledge a "role for the environment itself" (1996:214).

Entering the space of Herzfeld's " 'militant middle ground' " (2001:x) is political ecology's fate. For political ecology to do otherwise would be to undercut environmental social movements and oppositional campaigns (Peluso and Watts 2001; see also Demeritt 2001:28; Castree and MacMillan 2001:209), abdicate its responsibility to bear witness to environmental disasters and their human costs, limit the meaning of the word *political* to the power to name, an impoverishment of terrain that few would welcome, and handicap political ecology's explanatory power. And, so, for all the necessity of political ecology's anthropocentrism, it must also be ecocentric (see Vayda and Walters 1999), albeit in *re*constructed ways, ways that approach nature *in its sociohistorical context*, that is, as an aspect of *second* nature (see discussion in Dove 2001). Only if pursued as both an environmental science *and* a complex social-cum-human "science" of nature will it be possible to achieve the utopian collaboration imagined at the outset, a collaboration of "diverse networks of scholars and other concerned groups" (Blaikie 1999:131) on the terrain of culture/power/history/nature.

The Contributions

Although no collection can be comprehensive, this collection aims to promote the research agenda just outlined, and then some. The first section, "Beyond Modernist Ecologies," contains the contributions of Michael Dove and Gíslí Pálsson. Taken together these two essays provide a wide-ranging critique of modernist ecologies, and they explore the ways in which local knowledges and practices appear to contain a wisdom that science, in its hubris, lacks. Dove and Pálsson retrospectively review the modernist ecology of an earlier era, in several dimensions: its dichotomization of nature and culture, its faith in the scientific management of nature, and its scientism more generally, including its tendency to dismiss local knowledge as mere "emics" in need of "etic" correction.

The prestige modernism accords science is of a piece with the Eurocentrism of colonialism and other forms of Northern domination, and in "Equilibrium Theory and Interdisciplinary Borrowing," Dove implies that modernism has now yielded to a "late modern" (see Dove 2001), postcolonial era in which the wisdom of the South may be appreciated. Toward this end, he examines in his closing segment the augury practices of the Kantu' of West Kalimantan, Indonesia, establishing, first, that Kantu' augury practices have no function and, second, that their wisdom resides therein.

Resonating with Dove's chapter, Pálsson's "Nature and Society in the Age of Postmodernity" critiques the dualism of nature and culture as well as the related assumption that nature may be rationally managed by high science. His metaphor for modernist ecology is the aquarium, which boxes nature in and culture out, creating the illusion that an objective, omniscient study of nature is possible. But "humans are simultaneously part of nature and society" (Pálsson, this volume, 74), a premise that propels ecology from modernism to postmodernism. "If disembeddedness, dualism, certainty, and human mastery are the characteristics of modernism, *post*modernism suggests the opposite—namely, embeddedness, monism [refuting the nature/culture dualism], and the absence of certainty and human mastery" (ibid., 74). The preponderance of Pálsson's chapter is devoted to a critique of one particular effort to manage resources scientifically, an effort that had disastrous unintended consequences. In lieu of modernist managerial schemes, Pálsson proposes schemes rooted in pragmatism, which places the subject in his or her context or environs, natural and otherwise, and reasons from that vantage point (see Ingold 2000).

The second section, "Constructing and Appropriating Nature," examines, from varying perspectives, appropriations and constructions of nature and the political, historical, and/or cultural dimensions of these. Modernist ecologies place nature outside the human realm, but Berglund's, Greenberg's, Wilk's, and Robbins's essays begin to show how nature always exists within sociohistorical configurations, as a constructed or second nature.

The section opens with Eeva Berglund's contribution, "Ecopolitics through Ethnography," which picks up where Dove's and Pálsson's contributions leave off, on the threshold of postmodernism, in its striking case study of the *co*-construction of nation and nature in contemporary Finland. Berglund argues that Finland imagines itself as a nation of forests—indeed, as a forest-nation in which the Finnish identity becomes inextricable from the "virility and purity yet capacity for innovation in the face of a harsh but ultimately giving nature" (ibid., 105) that Finland's wooded landscapes impose upon its citizens. Under the circumstances, logging becomes an act of symbolic violence against the nation, sparking vociferous debate. One of Berglund's points is that the motivations and logics that come into ecological play are not, as modernist ecologies would have it, rational. Forest science has flourished in Finland in large part because of the symbolic load on forests, and the "forest group," a network of activists upon whom Berglund focuses, are emotionally involved in green issues, despite their thoroughly modern embrace of science.

Greenberg's essay implicitly continues in this vein, with a critique of modernist approaches to nature. His theme is the disconnect between political economic and ecological logics when nature is bureaucratized by the state. In the Gulf of California, marine resources are commodified through state-directed territorializations, which place rivers under one agency, fish under another, forests under a third, and so on, in violation of a natural order that has its own logic and functionality. As nature is dispersed across managerial structures and domains, natural resources fall subject to political and economic logics, with tragic consequences, a conclusion that Rappaport's later writings on capitalism and maladaptation adumbrated.

Like Greenberg, Wilk is interested in market penetration and its negative impacts upon the environment. Whenever the markets allowed a favorable conversion of labor into commodities, the Mayan Kekchi of Belize did not hold to local ecological limits but increased their consumption in pursuit of their consumer dreams. Without ignoring globalization, Wilk locates these dreams not outside but *within* a culture that over the long haul has altered under transnational pressures. "Culture does not disappear as people enter a cash and commodity economy; instead, new forms of consumer culture appear" (166, emphasis deleted), consumption itself being "everywhere highly cultural and specific to particular times and places." Since consumption places demands on resources, the study of consumption, in its cultural no less than in its economic dimensions, is critical to a political ecology that connects "the globalizing aspects of the modern world economic system to the very local level where real people make choices on a daily basis and within very particular circumstances" (167). While Wilk does not say as much, clearly he realizes that cultural studies and transnational studies, focused as they are on the nexus of capitalism, culture, and the media, are important resources for any political ecological probe into consumption and its mediation of human–nature articulations. The young men of Kekchi no longer want to farm. They want and seek wage work outside Belize, traveling as far as the United States to support a lifestyle they and their relatives desire but do not need—succumbing, then, to transnational pressures and imaginings.

Like Wilk, Joel Robbins, in "Properties of Nature, Properties of Culture," demonstrates the complicity of local actors in development and their role in the creation and exploitation of transnational spaces. Property is an appropriation of nature, one, moreover, that entails the assignment of rights in the nature that is thus appropriated, making property central to political ecology. Property is also culturally variable, a matter of rendering things significant in specific ways, making property irreducible to economic or ecological factors. Following G. W. F. Hegel's theory (expressed in the *Philosophy of Right*, 1942) Robbins argues that politics is "a matter of the pursuit of mutual recognition, not of the struggle for self-aggrandizement or self-protection" (Robbins 172), and shows how the Urapmin of Papua New Guinea use property in a bid for the recognition of foreign resource developers. From the perspective of the white developers, this effort is doomed from the start because property transactions are all about profit making at somebody's expense, exploitation so-called; they are emphatically *not* about mutual recognition.

The third section, "Ethnographies of Nature," offers "thick descriptions" (Geertz 1973) of the complex politics that comes into play regionally, nationally, and internationally when nature is brought within the human sphere — "humanized," in Lansing and Kremer's (1993) use of that term.

From its title and first note forward, Søren Hvalkof's chapter, "Progress of the Victims: Political Ecology in the Peruvian Amazon," sets itself at odds with the kind of master narrative that envisions "relatively isolated tribal groups" as "victimized by the cruel and genocidal expansion of Western civilization threatening their very existence" (this volume, 196). The "victims of progress" trope inscribes indigenous peoples as essentialized, isolated, and fundamentally passive others in a process that remains dominated by colonial and/or capitalist powers (cf. Sahlins 2000:chapter 14). But "the indigenous peoples did not vanish or assimilate as anticipated — on the contrary, many of them created their own political spaces for agency in the reconfiguring modern states" (Hvalkof, this volume, 196–97). This shift from the top-down structural approach of world system theory to a "practice theory" investigation of grassroots resistance establishes the platform for an "ethnography [and also history] of nature" focused on how the Ashéninka operate within local–national and local–global spaces to forestall the encroachments of cattle-raising colonists and preserve their way of life.

My chapter, "Red River, Green War," concerns the division between upstream and downstream Porgerans that gold mining has engendered. The resources of so-called Lower Porgerans have been jeopardized by the waste products of mining, which have discolored and contaminated the Porgera River and which have also buried the alluvial gold that has been the Lower Porgerans' livelihood since the 1960s. Years of negotiation have established no universally accepted standard of compensation, and as time has worn on, issues have festered and proliferated rather than been resolved. From a world system perspective, the animosity of the Lower Porgerans toward the mine and also toward those residing upstream, the principal beneficiaries of the mining, may be explained entirely in terms of the differential positioning of each group vis-à-vis the mine. But a political economy perspective would overlook the emotional charge on Lower Porgerans' censure of upstreamers *as bad kith and kin* and the cultural roots of this emotional charge. That upstream relatives benefit at the ecological expense of Lower Porgerans is morally offensive to Lower Porgerans. Hence, the "green war" of the title: that conflict that sets Porgerans against not only the mine but Porgerans themselves. The "politics of place" along the Porgera River must therefore be understood both historically and culturally, with respect to a *conjuncture* (of outside and inside forces) over the long run.[28]

As much as any ecologist, J. Peter Brosius has been conscious of the transnational alliances that are forged in the context of environmental social movements and oppositional campaigns. Caught up in the Penan's antilogging campaign have been NGOs, international activists, the international media, the anthropologist himself or herself. While "Between Politics and Poetics" expands upon Brosius's reporting on the transnational dimensions of the campaign of the Penan of Sarawak to check logging, its main focus is the relationship between meaning and politics, language and practice, within a new, culturally inflected political ecology. Brosius is interested not in symbolism as such but rather in "the . . . complex relationship between representation, discursive production, and political agency" (this volume, 282) that undergirds efforts by the Penan to convince a variety of audiences and political actors that logging violence threatens their identity and way of life.

The final section, "Between Nature and Culture," contains the only interdisciplinary essay in the book, an essay that builds on the work of the anthropologist J. Stephen Lansing. While the nature/culture binary framed much of Rappaport's thinking—underwriting his adaptationism, for example, and his distinction between "operational" (or "etic") and "cognized" (or "emic") perspectives—Lansing, Schoenfelder, and Scarborough recollect that Rappaport himself, in his "long struggle to reconcile his scientific methods with his humanist aims" (this volume, 325), recognized that the nature/culture dualism was difficult to uphold. The essay provides an ethnography of second (or, in Lansing's terminology, "humanized") nature centered on the Balinese irrigation system that has brought nature within the human realm. In a move that echoes Dove's and Pálsson's appreciation of the soundness of local practices, Lansing, Schoenfelder, and Scarborough uncover the sheer success of the way that the Balinese manage water. The bulk of the chapter demonstrates how decentralized decision making, aiming for local maximization, results in regional adjustments and adaptations, a demonstration that is unique in the ecological literature.

Conclusion

As environmental crises multiply and the ecological costs of capitalism compete with its social and human costs for practical and theoretical attention, political ecology is poised to make its strongest contributions to date. Refashioning itself in post-Marxist and postextremicist terms, political ecology engages with key contemporary debates but brings to them a measure of realism and materialism that it will not, cannot surrender and that is lacking in other frameworks. It thus reorients these debates away from Scylla and Charybdis extremes and toward Herzfeld's "militant middle ground." Given its interdisciplinarity, political ecology's contributions are not only theoretical but methodological (see Lansing et al., this volume). Moreover, its language is not only inter- but *post*disciplinary, intelligible to geographers, sociologists, anthropologists, political scientists, and historians alike. Political ecology is thus well positioned to become a premier domain of empirical inquiry and site of theoretical production for decades to come.

Notes

The Duke University readers were wonderfully helpful in pinpointing strengths and weaknesses in an earlier draft of this writing, and I would like to thank them for their committed and helpful readings. I also thank Arif Dirlik, Arturo Escobar, Jim Greenberg, Jerry Jacka, and Dianne Rocheleau for readings of drafts of this introduction. I have found useful prods in the finalization of this introduction the discussions of Pete Brosius and Jim Scott at the close of my panel "Political Ecology and the Politics of Place" at the 2003 annual meeting of the American Anthropological Association in Chicago. Further, I would like to thank Carolyn Cartier, Corinna McMackin, Dianne

Rocheleau, Kristina Tiedje, and the anonymous Duke University Press readers for bibliographic tips, and Wendy Harcourt for making available her special issue of *Development* ("Place, Politics and Justice: Women Negotiating Globalization") as this piece was still in progress. Many of the ideas expressed in this introduction have crystallized as a result of my research in Papua New Guinea, conducted most recently with Wenner-Gren, ACLS, Fulbright, and CSWS (the University of Oregon's Center for the Study of Women in Society) funding, and I am most grateful for the generous support of these agencies.

1. The term *political ecology* had some currency before it appeared in a paper by Eric Wolf in 1972. In the 1960s and 1970s it referred to a neo-Malthusianism that stressed the need to control population expansion and the pressures it placed on land utilization in the interest of solving a perceived environmental crisis (Bryant and Bailey 1997:10–11; see also Castree 1995:18–19). This " 'political ecology school' " was discredited across the political spectrum (ibid.:11). Geographers in particular dismissed it as too narrowly focused on demography and local practices (see Bryant 2001:152–55; Harvey 1974; Hecht 1985; Peluso and Watts 2001; N. Smith 1984; Watts 1983a, 1983b, 2000). Beginning with Wolf's use of the term, political ecology became Marxist in its orientation (Greenberg and Park 1994; Peet and Watts 1993:238–39, 1996:4–5; Scoones 1999; N. Smith 1984:53; Vayda and McKay 1975; Watts 1983a:234–39).

2. As a "green" Marxism, neo-Marxist political ecology offers *a heterodox rather than an orthodox* reading of Marx. However useful the Marxist legacy retrospectively appears, those looking for a systematic ecological framework have found the classic texts disappointing. Some even find them wide of the mark, inspiring drubbings as well as neo-Marxist revisions and post-Marxist departures (see Greenberg, this volume; see also discussions in Benton 1989; Castree 1995; Castree and Braun 1998:7–10; Eckersley 1992:chapter 4; Foster 2000; Grundmann 1991; Harvey 1996; O'Connor 1998; Peet and Watts 1996:28–30; Schmidt 1971; and N. Smith 1984). Perhaps the best-known critique of Marxist orthodoxy is that of the Frankfurt School, which faulted Marx for his promotion of progress, seemingly at all costs, and for his infatuation with an industry- and a technology-driven "domination" or "mastery" of nature, at the expense of nature itself and its ecovalue. The Frankfurt School replaced class conflict with "the larger conflict between men and nature" (Jay 1973:256; see Baudrillard 1975; Eckersley 1992:chapters 4, 5; Harvey 1996:133–39; Jay 1973:chapter 8; N. Smith 1984). Although a Marxist might counter that these two conflicts are inextricable, that class conflict and the conflict between nature and humanity alike derive from the mode of production, the Frankfurt School, in an unprecedented way, succeeded in putting the need to theorize nature and human–nature articulations on the historical materialist map. The Frankfurt School's critique reverberates in ecofeminist writings, especially in Carolyn Merchant's *The Death of Nature*, which locates the domination of nature in the domination of a *patriarchal* capitalism.

3. On the shift from neo- to post-Marxist political ecology, see Bryant 1998; Escobar 1995a, 1995b; Peet and Watts 1993, 1996; Peet and Watts, eds., 1996; and Peluso and Watts 2001.

4. A classic instance of materialist reasoning, one that is paradigmatic for cultural ecology, is Marvin Harris's (1966) account of why Hindus prohibit the eating of beef. Harris reasoned that cattle are a better resource alive than dead and that prohibiting the consumption of beef is a way of assuring that cattle will not be slaughtered. True, dead cattle are a source of leather and beef, but live cattle provide dung for fertilizer as well as milk, and they also serve as work animals, pulling the plows that furrow the fields that the dung fertilizes. An idealist, by contrast, would explain the Hindu prohibition on eating beef in religious terms.

5. On the constructionist turn in political ecology, see Alvarez, Dagnino, and Escobar 1998a, 1998b; Alvarez, Dagnino, and Escobar, eds., 1998; Anderson and Berglund, eds., 2003; Berglund and Anderson 2003; Brosius 1999c; Escobar 1995a; Gibson-Graham, Resnick, and Wolff 2001; Hajer 1995; Laclau and Mouffe 1987; Leach and Mearns, eds., 1996; Peet and Watts 1993, 1996; Peet and Watts, eds., 1996.

6. The critique of the nature/culture dualism is most strident in Descola and Pálsson 1996 and Lansing and Kremer 1993. See also Descola 1994; Pálsson and Lansing et al., this volume; and Soper 1995. On the term *social nature*, see Braun and Castree, eds., 1998; Castree and Braun 1998 and 2000; Castree and Braun, eds., 2001; Braun and Castree, eds., 1998. On the term *humanized nature*, see Lansing and Kremer 1993 and Lansing et al., this volume.

7. Reading *Pigs for the Ancestors* this way directs attention away from the environment and toward Maring politics, including gender politics. Although *Pigs for the Ancestors* was written before the great efflorescence of interest in gender studies and feminist anthropology, Maring gender politics is all but featured in Rappaport's account of how the *kaiko* is triggered. Of *Pigs for the Ancestors* it could be said that it offered the very first glimpses into the gender politics of production, warfare, and exchange in the New Guinea highlands, themes that would begin to engulf New Guinea ethnography in the decade following the book's publication.

8. Critiques of Rappaport's work, especially *Pigs for the Ancestors*, appear in Friedman 1974; Lees and Bates 1990; Moran 1990; Sahlins 1976; and Vayda and McKay 1975. See Rappaport's responses in the "Epilogue" to the 1984/2000 edition of *Pigs for the Ancestors* and Rappaport 1990; see also Kottak 1980:chapter 8.

9. In his "Epilogue" to the 1984/2000 editions of *Pigs for the Ancestors*, Rappaport rejected in no uncertain terms the reductive materialism of the first edition: "The emphasis put upon organic and ecological functions in explanations of cultural phenomena was too great in early formulations . . . , including that developed in *Pigs for the Ancestors*. There was a tendency to strip cultural phenomena of their distinctiveness as such and to grant to the possibly adaptive roles of some cultural forms a comprehensive signifi-

cance approaching explanatory sufficiency. The explanatory power of the general ecological formulation was, in short, exaggerated" (1984:333–34). Rappaport's signature
move consisted in replacing the reductions of *Pigs for the Ancestors* with an appreciation
of the incommensurabilities of the human condition (Biersack 1999c): "What seems to
me distinctive of humanity is that it lives in terms of meanings it itself must construct
but it is not fully constituted by those meanings, nor is the world in which it lives. . . .
The makers of meaning are organisms living in and absolutely dependent upon ecological processes, process constituted not by meanings but by natural law. . . . We are,
furthermore, only *loosely constrained* by our circumstances from constructing meanings
that do not conform to law or, for that matter, even to organic need. We are not, that
is to say, debarred from the construction of self-destructive or even world-destructive
follies" (Rappaport 1984:335–36; emphasis added).

10. Antecedents to this argument may be found in the writings of Benjamin Whorf,
who argued that a language that has twenty words for snow constructs a reality that
differs from the reality that a language having only one word for snow constructs. It
may also be found in the structuralist emphasis upon differences that make a difference. In his *Course on General Linguistics*, the structural linguist Fernand de Saussure
famously observed that the French term *mouton* and the English term *mutton* have different signifieds (that is, reference different realities) because the one refers to sheep on
the hoof and lamb on the plate but the other only refers to food (1966[1915]:115–16; see
discussion in Sahlins 1976:62–64). Instead of *reflecting* a reality that is *anterior* to signification, classification, the business of recognizing differences that make a difference,
signification *produces* a reality that is *posterior* to signification.

11. This distinction between sex/sexuality as a datum of nature and gender as a datum
of culture is itself now interrogated, queer theory arguing that sexuality is itself constructed.

12. In this regard, the term *transnational corporation* (TNC) suggests what the term
multinational corporation cannot: a displaced-replaced *emplaced* enclave that is enmeshed
not only in "specific social relations established between specific people, situated in un-
equivocal localities, at historically determined time" (Guarnizo and M. Smith 1998:11),
but also in the transnational circuits that are the condition of its own transplantation.
TNCs operate within local-regional/national/global matrices, and it is these matrices
and their dynamics that are the topics of a transnational, place-based political ecology.

13. On the concept of place as used here, see Biersack 1999b:81–82, 1999c:14, 2003,
2004; Dirlik 2001; Escobar 2001; Harcourt, ed., 2002; Harcourt and Escobar 2002;
Massey 1993; Moore 1998; and Prazniak and Dirlik, eds., 2001.

14. Harvey uses the term *place* to mean the local in the sense of a geographically
delimited, self-oriented and self-organizing entity, one that is "constructed out of an
introverted, inward-looking history based on delving into the past for internalized origins" (Massey 1993:64; see Harvey 1993). In this usage, *place* suggests an enclave "of

backwardness left out of progress," a "realm of rural stagnation against the dynamism of the urban, industrial civilization of capitalism, as the realm of particularistic culture against universal scientific rationality" (Dirlik 1996:23).

15. *Place* is not the only term that has been used to signify local–global intersections (and, admittedly, this is not the only meaning given to the word *place* [see Feld and Basso, eds., 1996, for another usage]). Thus, Featherstone writes of "third cultures," which emerge through the interaction of the global and the local (1993:174). Wilson uses "global/local" to refer to intermediacy—to suggest, as he puts it, "situated [global/local] interrelationships" (2000:250) in "third spaces" (ibid.:249) and the "impurity and synergy" (ibid.) inherent in the "global/local interaction" (ibid.; emphasis removed) of these "third spaces." Robertson is well known for his neologisms "glocal" and "glocalization" (1995) to suggest the spaces and processes of intermingling in and through which the peculiar mixture of homogeneity and heterogeneity (see Appadurai 1996:32–33) of the contemporary world takes shape. In his contribution to *Building a New Biocultural Synthesis*, Roseberry "reject[s] the attempts of world-systems theories to explain local processes and relations in terms of the dynamics and needs of global capitalism" (1998:75) and concentrates instead "on the specifically local construction and shaping of power relations, including those that have their source outside of particular regions" (ibid.). The "social field" approach that he recommends dispenses with the structural or "level"-based approach of world system theory, which privileges the global over the local, and considers instead the way in which external factors contextualize internal factors, which then respond to these external factors, etc. "The social field places the local within larger networks and therefore requires a knowledge of those networks. But the networks themselves are uniquely configured, socially and historically, in particular places at particular times." To the extent that this is true, "the local is global . . . , but the global can only be understood as always and necessarily local" (ibid.). Most recently, Raffles has promoted the notion of "locality" (1999, 2002). Differing from location, which is narrowly spatialized qua locale, locality partakes of "a chain and a series of ever-widening concentric circles" (Raffles 2002:70) and must be understood through these articulations.

16. Henri Lefevbre was the first to insist on the contingent and activity-dependent nature of space (*The Production of Space* [1991]).

17. There is no lack of terminology to talk about the contingent, historical character of space and its organization. Appadurai, for example, has recently coined the term *process geography* to refer to spatializations that precipitate out of "various kinds of action, interaction, and motion" (2001:7) and that establish, reinforce, or undermine the very articulations that define and make a place (ibid.:7–9). He prefers "process geographies" to "area" (as in "area studies"), a term that presumes geographical fixity and insularity and that is tied to an outmoded concept of culture and its territorialization (ibid.:7–9). James Ferguson and Akhil Gupta (2002), Anna Tsing (2000, 2001a,

2001b), and Neil Smith have written about "scale-making," "scale-jumping," and other spatialization practices. Actor network theory approaches space through its production, focusing on agents' networking activities (see Latour 1993; Law and Hassard, eds., 1999). Nancy Munn was perhaps the first anthropologist to provide an ethnography of the production of space—or, in her language, "spacetime"—in her phenomenological study of *kula* exchanges in the Massim area of coastal eastern New Guinea. Spacetime is "a lived world that is not only the arena of action, but is actually constructed by action" (1992:8). She elaborates in true Lefevbrian fashion: "sociocultural practices 'do not simply go on *in* or *through* time and space, but [they also] . . . constitute (create) the spacetime . . . in which they "go on"'" (Munn 1992, quoting Munn 1983:280). Munn does not consider (as N. Smith does [1992]) the possibly transgressive, subversive nature of the *kula*'s regionalism, but this regionalism emerges, and has emerged, in colonial and postcolonial contexts; it arguably constitutes an alternative, oppositional "politics of scale" (ibid.), one that installs itself transgressively in the interstices of colonial and postcolonial geographies (see ibid.).

18. Gupta and Ferguson (1997a) use *place* and *place-making* in a rather different way, in terms of the local and its construction (see also Feld and Basso, eds., 1996): "Too often . . . anthropological approaches to the relation between 'the local' and something that lies beyond it (regional, national, international, global) have taken the local as given, without asking how perceptions of locality and community are discursively and historically constructed. In place of the question, How is the local linked to the global or the regional? then, we prefer to start with another question . . . : How are understandings of locality, community, and region formed and lived? To answer this question, we must turn away from the commonsense idea that such things as locality and community are simply given or natural and turn toward a focus on social and political processes of place-making" (ibid.:6).

19. It could be argued that the theme of the production of space inheres in transnational studies. The various "-scapes" of which Appadurai has written over the past fifteen years (1996) are transnational spaces that are contingently created through the "flow" of images, capital, technology, ideology, and people.

20. Contributing to a critical understanding of the contemporary world, its marginalizations and injustices, environmentalist social movements and oppositional campaigns increasingly preoccupy today's political ecology (Alvarez, Dagnino, and Escobar, 1998a, 19998b; Alvarez, Dagnino, and Escobar, eds., 1998; Brosius 1999c, 2001b, and this volume; Escobar 1992; Escobar and Alvarez, eds., 1992; Greenough and Tsing, 2003; Greenough and Tsing, eds., 2003; Hvalkof and Escobar 1998; Kalland and Persoon, 1998; Kalland and Persoon, eds., 1998; Peluso and Watts, eds., 2001).

21. The social movements and oppositional campaigns of which political ecologists and others write today tend to rest upon a variety of differences other than class (gender, sexuality, age, ethnicity, "race," and the like) (see Moore 1998:349–50). In fact, they

rest upon a "discourse of difference" (Escobar 1995a:226) and a search for "collective identity" (Dirlik and Prazniak 2001) within a cultural politics that cannot be reduced to class and class struggle. They thus open a window upon how differences other than class mediate human–nature relations in the contemporary world.

22. The answer must be: in some times and in some places (see Ortner 1996; Mac-Cormack and Strathern, eds., 1980; Merchant 1980; Valeri 1990).

23. See Carney 1996; Escobar, Rocheleau, and Kothari 2002; Rocheleau, Thomas-Slayter, and Wangari, eds., 1996; Schroeder 1999; Schroeder and Suryanata 1996; Thomas-Slayter and Rocheleau 1995; Thomas-Slayter and Rocheleau, eds., 1995).

24. See Comaroff and Comaroff 1991; Gates, Jr., ed., 1985; Said 1978; Thomas 1994. Indeed, the critique of development, as proffered originally by Escobar (see also Gupta 1998), calls development discourse to task for its *cultural* politics, which cast as inferior the colonial and postcolonial Southern or non-Western world, converting spatial distance into evolutionary remoteness (Fabian 1983) and racial hierarchy. Several of the essays in this volume call attention to the invidious distinctions that lend a prima facie credibility to various "civilizing" missions, development among them, and that function powerfully to marginalize and disenfranchise groups. According to Brosius (this volume), loggers and their supporters conceptualize the Penan as near-animals in need of development's evolutionary boost and the forest as an atavistic, savage realm of particularism that undermines a "mainstream" vanguard of modernization, development, and Malaysian nationalism. In much the same way, the Ashéninka of Amazonian Peru are signified by mestizo-associated groups as primitive, backward, uncivilized, and the like (Hvalkof, this volume) and are handicapped through these cultural politics of denigration.

25. See Berkes 1999; Brosius 2000, 2001b; R. Ellen, P. Parkes, and A. Bicker, eds., 2000; Gupta 1998; Nazarea, ed., 1999; see also Dove; Lansing, Schoenfelder, and Scarborough; and Pálsson, this volume.

26. See Brosius, this volume; see also Brosius 2000, 2001b, 2003; Gibson-Graham, Resnick, and Wolff 2001; Hyndman 2001; Kirsch 2002.

27. On the debate between extreme realism and extreme constructionism in ecology, see Balée 1998; Blühdorn 2000; Braun and Castree, eds., 1998; Burningham and Cooper 1999; Casey 1996; Castree and Braun 1998, 2000; Castree and Braun, eds., 2001; Crumley 1994; Demerritt 1998; Rolston 1997; Watts 1998).

28. On the "politics of place," see Biersack 2003, 2004; Harcourt, ed., 2002; Moore 1998; and Prazniak and Dirlik, eds., 2001.

Beyond Modernist Ecologies

Equilibrium Theory and Interdisciplinary Borrowing: A Comparison of Old and New Ecological Anthropologies

Michael R. Dove

Introduction

The stochastic, discontinuous nature of theoretical development in anthropology has recently received some critical attention. Roseberry (1996), for example, has suggested that post–World War Two anthropological theory can be divided into three generational periods, each of which has ended in the perception by the succeeding generation of a crisis of theory in the discipline. Roseberry asks whether this tendency to discard what went before in the light of what has come next is not overly facile. Ecological anthropology can also be faulted in this regard. Brosius (1999c:278) has recently pointed out that there is little linkage between the old ecological anthropology of the 1960s and 1970s and the new ecological anthropology of the 1990s and 2000s. Is such discontinuity real or just apparent? Where does it come from? And what does it tell us about the evolution of the field and the wider relationship between science and society?

Rereading Ecological Anthropology

Such theoretical discontinuities are made possible by a curiously ahistorical academic stance in which the ideas of the past are measured against the ideas of the present without reference to their own time and place. The historian of science Bernard Cohen (1994:xii) calls this stance "Whiggism in history: the attempt to judge the ideas of the past by present standards rather than to explore such ideas in their historical context." What is needed in order to explore rather than judge the old, as Cohen suggests, is greater attention to how we read it. The past decade or two have seen increasing interest in how we read our works and those of others. Rosaldo (1993:184), for example, argues that new forms of social analysis require new habits of reading. Poststructural theory offers insights into how to discern what is truly new as opposed to simply reworked. Derrida (1978:282) thus writes of the inherent paradox in and challenge to critical thought of necessarily exploring some of the very concepts that are being critiqued.[1]

One subject that merits greater attention in new readings or rereadings of theory is the relationship between science and society. This is a subject that anthropology (like many other fields) has traditionally avoided. As Asad (1973:15) wrote, there is "a strange reluctance on the part of most professional anthropologists to consider seriously the power structure within which their discipline has taken shape" (cited in Nader 1997:42).[2] This reluctance was supported by an earlier generation's vision of the role of science in society. Thus, we see in the work of the sociologist Robert K. Merton and his peers in the 1950s and 1960s an assumption of a sort of pact between science and society that was thought to guarantee the autonomy of science. Any interest in the relationship between knowledge and power was written out of this conception of science from the very start. A new, post-Mertonian generation of scholarship rejects these assumptions, however, and argues that science is not autonomous from society (Lenoir 1997:3, 15). This critique is at the base of two important traditions of scholarship: on the one hand, a more conservative and positivistic school of science and technology studies and, on the other hand, a more humanistic and radical out-and-out critique of modern science.

This increasing attention to the relationship between science and society has offered new insights into the relations between disciplines, in particular the way that ideas are taken from one discipline and used, critiqued, and transformed in another. Over the past decade interdisciplinary relations have been the source of considerable ferment and even conflict. Debates between physical scientists and critics of science from the social sciences and humanities have earned the sobriquet "the science wars." The critique of concepts from the physical sciences by nonphysical scientists has been derided by the former as "higher superstitions" (Gross and Levitt 1994) and "fashionable nonsense" (Sokal and Brichmont 1998). Unheeded by either side in this debate, however, is the work of historians and other scholars of science on the everyday practice in which disciplines borrow from one another, and how this practice reflects the wider character of relations between science and society (Cohen 1994; Fujimura 1992; Lenoir 1997). An understanding of these borrowing practices can help us to understand the way in which individual disciplines and science as a whole evolve. It can help us better understand the ways in which ecological anthropology in the 1960s both differs from and yet resembles ecological anthropology today and what the implications of this are for the future development of the field.

From Equilibrium to Disequilibrium

I propose to explore here a particular transformation in ecological anthropology since the 1960s: the supplanting of assumptions of equilibrium with assumptions of disequilibrium in the systems we study. Ecological anthropology in the 1960s assumed that socioecological systems tended toward a state of equilibrium, and it tried to explain different aspects of society in terms of their contribution to this state. Ecological anthropology today, however, assumes that systems tend toward disequilibrium and asks how societies cope with this tendency. I will draw on Roy A. Rappaport's monograph *Pigs for the Ancestors* (1968) as an exemplary case of the equilibrium-based model, and I will draw on my own published work from the 1980s and 1990s to illustrate the disequilibrium model. Rappaport's work focuses on the Tsembaga, a tribal group in the interior of Papua New Guinea, whose basis of subsistence was the swidden cultivation of root crops for both humans and pigs; my work concerns the tribal Kantu' of West Kalimantan, Indonesia, who cultivate rice and a variety of non-rice cultigens in swiddens to meet their subsistence needs and who meet market needs by raising rubber (*Hevea brasilensis* [Willd. ex Adv. de Juss.] Muell.-Arg.) and pepper (*Piper nigrum* L. [Piperaceae]) for international commodity markets (map 1).

I will focus on the ecological functions of ritual in Rappaport's work and in my own. Rappaport (1994:167) noted in later years, "I had intended to study a local group of tribal horticulturalists in the same terms that animal ecologists study populations in ecosystems . . . [but] was therefore surprised, to say the least, to discover that environmental relations among the people studied seemed to be regulated by a protracted ritual cycle." In the wake of this discovery, he dedicated his research to explaining the relationship between ritual and ecology. I began my research among the Kantu' with a similar puzzle: I understood from Freeman's (1960, 1970) work that the Ibanic peoples of Central Borneo were consummate swiddeners, but I also gathered from the literature that their agroecological strategies were periodically and decisively

DOVE MAP 1. The Kantu' Territory in Kalimantan, Indonesia, on the island of Borneo.

deflected by seemingly unrelated bird omens (Harrisson 1960; Jensen 1974; Richards 1972; Sandin 1980). My research, then, was intended to explain this seeming lacuna in the indigenous resource management system.

I will begin with a discussion of my work on agricultural divination among the Kantu'. I will then examine the evolution in thinking regarding "perturbation" since the 1960s, compare its treatment in Rappaport's work with my own, and try to explain the difference in terms of the wider political and intellectual contexts in which the work was carried out. In the next section I will analyze the use of equilibrium versus nonequilibrium models in terms of the politics of interdisciplinary borrowing in Rappaport's time versus my own. I will conclude with a discussion of the changes as well as the continuities in interdisciplinary borrowing since the 1960s and the implications of this for our understanding of relations between anthropology and environmental studies, between natural and social science, and between science and society.

Analysis of the Ecological Dimensions of Ritual

Rappaport (1984:4) summarized his analysis of study of the ecological significance of Tsembaga ritual as follows: "It will be argued here that Tsembaga ritual, particularly in the context of a ritual cycle, operates as a regulating mechanism in a system, or set of interlocking systems, in which such variables as the area of available land, necessary lengths of fallow periods, size and composition of both human and pig populations, trophic requirements of pigs and people, energy expended in various activities, and the frequency of misfortunes are included." Rappaport's analysis was one of the chief sources of inspiration for my own doctoral research among the Kantu'. His analytic framework is reflected in the grant proposal I wrote to the National Science Foundation to fund this research, which proposed a "functional hypothesis (concerning bird augury as an ecologically adaptive, functional system) and a philosophical hypothesis (concerning bird augury as a deterministic belief system)." The analysis I eventually carried out is summarized below.[3]

Kantu' Agricultural Augury

Kantu' augury is based on the belief that the major deities of the spirit world have foreknowledge of events in the human world and that, out of benevolence, they endeavor to communicate this knowledge to the Kantu'.[4] If the Kantu' can read the intended meaning of these communications correctly, they believe that they too can possess this foreknowledge. The most common media through which the deities are thought to express themselves are seven species of forest birds, which are said to be the sons-in-law of the major deity, Singalang Burong.[5]

The Kantu' deem omens from these birds to be relevant to many facets of life, including travel, litigation, and especially swidden cultivation. Omens are observed through most of the stages of the swidden cycle and typically are honored by proscription of swidden work on the day received. The most important omens, however, are those received during the first stage of the cycle, selection of the proposed swidden site (color plate 8). The selection of swidden sites is problematic for the Kantu' because of the large number of environmental variables that differentiate sites and because the particular variables associated with swidden success change unpredictably from year to year. This stage of the swidden cycle, called *beburong* (to take birds or omens), consists of traversing a section of forest proposed for a swidden and seeking favorable bird omens. The character of the omens received at this time—*burong badas* (good birds) versus *burong jai'* (bad birds)—is believed to be a major determinant of the character of the eventual swidden harvest. Accordingly, if a sufficiently ill omen is received, the site should be rejected for farming that year.

The key to interpreting site rejection in particular, and the system of augury in general, is the indeterminacy of the physical environment of Borneo, the consequent impossibility of correctly predicting critical agroecological conditions, and the attendant need to devise pluralistic rather than deterministic agricultural strategies. The system of augury helps to construct the conceptual space required for such strategies by systematically frustrating deterministic agricultural decision making and undermining empirical linkages between the environment and human decision making.

Environmental Irrelevance of Augury

Critical to my interpretation of Kantu' augury is the fact that I could find no empirical linkage between the behavior of the omen birds on the one hand and the success or failure of the Kantu's swidden harvests on the other.[6] Whereas there is an empirical basis to the birds' behavior, in the sense that they have fixed and predictable habitats, feeding patterns, mating seasons, etc., there is no temporal or spatial pattern in the birds' behavior that correlates with temporal or spatial variables critical to swidden success.[7] In any case, the rules of augural interpretation thoroughly scramble any possible empirical linkage between bird behavior and swidden success. A linkage is ruled out not by ecology, therefore, but by culture. According to Kantu' augural lore, for example, some omen birds have more than one type of call, and the meaning of an omen varies according to which call is heard. Thus, the normal call of the Rufous Piculet is auspicious but its variant trill is inauspicious (cf. Freeman 1960:82–83). There appears to be no ecological significance to this variation. Similarly, there is great augural, but there can be no agricultural, significance attached to whether one or more calls of the Rufous Piculet (or other omen bird) are heard. Equally important to interpretation (and equally irrelevant from an agricultural point of view) is whether the call is heard (or the bird is seen) to the observer's right or left. Augural interpretation is subject to an extravagant number and variety of additional rules and caveats, all of which appear arbitrary in an agroecological sense.[8]

The agroecological arbitrariness of augury is most clearly illustrated in the performance of *betenong kempang* (to divine from the *kempang* tree), a variant type of augury that the Kantu' sometimes practice instead of seeking omen birds at the prospective swidden site (color plate 8). It consists in cutting a pole from the *kempang* tree (probably *Artocarpus elasticus Reinw. ex Bl.*) and measuring and marking one's *depa'* (arms-breadth) on it. The augurer then proceeds to cut some of the underbrush on the site, after which he or she remeasures his or her arms-breadth against the *kempang* pole. If this measurement exceeds the initial one (indicating that the pole has "shrunk"), this augurs ill for the proposed site; but if the measurement falls short of the initial mark (if the pole has "grown"), this augurs well. Although this procedure is susceptible to unconscious influence on the part of the augurer, it nonetheless represents a cultural statement regarding the lack of any link between the environment and the augural system.

Another relevant feature of the rules governing augural interpretation is the proscription of interhousehold sharing of omens. Augury is performed by each household on its own, usually by the eldest male.[9] "Omens cannot be shared," the Kantu' say. If an auspicious omen became known to a neighboring household, the latter would want to join in taking it. Such sharing might abrogate the auspiciousness of the omen or, minimally, make it difficult for the original recipient household to obtain that omen again in future years. The Kantu' minimize sharing of omens by the simple expedient of keeping their own household's omens secret from other households. Sharing is also minimized by augural rules that tie omen interpretation to the varying composition and fortunes of the individual household. For example, the meaning of certain omens (e.g., the *bacar* call of the Rufous Piculet) is said to vary depending upon whether elders live in the household. Of more importance, many omens have no meaning other than to signify a reversal of the household's prior swidden fortunes, regardless of whether these were good or ill (cf. Sandin 1980:104–8). For example, if a household hears the inauspicious *bacar* call of the Rufous Piculet when selecting a swidden site, they should abandon that site. But if the household has never gotten a good harvest of rice, then this call is auspicious and they can retain that site. This arbitrary reversal of the meaning of omens makes it difficult to share them, increases interhousehold diversity in responses to omens, and generally enhances the randomizing effect of augury.

Sharing of omens is also mitigated by the belief that augural interpretation is personal and idiosyncratic. The Kantu' say, *Utai to' ngau bidik kitai* ("This thing is a matter of our own fortune"). Each person builds up over his life-time a personal and distinctive relationship with each of the omen birds (cf. Metcalf 1976:108). It is quite possible, as a result, for two augurers to assign completely opposing meanings to the same omen. This personal relationship, coupled with the fact that there is considerable interhousehold variation in the knowledge and intensity of observance of augural rules, further ensures that there is considerable interhousehold variation in the seeking of omens and the interpretation of the omens obtained.[10] If omens conveyed to the Kantu' empirically valid information about the environment, we would expect inter-household agreement on what information is conveyed by what omen, and we might also expect interhousehold sharing of this information, but this is clearly not the case.

In summary, the evidence suggests that there is no systematic relationship between augury and favorable conditions for swidden cultivation, and that the lack of any such relationship is enhanced by the rules of the augural system itself. This system produces what amounts to a metaphoric throw of the dice at a critical point in the swidden cycle, which I interpret as a cultural state-ment about the indeterminacy of the environment, the imperfection of human knowledge of it, and the inappropriateness of systematic management strate-gies. The augural system of the Kantu' helps them address this indeterminacy by culturally constructing and supporting a nonsystematic pattern of swidden behavior. This is associated with both intrahousehold and interhousehold di-versity in swidden strategies that helps to ensure a successful adaptation to a complex and uncertain environment.

Augury Versus Modern Development

This traditional system of knowledge differs dramatically from modern development thinking in the way that it deals with the uncertainty that characterizes the tropical forest ecosystem.[11] Both approaches make some effort to cope with uncertainty, but while modern development tries to eliminate it, augury does not. Studies in a variety of fields suggest that we need to come to better terms with the limits of our ability to know, in a deterministic fashion, the complex and the unknown (e.g., Diamond 1990; Holling 1994; Holling, Taylor, and Thompson 1991). Common to these studies is the belief that embracing our ignorance is, paradoxically, the best way to overcome it. Thus, Ludwig, Hilborn, and Walters (1993:36) write, "Confront uncertainty. Once we free ourselves from the illusion that science or technology (if lavishly funded) can provide a solution to resource or conservation problems, appropriate action becomes possible." I suggest that Kantu' augury, by accepting uncertainty, thereby reduces its impact on agroecological futures in the tropical forest.

Analysis of the principles that underpin the Kantu' system of augury can help to defamiliarize and thus make more accessible to critical review the principles being used by contemporary scientists and planners to understand and manage tropical forests. The aspect of modern science and planning that stands out in greatest relief by comparison to Kantu' augury, and that would benefit most from such a review, is its linear, deterministic, and monistic character. Although some notable critiques of this character have appeared (e.g., Holling, Taylor, and Thompson 1991), "single vision" continues to dominate the thinking of scientists, international donors, and national planners working in the field of development.

Perturbation and the Research Context

The premises of my analysis of Kantu' augury differ in some notable respects from the premises of Rappaport's study of Tsembaga ritual, especially with respect to perturbation and equilibrium. The differences do not simply involve my more critical stance toward equilibrium theory, however. Rappaport's work was also, in a sense, a critique of equilibrium theory, in particular its implications for the role of people. His goal was to demonstrate how the perturbation of local relations between society and environment could self-regulate, ultimately leading both the social and nonsocial components of the environment back toward equilibrium. Accordingly, if equilibrium theory took humans out of the environment, then Rappaport put them back in; if equilibrium theory denaturalized humans in the environment, then Rappaport naturalized them. Whereas Rappaport proposed essentially a new take on the equilibrium model, however, I joined other, subsequent scholars in rejecting the overall model. Thus, my work has focused not on elucidating the processes by which local perturbation leads back to equilibrium states but rather the processes by which extralocal perturbation leads local systems *away* from equilibrium.

Perturbation and Equilibrium Models

The equilibrium model on which ecological anthropology like Rappaport's was based assumed stasis in both society and environment, and anything that disrupted this was problematized. Eugene P. Odum's (1971) work in ecology is particularly associated with this approach.[12] This equilibrium model was replaced over the past two decades, not just in anthropology but in most of science, by a nonequilibrium model. Worster (1990:11) writes that "Odum's ecosystem, with its stress on cooperation, social organization, and environmentalism" was replaced with an image of "nature characterized by highly individualistic associations, constant disturbance, and incessant change." Worster (1990:3, 11) summarizes the change as one from "a study of equilibrium, harmony, and order" to a study of "disturbance, disharmony, and chaos."[13] The shift in emphasis was early on characterized by one of Rappaport's interlocutors, Jonathan Friedman (1979:268), as a shift from regulation, maintenance, and negative feedback to trends, constraints, limits, crises, and catastrophe.

The adoption of the nonequilibrium model within anthropology was not an isolated event but part of a larger set of changes. First, not only did the emphasis shift from problematizing stability to instability, but this shift entailed greater interest in the representation of stability versus instability (Worster 1990, 1995). Second, the discipline became much more attentive to the linkages between local communities and wider political-economic systems. And third, there is much more explicit concern with structures and relations of power: there is greater interest in problematizing institutions of power, notably institutions of national and international development; and at the same time, there is increased interest in decentered studies of power.

As a result of all of these changes, anthropology began to treat perturbation less as something that disturbs the ethnographic object and more as an object itself. This led to a generation of studies in anthropology and allied fields that encompasses such subjects as natural disaster (Erikson 1976; Hewitt 1983; Oliver-Smith and Hoffman 1999; Solway 1994; Watts and Bohl 1993), famine (Hansen 1994; Sen 1995; Watts 1983c), refugees (Ebihara, Mortland, and Ledgerwood 1994; Malkki 1997), and illness and human suffering (Davis 1992; Scheper-Hughes 1995). In Bornean studies alone, we have seen studies of El Niño Southern Oscillation (ENSO) and other climatic perturbations (Knapen 1997; Nicholls 1993; Salafsky 1994; cf. Fox n.d.), drought and fire (Gellert 1998; Goldammer 1990; Harwell 2000b; King 1996; Leighton and Wirawan 1986; Mayer 1996), and ethnic violence (Harwell 2000a).

As suggested by the subjects of these studies, this paradigm shift has potential political implications—but there are differences of opinion about what these are. Many supporters of the postmodern turn argue, and often with good cause, that the result is a more engaged and thus more radical scholarship. On the other hand, activists and scholars doing critical research on issues like gender, race, and ethnicity argue that the loss of equilibrium and other "centered" models has meant the loss of authority for their critiques.[14] This debate is especially sharp in environmental studies. As Zimmerman (1994:12–13) puts it, "If in fact there is no such balance and if natural processes are constantly in flux, why should anyone take seriously radical ecology's warning that the practices of advanced technological societies are throwing nature 'out of balance'?" Some observers say that the emasculation of critical environmentalism is in fact in keeping with the turn to the political right that has occurred since the 1960s. Thus, Zimmerman (1994:8) writes that some critics ask "whether it is any accident that, at the very moment in which capitalism is transforming the planet into a homogenized production unit, many postmodern theorists encourage students 'to reject global and universal narratives in favor of fragmentary conceptions of the world as 'text.'" Worster (1995:77) argues along similar lines that "the newest ecology, with its emphasis on competition and disturbance, is clearly another manifestation of what Fredric Jameson has called 'the logic of late capitalism.'"[15] Rappaport (1984:402–3) himself wrote in the 1980s that whereas his ecological anthropology had been driven by the "ecological movement," it was succeeded by something that was driven by "neo-conservative developments." This suggests that Rappaport's (1984:xviii) scholarship, including his reliance on equilibrium models, may not have been as naive or politically conservative as our post-Odum hindsight suggests.

The Context of Rappaport's Work

In order to properly interpret Rappaport's use of equilibrium models, we need to understand the context in which he worked. There is an irony in many of the criticisms of Rappaport's work, in that the same scholars that criticized him for ignoring the wider political context of the Tsembaga themselves ignored Rappaport's own wider political context. These critics wanted to place the ethnography but not the ethnographer in proper political context. They wanted to know how wider systems affect our understanding of the Tsembaga, but they did not ask how wider systems affect our understanding of scholarship on the Tsembaga.

Rappaport himself emphasizes that at the time of his arrival, the Tsembaga had as yet experienced limited "disruption," except for the introduction of steel tools and pacification by the Australian authorities (Rappaport 1984:12, 411). He also notes that during the fourteen months he lived with the Tsembaga, much of daily life revolved around the postwarfare *kaiko* ritual cycle (ibid.:397). Rappaport frequently refers to these two factors (albeit after the fact)—namely, the "intactness" of the society and its preoccupation with ritual—in explaining the focus of his research.

Rappaport also repeatedly mentions several factors beyond his immediate field site that influenced his work. One such factor was the "ecology movement" as it was then called (1984:402–3), which led to Rappaport's career-spanning concern with the impact of Western industrialized society on the environment. In *Ecology, Meaning and Religion*, Rappaport (1979:140) characterized industrialized capitalism as "inappropriate, infelicitous, and maladaptive." Part of this maladaptation is, according to Rappaport, capitalism's premise that it is adequate to the task of designing linear, deterministic systems for managing the environment. As Rappaport (1978:68, 1984:444) saw it, however, the true management challenge is a more humble one: namely, to understand how not to destroy any system on which we depend but whose complexity exceeds our comprehension.

As this last comment suggests, implicit in Rappaport's critique of the development of Western industrial society is a critique of the associated ideology of modernity. When Rappaport carried out his field research for *Pigs for the Ancestors* from 1962 to 1964, it was a time of triumphant modernism, in which rational forms of social organization and planning were in almost unchecked ascendance (Scott 1998). The most important facet of this modernism was a postwar development discourse (Escobar 1995) that effectively problematized the rationality of indigenous societies such as the Tsembaga. *Pigs for the Ancestors* was one of a number of studies done at this time that in effect countered this discourse of high modernism with a discourse of their own. *Pigs for the Ancestors* was one of the most influential of these studies, for several reasons. First, its counterintuitive arguments argued for the rationality of what appeared to be the least rational aspects of indigenous systems (thinking here especially of ritual expenditure, which was always particularly vulnerable to modern economic critique). Second, it focused on the self-regulating character of indigenous systems, which implicitly undercut the modern argument for external intervention. And, third, it documented the awesome complexity of such systems, which was not to be fathomed without lengthy study, local residence, and reliance on local knowledge—all of which conferred greater authority on the indigenous systems. *Pigs for the Ancestors* was especially notable for its effective use of some of the key metaphors of high modernity (including finely crafted analyses of cybernetic feedback cycles) in arguing *for* the rationality of the indigenous system and *against* the need for an intervening developmental rationality.

Rappaport's critique of modernity and industrial society was thus based on a comparative analysis of environmental relations in what was then referred to as "primitive" and modern society. In his 1984 "Epilogue," for example, he contrasts the "ecological felicity" of tribal society and the "ecological destructiveness" of our own. This comparison of tribal and industrial society provides the implicit, discursive framework for the analysis in *Pigs for the Ancestors* (as is made more explicit in his later writings). Rappaport denies that this represented primitive romanticism on his part. He writes, "It does not seem to be invoking some lost wisdom of 'primitives' to propose that the relationships of members of tribal societies to their environments is such as to encourage ecologically sound thought and practice" (Rappaport 1984:319). We can see Rappaport's work as an attempt to redress the bias in policy circles problematizing the environmental relations of so-called primitives more than those of modern society.

Rappaport was one of the first anthropologists to argue for what came to be called the "repatriation" of anthropology (Marcus and Fischer 1986:135, 137). He argued that we need to look at our relations not just with our subjects but also with our society, to which we can offer what Rappaport (1979:170, 1984:430–31) called a "theory of correction." Rappaport's own acts of repatriation are visible in his extensive studies of the hazards of offshore oil drilling and nuclear waste disposal in the United States. Rappaport called engagement with such topics the "anthropology of trouble."[16] This sort of anthropology entails collapsing the separation within the discipline between theory and practice (Rappaport 1993:163, 1995:1). More broadly, it entails collapsing the separation between science and society, which is a recurring theme in Rappaport's writing.[17] As Rappaport (1990:68–69) puts it, "The concept of the ecosystem is not simply a theoretical framework within which the world can be analyzed. It is itself an element of that world. . . . The concept of the ecosystem is not simply descriptive. . . . It is also 'performative'; the ecosystem concept and actions informed by it are part of the world's means for maintaining, if not indeed constructing, ecosystems."

The Context of My Work

The context of my work in Indonesian Borneo from 1974 to 1976 and subsequent years can be compared with that of Rappaport's from 1962 to 1964. By the time of my fieldwork, *Pigs for the Ancestors* had been published and heralded as "the yardstick for studies in human ecology for a long time to come" (Wilson 1969:659). It was a major influence on my thinking about ritual and ecology (other influences included Conklin on swidden agriculture, Freeman on the Ibanic peoples of Borneo, and Vayda on the ecology of tribal peoples in the Pacific). My research proposal, as noted above, echoed Rappaport's rhetoric in proposing "a functional hypothesis (concerning bird augury as an ecologically adaptive, functional system) and a philosophical hypothesis (concerning bird augury as a deterministic philosophic system)."

My field situation resembled Rappaport's in some ways—focusing, as it did, on a marginal, horticultural, tribal people—and in some ways it did not. Thus, whereas the Kantu' were also swidden cultivators like the Tsembaga, they seemed to have a much more volatile subsistence system (which was likely associated, in part, with the difference in patterns of risk involved in cultivating tubers—as among the Tsembaga—versus grains—as among the Kantu'). My hospitable reception by the Kantu' was affected, perhaps decisively, by the fact that the harvest prior to my arrival in late summer of 1974 was bad, so bad that many households' rice supplies ran out months before the next harvest, and they were obliged to substitute tubers and maize as their starch staple. In contrast, the first harvest following my arrival, in spring 1975, was very good. I now realize that my good fortune was a function of the ENSO cycle (the poor harvest of 1974 was affected by the strong El Niño of 1973 [Fox n.d.; Nicholls 1993; Salafsky 1994]). My research among the Kantu' showed that this sort of perturbation in swidden fortunes was not unusual: the average Kantu' household meets both its consumption and seed requirements from its swiddens only one out of every three years (Dove 1985b:294).[18] This amount of volatility in the agricultural system stands in marked contrast to that of the Tsembaga; Rappaport (1984:64) maintains that the Tsembaga simply did not experience crop failures at all. Also distinguishing the Kantu' from the Tsembaga was a history of involvement in global trade that dated back to at least the mid–nineteenth century, which was one of the principal means for coping with the volatility of their swidden system. Originally involving the gathering of forest products for international trade, since the beginning of the twentieth century it had involved the so-called smallholder cultivation of rubber and pepper in a manner that was carefully integrated both spatially and temporally into the swidden system.

The political circumstances of the Kantu' at the time of my initial study were also quite different from those of the Tsembaga. It was apparent along a number of dimensions that I was working with a people tied into wider settings, in ways that had direct and often negative implications for the equilibrium of local life. One important tie stemmed from the proximity of the Kantu' to the international border between Indonesia and Malaysia, a mere two days' march away. This location had placed the Kantu', as recently as two years prior to my arrival, in the middle of cross-border guerilla warfare between so-called Malaysian/Chinese communists and the Indonesian army, the latter exacting reprisals from local tribesmen thought to be collaborating with the former. Indonesian army units still stationed throughout the region by the time of my arrival. The army operated in an often heavy-handed way that reflected the ambiguity of the state's stance toward the interior tribesmen, incorporating as it did attitudes of not just protection and paternalism but also suspicion and hostility. Tribal longhouses that were perceived as being averse to the state projects of nationalism, security, and development were given permanent garrisons of one or two soldiers, which was explicitly interpreted (by both sides) as a statement of lack of trust.[19] One of the features of the national military presence that was most resented was the monthly levy of tribal labor (one day per longhouse door [viz., household] per month) to carry supplies to remote military outposts, the practice of which was said to date from 1965.[20]

In short, the Kantu' were at the time of my study in regular contact with a centralized, hierarchical, authoritarian state that found much lacking in their way of life. Local representatives of this state deprecated Kantu' language,[21] culture, and religion and pressured them to abandon their traditional agriculture and settlement pattern[22] and adopt "modern" pond field agriculture and single-family houses. The deprecation of local systems of resource use was associated with the advancement of state-sponsored systems for managing people and resources, like transmigration and industrial logging, both of which were starting to making inroads into the area during my stay there (and have since been followed by the now-ubiquitous oil palm plantations). The Kantu' reciprocated these feelings by placing the Javanese—locally equated, not without some accuracy, with the Indonesian nation-state—well below the Dutch, although above the Japanese, in their ranking of foreign invaders and oppressors. The Kantu' view of the Javanese, of the state, was well expressed in an annual agricultural ritual wherein one representative of each swidden pest was placed on a wooden raft and sent downstream "to Java." The circumstances of my fieldwork thus placed me in the category of ethnographers who "have witnessed personally a threat to the people they study"—a circumstance Kottak (1999:25–26) sees as critical in redirecting focus away from the strictly local.

This wider context of my fieldwork with the Kantu' affected both my research and my writing. Thus, my initial write-up of my doctoral work focused on explicating the indigenous logic and rationale of the Kantu' swidden system, thus explicitly addressing the state's antipathy toward this system (e.g., Dove 1983b, 1985a, 1985b). My next series of papers dealt with ecological uncertainty and the consequent instability of Kantu' swidden returns, and the role in correcting it played by, first, local social institutions (Dove 1982, 1983a, 1984, 1988) and, second, commodity production for extralocal markets (Dove 1993a, 1994, 1996b, 1997). These two sets of papers were prompted by discourses at national as well as international levels that deprecated the rationality of indigenous social institutions and obfuscated the extent to which indigenous peoples are already tied into global market systems. A subsequent set of papers looked at Kantu' cosmologies of resource use and abuse and represented an attempt to problematize simplistic, cross-cultural use of concepts like sustainability by global environmentalists (Dove 1993b, 1996a, 1998, 1999a, 1999b; Dove and Kammen 1997)—and these papers also included, finally, my analyses of agricultural augury.

Interdisciplinary Borrowing

The extent to which ethnographic research and writing are thus affected by the wider social and political context is fairly obvious, even if infrequently studied. Less obvious is the way in which this context affects subtler conceptual dimensions of anthropological research and writing, such as the borrowing of concepts from other disciplines. Such borrowing is a common mechanism for increasing the efficacy of a particular piece of research and writing, when such an increase is demanded by political factors. The use of this mechanism is especially prominent in Rappaport's work.

Rappaport's Borrowing

Rappaport did not create de novo the analytical tools he employed with such ingenuity in *Pigs for the Ancestors*; he borrowed them from other disciplines. There are abundant precedents for doing just that in anthropology. Thus, Durkheim (1933/1964) drew from natural science organic metaphors for his analysis of the division of labor in human society. Similarly, Radcliffe-Brown (1952:12) borrowed from biology the metaphor of organic structure (of the human body or even a single cell) to illustrate his concept of "social function." Leslie White (1949) borrowed a focus on energy from thermodynamics to analyze the evolution of society. Conklin (1954), Berlin (1974), and others borrowed the tools of linguistics and systematic botany to develop the subdiscipline of ethnoscience. Most recently, anthropologists have borrowed methods for textual deconstruction from the humanities, in particular literary criticism, to construct postmodern critiques of science and society. Rappaport's own reliance on interdisciplinary borrowing is a salient characteristic—and it has proved to be both a strength and a weakness—of his work.

Perhaps the most striking example of Rappaport's borrowing beyond the traditional confines of anthropology involves systems theory. Rappaport drew from such authors as Bateson (1958),[23] Goldman (1960), Margalef (1968), and Wynne-Edwards (1965) concepts of cybernetics, feedback loops, and circuits, which he used to explain cognized models, adaptation, and ritual functions. His use of this language—for example, he suggested that "adaptive processes are cybernetic" (1984:416) and ritual "resembles digital computing machines" (1979:186) and may function as "homeostats and transducers" (1984:233)—was extremely novel and thus powerful. Another prominent source of Rappaport's borrowing was nutrition science. The first edition of *Pigs for the Ancestors* contained fifty-six pages of mostly quantitative appendices, of which seven pages focused specifically on Tsembaga nutrition. In response to criticisms of his nutritional analyses, he added thirty-five more pages on this subject in the second edition. Perhaps more important, if less sensational, was Rappaport's borrowing from ecology. As noted earlier, his intention in going to the field was "to study a local group of tribal horticulturalists in the same terms that animal ecologists study populations in ecosystems" (Rappaport 1994:167).

This interdisciplinary borrowing brought *Pigs for the Ancestors* the most praise for innovation but also, and inevitably, the most criticism for misapplication. Rappaport's effort to study a human population in the same way that animal populations are studied was rightly hailed as an innovative assault on artificial boundaries between nature and culture (e.g., Wilson 1969:659); but it also was criticized, and perhaps also with justification, for its unrealistic premises (e.g., regarding the culture, history, and political dimensions of human as opposed to animal populations). Rappaport's use of cybernetic language to interpret the role that Tsembaga ritual plays in regulating key environmental variables was applauded as a creative bridging of materialistic and symbolic analyses, but it was also critiqued as vulgar materialism and naive functionalism or simply "the use of fashionable metaphors from electronics" (Wilson 1969:529). Rappaport's pioneering efforts to document the regulatory role of ritual with detailed data on Tsembaga nutrition were praised for their rigor and boldness but also were attacked as being error-ridden and derided as "protein obsession" and "nutritional reductionism" (Rappaport 1984:369–70).

The most revealing of the critiques of *Pigs for the Ancestors* focused on its "fetishism" and its "analogic" and self-privileging character. Thus, Sahlins (1976:298) accused Rappaport of "a kind of 'ecology fetishism', whereby corn, beans, and squash become an 'unbalanced diet'"; Bennett (1976:181) said that *Pigs for the Ancestors* was "fundamentally an analogic operation, in which ecosystemic complexities and a generalized impression of ecological causation are plausibly suggested but never worked out in detail"; while others interpreted Rappaport's conversion of data into calories and proteins as merely "an attempt to dress up ethnography as hard science" (Rappaport 1984:370). Rappaport (1979:82) characterizes one critique (Bergmann 1975) as an injunction to "quit whoring after the strange gods of physics" (Rappaport 1979:82).[24] These pejorative critiques unwittingly address what is in fact the purpose of interdisciplinary borrowing like Rappaport's: namely, to draw concepts from other disciplines and refashion and employ them in an empowering way within one's own discipline.

There is contradictory evidence as to how conscious Rappaport himself was of the purpose of his interdisciplinary borrowing (and much of what I say here is inferred from his post–*Pigs for the Ancestors* writings).[25] On the one hand, his published rejoinders to attacks on *Pigs for the Ancestors* (including the 180-page "Epilogue" to the revised 1984 edition) take the attacks at face value and respond in kind, thereby seeming to cede the narrow framing of the argument to his critics.[26] On the other hand, some of Rappaport's writing seems to take a more distanced view of the argument and adopts a more objective tone to discuss the weaknesses as well as strengths of his approach. For example, he acknowledges that whereas his approach yielded tractable statements, they were not easily falsifiable (1979:68). More specifically, he is candid about the risks as well as the benefits of interdisciplinary borrowing. Thus, he writes that "attempts to generalize that have involved the application of principles developed in one field to others are often regarded [in modern science] with suspicion, and are likely to be dismissed as amateurish, reductionistic, or metaphysical" (1994:164). In the face of such suspicion, Rappaport seems to justify his interdisciplinary borrowing mostly on pragmatic grounds.[27] Thus, he writes that cybernetic models are "illustrative" (1984:359); that his emphasis on equilibrium (viz., as opposed to disequilibrium) had "heuristic" value (1984:viii); and that "biological and ecological considerations were emphasized largely because they were relatively novel and social considerations were not" (ibid.:393).[28]

Analyses of Borrowing

Since *Pigs for the Ancestors* was written, there has been increasing (albeit still limited) scholarly attention to the politics of interdisciplinary borrowing. Lenoir (1997), for example, has insightfully interpreted such borrowing in terms of Bourdieu's (1977) concept of "symbolic capital" (social prestige and renown that can be accumulated and is convertible into economic capital). Lenoir (1997:9) suggests that the symbolic capital that can be deployed by a given field at a given time can often be significantly augmented through strategic borrowing from other disciplines. He argues that such borrowing can invoke external values and create points of leverage in support of either orthodoxy or heresy (ibid.:17–18).[29] Rosaldo has interpreted the work of one of Rappaport's contemporaries, Harold C. Conklin, in a similar light. Like Rappaport, Conklin (1954, 1957, 1980) has been exemplary in drawing on the biophysical sciences (botany, agronomy, cartography) in his research and writing. Rosaldo (1993:185) places a strategic interpretation on the role this has played in Conklin's construction of his ethnographic discourse. Rosaldo (ibid.) writes, "Conklin has chosen a rhetoric designed to persuade an audience of ethnographers, botanists, and agronomists, who conceivably could in turn convince policy makers." Rosaldo (ibid.:186) suggests that by adopting the language and concepts of the physical sciences, Conklin could assume the "authoritative high ground" and adopt a guise of "self-effacing detachment and scientific authority" in what was essentially a political defense of his subjects. A guise of "detachment and scientific authority" lent weight to Conklin's work because the conventions of the biophysical sciences were then (as they are still) held in greater esteem by the policy audiences to which Conklin was, at least partly, addressing himself.

Some such asymmetry in public esteem—in symbolic capital—is integral to the dynamics of all interdisciplinary borrowing. Thus, scholars tend to borrow up, not down; they tend to borrow from fields perceived to be ascendant to their own.[30] One example of this, the ascendancy of theoretical physics since World War Two (and the associated "physics envy"), has been discussed by a number of observers (Lenoir 1997; cf. Ludwig, Hilborn, and Walters 1993). "Borrowability" may indeed be taken as one measure of a discipline's current ascendancy (or at least of the ascendancy of particular conceptual "packages" within it [Fujimura 1992]).[31] Ultimately, of course, individual disciplines compete for the status of borrowee rather than borrower (Lenoir 1997:12). Whereas the discourse of the science wars represents current interdisciplinary tensions as a contest over the "knowledge of knowledge, the nature of nature, the reality of reality, the origin of origin, the codes of codes" (Franklin 1995:166), the present analysis reminds us that it is also, if not only, a contest over the relative symbolic capital of individual disciplines and their "rates of exchange" with other disciplines.

Rappaport's (1979:61) statement that one of the primary advantages of his approach (specifically, his use of systems theory) was that it linked the social with the biological sciences must be interpreted in light of these dynamics of interdisciplinary borrowing. More so than is the case today, in the 1960s the biological sciences were in the ascendancy over the social sciences, and the borrowing of their concepts and language was thus empowering for an anthropological argument. Such borrowing made it more likely that Rappaport's arguments would be accorded greater weight by other scientists as well as policy makers. The lack of hearing accorded by policy makers to arguments not put in the reigning language of modern policy science was characterized by Rappaport himself as "institutional deafness" (Rappaport 1993:300 [cited in Brosius 1999c:50]).

My Borrowing

Although the symbolic capital of the social sciences is higher today than it was at the time *Pigs for the Ancestors* was written, work by anthropologists on environmental subjects is still strengthened by borrowing from the biophysical sciences.[32] In laying out my analyses of Kantu' divination, I too drew from the biological sciences. For example, in suggesting that the Kantu' took a pluralistic and nondeterministic approach to managing tropical forest resources, which I compared favorably with the monistic and deterministic approach of modern science, I drew on a critique of "single vision" by the ecologist C. S. Holling (Holling, Taylor, and Thompson 1991). Further, I suggested that whereas modern development tries to overcome and deny all environmental uncertainty, Kantu' augury "normalizes" it; and I cited in support of the wisdom of this position a historical analysis of tropical forest product use by the biologists Ludwig, Hilborn, and Walters (1993). Finally, in discussing the challenge to comprehension of the environment posed by the human consciousness itself, I cited the biologist Jared Diamond's (1990) work on the complexity of the rain forest and the difficulty of discerning its underlying patterns.

The natural scientists upon whom I drew for support themselves reached across disciplinary boundaries. For example, the central image used by Diamond (1990:27) to illustrate the complexity of the rain forest is Bach's composition the "Lord's Prayer":

> When, late in life, Bach wrote his Lord's Prayer, I suspect that he was trying to express the view he had reached of nothing less than life itself, and of his own struggles to hear God's voice despite the obstacles that life poses. . . . It's as if Bach were praying: yes, yes, by all means forgive us our trespasses, and all those things— but above all, God, give us the will and ability to hear Thy voice through this world's confusion. With this metaphor, Bach also unwittingly captured better than any other metaphor I know, the sense of what it's like to come to know the rain forest. This conclusion is neither blasphemous nor trivializing, because to biologists the rain forest is life's most complex and wonderful creation. It overwhelms us by its detail. Underneath that detail lie nature's laws, but they don't cry out for attention. Instead, only by listening long and carefully can we hope to grasp them.

Similarly, Holling, Taylor, and Thompson (1991) built their essay on the folly of equilibrium models around Blake's poetic critique of Newtonian thinking:

> Now I a fourfold vision see,
> And a fourfold vision is given to me;
> 'Tis fourfold in my supreme delight
> And threefold in soft Beulah's night
> And twofold Always. May God us keep
> From Single vision and Newton's sleep!

It is noteworthy that one of Rappaport's principal mentors, Gregory Bateson (who receives, along with Theophile Kahn, the dedication of *Ecology, Meaning, and Religion*), also was famous for reaching across disciplinary boundaries, extending his reach to psychiatry and animal behavior, among other fields. The salience of cross-disciplinary argument in all of these examples may only reflect my own (and Rappaport's) partiality to such practices. But it also may suggest that these scholars obtained leverage in their own disciplines, and at the same time became "packageable" and "borrowable" vis-à-vis other disciplines, in part by virtue of this borrowing.

Discussion and Conclusion

This analysis of the way that the wider context in which we work has affected research in ecological anthropology, in particular how it has affected our use of the concepts of other fields, has several important implications regarding the evolution of science in general and ecological anthropology in particular.

In recent years numerous authors, including Rappaport, have voiced anxiety over serial faddism in anthropology. Decrying "revitalist movements" of anthropology (1979:87; cf. Roseberry 1996), Rappaport writes, "We continue to move without advancing, without having learned all we could, or should or need to, from our experience, our knowledge, and our mistakes" (1984:xv). The analysis presented here suggests that there is indeed more to intradiscipline paradigm succession than simply the replacement of the incorrect with the correct, or even the less correct with the more correct. This analysis suggests that paradigm succession must be interpreted within the wider context of relations between disciplines and also between science and society.

Compare, for example, the role of the equilibrium model in Rappaport's early analyses of the ecological functions of ritual with its role in my own, later analyses. When indigenous peoples following non-Western management traditions were popularly perceived as a threat to the environment, Rappaport's use of an equilibrium model to naturalize and rationalize their behavior was empowering for them. But after equilibrium models had fallen into disrepute, it was more empowering for me to portray indigenous peoples as having something to tell the West about *dis*equilibrium.[33] This reversal has continued to the point where today's environmentalists are borrowing anthropological work on indigenous environmental knowledge (e.g., the concept of "primitive environmentalism") to use in their critiques of modern, industrial systems of resource use.[34] Similarly, during the early days of the computer age in the 1960s, Rappaport could draw on the theory of cybernetics to compose a radical critique of modernity and defense of traditional societies, whereas today, a scholar like Haraway (1991) can turn a critique of cybernetics into a powerful critique of modernity. Another example is economics: in the 1960s, the symbolic capital of economics was so high that it stimulated the development of a powerful subfield of anthropology. The situation has so changed today that economic anthropology is in danger of disappearing as a named subfield.[35]

In each of these examples, the political loading of the metaphor has changed or even reversed between the early and later periods, but the associated scientific discourses are not unrelated. Just as different disciplines can be "homologous" (Lenoir 1997), so successive models or paradigms within the same discipline can be homologous—meaning that there is continuity through time of position or structure but not of composition or function. Some analysts suggest that the homologous transformations within disciplines track political transformations in the wider society, that the politics of science and society basically coevolve. As suggested earlier, for example, a number of analysts believe that poststructural critiques (like the related critiques of equilibrium theory discussed earlier [Rappaport 1984:402–3; Worster 1995]) have developed in concert with a turn toward the political right in Western industrialized countries over the past two decades (Jameson 1984). Within anthropology, Roseberry (1996:21) suggests that the rise in postmodern theory "in spite of its political claims . . . [has] succeeded in accomplishing what generations of university administrators and Republicans could not accomplish—purging a whole range of politically engaged anthropologies."

There is some evidence that just as orthodox science transforms itself in concert with the norms of mainstream society, so radical science transforms itself in an obverse relationship to these norms. There is evidence, that is, of a dialectical relationship between critical science and society, which periodically brings about a reversal of both their value systems. Thus, Roseberry (ibid.:23, n. 2) suggests that radical critiques alternate in their reliance upon scientific versus hermeneutic approaches according to whether the latter versus the former, respectively, is currently in the ascendance in the society being critiqued.[36]

This analysis leaves us with a number of new questions for further study. The key questions are, How do the politics of science and society comingle? And to what extent is this responsible for homologous developments within individual disciplines? What are the implications of the fact that political currents transform the composition or function but not the position or structure of reigning paradigms? How does the comingling of science and society affect interdisciplinary relations and the dynamics of interdisciplinary borrowing? How does the pattern of borrowing vary with the tenor of relations between science and society? What sort of interdisciplinary borrowing is supportive of the donor (as well as recipient) discipline, and what sort is not? And what determines the occurrence of one versus the other? How aware are the scholars involved of these dynamics? The answers to these questions will tell us what role anthropology will play in environmental studies in the future.

Notes

I carried out research on the Kantu' of West Kalimantan from 1974 to 1976 with support from the National Science Foundation (Grant #GS-42605) and with sponsorship from the Indonesian Academy of Science (LIPI). I gathered additional data on local systems of adaptation to the tropical forest during six years of subsequent work in Java between 1979 and 1985, making periodic field trips to Kalimantan, with support from the Rockefeller and Ford foundations and the East-West Center and sponsorship from Gadjah Mada University. A recent series of field trips to Kalimantan, beginning in 1992, has been supported by the Ford Foundation, the United Nations Development Programme, and the John D. and Catherine T. MacArthur Foundation with sponsorship from BAPPENAS and Padjadjaran University. Portions of the analysis of Kantu' augury have been published in Dove 1993b, 1996a, 1999b. I am grateful for comments on an earlier version to Aletta Biersack and James B. Greenberg. I alone am responsible for the analysis presented here.

1. Cf. Tsing 1993:268.

2. Studies like Nader's (1997), for example, are the exception rather than the rule.

3. This account draws on Dove 1993b, 1996a, and 1999b.

4. Detailed descriptions of Bornean augury have been provided by Harrisson 1960; Jensen 1974; Richards 1972; and Sandin 1980. King 1977 and Metcalf 1976 debated whether augural interpretation is fixed or subject to individual interpretation; and Freeman 1960 suggested that augury has a psychological explanation.

5. The birds vary in age and hence in authority. In ascending order they are the *Nenak* (White-rumped Shama [*Copsychus malabaricus Scopoli*]), *Ketupong* (Rufous Piculet [*Sasia abnormis Temminck*]), *Beragai* (Scarlet-rumped Trogon [*Harpactes duvauceli Temminck*]), *Papau* (Diard's Trogon [*Harpactes diardii Temminck*]), *Memuas* (Banded Kingfisher [*Lacedo pulchella Horsfield*]), *Kutok* (Maroon Woodpecker [*Platylophus galericulatus Cuvier*]), and *Bejampong* (Crested Jay [*Blythipicus rubiginosus*]). In practice, the Kantu' take most of their omens from the first three birds or from three variant ritual practices called *beburong besi* ("taking omens from iron"), *betenong kempang* ("taking omens from the *kempang* stick"), and *beburong pegela'* ("taking omens from an offering").

6. The absence of an empirical association between omens and agricultural ecology is in fact a prerequisite to Kantu' belief in the supernatural import of omens. If a particular omen is obviously associated with some spatial or temporal variable relevant to swidden success, it undercuts its own supernatural character. In most systems of divination, indeed, it is precisely the impossibility of any such empirical connection that confers supernatural authority on the system (Aubert 1959:7, 8). This explains why any systematic ecological information the birds might convey to the Kantu' must be obscured by the investment of meaning in such random phenomena as the number, type, and direction of their calls.

7. Cf. Harrisson (1960:23) on another Dayak group: "Nor do the Kayans use as omen birds . . . any that have anything actually 'to do' in fact with the operations (house building, marriage, canoe journeys, rice planting, etc.) which these birds powerfully influence and not infrequently decide."

8. Gomes (1911:159) writes, "The intricacies of the subject are great. The different combinations of these voices of nature are endless, and it is difficult to know in each special case whether the spirits intend to foretell good or bad fortune. It is not an unusual thing to see old men, industrious and sensible in ordinary matters of life, sitting down for hours discussing probable effect on their destiny of some special combination of omens."

9. The only exception to this occurs when the longhouse farms for the first time in a tract of old forest, when augury may be performed on a longhouse-wide basis in a ritual called *ngali tanah* ("digging the earth").

10. Freeman (1960:90) writes, "Despite a general acceptance of the meaning of augural signs it is not unusual, therefore, for the recommendations of one augur to differ from those of another."

11. Holling (1978:107) maintains that deterministic thinking is unsuited to environments characterized by uncertainty.

12. Ecological studies were then dominated by the concept of the "climatic climax community," which was believed to prevail unless something out of the normal nature of things occurred. Human environmental relations could only "deflect" this commu-

nity away from its ideal climax, by definition, so human society was not part of this community.

13. The shift in emphasis is exemplified in Holling's (1994) suggestion that ecosystem change is controlled not just by exploitation and conservation but also by creative destruction and renewal.

14. For example, see Parpart (1993) on postmodernism and gender studies.

15. Jameson (1984). Cf. Söderqvist's (1986:281) comment that "the transition from ecosystem ecology to evolutionary ecology seems to reflect the generational transition from the politically consciousness [sic] generation of the 1960s to the 'yuppie' generation of the 1980s" (cited in Worster 1990:12).

16. Rappaport's (1993:301–2) most eloquent statement on this subject is perhaps his Distinguished Lecture, entitled "The Anthropology of Trouble," for the American Anthropological Association (1993), in which he (1) calls for ethnographic discourses to be not just intelligible but also audible, (2) challenges us to be citizens as well as anthropologists, and (3) pointedly reminds us (and especially those who would hide behind the specious query, What right have we to intervene?) that if we abdicate the field, then social policy will be set by "other, narrower disciplines no better founded than our own, and considerably less humane."

17. One of Rappaport's principal sources for this idea is Gregory Bateson (1958, 1972). In a famous line, Bateson (1972:504) writes, "We are not outside the ecology for which we plan—we are always and inevitably part of it. Herein lies the charm and the terror of ecology—that the ideas of this science are irreversibly becoming a part of our own ecological system."

18. Over half of the households in my study village did not reap sufficient rice for the following year's seed in 1974, whereas all did in 1975 (Dove 1985b:293).

19. While visiting a police office on the coast during this period, I saw a map of the interior that categorized all of the tribal regions of the interior as potentially communist.

20. The Indonesian invasion and annexation of East Timor in 1974 led to a heightening of military security in this border region (among others), which further added to my impression of the region and people as a beleaguered state margin.

21. Extralocal Javanese and Malay speakers were particularly derisive of the fact that the Kantu' "counting term" for people is iko' (cf. Richard 1981:113). Because this is cognate with the Indonesian/Malay term ekor, which means "tail" and is a counting term for animals, this was interpreted as meaning that the Kantu' equated one another with apes and monkeys (Echols and Shaddily 1992:154; Wilkinson 1959, I:297–98).

22. The stereotypical critique of longhouse life that I heard from representatives of the state was that it was "boring, dirty, and smelly."

23. Rappaport wrote, "I met Gregory Bateson in Hawaii in 1968 and he immediately became—and has remained—the most profound of influences upon me" (1993:167).

24. Cf. the concluding sentence in MacArthur's critical 1974 review (p. 121): "Unless anthropologists are prepared to undertake a thorough search of the relevant medical and biochemical literatures—and that can be a formidable task—they should be wary about offering 'solutions' to problems that baffle the specialists."

25. Andrew P. Vayda, who supervised Rappaport's doctoral research, says (personal communication) that neither he nor Rappaport was consciously borrowing from other disciplines for the strategic, political reasons suggested here. But, of course, most such behavior is not self-conscious.

26. The 1984 "Epilogue" drew heavily on (and in many cases repeated verbatim) Rappaport's 1979 book, *Ecology, Meaning, and Religion*.

27. Cf. the recent argument by one of Rappaport's colleagues at the University of Michigan, Conrad Kottak (1999), regarding the value of interdisciplinary "linkages."

28. The suggestion that there was more pragmatism than dogmatism to Rappaport's borrowing from the harder, more positivistic sciences is perhaps supported by the concern he showed throughout his career with the limits to knowledge.

29. As a result of such interdisciplinary borrowing, no field is autonomous: each is a transformed version of all others; each is "homologous" with all others (Lenoir 1997:16, 17).

30. This is not to suggest that what is borrowed is not altered. The success of interdisciplinary borrowing tends to vary, in fact, with the extent to which borrowed concepts are transformed (Cohen 1994:63, 65; cf. Fujimura 1992:176, 203–5).

31. Cf. Fujimura (1992:176, 178, 205) on "standardized packages" as an interface between the "multiple social worlds" of different disciplines.

32. Note the recent enthusiasm within anthropology for such tools as geographic information systems (GIS) and such subjects as global climate change.

33. Less than a decade after *Pigs for the Ancestors* was written, Jonathan Friedman similarly argued that a disequilibrium model made for a more empowering analysis of an upland minority people like the Kachin (Friedman 1975).

34. Cf. Brosius's (1997a) critique of the use of ethnographic analyses of indigenous environmental knowledge by environmentalists.

35. I am grateful to Eric Worby for this observation.

36. Roseberry (1996:23, n. 2) writes, "In periods dominated by obscurantist approaches . . . a 'scientific' examination of the relations and structures of power may be the most important step a politically engaged anthropology can take. In periods dominated by scientific positivism that serves to rationalize structures of power, a hermeneutic critique is necessary."

Nature and Society in the Age of Postmodernity

Gísli Pálsson

As terrestrial mammals, we humans stake our differences on the land; the
sea, however, is a great dissolver—of time, of history, of cultural distinction.
It is most fitting, therefore, that we should turn seaward to rediscover the
continuities of the dwelt-in world.
—Tim Ingold, 1991

The Regime of the Aquarium

This chapter discusses the dualism of nature and society in the age of postmodernity, focusing on the practical and theoretical implications of anthropological attempts to go beyond it. I shall illustrate my general argument about
the nature-and-society divide with reference to what I call the regime of the
aquarium, emphasizing the growing role of the state in coastal management
and the construction and acquisition of knowledge about marine habitat, particularly in the context of Icelandic fishing. In Iceland, the state has played
an increasing role in fisheries management, with the so-called Cod Wars and
the successive expansion of the national fisheries limits. This development has
culminated in a system of individual transferable quotas (ITQs), a highly modernist regime that privileges capital, boat owners, and scientific expertise, marginalizing labor, crews, and practical knowledge. The anticipated benefits of
the ITQ system—in terms of economic efficiency, ecological stewardship, and
safety at sea—are less than impressive. More important, the system has had
far-reaching social implications. For one thing, over time quota shares have
been rapidly concentrated with the largest companies. Also, a semifeudal system has developed with a fundamental division between quota holders and

those who have to rent quota—between "sea lords" and "tenants," to borrow local jargon. A small class of boat owners has become the de facto owner of the fishing stocks in Icelandic waters. Similar developments can be observed in several other fisheries (*Sharing the Fish*, 1999). The relative failures of current fisheries management, I suggest, invite a rethinking of the modernist regime and its assumptions of discontinuity, control, and hierarchy. The dualism of nature and society is part of the environmental problem. Unfortunately, the ecological theory that informs much radical environmentalism, including the animal rights movement, tends to reproduce the dualistic perspective rather than resolve it; informed by objectivist, Western discourse on science and the Other, animal rights activists often make a fundamental distinction between them (indigenous hunters and first nations) and us (Euro-Americans), nature and society, animals and humans.

Color plate 1 helps to illustrate some of the aspects of the modernist regime. This powerful image, first of all, underlines a conceptual distinction between nature and society. Also, it emphasizes the notion of control and captivity. One species is awaiting exploitation, while another occupies a privileged position, the position of the observer and manipulator. Implicit in that distinction is the separation of the inside and the outside and the related distinction between practitioners and experts. Finally, the presence of the aquarium in the dining space, containing samples from the ocean in the background, naturalizes the artificial human world. The aim of the artist, apparently, is to produce an "environmental" message. By reversing the roles of humans and aquatic animals, he seems to call attention to our implicit, subconscious positioning of the human and the natural.

Aquaria usually owe their construction to the fascination with single species and individual animals. Like keepers of aquaria, marine biologists have typically focused on one species at a time—modeling recruitment, growth rates, and stock sizes—although recently they have paid increasing attention to analyses of interactions in multispecies fisheries. Fisheries management seeks to affect systematically the structure of fish populations by controlling the relative sizes of different species and year classes, through regulations concerning fishing effort, gear, mesh sizes, territorial restrictions, etc. They may be difficult to administer at times, and the results are not necessarily along the lines envisaged by those in charge, but it is generally assumed that things are under control. The dominant management response to the current problem of overfishing in Western countries, including Iceland, is characterized by a preoccupation with single species, certainty, and expert control. That response, I suggest, is part and parcel of the dualistic, modernist project. Not only does it underline the boundary between the inside and the outside, observers and the observed, it fails to appreciate the nature and role of practical knowledge, misconstruing the relationships between humans and the environment.

The regime of the aquarium is not restricted to fisheries. As Scott has shown (1998), it goes with state power in high modernity. Indeed, some of the properties of that regime were laid out early on in Western history. Foucault has argued in his work on the "birth" of the medical clinic that modern medicine signified a fundamental shift in the understanding of the human body, a "mutation in discourse" (1973: xi); in particular, the body was dissected and subjected to the scientific gaze and manipulation of supposedly detached observers. Western understanding of the ocean and its inhabitants has undergone a similar transformation. It is pertinent, paraphrasing Foucault, to speak of the birth of the aquarium. The oceans tend to be seen as a gigantic fish tank, scientifically managed for human purposes. Such a notion is the culmination of a complex cognitive and political history. Until fairly recently Westerners typically assumed that the supply of living resources in the ocean was a boundless one. Thus, Thomas Huxley wrote in 1883, "I believe that the cod fishery . . . and probably all the great sea-fisheries are inexhaustible; that is to say that nothing we can do seriously affects the number of fish" (cited in McGoodwin 1990:66). Such a position, of course, was untenable in the long run. Many of the world's major fishing stocks are threatened with both overfishing and pollution—oil, radioactive waste, and other by-products of human activities— and fisheries more and more resemble other branches of industries in that the resource base is increasingly subject to deliberate human impact. For one thing, the boundaries of so-called wild fisheries are increasingly becoming blurred, with exponential growth in sea ranching and fish farming, not to mention genetic intermixing and engineering. Consequently, to think of the oceans as a boundless storehouse of living resources unaffected by humans really does not make much sense. It would be far more appropriate to speak of the regime of the aquarium.

Modernist and Postmodernist Ecological Anthropology

The concept of modernism usually connotes at least three related characteristics: the dualism of nature and society, the notion of objective science, and the assumption of linear control. Thus, Gudeman defines the "modernist pro-

duction regime" (1992:151) as a regime based on the idea that "the human
and natural world can be organized and subjected to rational, totalizing control." Scott (1998) uses similar terms. For him, "high modernism" is represented by "supreme self-confidence about continued linear progress, the development of scientific and technical knowledge, the expansion of production,
the rational design of social order, the growing satisfaction of human needs,
and, not least, an increased control over nature (including human nature) com-
mensurate with scientific understanding of natural laws" (Scott 1998:89–90).
Nature, then, is presented as an inherently logical and linear domain and, accordingly, the project of the resource manager is likened to that of the engineer or the technician. The modernist approach to environmental problems,
with its separation of nature and society, draws upon textual notions of scientific practice developed during the Middle Ages, when it was customary
to speak of nature as "God's book" and to regard science as the "reading of
the book of nature." Before the advent of modernism, there was no radical
separation of nature and society in European thought. People saw themselves
as integral parts of the world, embedded in nature. In a brief period, nature
became a quantifiable, three-dimensional universe appropriated by humans.
This universe represented a radical departure from the earlier, enclosed universe of the Aristotelians constituted by the earth and its seven surrounding
spheres.

The distinction between nature and society is central to both modern science and modernist culture. Such a dualism has not only been reinforced by a
rigid academic division of labor and massive institutional structures, but also
tends to be engraved in the financial and spatial organization of universities
and campuses, in their architecture, layout, and budgets. Much social scientific
thinking shares the main tenets of the modernist perspective, assuming a fundamental distinction between nature and society. Interestingly, the prologue
to Mary Catherine Bateson's memoir (1984) of her parents, Gregory Bateson
and Margaret Mead, is subtitled "The Aquarium and the Globe." Evidently,
the parents used globes and aquaria to give their daughter a sense of the integrity of the biosphere and the necessity of building a rational world for future
generations, "to balance the needs of living creatures and their relationships
with each other, the cycles of growth and respiration and decay" (ibid.:5). As
metaphors, both globes (Ingold 1993) and aquaria are highly modernist constructs; most important, they position the observer outside the system observed, gazing at a separate reality, much like the medical practitioner in the
Foucauldian clinic or the guests in the restaurant of color plate 1.

If disembeddedness, dualism, certainty, and human mastery are the characteristics of modernism, *post*modernism suggests the opposite—namely, embeddedness, monism, and the absence of certainty and human mastery. For me, postmodern social science is committed to continuity, engagement, and the negation of the idea of the detached observer. It seems that at the dawn of a new millennium anthropological theory on human–environmental relations is rapidly moving in such a direction, echoing the *condition* of postmodernity (Harvey 1989): the declining faith in rigid dualisms, hierarchy, and the tendency to conflate theoretical spaces previously kept separate. In recent years, indeed, the distinction itself between nature and society has increasingly been subject to critical discussion in several fields, including anthropology. And there are good grounds for second thought. For one thing, humanity has an embodied physicality that, by definition, naturalizes it, as Marx maintained long ago. Also, modern humans are presented with a "nature" very different from that experienced by earlier generations. Biotechnology and genetic engineering have revolutionized our capacity to analyze and alter DNA material, raising new and fundamental questions as to what constitutes life and nature; organisms are engineered and manufactured according to human designs and for human purposes (Pálsson and Harðardóttir 2002). Human nature, then, must be a fleeting category.

Moreover, recent theoretical developments in biology have questioned the classic argument of Mendel and Darwin that organisms are autonomous objects dictated by genes and selective pressures. An emerging alternative model emphasizes that the organism is empowered to shape its own development, that it is the *subject* of evolutionary forces. "Once it is realized," Ingold argues, "that capacities are constituted within developmental systems, rather than carried with the genes as a biological endowment, we can begin to see how the dichotomies between biology and culture, and between evolution and history, can be dispensed with" (Ingold 2000:385). The dialogic vocabulary of "co-evolution" and "niche construction" (Odling-Smee 1994) seems to be emerging in the place of mechanical Newtonian notions. Any distinction between inside and outside (and, by extension, between nature and society) seems beside the point. It seems reasonable to assume that humans are simultaneously part of nature and society and that modern policy on the environment should be based on that premise, and not on the idea that humanity, or some part of it, is suspended above nature.

While criticism of the modernist project and its separation of nature and society has been fueled by recent developments, including the greening of public discourse, it is not a brand-new phenomenon. The sixties and seventies, in particular, were characterized by growing doubts and discontent. Bateson, for instance, offered an early warning about the nature/society divide and the idea of absolute human domination, emphasizing that humans are part of nature, not external "autocrats." The "arrogant" Western notion of "complete power over the universe," he argued, was obsolete; in its place there was "the discovery *that man is only a part of larger systems and that the part can never control the whole . . . he cannot have a simple lineal control.* . . . Life is not like that" (Bateson 1972:413, emphasis added). Vayda and McCay (1975) challenged the cybernetic notions of homeostasis and explanation in the so-called new ecology of the time. And Wagner argued—from a different, "semiotic" perspective—that the distinction between the environment and the environed was an arbitrary one, fixed for the sake of analysis. As he wrote in an important and somewhat neglected paper, "Positivistic epistemology has generally favored the notion of 'levels' in the sense that the cultural is said to be an 'abstraction from' nature—a replication of its 'orders' via human artifice. . . . The arbitration of this limit, forging a literalistic culture that continually separates itself from a figurative nature that continually encompasses it, is the key to the 'environment' problem. In fact . . . the distinction is itself non-locatable, . . . nature is as much abstraction from culture as the cultural is an abstraction from nature" (Wagner 1977:395–96). Wagner's conclusion has a clear postmodern twist. In his view, nature and semiotics are so "completely and mutually continent of one another . . . that no boundary of any sort can be established between them." This implies, he argues, that "the Cartesian duality is at once completely insoluble and largely irrelevant" (ibid.:409).

Postmodern criticism has undoubtedly enriched anthropological theorizing on environmental issues, drawing attention to relations of power, to Western anthropocentrism, to the problems with dualism, and to the inadequacies of the correspondence or mirror-of-nature theory of truth and of the grand narratives of modern science on progress and control. Some postmodernist thinkers, however, leave it unclear how people should act with respect to the environmental crisis, dismissing the environmental problem as a "social construction" (see, for example, Hannigan 1995). As Gare argues (1995:97), while the idea of a "global environmental crisis" can be shown to serve those who are attempting to mobilize people to address it, with their hostility to grand narratives radical postmodernists "leave environmentalists no way to defend their belief that there is a global crisis or to work out what kind of response is required to meet it. . . . They are bound by assumptions which make the idea of a global environmental crisis incomprehensible." One wonders, indeed, given the social-construction perspective, how humans could possibly stumble on solutions to their problems.

Recognizing the contributions of postmodernist approaches to environmental issues, I suggest they also may have important drawbacks. I fail to see how one can develop an effective politics of the environment without some grand narrative, in the absence of any kind of theoretical authority in which we could ground reasonable and responsible claims about the nature and scale of the environmental problems we face. The earth is a place to live in, and to maintain its integrity and avoid ecological bankruptcy we have at the same time both to dwell and attempt to manage. Grand narratives, whether we like it or not, seem to be a political and ecological necessity. Such narratives, however, should be constructed through a democratic process and, moreover, they should combine theoretical expertise and practical knowledge, the "cunning intelligence" summarized in the Greek term *mêtis* (Scott 1998). And that brings me to my empirical example: modernist approaches to fisheries and their problems.

Icelandic Fisheries

Icelandic production discourse has undergone a series of successive changes as Icelanders have assumed new kinds of relations in the course of appropriating marine resources. To each phase in the development of Icelandic society corresponded a particular dominant paradigm, an underlying framework of understandings and assumptions with respect to what constitutes production and ecological expertise. One of the important changes concerns the discursive shift from land to sea at the end of the nineteenth century. During earlier times, Icelandic farmers and landowners occupied a central position, and consequently fishing was regarded as merely a supplementary subsistence activity. Fishing was not just a marginal occupation; it was also the subject of a cultural struggle. This can be seen from the fact that in the nineteenth century and the early twentieth those in power tended to present fishing communities as "devoid of culture" (*menningarsnau*), the source of degeneration, alienation, and deficient language. Finnur Jónsson, an Icelandic ethnologist, remarked in 1945 with respect to a fishing village on the southwest coast that while it was always regarded "as one of the best fishing places in the south, . . . its culture was at a rather low stage of development" (quoted in Pálsson and Helgason 1996). In the nineteenth century, however, as new markets for Icelandic fish were developed, especially in Spain and England, fishing villages grew, and there emerged an expanding market economy. While for many Icelanders the agricultural community continued to provide the dominant cultural framework, the essence of the Icelandic way of life, the focus of discussions on economics and production inevitably shifted from the landed elite to the grass roots of the fishing communities as fishing became a full-time occupation and a separate economic activity. Early in the twentieth century, fishers and boat owners gradually became the central agents of production discourse, replacing the landed elite as the economy shifted from stagnant agriculture to expansive fishing. In the process, agriculture was redefined as a burden to the national economy. Now, once again, with scientific management and a quota system in the fisheries, the discursive pendulum has swung in the opposite direction—from sea to land. Fishing remains a major economic enterprise, but the makers of knowledge and economic value are no longer fishers but the land-based owners of boats and fishing plants and the holders of scientific, textual knowledge.

Following Iceland's independence in 1944, fishing effort on Icelandic fishing grounds multiplied. In 1948, the Icelandic Parliament passed laws about the "scientific protection of the fishing grounds in the coastal zone," to be able to prevent overfishing of its major fishing stocks, particularly cod. Four years later, Iceland announced that it would extend its territorial jurisdiction from three to four miles, and in 1958 it unilaterally extended its jurisdiction to twelve miles. In 1976, the Icelandic government extended the national fishing limits to two hundred miles, which marked the end of the last Cod War with Britain and West Germany. The domestic fishing fleet, however, continued to grow, and catches, relative to effort, continued to decline. The first serious limitations on the fishing effort of Icelandic boats were temporary bans on fishing on particular grounds. By 1982, politicians and interest groups were increasingly of the opinion that more radical measures would be needed to limit effort and prevent the collapse of the cod stock. A boat-quota system was suggested in 1983 to deal with the ecological and economic problems of the fisheries, a system that would divide this reduced catch within the industry itself. The precise allocation of catches was debated, until it was agreed late in 1983 that each boat was to be allocated an annual quota on the basis of its average catch over the past three years. This meant that some boats would get higher quotas than the rest of the fleet, a fundamental departure from traditional policy. And quotas were allocated to boat owners, not crews. These developments highlight two important points, as the following discussion will show: the relative marginal-ization of the practical knowledge of fishers and the shift in the locus of power from labor to capital.

Experts and Laypersons

In Iceland, some marine biological research had occurred by the end of the nineteenth century, but full-time research did not start until the 1940s. At the beginning of the twentieth century, most of the contributions to *Ægir*, the journal of the Icelandic Fisheries Association (which embraces most interest groups), were by fishers, but gradually marine biologists entered the scene. With fishers being important agents in the expanding economy, marine scien-tists had to carve a space for themselves in the role of collaborators and ap-prentices. This is especially clear in the writings of Bjarni Sæmundsson, the pioneering ichthyologist. In the 1890s he traveled throughout Icelandic fish-ing communities to learn from practicing fishers: "I had the opportunity to observe various kinds of newly caught fish, to look at fishing gear and boats and to listen to the views of fishermen on various matters relating to fishing and the . . . behavior of fish" (*Ægir* 1921, 14:115). Sæmundsson seems to have thought of himself as a "mediator" *(millilidur)* between foreign scientists and Icelandic fishers (*Ægir* 1921, 14:116), eager to learn from both groups. Scientific knowledge, along with the "practical knowledge" *(reynsluflekking)* of fishers, he suggested, was "the best foundation for . . . the future marine biology of Iceland" (*Ægir* 1928, 21:102).

The pioneering biologists not only regarded themselves as humble appren-tices, but were moderately optimistic about the immediate achievements of the scientific enterprise. Referring to the prospects of dealing with "the old mys-tery, the migration of fish," Sæmundsson comments, "We should not expect . . . to be able to deal with everything and, thus, to answer whatever question we may have, for instance to establish the location of herring . . . at a particular time. That kind of knowledge is far away, although it is our mission [*hugs-jón*] to be able to provide it in the future" (*Ægir* 1924, 17:144). Such a mixture of mission and modesty was no doubt necessary in the beginning in order to ensure political and financial support for marine science. Gradually, the neces-sary trust and confidence were attained; fishers, boat owners, and the general public participated in establishing fisheries science. Significantly, in 1931 one of the regional fisheries associations resolved as follows: "The behavior of most of the fish species we exploit is now known in most respects. The place and time of spawning . . . are topics which science has for the most part mastered. Nevertheless, there are many 'dead spots' in our knowledge of fish behavior. Little or nothing is known about what determines fluctuations in the catch" (*Ægir* 1931, 24:29). At the same time, however, another discourse emerged that downgraded the expertise of fishers. While the editor of the fisheries journal urged fishermen to participate in discussions on the fisheries, he sometimes reinvented the biases of the earlier agricultural elite: "You fishermen! This journal is intended for you, it should be your guide and your voice . . . it should speak for you when you are busy at sea . . . it should enlighten those of you who live at the outskirts, at the margin where the profit is, but often, too, unfortunately, ignorance and poverty" (*Ægir* 1932, 25:159).

By the middle of the century, the subtle competition of the discourses of fishers and biologists seems to have developed into open confrontation. In 1947, the fisheries journal published an article that found it necessary to remind readers of the significance of practical knowledge:

> Fisheries research is . . . intimately connected to fishing . . . and naturally . . .
> it should be carried out in collaboration with perceptive fishermen and boat
> owners. . . . *This may not be particularly scientific, but we should keep in mind that the
> experience that perceptive fishermen have acquired after years of practice . . . must provide
> some kind of guidance to the scientists. It is no coincidence that the same men catch more
> than others year after year.* What matters most is their attentiveness and their percep-
> tiveness with respect to the behavior of cod and herring. Icelandic ichthyologists
> should recall Bjarni Sæmundsson, who once remarked, in his well-known humble
> spirit, that he owed most to the fishermen of this country. (*Ægir* 1947, 40:159,
> emphasis added)

During the Cod Wars, the biologists at the Marine Research Institute, established in 1965, emphasized the prospects of estimating the composition and size of the cod stock: "In recent years, the success of spawning for a given year has been extensively studied. We have obtained tentative estimates of the size of different year classes, but since such research only began recently . . . it is not quite clear . . . what each year class will supply for the fisheries. Before long, however, we should know, and then we expect to be able to predict, only a few months after spawning, the real size of the year classes. I am optimistic that in the future we will be able to make forecasts with more accuracy than at present" (Schopka 1975:48). Now, more than two decades later, these words sound overly optimistic. Fundamental ecological relationships—including the relationships between the size of the spawning stock, the success of spawning, the size of the future fishing stock, and fishing effort—have turned out to be far more complex and difficult to establish than the biologists estimated.

The tone of humility and mutual learning typical of the pioneering biologists during the first half of the century has been replaced by claims about scientific certainty and folk "misunderstanding" (see *Ægir* 1964, 57:109). The element of trust that characterized relations between scientists and fishermen has evaporated. One skipper offered the following observation: "When fisheries biologists realize that fishermen possess knowledge which they themselves do not have, and when these two groups begin to cooperate on the basis of each other's knowledge, then we may envisage realistic knowledge about the quantity and behavior of cod on Icelandic grounds" (Guðjón Kristjánsson, *Ægir* 1979, 72:595). Another skipper (Guðjón Sigtryggsson) remarked a few years later, "Fisheries biologists have no possibility of finding or counting the fish in the sea. They have no equipment for this purpose beyond those that fishermen have" (*Ægir* 1986, 79:33).

The skippers' approach to the environment and the acquisition of ecological knowledge is very different from that of marine biologists. Formal schooling is essential for Icelandic skippers, but they all seem to agree that most of their learning takes place outdoors, in the course of fishing. Skippers' extensive knowledge of the ecosystem is the result of years of practical enskillment, the collective product of a community of practice (Pálsson 1994; Pálsson and Helgason 1998). Skippers discuss their own research strategy as a dynamic, holistic one, allowing for flexibility in time and space. Usually, their accounts emphasize constant experimentation in the flux and momentum of fishing, the role of perpetual engagement, and the importance of hunches, intuition, and tacit knowledge. Somewhat ironically, the skippers' approach is much closer to the postmodernist paradigm than is the approach of marine biologists.

Skippers rarely mention how they actually make decisions. One reason is that they are guided more by practical results than by an interest in theoretical advancement. Often they simply notice that a particular strategy seems to work, without worrying about why that is the case. The skippers' reluctance to discuss their fishing tactics is not just the result of competition and secrecy and the value they generally place on independence and modesty; they have difficulty verbalizing their complex experience and intuition. What fishers label as

·hunches and fishing mood is particularly difficult to put in words, and some important decisions are made "out of the blue." Decision making, then, is based less on detached calculation or mental reflection than on practical involvement. Similarly, the process of enskillment is not just a cognitive one; rather, it involves the whole person interacting with the environment.

The education of skippers recognizes the importance of situated learning. Earlier participation in fishing, as a deckhand (*háseti*), is a condition for formal training, built into the teaching program and intended to ensure minimum knowledge of the practice of fishing. Once students in the Marine School have finished their formal studies and received their certificate, they must work temporarily as apprentices (mates [*stýrimenn*]), guided by practicing skippers, if they are to become fully licensed as skippers. According to many skippers the period of apprenticeship is a critical one. Reflecting on his mentor, with whom he had spent several years at sea, one skipper explained, "I acquired my knowledge by working with this skipper, learning his way of fishing. I grew up with this man." It is precisely here, in the role of an apprentice at sea, that the mate learns to attend to the environment *as a skipper*. Working as a mate under the guidance of an experienced skipper gives the novice the opportunity to develop self-confidence and to establish skills at fishing and directing boat and crew. The role of the mate, in fact, institutionalizes a form of apprenticeship that allows for protection, experimentation, and varying degrees of skill and responsibility. This is not a one-way transfer of knowledge, as the skipper frequently learns from the cooperation of his mate: mate and skipper—in fact, the whole crew—educate each other. In the beginning, the mate is just like an ordinary deckhand; in the end he is knowledgeable enough to have a boat of his own. At first he is of little help to his tutor but later on can be trusted with just about anything. Occasionally, the skipper may even take a break and stay ashore, leaving the boat and the crew to his mate.

The skipper's knowledge is a complex one. A skipper must choose times and places to fish on the basis of a serial accumulation of detailed environmental information. It is not surprising, therefore, that fishers often refer to the importance of "attentiveness" (*eftirtekt*) and "perceptiveness" (*glöggskyggni*): the ability to recognize and apply an array of minute but relevant details. Attentiveness is a complex ability and includes, for example, being able to read the sky and predict the weather, to participate in discussions within the local fleet, to understand the "sparks" of electronic instruments, and to be able to coordinate crew activities. All of this is essential in order to stay tuned to the realities of the local fleet and the fishing grounds.

The practical knowledge of modern-day skippers and their crews, of course, is just as essential to the success of fishing expeditions as it was to fishers in earlier times. As we have seen, however, within a few decades fishers' knowledge has increasingly been marginalized in public discussions and policy making. Why did this shift in discourse take place? One reason may have to do with changing paradigms in marine biological research (Deacon 1997). More important, though, Icelandic high modernity gradually ensured a strong connection between the state, capital interests (the owners of vessels), and marine science. During the Cod Wars of the 1970s, marine science played an important role, as scientists supplied the arguments that were used to support the notion of the "rational" management of the fisheries. In the words of Jón Jónsson, formerly director of the Fisheries Research Institute, "Our rights will never be accepted internationally unless we are able to supply solid evidence, based on scientific research, for the dangers posed to our fisheries and our whole cultural existence" (*Ægir* 1947, 40:258). With the birth of the modernist fisheries regime and the grand narrative of marine science, the voice of fishermen was gradually subdued, if not silenced.

While the present management regime represents the apex of modernist management, with science in the leading role, there is a growing recognition of the rhetorical context and the political role of marine science. Significantly, the Boat Owners' Association has hired a marine biologist on a permanent basis to reanalyze the data of the Marine Research Institute and to facilitate a "better understanding" among politicians and the general public of the cause of boat owners. This decision was triggered by discontent with the prognoses of the institute and its conservative recommendations regarding the total allowable catch. At the same time it illustrates the thin line between marine science and politics. The results and recommendations of both the Marine Research Institute and the economists responsible for the establishment and design of the ITQ system have also been challenged from within the scientific community, notably by researchers at the University of Iceland.

Relations of Power

Since the introduction of ITQ management in 1984, and particularly in the years following the enactment of the fisheries legislation of 1990 whereby fishing rights became true commodities (fully transferable), the Icelandic fishing industry has undergone a radical transformation. ITQs have become increasingly concentrated in the hands of large, vertically integrated companies, while the number of smaller operators has diminished (see Pálsson and Helgason 1995 for a detailed account of these structural changes). In 1991, there were 1,155 ITQ-holders, of which 16 "giants" (those with more than 1 percent of the ITQs) controlled about a quarter of the total Icelandic quota. In 1997, the number of ITQ-holders had decreased to 706, with 22 "giants" now controlling about half of the quota. A large majority of participants in the fishing industry and the Icelandic public are deeply concerned about the concentration of fishing rights in the hands of a few. In public discourse the owners of the biggest companies are habitually referred to as "quota kings" (*kvótakóngar*) and "lords of the sea" (*sægreifar*). Complaints are often raised that while fishing rights were traditionally the birthright of all Icelanders, now that they have become commoditized they will be inherited by the holders' descendants like any other privately owned item.

Not only are quotas being concentrated within the biggest companies, but new relations of "tenancy" have developed. These typically involve long-term contracts between large ITQ-holders and smaller operators, where the former provide the latter with ITQs in return for the catch and a portion of the proceeds. One such arrangement, usually referred to as "fishing for others" (*veiða fyrir aðra*), is becoming increasingly widespread. In such transactions, the supplier of the ITQs is a large, vertically integrated company that controls a processing plant and a trawler. A contract is arranged whereby the large ITQ-holder transfers ITQs to the smaller operator's boat. The latter then fishes the ITQs and delivers the catch to the supplier's processing plant for a price way below the free market price. Understandably, the lessee boat owners cannot make the same level of profits when fishing for others in comparison to fishing their own ITQs. As a result, they try to compensate for their losses by reducing the wages of fishers. Another form of ITQ leasing, generally referred to as "ton-for-ton fishing" (*tonn á móti tonni*), takes place when a large ITQ-holder offers to pool one ton of his ITQs against every ton put forward by the lessee. The latter then goes out and catches the fish and delivers the catch to the lessor's processing plant. In some cases of ton-for-ton fishing, regional fish markets act as the ITQ-brokers. Like the processing plants, the fish markets require a steady supply of raw material, and in order to achieve this they sometimes buy a small "surrogate" fishing boat on which to "store" their ITQs (to hold ITQs an operator must control a fishing vessel). These surrogate boats are rarely used for fishing and in fact are often unseaworthy.

The typical lessee operator is either an owner of a relatively small vessel with a meager supply of ITQs or the owner of a so-called eunuch (*geldingur*), a boat that has virtually no ITQs of its own and is solely operated on leased ITQs. Through ITQ leasing, boat owners with small ITQ holdings manage to prolong their fishing operations throughout the year. For the lessors of ITQs, however, participation in these new relations of production represents a rather lucrative business. By leasing its ITQs, a company can free itself from the expenses of actually catching the fish, while still procuring up to half of the market value of the resulting catch. These developments have led fishers to augment existing feudal metaphors by referring to the ITQ system as a tenancy system (*lénskerfi*). In this conception the quota kings are likened to medieval landlords, with the fishing grounds as their estate (*óðal*). Conversely, fishers and small-scale lessee operators become the "tenants" or "serfs" (*leiguliðar*), who are granted access to the fishing grounds on the prerequisite that they hand over their catch to the lessor's processing plants. The lessor controls not only how many tons a tenant boat is allowed to fish, but also the duration and location of each fishing trip. As one skipper put it, "One must give in to almost every demand, because the quota king makes all the rules, sets the price and everything."

The discourse of resistance briefly described above seems to highlight the issues of agency and a labor theory of value (Helgason and Pálsson 1997, 1998). In the case of the Icelandic ITQ system, the allocation of commoditized fishing rights to boat owners has resulted in a privileging of capital over labor, shifting power from sea to land and widening the economic rift between boat owners and their employees. Commenting on a young boat owner who had given up fishing and turned to renting out his ITQs, one fisher remarked, "He isn't working, and that's unnatural, a young man like him!" In the words of another fisher, "It necessarily adds a devilish aspect to the system when people can rent their quota and then just relax in bed." These and related statements testify to a powerful folk concept of work, bodily experience, and labor value that resonates with the so-called medieval house view of production and exchange, wherein the merchant and the usurer were not held to be creating anything but immorally breeding money from money.

The issue of the ownership of fish and quotas is frequently contested. ITQs remain, according to the first clause of the fisheries management legislation of 1990, the "public property of the nation." During debates on these fisheries laws, some members of the Icelandic Parliament raised doubts about the legality of the ITQ program, arguing that proposed privileges of access might imply permanent, private ownership that contradicted some of the basic tenets of Icelandic law regarding public access to resources. The laws that eventually were passed categorically stated that the aim was *not* to establish private ownership. The real world of legal and economic practice, however, seems to have a momentum of its own. While quotas, according to the law, are not to be regarded as the private property of quota holders, quota shares may achieve the characteristics of private property as time passes. There has been a long discussion over whether quotas can be used as collateral for obtaining loans. The law seems unclear on this point, but economic and legal practice seems increasingly to recognize quotas as collateral, which is a further step in the recognition of quotas as private property, undermining the significance and effect of the statement in the current law on public ownership. Some evidence indicates that quota shares are gradually acquiring the characteristics of full-blown private property.

In December 1998, the Icelandic Supreme Court came to a stunning conclusion concerning the legality of the quota system—stunning both in the sense that few people seem to have anticipated the verdict and because the immediate political fallout was massive. It is hard to find a parallel example in the entire history of the court over seventy-eight years. The Supreme Court unanimously concluded that the clause in existing fisheries laws that privileges those who derive their fishing rights from ownership of vessels during a specific period (three years prior to the establishment of the ITQ system) (Article 5, 38/1990) is unconstitutional. This privilege, the court concluded, violates both the constitutional rule against discrimination (Article 65) and the rule about the "right to work" (Article 75). The rule against discrimination specifies that all citizens shall enjoy equal rights (irrespective of sex, religion, worldview, ethnicity, race, color, wealth, family, and status in other respects), echoing the European declaration of human rights (Article 14) and the international agreement of 1966 on human rights. The latter rule, concerning the right to work, specifying that each citizen is free to enjoy the work he or she may choose, derives from the constitution of 1874, which, in turn, was modeled on the Danish constitution and the constitutions of other states. The court reasoned that temporary measures to limit fishing effort by restricting licenses to particular classes of vessels may have been both necessary and constitutional in the beginning, as long as they were in the interest of the general public. While, however, restrictions to the right to work may have been justifiable at some point, given the threat of collapse of fishing stocks, the indefinite legalization of the discrimination that follows from Article 5 38/1990 was not justified. That article, in principle, the court went on, prevents a substantial part of the public from enjoying the right to work in fishing and the relative share in the common property represented by the fish stocks, to which they are entitled.

Following the Supreme Court's ruling several fishers in the rural communities of the Western Fjords announced they were going fishing even though they did not have a quota. Their aim was to be taken to court to be able to challenge the law, and indeed the authorities were forced to respond by withdrawing licenses and threatening arrests. Such a rebellion, unparalleled in the history of the Icelandic ITQ system, is reminiscent of the oyster wars of colonial New Jersey (McCay 1998). In both cases attempts were made to defend common resources against enclosure and privatization, to establish or maintain some form of public trust doctrine. The ruling of the Icelandic Supreme Court has not only set the stage for intensive legal and political discussions about ITQs in the domestic context, but also has raised potential implications for the discussion of the constitutionality of similar systems elsewhere.

Beyond the Modernist Aquarium

The currently fashionable approach to fisheries in many Western countries, typically based on the allocation of individual property rights to fishing stocks in terms of shares in the total allowable catch (TAC) for a given species, has been developed in several contexts besides Iceland's, including Canada, New Zealand, South Africa, and the United States. By instituting private property rights to the fishing stocks in the form of quotas and letting the market regulate their distribution, it is claimed, rational production will theoretically be attained. Assuming a sense of responsibility among the new "owners" of the resource (the quota holders) and an unhindered transfer of quotas from less to more efficient producers, it is argued, privatization both encourages ecological stewardship and ensures maximum productive efficiency. The regime of fisheries management discussed above is informative in this context. The Icelandic ITQ system is one of the pioneering systems in the world, and as a result, perhaps, it reveals both the explicit and implicit assumptions of the theory of ITQs and the modernist perspective, with its emphasis on control and dualism. Also, in Iceland it may be relatively easy to detect and observe both the intended and unintended consequences of modernist fisheries, since here, unlike many other contexts, including those where ITQs have been practiced, fishing is of central importance to the national economy. The ITQ experiment in social, economic, and ecological engineering, in a sense, is relatively uncontaminated by confounding factors.

As we have seen, the Icelandic case illustrates many of the pitfalls of modernism: the radical separation of nature and society and the preoccupation with order, hierarchy, scientific privilege, and control. Here a totalizing regime that concentrates wealth and power in the hands of a few boat owners and marginalizes the practical knowledge of fishers and other laypersons has been established under the banner of progress and modernist science. Not only is this regime grossly unfair, engendering inequality on an unprecedented scale, but there are good grounds for questioning its reported beneficial role for sustaining fishing stocks.

First, in attempting to remove both the economic actor (the quota holder) and the observer (typically the economist) from the realm of social relations and communitarian concerns, implementing the autonomous *homo economicus* of neoclassical economics and theorizing of "tragedies of the commons," ITQs tend to manufacture irresponsible resource users. Where ITQs have been instituted, cheating (the underreporting of catch) and the dumping of bycatch (low-value species and fish for which the producer in question has no quota) are identified as major problems of monitoring.

Second, given the chaotic processes of marine habitat, there is no guarantee that the practices of allocating total allowable catch and individual transferable quotas have the consequences anticipated by theorists and policy makers. Many environmental goods, it may be argued, need to be understood in a holistic manner, not as atomistic objects but as parts of a larger complex. Acheson and Wilson suggest (1996) that the numerical approach of current resource economics and marine biology—an approach that has much in common with the regime of the aquarium, emphasizing single species, linear relationships, and states of equilibrium—fails to account for the realities of many fisheries. Their empirical work shows that while fisheries are deterministic systems, because of their extreme sensitivity to initial conditions ("butterfly effects," in the language of chaos theory), even simple fish communities have no equilibrium tendency. As a result, management faces forbidding problems when trying to explain the noise in ecological relationships. For example, it has been said about the relationship between recruitment and stock size, often a key issue for managers, that the degree of accuracy required for prediction is beyond any capabilities we might expect to achieve in a fisheries environment. Therefore, it becomes difficult, if not impossible, to know the outcomes of management actions such as quotas. This partly accounts for the failures of many attempts to manage fisheries, including the Icelandic ones, although the sheer level of fishing effort is, no doubt, a major problem generally.

The relative failure of the modernist regime and of individual quotas in recent years to deliver the goods they promised and the social repercussions they entail suggest that it may be wise to look for alternative management schemes and alternative ways of understanding the human engagement with nature. Pragmatism—with its emphasis on phenomenological perspectives, practical engagement, and direct perception—offers a way out of the modernist regime. According to the pragmatist school, the practitioner's knowledge is an emergent phenomenon, situated in immediate experience and direct engagement with everyday tasks (Pálsson 1994). Such a view, which starts with the assumption that all behavior is the result of the collaboration of person and context and that "personal" capacities arise from the mutual relations of individual and environment, suggests a radical break with the Cartesian tradition, the detachment of the subject. A similar perspective may be applied to scientific practice. Thus, the idea of some Archimedean standpoint outside nature and history is frequently subject to critical discussion on empirical, ethnographic grounds, with the growing awareness that the modernist perspective fails to account for the actual practice of modern science (see Irwin and Wynne 1996). The proper focus should not, therefore, be the passive, autonomous individual, but the whole person acting within a particular context. The Cartesian project has also been challenged by another related development: recent theorizing on the human body that emphasizes the embodied grounding of cognition, experience, and learning. Much of our knowledge, according to this perspective, is tacit, dispositions engraved in the habitus of the mindful body (Bourdieu 1990; Lave 1988).

The denigration of practical knowledge, evident in the Icelandic case, is a byproduct of high modernism. Scott argues (1998:305) there are three reasons for this: the professional concern that the more the practitioner knows the less the relative value of the expert, the general modernist contempt for everything having to do with the past, and, finally, the fact that practical knowledge tends to be codified and represented in a form that is alien to science. While *métis*, the intuitive intelligence of the practitioner and the painstaking attention to detail and the demands of the here and now, is indispensable for the success of any kind of practical enterprise, it tends to be discursively relegated to the margin. High modernism, Scott suggests, "has needed this 'other,' this dark twin, in

order to rhetorically present itself as the antidote to backwardness" (1998:331).
The proper response to the modernist agenda is not to adopt a romantic adherence to the past or make a fetish of traditional knowledge, but rather to
construct a management framework that is democratic enough to allow for
a meaningful dialogue between experts and practitioners and flexible enough
to allow for a realistic adaptation to the complexities and contingencies of the
world—in sum, a communitarian ethic of "muddling through." Those who are
directly involved in resource use on a daily basis may, after all, have highly valuable information as to what goes on in the sea at any particular point in time.
It is important to pay attention to the practical knowledge of skippers, allowing for contingency and extreme fluctuations in the ecosystem. Some form of
self-governance in fishing may be a practical necessity.

Self-governance, however, on the basis of practitioners' knowledge, may invite a dubious commodity fiction of its own. In orthodox theories of learning,
knowledge often becomes analogous to grammar or dictionaries. Given such
a perspective, indigenous knowledge is sometimes presented as a marketable
commodity—a thinglike cultural capital. Much of the practitioner's knowledge is tacit—dispositions inscribed in the body in the process of direct engagement with everyday tasks. A thorough discussion of what constitutes tacit
knowledge and how it is acquired and used seems essential for both renego-
tiating the hegemony of scientific expertise and rethinking the relationships
between humans and their environment. In this process, anthropologists can
have a crucial role to play, given their ethnographic method and their routine
immersion in the reality of the practitioners.

Many anthropologists have recently drawn attention to the importance of
developing an anthropological approach that combines human ecology and
social theory, and similar developments are taking place in some of the humanities, including environmental history (see, for example, Cronon 1996). Several
edited volumes (Croll and Parkin 1992; Descola and Pálsson 1996) give an impression of an emerging anthropology that is rapidly moving away from dualistic, modernist perspectives. One sign of a change in perspective is provided
by significant and rather sudden shifts in the views of many contemporary anthropologists—for instance, those of Ellen and Ingold, two important figures
in the anthropology of the environment. In some of their earlier writings both
made a rather rigid distinction between social and ecological relations, a distinction which they later seemed to feel uncomfortable with, if not to abandon.
Ellen (1996) emphasizes that nature is a social construction and that our dis-

tinction between nature and society is necessarily ethnocentric, adding that dichotomies are a "tyrannical necessity" (ibid.:28) and that "even if nature is a semantic fiction, it is a very convenient one" (ibid.:30); Ingold (2000) wants to dismantle the nature/society divide altogether. Whatever their theoretical disagreements in other respects, for Ellen and Ingold the distinction between social and ecological relations no longer suggests separate realities; it is an analytical device that is either useful or misleading.

No doubt the dualism of nature and society was highly useful in the sense that it made room for social scientific approaches to the environment within academies and universities traditionally dominated by natural science. As Benton argues (1991:25), "Dualistic, anti-naturalistic programmes in the contemporary human sciences are best understood as primarily defensive reactions to the intellectual imperialism (and, in many cases, moral and political conservatism) of biological reductionist programmes." Just as the dualism of modern social science was necessary to draw attention to the collective aspects of social life, to confront the individualistic bias of psychology, a dualistic academe with a relatively autonomous wing for social science was necessary to facilitate systematic discussion of some of the social aspects of the environment previously neglected by the paradigms of natural science. We may wonder, therefore, what the consequences of suppressing the nature/society dualism will be. Will it mean that the projects of development and the environment become, once again, subject to technological fetishism and green revolutions, relegated to biology, genetics, and engineering—with all the (im)practical implications such reductionisms have had in the past? Is it necessary, perhaps, given potentially shrinking budgets for social scientific research and the power struggle within Western universities and bureaucracies, to staunchly defend a well-demarcated social scientific camp? Surely, budgets are important, but I don't think that stubborn adherence to the dualisms of the past is a realistic defense strategy to address current problems of funding. Social scientists, in fact, might have been more successful lobbyists had they rejected the duality of the individual and the collective, the natural and the social.

Conclusions

There are profound problems, as we have seen, with modernist approaches to the environment. Icelandic fisheries management demonstrates many of the results. The system of individual transferable quotas, with its radical separation of nature and society and its division of winners and losers, both manufactures environmental irresponsibility and privileges capital and scientific expertise, marginalizing labor and practical knowledge. To move beyond the modernist approach represented by what I have termed the regime of the aquarium, it is essential to rethink human–environmental relations, including the nature–society divide. I have argued for a fundamentally revised division of academic labor—in particular the removal of the disciplinary boundaries between the natural and the social sciences. Such a move should not be seen as violating the integrity of the discipline of anthropology. On the contrary, from early on anthropology refused to be categorized as either natural or social. Anthropological practice, in my view, should be broadened, emphasizing intensive collaboration with a variety of other disciplines touching on environmental issues. The anthropology of the environment should be a dialogic affair.

Ellen has suggested that "the more you talk about nature the more you create a meta discourse which relies upon its existence, and the more you give it a life as a ruling concept; in trying to get *beyond* nature and culture we reify an opposition" (1996:29). That metadiscourse, of course, as Ellen implies, is not an end in itself. However, it has been around for quite a while, and silencing it is unlikely to dissolve the opposition of nature and society; dualisms don't disappear just because people stop talking about them. More crucially, there is an important sense in which this critical discourse *is* a highly useful one in that it provides a framework for identifying and removing persistent obstacles to the understanding of human engagement with the environment. An important item on the management agenda is to understand practical ecological knowledge and the ways in which it might be brought more efficiently than at present into the process of resource management. Given the perspective of practice theory, practical expertise is the result of a simultaneous engagement of the human actor with fellow humans and the rest of the material world.

Why, one may wonder, has the long theoretical conversation that sees humans in nature, engaged in situated, practical acts, been subdued most of the time in Western thought? While the dualism of nature and society has a dynamics of its own, driven by industrial capitalism and the successes of modern science, monism, too, has its critics. Plumwood, writing on gender and ecology (1991), suggests that one cannot really care for the environment if it is simply an unbroken extension of oneself. Such a position echoes the developmental views of Grimshaw (1986) with regard to dependent selves, the argument that too much conflation in a dyadic relationship (in marriage or a parent–

child relationship, for instance) may have detrimental effects for the personal development of one or both of the partners—namely, a loss of autonomy or maintenance of dependency. Grimshaw suggests that care and understanding "require the sort of distance that is needed in order not to see the other as a projection of self, or self as a continuation of the other" (1986:182–83). For Plumwood these points "seem to . . . apply to caring for other species and for the natural world as much as they do to caring for our own species" (1991:14). While the loss of self-boundaries may hinder personal growth, resulting in neglect rather than care, Plumwood's environmental argument is not convincing. After all, the extended notion of the embodied self—of *being* a body and not simply having it—does not preclude the idea of bodily concern. Indeed, caring for one's health and fitness is a major, if not obsessive, preoccupation nowadays, and not simply among those who project their body as a fetish external to themselves. The dissolution of the mind/body dualism, currently fashionable among Euro-Americans, is frequently associated with healthy diets and care for the body. And if, for many people, the incorporation of the body into their notion of self signifies intensive bodily care, why should they neglect the environment once they reject the dualism of nature and society?

I have found it useful to draw upon Scott's treatise about high modernism (1998). Scott's work tends to focus on agrarian discourse and the metaphor of gardening, a metaphor underlining the reconstruction of natural sites and the designed terrestrial space of botanical order, although it also refers to fishing. As a metaphor, the aquarium is no less compelling than the botanical garden. I hope to have shown that the dualism of nature and society, one of the cornerstones of the modernist perspective and the regime of the aquarium, is part of the environmental problem in that it both obstructs understanding of the human predicament and the kind of change in human-environmental relations that is needed. It is important to develop an approach that fully integrates human ecology and social theory, adopting a monist perspective that conflates nature and society. Given such a perspective, the aquarium may be an effective key metaphor for the interconnectedness of the biosphere. For such a metaphorical association to make sense, however, one would have to relax some of the modernist assumptions. The aquarium will have to include the practitioner of science as well as the layperson, swimming—along with fish and other earthlings—in the household of life. For me, that amounts to a postmodernist anthropology of the environment, an anthropology sensitive to interconnections, relations of power, and social discourse.

Notes

This article is based on my Kaspar Naegele Lecture at the Department of Anthropology and Sociology, University of British Columbia, on 15 October 1998, and a paper I presented at the Symposium on Cognition and Representation of Living Kinds: Towards a New Ecological Anthropology, University of Kent, 25 February 1997. I thank my hosts on both occasions for their invitation and hospitality and their comments upon some of the arguments presented. Also, I acknowledge the help of the editors, A. Biersack and J. Greenberg, who provided extensive and thoughtful comments upon earlier drafts. Agnar S. Helgason and Jónas G. Allansson provided valuable help as research assistants, collecting and analyzing historical and numerical data.

Constructing and
Appropriating Nature

Ecopolitics through Ethnography: The Cultures of Finland's Forest-Nature

Eeva Berglund

Accounting for Bias

Prominent images of Finland remain wedded—or shackled, depending on one's disposition—to forested landscapes. The following, from an English-language brochure, is typical of the rhetoric: "Forests cover more than two-thirds of Finland's land area. Over 26 million hectares of land are devoted to forestry, an area larger than several of the countries of Europe. The Finns have always relied on the forest for their livelihood. From using the forest as a source of fuel, food and shelter, over the decades Finland has become a supplier of highly processed top-quality forest products."

Another brochure proclaims, "Renewable, recyclable, responsible" and goes on to say that nobody is more concerned with the health of the environment than the Finnish forest industry. "Facts, not fiction" is what they offer the reader interested in assessing the state of forestry (*Finnish Forest Industries Federation* 1994). Meanwhile, dozens of articulate activists have involved themselves in repudiating such assurances under skeptical headings like "Finland and Forest—A Success Story?" (Karjalainen et al. 1993). Such claims and counterclaims are made on the terrain of ecopolitics.

The politics of ecology—such as campaigns to save old forests, to protect endangered species, and to ensure the continued existence of robust ecosystems—has transformed ways of thinking about and interacting with nature. Through ethnographic research on forest politics in Finland, this chapter argues that ecopolitics is a significant site of cultural innovation, but that the creativity of ecopolitics is embedded, nevertheless, in older political values.

The research focus is inspired by a sense that, despite a flurry of work on environmental politics, the social and cultural aspects of ecopolitics are still poorly documented and understood. Moreover, since views that influence the management of nature globally continue to be generated in northern Europe, the emergence of these views needs to be better understood.[1]

Ecopolitics, after all, has become a household term in many European languages—*ympäristöpolitiikka*, *Umweltpolitik*, and *miljöpolitik* in Finnish, German, and Swedish, respectively. Anthropologists, however, are particularly sensitive to the fact that although the term *ecopolitics* evokes resistance and opposition to power, many forms of environmentalism support conservative as well as exclusionist agendas, which can further disempower already marginalized people. It is all the more important, then, to be clear about what is being proposed in the name of ecology. A significant aspect of ecopolitics is the role of social movements, those fluid sociopolitical spaces where shared fears and desires are articulated. Social movements not only voice claims on behalf of nature, but also create new forms of collective association and division.

If public debate on nature is often characterized by strong reactions, recent academic debates around the construction of nature have also given rise to many misreadings as well as to genuine theoretical impasses (Escobar 1999a).[2] What is interesting is that, while anthropologists are at least groping toward, if not embracing, concepts that seek to transcend the radical separation of nature and culture,[3] environmental politics often reinscribes nature into the discourse through the idea of "eco" as an immutable domain separate from human folly. Finnish forest activists, too, who pose the most prominent challenge to the forest industries in Finland, love the "eco" of ecology. For them, ecology is the science of nature's web, privileged knowledge of life itself, and it is best apprehended in old growth forests, devoid of human interference.[4] Thus, two separations—recently interrogated by academics such as Tim Ingold (1995), Marilyn Strathern (1980, 1992), and Bruno Latour (1993)—are in fact right at the heart of environmentalist agendas: first, that between nature as passive object and culture as active subject and, second, that between the human and the nonhuman.

Despite this conservatism, activism manages to appear conceptually novel at the same time as it poses a threat to existing expert regimes. This begs some important questions: what does environmentalism gain from clinging to the problematic separation between humanity and the rest of nature? What kinds of understandings and experiences of nature have legitimacy and why? How do these tie in with scientific expertise? And, further, given that it is possible to phrase the problem in such constructionist terms, what does this do to the idea of nature as such?

This chapter seeks answers, but also new, more fruitful questions, through exploring the nature–culture divide in Finland. Its claim is that although activists are well versed in scientific expertise and treat forests as an object, their impetus for protecting nature arises from experiencing forests as something other than inert and passive. One important implication is that as part of ecopolitics, forest activism transforms the way people place themselves within the world, but it does so in complex and sometimes self-contradictory ways. A sketch of the historical emergence of a particular set of truths about what in Finland is known as "forest-nature" will make clear that understanding the use of the concept of nature has to be situation-specific but also that its use is related to ideas with universal pretensions, such as democracy and citizenship.

It seems that both empirically and conceptually it is hard to do without nature, but ecopolitics proves that nature is incredibly contested. Yet the sensitivity about how nature is or is not constructed points to the importance of nature construction as such. If nature can no longer be taken for granted, or if political power dictates what counts as nature, then this is a political problem as well as a philosophical and existential one. This suggests a reframing of the issue. Some anthropologists now claim that the world, or Europe, or the North Atlantic is "after nature" (Strathern 1992; Escobar 1999a).

Most obviously, it is impossible to establish the boundary between nature and culture empirically. Landscapes have been transformed by domestication and resource extraction, and from transboundary risks to the manipulation of genetic processes, technology invades nature's creatures at all scales. Technical capacity and human ingenuity have rendered nature unrecognizable and indistinguishable from culture—that is, from human creativity.

Anthropological comparisons have shown that the divide between nature and culture that orders Euro-American cosmologies is not found everywhere (MacCormack and Strathern 1980). Strathern (1980, 1988) has demonstrated how Melanesian cosmologies fail—if that is the correct word—to conceptualize human actions as cultural, somehow manipulating and directing an inert realm of nature. Here subjectivity and agency are not the privilege of humans, let alone of particular kinds of humans.[5] For Melanesians a division between subjects and objects (those who act and that which is acted upon) is neither clear-cut nor permanent. The mysteries of the world do not seek explanation in appeal to natural processes or human intentions, and, correspondingly, things do not happen because *either* a person intends them to or nature dictates. Rather, life unfolds in contexts, relationships, and complex interactions among and between persons and things, confounding a division into a natural realm and a cultural realm. There is, Strathern claims, no nature and no culture in Melanesian cosmology. These are more appropriately considered European folk models that anthropology has unreflectingly employed as tools of analysis.

In her book *After Nature*, Strathern applies these insights to exploring English, and by extension Euro-American, notions of the natural. She contends that a number of key concepts like family, society, the individual, and nature are in crisis. States of affairs no longer acquire legitimacy simply through being "naturalized" and based in biology (1992:151); instead, people have to make ever more conscious choices about what is right and good.[6] This contrasts with how, at the height of modernity, Euro-Americans thought that—although they were destined to organize, manipulate, and consume it—nature itself would always provide a stable context for human endeavor. A division was made between a resource and the tools for manipulating it, a division related to an ontology of nature as given and culture as innovative. But, Strathern suggests, this modern separation is proving volatile and problematic. Technology has increasingly become something that enhances or mixes with nature, and the distinction between technology as human innovation and nature as precultural seems to have imploded. For example, machines now help people live out their "natural" capacity to be parents (Strathern 1992:177). The final crisis, though, is primarily conceptual. Nature, which used to provide the ontological grounding for human endeavor, actually now requires culture in the form of environmental protection simply to continue to exist. If nature needs cultural manipulation, this makes it impossible to conceptualize it as foundational or prediscursive.

Nature, then, is in a process of being rethought and—pardon the awkward term—repracticed. From the molecular level to interplanetary scales, conditions for living are being reconstituted. As proponents of technological and especially medical development point out, being after nature in this sense generates exciting new horizons. However, it also produces "unequally distributed chances of life and death" (Haraway 1997:269). In this context, ecopolitics as a struggle over the management of nature appears to be going in opposite directions: it seeks reassurance in the ontological primacy of nature, but it is also a challenge to such primacy.

Clearly this is disorienting. It would be easier to revert to the position that nature is simply out there, an unchallenged given of life on planet Earth and a prediscursive or extrasocial fact. But from the standpoint of sociocultural anthropology, there can be no such thing as a prediscursive nature because all practices of nature, including those of the technologically sophisticated Euro-American cultures, are historically created and upheld through social interaction. But although "natural conditions" are always already cultural, this does not mean they are less real. It does mean that anthropology is well placed to elucidate some of the paradoxical aspects of the environmental crisis.

Given the shifting terrain not only of ecopolitics, but also of scholarly examinations of nature and culture, anthropologists venturing into this area have to be explicit about their positions and perspectives. Here my standpoint is that of an embodied and, not insignificantly, Finnish citizen for whom the idea of culture being opposed to nature is a product of an English-language anthropological formation. It is not part of Finnish vernacular usage, though the Finnish language does have more or less equivalent terms: *luonto* and *kulttuuri*. My analysis thus produces a historical and objectifying narrative of how understandings of the natural and the cultural have emerged and of what meaning and use people give these concepts today. In some parts of this chapter, therefore, the role of these terms is closer to that of object than of instrument of analysis, though the two inevitably shade into each other.

For the first nine months of 1996, I interviewed and spent considerable time with a group of activists working to prevent logging of old growth areas across the country at a time when Finland's forestry and conservation policies were, as they still are, being redrafted.[7] I can count my "key informants" on the fingers of two hands, but I conducted over thirty open-ended interviews and took part in countless public gatherings as well as, with their permission, meetings open only to activists. The most illuminating insights were acquired, however, not with a notepad or tape recorder, but in informal meetings over beer or in forests and also through some of the letters the activists wrote and the comments they made in respondse to my earlier efforts (1997) to write about their work.

As elsewhere, social movement groups in Finland are loose networks of people with varying degrees of commitment and resources to bring to the work; but there continues to be an identifiable core. Throughout the 1990s, this core, known as the forest group, has worked under the loose sponsorship of an organization, partly state funded, called the Nature League. The group is a mix of voluntary and paid environmentalists. In 1996, I "hung out" in their office, which was provided for them by the Nature League, but because of the sensitive relationship between social movement groups and researchers, whose work frequently turns into a critique or exposé of activism (Brosius 1999c), I did not seek to "infiltrate" the forest group's inner sanctum. Nor have I subsequently sustained more than sporadic direct contact. Instead I have compiled my data through a variety of channels, including historical and publicly available materials, which, as I shall show, provide important insights into ecopolitics.

I also interviewed administrators and top executives in the forest sector, but the relationships I established with activists (despite some suspicions) were much closer, and I found archival and published sources a more satisfactory avenue for building a sense of the forest sector's side of the controversy. As well as continuing, if sporadically, my contacts with activists, I have followed the debates through the national and even international media, including the Internet as well as public meetings. However, the ethnographic material collected in the spring and summer of 1996 lies at the heart of the claims I make. Indeed, without a participant-observation component, the research could not have generated the insights about commitment to and personal relationship with the forest that it has. Without the historical understanding of Finland's emergence as a forest-state, the ethnography would not have been so suggestive.

The role of forests in narratives of Finnishness in the twentieth century cannot be overestimated.[8] I shall show how the forest sector and forest science helped create a nation–nature dyad in which opinions about forests are interpreted within a framework of national belonging. From the beginning of my research, my conversations with nonactivists in Finland have often resulted in unsolicited commentary on the debates. The forest sector is undergoing economic restructuring (downsizing and relocation overseas), and the successes of information and communications technologies have already altered the economic profile of the country; but through work, leisure, or ownership, almost every Finn is still somehow linked to industries and services related to timber resources. It is possible that conversations about forests have always characterized socializing, but that only a research interest in the sociocultural effects of a forest-based economy made me aware of this. It also seems likely, however, that as legislation about forests has been redrafted in the 1990s and as criticizing the forestry sector has become acceptable, the lid has been lifted off and simmering discontent with the forest sector has boiled over.

Expertise in the Finnish Forest-State

Finland is a generally quiet country at the meeting point of the European Union and Russia, formerly the communist Soviet Union. Compared to the rest of Europe, it is very sparsely populated, with only five million people inhabiting its roughly three hundred thousand square kilometers. About three-fourths of the country is productive forest, mostly of the boreal coniferous type. Almost 60 percent of this is in small-scale private ownership, but it has overwhelmingly been managed by state-sanctioned experts for the purpose of turning it into paper and pulp. This industry helped create affluence and security throughout the twentieth century. Recently it has transformed itself in preparation for globalization, enthusiastically mechanizing, merging, and rationalizing (as it is called) production.[9] The industry's concerns about efficient resource use and competitive advantage are not about to disappear.

What some people refer to as Finland's forest war is taking place amid significant political, economic, and social change, in which what I call the nation–nature dyad is bound to shift. From independence in 1917 until the mid-1970s, forests could easily be invoked as national patrimony, the common inheritance that defined Finland and created its enviable affluence and modern infrastructure. By the 1980s other industries and a new, urbanizing ethos began to overshadow the forest sector. The country's economy seemed to enjoy permanent growth, but by the early 1990s, Finland, like other European countries, suffered debilitating recession. Unemployment soared from below 5 percent to a staggering 19 percent.[10] Further uncertainties continue to attend Finland's adaptation to membership in the European Union, which it joined in 1995.

Through the 1980s forest conservation was supported by officialdom, and environmental values were recognized by industry. By the mid-1990s, however, those in charge of the forest sector dismissed calls, as they had repeatedly in the past, to curtail industrial use of forests and increase ecological awareness as naive and misinformed. In a context of competition over who is informed and misinformed and over how much forest Finland can afford to turn over to conservation, predominantly young forest activists intensified their interest in creating exact and authoritative knowledge about the importance of biodiversity and of unfragmented old growth forests. Environmentalists were also spurred on by the pressures put on industry in the wake of the Earth Summit of 1992.

In ecopolitics across Europe, the divide between expert and lay knowledge has become blurred as environmentalism makes one successful challenge after another to official declarations that everything is fine (Berglund 1998, 2001; Wynne 1996). From a constructionist angle, it is easy enough to argue that public officials have in fact sustained falsehoods because they have political power. For instance, Finnish forest science was good for the paper and pulp industry and by extension for a good number of Finns, but it did uphold a narrow view of a forest as raw material for paper and pulp. Built-in biases and systematic misrepresentations of reality in the field known as forest science can be traced to its goal of maximizing utility and profit.

Yet in significant ways the science of biodiversity upon which activism draws is also historically constituted, and it too reflects the concerns of the socio-cultural milieu within which it emerged. Studies of scientific knowledge by sociologists and anthropologists and critical analyses of the uses of maps provide tools to show that forest activism is not innocent, although its politics are perhaps not as apparent as those of the forest sector's appointed experts. It is the politics that underlie activism that ultimately interest me here. But first, I must provide the necessary historical context.

The Finnish nation-state was co-constructed with what is now routinely called Finland's forest-nature, a wooded landscape interspersed with lakes and waterways. Its image is one of simplicity and strength, which is also, as advertising reminds us, one of purity (*puhtaus*). Forests are ubiquitous in the proximate surroundings, even in urban and suburban environments, which, since postwar urbanization, are home to the majority of people living in Finland. Images of forests permeate national high culture, for instance, in the national epic, *Kalevala*, in music, and in painting. But everyone knows that the Kalevala and other celebrations of Finnish creativity are products of high culture. In contrast, as a symbol of national unity, forests evoke naturalness and rootedness, offering themselves as natural protectors of the nation. From an anthropological perspective, just as the forests in which Finns from different walks of life seek reassurance undergo transformations, so too do the groups that collectively mirror different aspects of forests in their identities as they (re)constitute themselves daily. A history of state-led narratives and collective practices means that regional, occupational, generational, or gendered positions across Finland are defined against, and partake of, forests.[11]

At the end of the nineteenth century, socioeconomic life diverged ever more from that of the imperial Russians. Ironically, in taking over Finland from the Swedish crown in 1809, Russia had provided Finland with social conditions that increased prosperity and, by the late nineteenth century, fueled desires for political independence. By then educational developments and the novelties of industrial capitalism began to make themselves felt across Finland, a society that was predominantly rural and characterized by individualism. In the early twentieth century, proponents of the forest industries helped create a sense that there was an intimate link between the well-being of the people, who suffered periodic waves of oppression by the Russian administration, allegiance to local timber companies, and care for the forests of the emerging nation. This merged with ideas of essential Finnishness: virility and purity yet capacity for innovation in the face of a harsh but ultimately giving nature.[12] These values are still lived out, as Finns spend summers in self-consciously simple summer cottages at a distance from urban life (which, nevertheless, hardly qualifies as bustling for North Atlantic people from more densely populated regions!).

Finnish forest science is now widely considered both a national achievement and a body of knowledge of global significance (Michelsen 1995), and sustained yield silvicultural know-how has been an export item for decades. From its early days, appointments, financial support, and research agendas in forestry have been financed and administered by the state. Throughout the nineteenth century, power to mold the land was taken out of reach of unscientific and supposedly undisciplined peasants, even if, as today, the land was predominantly in private ownership. The National Board of Forestry was consolidated in 1859, and forestry education was established in the late nineteenth century. Karl-Erik Michelsen's English-language history of the Finnish forest sciences makes clear that the emergence of economic and political institutions and the creation of the physical landscape and its guardians were intimately connected.

A state-led forestry profession developed to serve the requirements of industry, but the conservation of the national heritage was also taken up by the state (Laitakari 1961). Nineteenth-century Finland forged its collective symbols and national identity with reference to its biophysical landscape. Not unlike America's worship of natural monuments, Finns celebrated the landscape as guarantor of national genius. Creating and sustaining national political consensus, corporatist forestry interests have long been able to project a benign image. It has been easy to draw on people's affections for wooded landscapes to secure continued support for industrial forestry. In his work on the construction of Finnish nature, A. A. Lehtinen has demonstrated how Finland's "conservation was an inseparable part of the forestry administration" (1991:79). And an American popular text echoes the predominant tone of the twentieth century: "Finland is not going to let her green gold vanish . . . she has very strict rules for reforestation and conservation. In addition, though most of her wooded country is in the hands of private citizens, this means it is controlled by cooperatives working together for the good of the whole" (Berry 1972). True, the destroying of stands has long been a criminal offense, but nonintensive, environmentally sensitive management has also been punished in the courts.[13] With the help of an impressive mountain of research data, professionals have claimed to know everything worth knowing about forests.

As a way of both representing and intervening in the landscape, surveying, whether for conservationist or industrial purposes, developed together with the professionalization of timber extraction. The effect of the constant surveying of Finland's landscape has been to establish a set of truths about Finland's forests in a quintessentially modern idiom in which expert representations such as inventories and maps are crucial. The Finnish Forest Research Institute, established in 1917, enjoyed the prestige of modern scientific credentials and helped establish Finland's "forest consensus," an implicit as well as explicit ideology that continues to identify forests as the everlasting source of national security. Not only does the institute publish annual reports of cubic meters and annual increment, etc., but it has surveyed the population on its attitudes toward forestry, willingness to sell timber, and size of landholdings. Employing a disinterested, scientific tone, it continues to collect, collate, and publicize authoritative data on everything related to forests.[14]

The Finnish geographer Anssi Paasi (1996) argues that national identification was finally consolidated in the wake of the traumatic World War Two. Likewise the corporatist forest sector secured its place at the heart of the country's political economy. In the 1950s, alongside other efforts to rebuild the war-torn country, hundreds of thousands of people joined so-called forest marches, planting, thinning, and generally improving growth conditions. Investments in silviculture and new appointments of forest professionals increased into the early 1970s. The efforts seemed to pay off. Government-sanctioned expertise in sustained-yield forestry has ensured that since the 1970s more wood than ever has grown in Finland's forests (FSIS 1995:40). If it is not harvested, all the hard work would go to waste, or, to paraphrase a leading forest official, this timber will be left standing to rot in the forest. Such rhetoric shows just how embedded forest expertise became in a capitalist scheme of resource use. Only potential profits count(ed) as forest.

The Finnish Forest Research Institute, together with the experts it authorizes, directly or indirectly, provides an example of how a scientific establishment can claim a monopoly on knowledge.[15] So long as the justifications for the hegemony of the forest sector were congruent with the nation's experiences, and its fruits were equitably distributed, critics inside and outside could be muted. Ample anecdotal evidence and hindsight, though, suggest that considerable effort was invested in creating Finland's forest consensus.

In the mid-1980s, cracks in the consensus became visible as the prospect of forest dieback caused by pollution became a public concern. Events in Finland echoed the broader debates on acid rain damage, which brought the German concept of *Waldsterben*, or "forest death," into European ecodiscourse. Also, an open debate between two scientists working for the institute helped crystallize emerging environmental fears (Väliverronen 1995). At the same time, a series of new environmental protection institutions were created in Finland, as elsewhere in Europe (Munk Christiansen et al. 1996). The Environment Ministry started in 1983, and in the late 1980s the Green Party consolidated itself as an alternative to the traditional social democratic, center-agrarian, and coalition (conservative) parties. Environmental concern is now part of politics at both the national and the local level. Explicitly green concerns even entered the vocabulary of the former National Board of Forestry, accordingly renamed in 1992 the Forest and Park Service.

As UN-sponsored international environmentalism increased visibly, Finns could be proud that they were able to subordinate internal disagreements to the needs of what presented itself as a global threat. Government and most sectors of society came to support environmentalism. Political and technical interventions to prevent global environmental catastrophe were promoted, enhancing the sentiment that Finns are somehow privileged in both accurately understanding and being in a position to influence the trajectory of this crisis. Not only should Finland be concerned with its own forest-nature, it should carry responsibility for the entire globe. The imagery with which the forest sector now promotes itself conforms to the ideals of this global, supposedly planet-embracing vision: "Renewable, Recyclable, Responsible!" And despite the recession and the waning of concern for environmental politics worldwide after Rio, Finnish officialdom enthusiastically answered calls to renew forest policies, and several high-level conferences were convened in Helsinki.[16] In promoting environmentalist claims, the forest sector has fed into as well as drawn upon collective representations of Finnishness.

The idea of an indigenous respect for nature continues to be consciously promoted in the media. Books and films about lumberjacks and wilderness-dwellers have a steady following, and advertising evokes experiences urban and suburban Finns have of being in rural environments. In 1998, a television campaign presented images of pure nature, reminding viewers that the Forest and Park Service's experts were hard at work caring for the national, natural heritage. Such explicit reminders have seemed ever more necessary as the paper and pulp industry has faced mounting criticism at home and abroad for its polluting and energy-intensive production methods, for practicing ecologically harmful forestry, and for disregarding the importance of unfragmented old growth forests.

Importantly for the current topic, the character of ecopolitics has been transformed by ongoing economic restructuring since the 1980s. In 1990, after massive capital investments and a period of sustained growth, the country plunged into severe recession. To keep exports of paper and pulp moving, the currency, the markka, was allowed to float, effectively reducing its purchasing power. As economic crisis continued, so did changes in environmental administration, only now spurred on more by the need for frugality than by the imperative to be a beacon of progressive, eco-aware politics.

The economy took an upswing in the second half of the decade, but youth unemployment has remained higher than the overall figures, at around 15 percent. In the political-economic juncture of the early 1990s, hundreds of mainly young people became involved in protesting the logging of old growth forests in Finland and subsequently, as the border opened up, in Russia. Dozens have made forest campaigning their key occupation and a crucial aspect of their identity. Activism has taken many forms, but one result has been to alter collective representations of forests. By 1995, the scientistic approach I describe next had taken center stage.

Maps, Species, and Activists

Grubs and polypores have often made it into Finnish headlines.[17] Environmentalists see them as indexical of the health of forests, nature, and of life. But while activists rejoice in rare epiphytes, many, including state-level politicians, ridicule such concern for "creepy crawlies." Behind the scenes, maps and survey data shuttle back and forth among government, industry, activists, and overseas consumers of paper. There is more to this emphasis on counter expertise than the fact that it appears to work, as new conservation programs attest.[18]

The rest of this chapter explores how activism sustains nationally legitimated social commitments in the name of biology, and it offers a qualified critique of anthropological constructions of eco- and biopolitics as primarily and dangerously conservative.

The most vociferous protest against the industrial use of Finland's forests has, in the past decade, come from activists affiliated with the forest group, but the networks that operate on behalf of old growth forests defy institutional definition. As is characteristic of social movements, the forest group at the heart of the protest is fluid. In 1996, six or seven young people (those most prominent tended to be men) coordinated nationwide protests and vigilance over the activities of logging companies. Their headquarters were in Helsinki but they connected through personal relationships to most regions. Their work consisted of alerting the public to the dangers of excessive logging as well as helping concerned members of the public put pressure on authorities and industry to examine and protect specific forests. Several activists complained that working with, against, and between the various authorities made them feel like petty bureaucrats—yet they feel the job must be done.

The language of biodiversity, adopted by the Environment Ministry and international treaties, is ubiquitous. In Finnish, both spoken and written, *biodiversity* is used interchangeably with its Finnish translation, which, word for word, is "nature's variation" or "nature's diversity."[19] As specific plots are evaluated for inclusion in conservation, the terminology quickly switches to talk of "nature's values." The debate is phrased overwhelmingly in words that include or directly invoke the word *luonto*, "nature," and so make connections to familiar experiences.

The concept of sustainability also carries well in a country with decades of legislation on sustainable-yield forestry. Environmentalists, however, charge that a sustainable yield as the forestry profession understands it has little to do with biological integrity. What is being sustained is the capacity of the land to reproduce cubic meters (board feet) of timber. This often means loss of biodiversity as dead and rotting trunks are removed. As elsewhere, interested parties also worry about how economic and social systems can be maintained, and facts and figures continue to be produced and publicized.

Still, activism easily presents ecological sustainability as the encompassing context for other concerns. This both depends on and generates ecological knowledge. "We have the best knowledge base about natural values of any environmentalists in Europe," one young man boasted to me, referring to the piles of maps, pictures, and surveys of old growth forests that he and his co-activists had amassed. What activists refer to as "knowledgeability" is expertise regarding biodiversity, including mapping and survey skills. Their own expertise has become an extension of the interest in nature as a hobby, something that characterizes almost all activists, if not before their involvement, then at least as long as they remain active. Activists are excited to talk about species, and all are angry and frustrated at the lack of respect for the importance of species by those officially in charge. Forestry expertise, they claim, has been made to appear inevitable and good for everyone—including the forests themselves—but in actual fact it has created a monotonous and fragile landscape. Their critique is fully borne out by the historical record within Finland and is echoed, for instance, by James Scott's (1998) critique of modernist planning, one that does not denigrate science as such but that focuses instead on the universalist pretensions and authoritarianism in the social sphere of such planning (ibid.:340).

A salient characteristic of modern knowledge practices is the belief in progress through critique. It is not surprising, then, that expertise has bred counter-expertise in Finland's forests too. In 1991, a state-funded process of charting old growth forests began, seeking to reintegrate the ever more conflicting agendas of the Environment Ministry and industrial forestry. The authorities hoped that a new consensus could be reached, and a rigorous basis established for land use decisions. The Forest and Park Service (then still the National Board of Forestry) employed young people to carry out the surveys, and now many who took part are expert at surveying as well as at producing and using maps, satellite images, and other representations of the landscape. These constantly clutter their office, where the walls are lined with files and memos, newspaper archives and research reports; the tables are covered with maps, and the chairs often with compasses, rumpled backpacks, and half-empty lunch boxes.

News coverage and research papers have criticized the narrowness of activist enthusiasm for ecological fact finding. But far from being a cold, bureaucratic practice, the continuing insistence on mapping is closely entangled with privately articulated as well as unspoken respect for ecological processes that defy static representation. In one-on-one interviews, activists expressed aesthetic and highly personal motives for their protest. I have also received a letter whose writer takes issue with one social scientist's interpretation—that environmentalists' focus on species is "capitulating in the face of globalization." My friend writes,

I continue to find this statement utterly absurd. . . . Recently as I've contemplated the problematique of species- and forest-protection, I've started to feel that species-thinking made a breakthrough because it felt novel. The inhabitants of the dusky backwoods actually sensed a freshness in the pines. I remember [a prominent activist] announcing in 1989 on the steps of parliament that at Talaskangas[20] in a rotting fungus, they'd found a rare creature, an endangered mosquito, a gnat, a teeny-tiny devil of a thing which provided a political hobbyhorse, something quite new and revolutionary in Finnish environmentalism.[21]

One young woman mused on the practical and philosophical plausibility of something like a science of biodiversity, stressing the irreducibility of nature's complexity to scientific formulae, echoing comments I often heard: that nature is a process, not an object. In interview she said, "You won't catch me out for positivism. J. criticizes me for positivism just because I'm a biologist, and a lot of them are [positivists]." She sought to distance herself not only from official forest science, but also from uncritical and narrow faith in biology. But, as for so many others, it seemed to be the experience of doing surveys that provided an impetus to her efforts toward conservation. She had taken part in old growth inventories in Russian Karelia, across the Finnish border, where forests were long untouched by industry because the area was a closed-off military zone. She commented on the striking differences between the forests on the two sides of the border.[22] It disturbed her, and she articulated her concern specifically as a Finnish citizen—that "we" should do better. Such an attitude is common among activists.

A short account of a trip to Russian Karelia, emphasizing my own reactions, will illustrate that activist science can be understood only in conjunction with its visceral element (Berglund 1997). From satellite images and aerial photographs one can see how the boundary between Finland and the Soviet Union, now Russia, became clearly demarcated in the landscape. The Russian side, unlogged for most of the twentieth century, is densely forested, while Finland is characterized by meager biomass. From the road a trained eye can apparently also tell from the height of the trees whether a stand is managed or not. On both of my short trips to this part of Karelia, near Kostamuksha, my guides commented on the sadly uniform Finnish forests. Eagerly they anticipated the variety in Russia's untouched woods. Once we were well across the border, there was a feeling of happy return as we saw, felt, smelled, and heard the luxuriant forests.

If I could not fully comprehend the joy of being there, I was able to share in the sadness of apprehending a clear-cut. A western preoccupation has introduced to Karelia the habit of leaving a camouflage strip of forest alongside a road, but a keen eye—for heavy-goods vehicle tire tracks—can help spot places where paper and pulp producers have "harvested." Within hours of my first trip behind such a strip of trees, a scene of devastation reduced our party, eight activists and myself, to the verge of tears and angry, compulsive smoking. A few grand pines remained standing in the middle of a clearing that, extrapolating from the Finnish vehicles at the scene, was at least partly the doing of a Finnish company. The trees were presumably left because machinery designed for Finnish sustained-yield conditions is unable to deal with such thick trunks.

There are phenomenological aspects of the forests that can be communicated even in the absence of ecological training. An account of activism that omits this visceral element would be a distortion. At the same time, visceral responses say nothing about the moral value of activism, even if it is tempting to jump to conclusions about right and wrong here.

Nature Reconstituted

Recent scholarship has emphasized that environmentalism, as benign as it seems, and science, as neutral as it appears, are never innocent (Cronon 1996; Escobar 1999a; Haraway 1997). Echoing anthropologists like Marilyn Strathern, whose work I considered above, this new scholarship demonstrates the dangers of employing Western folk notions of common sense as universal analytic categories. It highlights the point that cultural and political commitments underpin all agendas articulated in the name of nature.

In particular, social and cultural studies of science (Haraway 1997; Latour 1987) provide an empirically grounded and theoretically fruitful starting point for understanding the complexities involved in acknowledging that nature and science are shaped socially. In fact, many scholars prefer the term *technoscience* to *science* because it highlights the simultaneously cultural and technical (natural) elements of what today counts as science. Technoscience is a set of practices embedded in ever more complex institutional, financial, and political as well as interpersonal networks and is never simply the discovery of existing powers and essences.[23] Ethnographic attention to the everyday practices of scientists and their helpers, funders, and clients shows how technoscience is created through human and nonhuman activity in processes that are always both technical and political. Only rhetoric makes it possible to present an audience with either a purely technical or a totally political claim. Importantly, though, the idea of rhetoric should not automatically, if at all, be construed as pejorative. Since objects do not speak for themselves, people do, and thus rhetoric and persuasion are always necessary to technoscience, good and bad. Broadly speaking, the authority of technoscience derives from a combination of trust in the coherence and consistency of mechanical or technical systems and belief in the good faith of those making claims. Such trust itself is informed by what is collectively held to be "how the world is." In Euro-American terms, this is the realm of nature.

It requires political power to purify the domain of the technical—say, the condition of a stand of trees—from the "merely" social and political—say, how laypeople think about the stand—and mapping this distinction onto nature and culture. But however much human effort goes into creating this distinction in practice, conceptually the technical and the political cannot exist independently of each other. In Donna Haraway's words, "The technical and the political are like the abstract and the concrete, the foreground and the background, the text and the context, the subject and the object" (1997:37), and they need each other. Haraway reminds us that scientific expertise relies on rendering itself invisible, making the human experts and their arguments completely disappear into the background, leaving only established facts visible. A scientific claim about nature is at its strongest when the scientist(s) who created and authorized the claim act as if the facts spoke for themselves, as if science could be mapped onto a preexisting nature out there. We know, however, that scientific knowledge never just is, it is always somebody's, always apprehended from a human perspective and therefore linked to social positions (Haraway 1991). By the same token, graphs, surveys, and maps are always created by and for somebody.

Another way of understanding how modern forms of knowledge can be imagined as neutral and accurate is to theorize mapping. Maps are convenient tools that tell us about space and the relationships between spaces, but connecting maps to the things they represent is more complicated than at first appears. Until recently, anthropology had contributed surprisingly little to understanding how disembodied knowledge of the kind inscribed in maps affects people's lives.[24] Elsewhere, however, the connection between a thing and its representation has long commanded attention.

In work influenced by Martin Heidegger and Michel Foucault, the political scientist Timothy Mitchell (1988) provides one of the clearer analyses of the modern dilemma of representation. He elegantly describes how the use of plans makes the world appear to a person, in his role as observer, as a relationship between picture and reality. The modern subject stands back and contemplates his object of study from a distance. The object will be framed so as to include only what is relevant and exclude the rest. At the same time corporal discipline can be established, and the total environment—late nineteenth-century colonial Egypt in Mitchell's example—can be transformed into "a place . . . of continuous supervision and control, of tickets and registration papers, of policing and inspection" (1988:97). Everything must have its place. Frameworks like the urban plan, the map, and the school curriculum make the world something to be managed through knowing the relationships that obtain between things. The mechanics of fixing relationships and keeping them under constant administrative surveillance created a distinctive appearance of order, one which positioned the subject in a separate place from the observed object, but also one which made apparently irrelevant detail vanish.

Mitchell's historical example also demonstrates how foundationalism symbolized by science has provided moderns with a formidable Natural Order of Things. The politics of environmental protection still largely works on the principles that have given modern people a sense that beyond the representation or map there is a separate realm of the really real (Mitchell 1988:60). Another way of putting this is that experiencing the world as a picture produces a separation between the world and the word or map, a distinction that fixes nature and culture as separate realms. However, being in possession of scientific knowledge, what they consider accurate representations, moderns have believed that they/we are privileged in having better access than others to truth about real nature. Correspondingly, some maps carry more authority than others. And often maps are more powerful than no maps.

This excursion into mapping helps us understand how a Finnish state forester's image of forest-nature long counted for so much more than a small-holder's or an environmental activist's view (a view that was relegated to the status of uneducated opinion), and why it carried cognitive and not just political authority. But it also suggests that activist claims to knowledge work through the same principles. Like foresters before them, today's environmentalists have power through scientific knowledge, and analogously they consider their expertise to be more rooted in the reality of nature than what they perceive as the merely cultural values of those seduced by the promises of economic growth or swayed by aesthetics. If the forest scientists have failed to "see" biodiversity, activism, too, often uninterested in local social conditions and focused on individual forests, also has its blind spots. An anthropology of environmentalism needs to consider these blind spots without collapsing possibly significant distinctions between various kinds of claims to truth.

Let me return to science studies to explore the similarities and distinctions between the discourses that operate in Finland's forest debates. If the forest sciences have been dethroned, it is also possible to deconstruct biology at the molecular level in ways that are relevant to this discussion. Sarah Franklin (1996), Donna Haraway (1991, 1997), and Arturo Escobar (1996, 1997, 1999) have linked the fetishization of the biological to the promises of biotechnology. Their work draws attention to the usefulness of ecopolitics to the profit-seeking aims of the biotechnology industries. They show how the gene is a symbol or trope that captures nature "out there" and nature as it must be, which, with the help of technology, in fact becomes nature as the biological sciences decide. As these authors point out, in the (North Atlantic) public imagination as well as in international policy, the gene has become the thing-in-itself, irreducible to tropic or relational understanding or historical construction. This means that nature, far from being thought of as a process, as activists claim, is now identifiable and mappable as the genetic code that is the key to life itself. The frightening drawback is, of course, that this nature is in the hands of a few powerful biotechnology institutions. Unwittingly, it would seem, activism in the name of biodiversity supports the ideology that places nature in expert hands and not only turns fields, oceans, and mines into resources, but puts the very tissues of each and every body into a framework of management and profit seeking.

I want to shift this anthropological emphasis. Rather than identify ecopolitics as techno-managerial expertise—globally often associated with exploitation, racism, and imperialism—or as concern for biodiversity with genetics, I wish to consider an alternative direction for further exploration in the anthropology of environmentalism. For ecopolitics in Finland may well be related to the fortunes of genetic engineering worldwide, but it is not the same thing. Collective, specifically national commitments have more to tell us about these environmental debates than how we understand the quasi-globalized worship of the gene. A set of nationally explicit values underpins both the enthusiasm for ecological expertise and the delight of being in a forest that inform Finnish old growth activism.

I have argued that activism proceeds along two tracks. On one hand, through the scientific idiom of biodiversity it claims to draw on a global discourse supported by the authority of technoscience. On the other hand, in being inside an old growth forest activists enter into a visceral relationship with nature. The scientifically argued rationale is so self-evident that it is hardly possible even to articulate it; extinction is, after all, forever, and the biological facts should speak for themselves. In contrast, the emotional rewards of appreciating forests are recognized as partly cultural and are thus amenable to self-conscious explanation or at least to frequent references to the Finnishness of the issues or statements such as "going into a real forest for a week transforms you." Activists draw simultaneously on the collectively recognized authority of technoscience and on the national salience of forests as places of comfort, regeneration, and true Finnishness. For them, forests are irreducible to lists of species, genes, or static representation. Unlike in the world of genome mapping, in the world of environmental activism the map is not the prize (cf. Haraway 1997), although a map remains a forceful argument. Ecology of the variety espoused by forest activism proclaims a priori the impossibility of an accurate, adequate map. The real thing defies representation. Unlike the understanding, nourished by administration and industry, that laboratory science and its relative, forest science, are transparent, the science of ecology, activists claim, denies the possibility even that expertise could grasp nature in anything but the most abstract formulae. Ecological science may reify nature, but it does so in order to emphasize its irreducibility to the spatiotemporal categories of expertise designed for capitalism. If positivism, as activists use the term, stands for misplaced confidence in modernity and capitalism, then by implication if not explicitly, the phrase "I'm not a positivist" echoes throughout the forest group.

A concomitant of this attitude is that even as they seek political control through mapping, activism affirms agency in nonhuman nature. Borrowing from Haraway, I would say that forests have the power to interpellate people.[25] They hail them and draw their attention. In parliamentary terms, interpellation means calling on a minister to explain publicly current government policy. Hence, it is also "an interruption in the body politic that insists that those in power justify their practices, if they can" (Haraway 1997:50). Such a two-way concept applied in this context blurs the divide between active humanity and passive nature. Nature calls attention to itself, and activists respond as best they can.

Conclusions

Supported specifically by ethnographic work, I have argued that activism creates a moral universe that includes both humans and nonhumans. The history of Finland as a country dependent on forests thus acquires a new twist, as decades of forest management and its attendant narratives foster new affective responses. For many in Finland today, the collective life is characterized by underemployment, information overload, and accelerated resource exploitation, and activism, as I see it, is one way of dealing with these conditions. It does so by drawing on what was made explicit by earlier generations: that Finland lives off the forest.[26] Activism continues a tradition of recognizing nature as timeless and inherently separated from humanity (and its stupidity), at the same time it celebrates a connection with it. Activist science does constitute nature as external, but not as a resource, as forest science or biotechnology would.

After all, activism eschews the confidence of positivism, though it still trusts in science just as, like all social movement groups, it trusts in progress. Technoscience still partakes of shared and quite ancient principles of knowledge production that enable two fundamental claims to be made. First, that data processed in controlled and rigorous conditions by competent practitioners are valid. Second, that these data are always open to improvement—that is, to progress.

Apart from the tangible rewards provided over the past one hundred years through the forest sector, the history of Finland as a constitutional state may further clarify why technoscientific knowledge of nature specifically is so cherished. Finns' self-image is that they/we are free of the fetters of tradition and cultural bias and are always ready to move forward and discard old ways when necessary. Finns also, erroneously or not, value parliamentary democracy as something indigenous.[27] Its early successes came in 1906, when universal suffrage—all men and women over twenty-four—was introduced. This was a time when national identity was an urgent concern and was crystalized in the worship of justice, economic security, and technical progress. From independence in 1917 until the relative decline of the forest industries in the 1970s, forest-nature was the foundation that would always guarantee these desirables. And forest science could present itself as a unifying, shared, and democratic institution that would secure the well-being of each Finnish citizen.

The ethnography and history presented here suggest that the discourse of ecopolitics concerns technoscience and politics as well as nature and culture. In a sense I have argued that, of the four pivots around which activism revolves, one of these, the national economic relationship to forests, can be deconstructed by activists, and two others, ideas of presocial nature and the faith in transparent science, can be deconstructed anthropologically. The fourth pivot of ecopolitics, I suggest, is the implicit nexus between progress and citizens' participation in the institutions of democracy. Despite the battering they have received over the past century, the ideals of democracy and citizenship continue to have a powerful hold. As Haraway claims, "Science projects are civics projects" (1997:175), and forest activists might simply lose too much in the realm of civics if they capitulate to the idea that science is cultural and nature is constructed.

In contrast, social scientists writing about ecopolitics take such conceptualizations almost for granted. In so doing, however, they may find their work maligned by those with whom they would sympathize. To move on, new ways of questioning need to be devised that respect situation-specific articulations not only of nature, culture, and technoscience, but also of political and economic processes. Fortunately, anthropologists and social scientists are already in a position to ask, Is there not more to the social side of technoscientific knowledge than its links to profit? How is activism in different situations experimenting with alternative understandings not only of science but also of citizenship? Anthropologists, I believe, need to unpack the differences as well as the similarities in the ways scientific knowledge of nature continues to be invoked for political ends because nature still matters and ecopolitics continues.

Notes

Thanks to members of the Department of Geography and the College of Natural Resources at the University of California at Berkeley for comments on seminars given in 1998 on the material presented here, to Sakari Virtanen for invaluable feedback, and to James Greenberg and Aletta Biersack for editorial help. Part of the research upon which the chapter is based was funded by the Emil Aaltonen and Ella and Georg Ehrnrooth foundations.

1. Although the ethnographic research for this chapter was done in the mid-1990s, when social science interest in ecopolitics was less established than it is today, the need for empirical accounts remains.

2. See the introduction to the second edition of Cronon's *Uncommon Ground* (1996).

3. For examples, see Ingold 1995 and Escobar 1999a.

4. This ethos is also apparent in the discourses of many English-speaking environmental organizations.

5. Ortner (1974) famously argued that women tend to be associated with nature as a passive, objectified realm in contrast to men, who transcend their naturalness through the innovations of culture. Merchant's historical argument shows how modern science turned women into passive objects in Europe (Merchant 1980). Later the poor and colonized were similarly pacified/passified.

6. See also Berglund (1998), especially chapter 8, for a longer discussion.

7. European Union conservation directives, specifically the Natura 2000 project, continue to be debated and contested. The Ministry of the Environment, the European Forest Institute, and the Finnish Forest Research Institute among others continue to publish relevant studies and policy documents, as they have since the mid-1980s.

8. Interested readers will find state-sanctioned narratives on the numerous ministerial Web pages. The following was found on http://virtual.finland.fi/info/english/metsaeng/html: "Forests are close to every Finn. They are an important element in the daily life of virtually each one of us. . . . Finnish forests are producing more wood than at any time in this century. The growing stock countrywide currently outstrips use, not least because of intensive silviculture. . . . With almost two-thirds of its total area, or over 200 000 km^2, covered by trees, Finland looks like one great forest. The forest cover extends for a good 1000 km from north to south right through the boreal coniferous zone."

9. Things move quickly in this domain, as daily newspaper reports attest. Marchak (1995) provides an overview of the global situation in the mid-1990s. Lehtinen (2001) offers an overview from Finland's perspective.

10. According to Finnish Forest Research Institute figures, unemployment in the forestry sector rose as high as 28 percent. Youth unemployment continues to be a severe problem, hovering around 15 percent, according to the Statistical Bureau's Web page.

11. My own narrative here is a rough sketch of forest relations. I am grateful to Sakari Virtanen for reminding me that nationalist rhetoric and the actual forestry practices carried out across the country have not always been congruent with each other. Despite apparent consensus, the history of Finnish forests, like that of Finnish society, has been one of negotiation and even discord, and my account is not meant to suggest otherwise.

12. Persuasive Finnish-language accounts include Mikkeli (1992) and Laaksonen and Mettomäki (1994).

13. Erkki Lähde, interview Finnish Forest Research Institute, March 1996.

14. See the institute's expansive Web site at http://www.metla.fi/METLA.html.

15. Palo and Hellström (1993). The institute undoubtedly deserves its academic reputation. My point here is to emphasize its reach into every aspect of people's relations with forests.

16. For instance, the Ministerial Conference on the Protection of Forests in Europe in 1993 and the Intergovernmental Seminar on Criteria and Indicators for Sustainable Forest Management in 1996. For more detail on the drafting of new legislation, see Berglund (2001).

17. Polyspores are bracket-fungi commonly found in Finnish forests.

18. An overview is available at http://virtual.finland.fi/info/english/metsaeng/html.

19. Finland's only national newspaper has banned the use of the Latin-based word (Jani Kaaro, personal communication).

20. One of the prominent sites of conflict in the late 1980s.

21. My translation, with the author's permission.

22. Russian Karelia's old growth forests became an attraction for Western forest industries as the Iron Curtain was dismantled. An international coalition of environmentalists has been seeking to ensure that these vast areas are not denuded. See Berglund (1997).

23. My understanding of the construction of science owes much to the work of Bruno Latour, especially *Science in Action* (1987).

24. James Scott's *Seeing Like a State* (1998) is a survey by an anthropologist of the consequences of large-scale mapping exercises.

25. Haraway claims to be "warping" it from Louis Althusser (Haraway 1997:49).

26. This formulation owes much to the work of Marilyn Strathern.

27. Non-Finns have noted this too. For instance, W. R. Mead (1968) wrote that the Social Democratic group has been continuously strong in Finnish electoral politics.

The Political Ecology of Fisheries in the Upper Gulf of California

James B. Greenberg

Introduction

Between 1989 and 1990, the shrimp catch in the upper Gulf of California dropped drastically, nearly 60 percent from previous levels, and yields for the next three years remained low. By 1992–93, commercial shrimpers and shrimp cooperatives were deeply in debt to banks and marketers and had defaulted on their loans. Many shrimpers had their boats seized or were forced to sell them to meet their financial obligations. Conservationists at the time blamed fishermen for the ecological problems in the upper gulf, contending that problems there represented a "tragedy of the commons." They alleged that fishermen, even in the face of declining stocks, continued fishing rather than exercise restraint; and, as Hardin's (1968) model of the commons would predict, the crash was the result of each fisherman trying to maximize his own individual benefit lest, in a zero-sum game, such gains went to another.

Evidence suggests, however, that the economic and ecological problems in the upper gulf were not this simple.[1] Hardin's model, in which individual users maximize their own benefit at the expense of the commons, has been extensively criticized, primarily for its assumptions of competition rather than cooperation in the management of common resources (McCay and Acheson 1987; McC. Netting 1993). Here, I shall argue that the problems of the upper gulf cannot be understood at a local level but are rooted in wider processes that stem from the way the upper gulf's fishery and Mexico, for that matter, are integrated into larger political and economic orders. The natural world, in this larger political ecology, is divided among a hierarchy of territorial entities from local communities to nation-states as well as among a variety of local, state, and federal agencies that claim jurisdiction over particular resources. While divide and rule may be sound statecraft, the gerrymandering of nature leads to poor environmental management. The real tragedy, I contend, is not one of the commons but of commoditization. This is a tragedy that often results if natural resources are managed not as integral parts of particular ecologies but as so many individual commodities. The tragedy (and the problem) is that the economic rationality that markets display in aggregate is very different from that which controls biotic relationships. Sadly, as Rappaport observes (1979:167), where market forces price selective parts of the ecosystem in terms of the demand for particular commodities, they do so without regard for their ecological function or importance.

The Tragedy of Commoditization

The tragedy of commoditization is not simply a result of market integration; it is also the product of the complex way in which nation-states formulate and enforce the policies and regulations used to manage natural resources. Such policies are often the outcome of political and economic machinations that take place far from the ecologies they affect. Moreover, such policies are commonly driven by logics that are alien to the environment—such as the need to pay off foreign debts. In such political processes, local populations, who may have both a greater knowledge and a greater stake in particular environments, often have little voice in policy formulation. And, haplessly, even when governmental policies and regulations attempt to strike a balance between the "conservation" of natural resources and the economic interests of various competing groups, such efforts too frequently are either poorly coordinated or have contradictory effects on the environment.

The economic and ecological problems of the upper Gulf of California are, of course, by no means unique; they represent inherent problems of capitalism. Capitalist growth often undermines its very foundations. Indeed, that economic development is commonly predicated on nonsustainable use of natural resources appears to be a fundamental contradiction of capitalism (O'Connor 1998:165). Rappaport proposes that such problems are created by fundamental conflicts between very different forms of logic that underlie and order natural and capitalist systems. These logics are not just based on very different premises, but ultimately on premises that are fundamentally at odds and deeply incompatible (Rappaport 1999:454–55). The logic of ecosystems, he argues, upon which life depends, is based on a great range of qualitative distinctions among natural processes, organisms, and their material requirements. Monetary systems, by contrast, are based on quantitative differences. When applied to nature, he argues, monetary metrics arbitrarily equate and transform qualitative distinctiveness into mere quantitative differences—reducing them to the bottom line. Such operations are not just epistemologically flawed, they are stupid, both in terms of being incapable of handling even a fraction of the information that natural, self-regulating ecosystems process and also in the conventional sense of often leading to destructive decisions (Rappaport 1994:263–64).

Although the destructive tendencies of bottom-line logics are certainly apparent in the upper gulf, the environmental problems evident there are not merely a consequence of applying a monetary metric to nature. They are, I argue, deeply rooted in the political processes through which access and ownership rights to natural resources are established, and in the economic processes through which control over the distribution and consumption of natural resources is executed. Controls over these processes are highly contested, and the battles for that control are fought not just in the market but also in the political arenas of state and suprastate organizations.

Approaches to Global Capital and Its Disorders

Rappaport's (1979:161–67, 1994:273–81) notions of systemic disorders (such as usurpation, meddling, overcentralization, oversegregation, undercentralization, and hypercoherence) would seem to offer some insights into the problems created by capitalism and globalization. He defines usurpation as the capture of regulatory systems by lower-order subsystems. His famous example of this is the proposition that "what is good for General Motors is good for America." Meddling, by contrast, involves higher-order regulatory systems taking over the management of lower-order subsystems. An example of this might be overregulation by a central government agency—such as a department of fisheries that takes over the control of the who, where, when, and how of fishing at the local level. For Rappaport, overcentralization is a special form of meddling in which control moves away from local levels and is centralized, as in the case of upper gulf fisheries in places like Mexico City. Rappaport specifically addresses issues of globalization in his discussion of disorders of oversegregation, undercentralization, and hypercoherence. He defines oversegregation as overspecialization at the expense of stability, as when a region or country specializes in one crop or product. This involves a loss of local self-sufficiency and regulatory autonomy, as well as increasing economic vulnerability. If overcentralization is the result of moving regulatory control from a local setting to, say, Mexico City, undercentralization is a direct consequence of globalization, in which decisions are no longer made by centralized powers but in world markets, and thus represents a state form of loss of regulatory control. Globalization, it would seem, also carries with it problems of hypercoherence, in which, as Rappaport notes, increasing integration and the lack of local autonomy mean that disruptions originating anywhere may spread rapidly everywhere throughout the system. Thus, economic problems in Japan might hurt U.S. markets and spread to the Mexican economy, where they might even be felt in the upper gulf.

A good case probably can be made for state meddling in Mexico's fisheries. Almost from the beginning, I shall argue, the efforts of the Mexican state went far beyond merely regulating fish stocks. The central government sought to control all aspects of fishing: organization, management, marketing, and so on. Its meddling both led to overcapitalization of the fleet, and encouraged fishermen to borrow heavily; so when its policies changed, they were left with ruinous debts. The problems of meddling were further compounded by the Mexican state's overcentralization, long acknowledged as a serious problem. Overcentralization has meant that the Mexican government, in addition to being insensitive to local problems, was slow to respond to them. For example, as I shall argue, despite evidence that expanding the shrimping fleet was eroding the profitability of each boat, government policies continued to encourage further expansion. As Mexico's debt crisis deepened, the pendulum swung toward undercentralization. Mexico's major trading partners, such as the United States, and major lenders, such as the World Bank and the International Monetary Fund, forced the Mexican state to downsize the government and privatize the economy. As foreign capital was needed to do so, the Mexican state was forced to loosen its regulatory restrictions of foreign investment. This swing, of course, led to the withdrawal of credit from the cooperatives, their defaulting on loans, and the sale of their boats at bargain-basement prices to private capitalists, foreign and domestic. Finally, the problems plaguing Mexico's shrimping industry also illustrate hypercoherence. When government withdrew its various subsidies, fishing costs rose rapidly. However, since the price of shrimp is determined on a world market, fishermen were unable to obtain a better price, and shrimping for the bloated fleet became increasingly unprofitable.

As valuable as Rappaport's notion of systemic disorders is for understand-ing some of the problems created by capitalism and globalization, their very systemic assumptions, generality, and ahistoricity limits their analytical utility. Part of the problem stems from the systemic characteristics of his model. Al-though when building models for heuristic purposes it may be useful to assume an integrated and self-regulating system, there is little evidence to suggest that real systems are "wired" together and integrated this way, let alone that they maintain stable equilibriums. The second law of thermodynamics would sug-gest instead that systems are always running down and are maintained only by expenditures of enormous energy, so that steady states are the exception rather than the rule. A much more fundamental problem, however, is that these models lack true historical dimensions. Although such models identify forms of disorder that are indeed deeply problematic, because at root they are ahistorical, such diagnoses are of little value in understanding the etiology of disorders and tell us virtually nothing about how and why such disorders arise.

If Rappaport's notions of systemic disorders seem only partly to engage the range of problems that we see in the upper Gulf of California's fisheries, simi-lar shortcomings also plague the approaches of political economy. Although world systems and dependency theories, for example, discuss the role of colo-nialism and dependent capital in extracting from developing countries the raw materials needed to fuel more industrialized economies from developing coun-tries, their analyses give ecology and nature surprisingly short shrift and pay scant attention to actual impacts on real environments. In fact, under the rubric of metropolis and satellite—core, periphery, and semiperiphery—the distinc-tiveness of particular places, ecologies, and even of whole continents and coun-tries disappears.

Much of the recent anthropological literature on globalization seems equally distant from the problems of real people and places. Instead of wrestling with how nation-states are variously embedded in a complex world order or with how the interactions between local and global systems create shifting demands on nations, particular places, and populations and on specific natural resources, species, and ecologies, globalization is framed in terms of decentered transna-tional processes taking place in various and sundry "scapes and hyper-spaces" in which faceless actors meet in mysterious global marketplaces (Appadurai 1990, 1991; Basch et al. 1994:5–10; Hannerz 1989; Kearney 1995:548–50). Even in traditional Marxist political economy the attention paid to nature has been fairly minimal (see O'Connor 1998 for a review of Marx's and Engels's ideas on nature). Marxist analyses of commodities, for instance, focus on how labor power transforms nature into commodities but gives surprisingly little importance to the fundamental processes by which living things are reproduced or to how claims to things like land and water (which need not be products of labor) are established and legitimized.

The Political Ecology Approach

Political ecology seems to offer a way around such problems. Unlike an earlier cultural ecology that framed the relation of human beings to nature within an adaptive evolutionary framework, political ecology seeks instead to understand how human societies use and shape nature to their own ends. Rather than attempting to explain human culture with problematic assumptions about adaptation, homeostasis, functions, and bounded ecosystems taken from natural sciences, political ecology focuses on human institutions and actions through which a "humanized" nature is constructed, transformed, and managed. Whereas political economy looks at the historical intersection of capital and the state, political ecology adds nature to the equation. In doing so, it addresses the lack of attention paid to the natural world by traditional political economy approaches and avoids making unnecessary assumptions about forms of integration or previous ecological equilibria. It simply examines how real political and economic systems interact with nature through time.

From this perspective, the central problem is to understand the processes by which human beings transform and reshape nature and, as Marx and Engels (1845–46) observed in *The German Ideology*, in the process transform themselves. And the central question is, how is nature transformed into commodities? In particular, how is it that land and labor—which, as Karl Polanyi (1944:131) points out, are not produced and reproduced in accordance with market forces or the law of value—are transformed into pseudocommodities made available for sale? In a capitalist economy, the answer is that it is the state that creates, through its legal systems and bureaucracies, the needed definitions of property rights, ownership, and procedures of transference that make human labor power, and nature, available to capital in the needed quantities and qualities in the required places and times (O'Connor 1998:164).

In complex societies, as Wolf observed, the ownership of property is a battleground in which "contending forces utilize jural patterns to maintain and restructure the economic, social, and political relations of society" (1972:202). From this perspective, the processes through which rights of access, control, and transfer of ownership are organized and contested have profound implications for commoditization. As I shall argue, commoditization involves two processes: first, territorializations of nature through which rights of access and control over the means of production are defined; and second, processes of exchange that are fundamental to globalization and that entail the definition and transfer of ownership rights, which determine how commodities will be treated as they enter ever-wider markets.

Territorialization and Globalization

Although territorialization and globalization may appear to be opposed concepts, they are, in fact, two halves of the process through which nature is transformed into commodities exchanged in globally integrated market economies. Territorializations, however, are not simply a product of the political geography of nations; they also are key to their internal dynamics and so govern the national processes whereby nature is fractured and transformed into separable commodities. It is through internal territorializations that states govern the processes whereby legitimate access and ownership of natural resources are established.[2] By imposing administrative and territorial hierarchies, nation-states attempt both to control the assignment of rights to natural resources and to set the "rules of the capitalist game" within their boundaries (Heyman 1994:13–14; Mann 1993:44–91). Territorialization is an essential technology of power, by which I mean that it is a means through which the field of play that defines the possible actions of others is structured (Foucault 1982:221). As such, contending classes and groups that vie for control over natural resources often seek to change policies and law that define and govern access to natural resources. As a result, administrative and territorial hierarchies through which natural resources are governed are constantly being redefined. Such territorializations and reterritorializations, of course, may occur within states that are themselves historical products of previous territorializations, frequently forged in the collapse of earlier empires or created as colonial or postcolonial products.

If territorializations establish "the local rules of the game," globalization entails the dance of commodities as they enter markets. This game is governed not only by the technologies of power imposed by states (Biddick 1990:3–4; Wolf 1990, 1999a) but also, in an increasingly integrated global economy, also by decisions made in distant markets, boardrooms, and halls of power. In these global spaces, economic processes that transcend nation-states control commodities. These processes rest on policies, laws, codes, agreements, and practices that emerge from a variety of global institutions, transnational corporations, the World Bank, the International Monetary Fund, etc. (Ghai et al. 1987). Moreover, such actors often have sufficient power to force states to restructure their political, legal, and economic system—that is, to reterritorialize their economies. Although such reterritorialization arguably may facilitate international trade, as commodities move into such circuits any links to the specific landscapes and ecologies from which they derived all but disappear.

Although territorialization and globalization are distinct processes, their effects on local ecologies are closely related. Territorializations seldom follow the contours of nature. Thus, political entities seldom control key elements or parts of ecologies upon which they depend. As nature is carved up among administrative and territorial units, actions that may be advantageous for one entity may damage another. Where pulverization of nature is extreme, territorial units may be less and less viable both economically and ecologically. The physical space is divided among political entities and fractured into various kinds of property and regimes, but in addition nature is conceptually fractured as it is divided among various agencies whose jurisdictional domains govern particular natural resources, such that a region's forests may be controlled by one governmental agency, its wildlife by another. Although agencies attempt to manage their particular resource, what may be rational management of one resource may have a negative impact upon other resources (Greenberg 1998).

Again, although territorializations may set the local rules of the capitalist game, globalization ensures that the game is played on a worldwide field (Braudel 1986; Frank 1978; Wallerstein 1974; Wolf 1982). Historically, incorporation of local systems into national and world metropoli not only increases demands on local natural resources, but also frequently entails a steady loss of local control over them. In turn, this increases the dependence of local economics on the wider society. Because global capital is constantly searching for higher rates of profit, investments shift from place to place. The result is uneven development. Regions prosper as long as there is money to be made but are left to languish when profits fall. Globalization thus creates a succession of territorializations and reterritorializations as various local, national, and international groups compete over the control of resources. As globalization proceeds, although the exploitation of natural resources is increasingly driven by prices set in global markets, national action cannot be understood entirely in terms of international capital and its logic. Although national economic policies are sensitive to such things as world prices, balances of trade, employment, and exchange rates, because nation-states have their own self-interests, national political processes in the end determine how national resources are used.

As landscapes are fractured, territorialized, and commoditized, their management becomes more complex, harder to coordinate, harder to change, and slower to respond. When ecological problems do arise, they often entail complex legal and political disputes that may involve a host of local, state, and national bureaucracies. Years may pass before any solution or agreement is reached. In the meantime, irreversible environmental damage may continue despite all efforts.

In the following case study, I will argue that the present problems of the upper Gulf of California represent not a tragedy of the commons but a tragedy of commoditization that can be understood only by historically examining how Mexico's relationship to capital has shaped the way in which the country has territorialized and managed its natural resources (Alvarez Jr. 1994; Engel 1989:27). In making this argument, I shall attempt to show how dependent forms of capitalism produce tragedies of commoditization by their heavy reliance upon extraction of natural resources to pay for the nation's economic growth. I shall further show how repeated territorializations and reterritorializations in response to national and global pressures have historically shaped the political ecology of the upper gulf to produce these tragedies (Alvarez López 1988:58; McGoodwin 1990:85).

Territorializing the Upper Gulf

Early History

Mexico's fisheries have been enmeshed in a complex political economy almost from the beginning. At the end of the nineteenth century, Mexico's leaders, determined to foster capitalist growth and turn their nation into a developed country, enacted a series of policies designed to privatize lands and natural resources. During the presidency of Porfirio Díaz (1876–1911), the government, in line with the liberal philosophies of the day, began to territorialize its waters and issued federal fishing permits to small companies that granted them exclusive fishing rights to especially productive estuaries and lagoons. These permits effectively prohibited local fishermen who were not working for these companies from fishing for subsistence in these estuaries and lagoons. Compared to the vast program of Liberal reforms used to carve large haciendas and plantations from communal lands of Indian and peasant communities, the reterritorialization of Mexico's fisheries was of minor consequence; however, the effects were much the same. Just as reform policies concentrated land in the hands of a small elite, leaving millions of smallholders landless, the reterritorialization of Mexico's waters left small fishermen little prospect of earning a livelihood.

When Mexico's masses rose in revolution (1910–17), their cries were not just for land and liberty, the return of their communal lands and freedom from peonage, but for *libre*, or "free," access to Mexico's waters. During the revolution, President Francisco I. Madero's administration (1911–13), responding to the demands of local fishermen, issued a proclamation declaring that fishing companies no longer held exclusive rights and that Mexico's waters would be free and open to all for subsistence fishing.

Postrevolutionary Policies to 1940

At the end of the Mexican Revolution, the Constitution of 1917 set the stage for another broad reterritorialization of Mexico's natural resources. Article 27 not only laid the foundation for land reform, but in declaring that "henceforth all lands, waters, minerals, and natural resources were property of the nation to be used for its benefits" clearly expressed the nation's intent to take over the management of its natural resources. Although free subsistence fishing rights continued to be recognized, postrevolutionary administrations, in a change from Madero's policy, used Article 27 to assert that federal rights to regulate fisheries superseded those of states, *municipios*, towns, or any other entity (McGoodwin 1979, 1987:222).

Prior to the revolution the fisheries of the Gulf of California were very primitive. Soon after, however, the Mexican state began experimenting with ways to control and develop its fisheries. Thus, from the beginning federal regulations and government interventions have played an important role in the development and management of the gulf. During the 1920s and early 1930s, pushed by contending political interests, government policies vacillated between territorializations that favored local fishing communities and those of open access that favored commercial interests. In 1923, for example, General Abelardo Rodriguez, then governor of Baja California, created the first cooperative in Ensenada in an attempt to stimulate production by encouraging the collaboration of fishermen and seafood truckers. This cooperative was so successful that it quickly drew the attention of the federal government, which saw in such cooperatives the means of both regulating its fisheries and expanding production (Meade 1986:198). In 1925, President Plutarco Elías Calles proclaimed the first fishing law, or Ley de Pesca, to encourage and regulate such activities. This law provided the legal basis for establishing reserve zones and periods of bans for specific species. As postrevolutionary regimes consolidated power, other legislation regulating fisheries followed. Initially federal policies sought to guarantee local fishermen a minimum standard of living by territorializing the fishing rights of coastal communities. In 1928, a decree was issued that divided the fisheries on the coasts of Sonora, Sinaloa, and Nayarit among coastal communities.

By the 1930s, however, federal policies again began to shift. In part, the shift reflected changing technologies of exploitation. Early cooperatives depended on artisanal technologies—small boats, hand nets—and primarily exploited near-shore resources. As cooperatives became more capitalized, larger, seagoing vessels came to predominate the commercial sector of the market. In part, this shift also reflected the intense competition Mexican fishermen faced in international waters, beyond the three-mile limit. In the early 1920s, Japanese and American ships were actively trawling Mexico's Pacific coasts for shrimp. In 1930, an American company, La Compañía Panamericana, began operations in the Gulf of California. It was among the first to use dragnets and to export shrimp to the United States. By 1931, Japanese ships too were fitted with dragnets and began to compete with Panamericana. Soon the Japanese dominated the international shrimp market, becoming so successful that by 1938 they had driven their competitors from Mexico's Pacific coasts (Mercado and Leanos 1976:517).

In response to such competition, the federal government in 1930 issued a new decree that defined areas of the Gulf of California as open fishing grounds for totoaba, corvina, and cabrilla (Quesada 1952:204). During the administration of President Abelardo Rodriguez (1930–32), the Ley de Pesca was used to push the creation of cooperatives and the development of large-scale fishing on the Pacific coast of Baja California and in the Gulf of California. In 1933, the Mexican government, invoking Article 27, declared that the inshore fishery was a federal district and claimed exclusive rights to commercial exploitation of lagoons.

Although the reterritorialization of Mexico's waters may be seen as an effort both to defend its waters from foreign encroachment and to promote the development of its fisheries, it also was part of President Lazaro Cárdenas's (1934–40) much larger national project to forge Mexico into a corporatist state in order to further solidify state power (Paré 1986:49–53, 1990:81). Thus, the same year the Ley General de Cooperativas, which organized significant sectors of the population into corporate structures, was also passed. This law was used, for example, to organize peasants into the National Confederation of Peasants (CNC); workers were encouraged to join the Confederation of Mexican Workers (CTM). The Ley General de Cooperativas was also used to undertake an aggressive program of state participation in selected enterprises. The Mexican government bought out private companies operating within inshore waters and established fishing cooperatives in which it retained the majority of stock (McGoodwin 1979:54, 1987:222). By 1936, twenty-six such cooperatives had been formed (Gatti and Alcala 1985:31). To further reinforce its control over fisheries, the federal government passed a tariff law on fish products that required permits for all national waters. It fixed tariffs for identification cards, fines, and for registry of boats and fishing gear and equipment (Quesada 1952:204).

During the Cárdenas administration, Mexico's efforts to territorialize its national waters and to centralize control over them in federal hands saw the passage of a number of other acts. In 1934, President Cárdenas created the Departamento Autónomo y Forestal de Caza y Pesca (Department of forestry, hunting, and fishing), the duties of which included encouraging and protecting national fishing. Under Cárdenas, fishing cooperatives were granted exclusive rights to specific species such as shrimp, lobster, oyster, abalone, and snails (the totoaba was incorporated years later). They also were given quick and easy credit to buy modern equipment (Gatti and Alcala 1985:31). Although the government granted exclusive territories to fishing cooperatives, ultimately the federal government retained control. Fishing cooperatives were closely bound to regional packing plants and were required by their charters to deliver their entire catch to these plants at prices fixed annually by the government (McGoodwin 1979:54–55). The effect of these regulations, of course, was to render subsistence fishing less free. The legislation favored the development of fishing cooperatives; the privileges granted to them also tended to put pressure on allegedly free fishers to join cooperatives that initially offered better prices, credit, and guaranteed access to productive fishing areas (Quesada 1952:34).

World War Two and Its Aftermath

On the eve of World War Two, the Cárdenas government expelled the Japanese fishing fleets from its coastal waters. In the absence of Japanese competition during the war, the way was opened for Mexico to develop its offshore fishing fleet. The Mexican state under President Manuel Avila Camacho (1940–46) moved aggressively to create the institutions and infrastructure needed to expand its fishing sector. In 1941, the Banco Nacional de Fomento Cooperativo (National bank for the support of cooperatives) was created and began to finance fishing cooperatives through a branch in Ensenada (Quesada 1952: 26). In Sonora, General Abelardo Rodriguez was a key player in the drive to expand Mexico's offshore fleet. As the governor of Sonora during the Cárdenas administration, he helped establish the company Guaymas, S.A. to exploit shrimp and other fish.[3] During the war, he created the Financiera del Golfo de Cortés (Finance company of the Gulf of Cortés), later called the Financiera y Fiduciaria de Sonora, S.A. (Finance and trust company of Sonora). In partnership with local investors, General Rodriguez also organized Productos Marinos de Guaymas, S.A. (Seafood products of Guaymas), a refrigeration and freezing plant. By 1943, the plant had a contract with five fishing cooperatives and monopolized seafood production in Guaymas, making impressive profits for all parties concerned. This activity revitalized the port of Guaymas: new facilities for ship construction and repair soon employed one hundred men (Guadarrama 1985:156). In 1944, General Rodriguez, on the basis of his work with fishing cooperatives, created the Cámara de la Industria Pesquera (Chamber of commerce for industrial fishing).

Although fishermen were first attracted to the upper gulf in the early 1920s, from the beginning the development of the fisheries there was closely linked to international demand. Initially, the upper gulf's fishermen supplied totoaba, an endemic species of sea bass, to Chinese living in Mexicali, San Diego, and Los Angeles.[4] Early fishing techniques, however, were extremely crude and destructive. Fishermen used dynamite to mine the seas. They threw sticks of dynamite into the water, and the stunned and dead fish floated to the surface, where they could be hauled in. By World War Two, in part because of such destructive techniques, totoaba stocks began to decline.[5] As offshore fishing in the Gulf of California expanded during the 1940s, fishermen began to target other species. During World War Two, a market for shark livers as an ingredient in vitamins for U.S. soldiers developed briefly but collapsed soon afterward (Equihua Ballesteros 1983:513–14). Following the war, fishing efforts began to shift rapidly toward shrimp. In 1946, the first shrimp cooperative, Elias Calles, was organized in Guaymas. The venture was so successful that by 1948 Sonora's fishing cooperatives captured and processed more kilos of fish than any state in the country (Ramirez and Guadarrama 1985:183). The national production of shrimp rose between 1945 and 1950 from 7,401 to 20,373 metric tons (Instituto Nacional de Estadística, Geografía, e Informática 1990: 1:432–33).

The Mexican State, Foreign Debt, and Development Policies

Mexico's experiences with foreign capital during the Porfiriato made post-revolutionary governments profoundly suspicious of foreign investment and deeply nationalistic. During the Cárdenas administration, influenced by the current dependency theory, Mexico adopted development policies based on a model of import substitution industrialization (ISI) to which the Mexican state continued to adhere until the mid-1980s. Guided by these policies, the Mexican government sought to promote the manufacture in Mexico of goods imported from abroad; in so doing they aimed simultaneously to break dependencies on foreign nations and to become industrialized in the process. These policies had a profound impact on the development of Mexico's fisheries.

The Mexican state not only intervened heavily in key industries, including fishing, during these years, but also organized parastatal companies to which it provided credit and other subsidies. As well, the Mexican state attempted to limit foreign investment by requiring a minimum of 51 percent Mexican ownership of companies and to protect Mexican markets from foreign competition by imposing tariffs, duties, licenses, and other measures. As key to ISI, the state also tried to maintain favorable trade balances. Although through the 1930s and 1940s, Mexico maintained a favorable balance of trade and relatively small foreign debt, in the early 1950s, it began to experience foreign trade deficits and an ever-growing foreign debt. Ironically, such debts and deficits were largely a product of ISI policies. In hindsight, one can see that the major flaw in Mexico's policies was to leave to private capital the decision as to what goods should be manufactured in Mexico. Being good businessmen, the capitalists opted to produce highly profitable consumer goods rather than invest in less profitable areas of production such as machine tools, which would have given Mexico the capacity to produce its own factories. Unfortunately, this meant that Mexican companies producing consumer goods often had to import all their manufacturing equipment, raw materials, and components. Sadly, rather than making Mexico independent, ISI policies made Mexico more dependent and generated increasing economic inefficiencies to boot (Gould 1996:19–27; Russell 1977:66). As trade balances began to sour in the early 1950s—a trend that was to continue (Instituto Nacional de Estadística, Geografía, e Informaática 1990: 2:661)—Mexico made economic growth its top priority.

Under Mexico's form of state capitalism, even though the state controlled key industries, its control was rife with contradictions. While some industries were profitable, many required heavy subsidies. Although such subsidized industries made private capitalist ventures that much more profitable, paying for them was problematic. Like most developing countries, Mexico's domestic market and tax system were notoriously weak, so the burden of paying for industrial development fell on the exploitation of its natural resources. As the pace of industrialization increased, so too did its rapacious demands on nature.

Mexico's March to the Sea

As Mexico cast about for the means to promote economic growth, it looked increasingly toward the sea. Although efforts during World War Two and through the late 1940s increased fish production dramatically, many argued that a country with ten thousand kilometers of coast could produce much more. To increase fish production, President Adolfo Ruiz Cortinez (1952–58) launched a program known as "the march to the sea" (Gatti and Alcala1985: 31). This program, continued by subsequent administrations, not only pushed the expansion of commercial fishing, but also led to new reterritorializations of Mexico's waters. The aim of the Mexican state was to increase production, while extending its control over the sea. During the administration of President Gustavo Díaz Ordaz (1964–70), Mexico extended its territorial waters from three to twelve miles. Under President Luis Echeverría (1970–76), Mexico further expanded its territorial waters to a two-hundred-mile-wide zone in which it claimed exclusive rights (Gatti and Alcala 1985:31).

Once the Mexican state owned the fish, a massive administrative reterritorialization of agencies regulating fishing moved forward. Federal regulations that radically modified fishing were passed. Norms for conservation were enacted that defined fishing seasons, established bans, regulated the size of fish and volume of fish caught commercially for each species, and established what kinds of fishing gear were permitted (Mercado and Leanos 1976:527). A series of new institutions were created to enforce and administer such regulations. In 1970, a new Subsecretariat of Fishing (SEPESCA) was established under the Secretary of Industry and Commerce. SEPESCA's task was to promote development of fishing, cooperatives, and the uses of advanced technologies. By the 1970s, state efforts had induced 75 percent of some seventy thousand fishermen in communities around the Gulf of California to join the 139 fishing cooperatives in the region (Mercado and Leanos 1976:534).

Echeverría's administration (1970–76) also moved to formulate the National Fishing Program, giving special attention to the Gulf of California. This program created an administrative framework that encouraged cooperation between private and cooperative sectors. This, of course, helped the government to further consolidate its control over the fishing sector. For example, many private firms were absorbed by the state and converted into parastatal companies (Moctezuma-Hernández and Alvarez López 1989:129–30). To further broaden its control, the government helped establish a nationwide network of distribution for Mexican fish products through fish shops and state-subsidized CONASUPO stores (Mercado and Leanos 1976:530). As part of its efforts to expand the Mexican fishing industry, the government used its Banco de Fomento (Development bank) to provide credit to modernize the fishing fleet and port facilities and to offer greater financial support to cooperatives. At the start of the march to the sea, most shrimp trawlers were wooden boats with gasoline engines and capacities of eleven tons. As the government made credit increasingly available, larger, steel-hulled shrimp boats of up to one hundred tons with diesel engines replaced the older, smaller boats.[6]

The impact of these programs is readily seen in national production figures. During the 1950s, with the start of Ruiz Cortinez's march to the sea, total fish production averaged 148,000 metric tons a year (figure 1). Through the 1960s, production continued its upward trend, averaging 170,000 tons annually. During the 1970s, after extending its coastal waters to two hundred miles, Mexico established a National Fishing Program that pushed to increase yields. As a result, total fish production rose to an average of 468,000 metric tons. In 1982, when the dramatic drop in the world price of oil sent Mexico's economy into a tailspin, fish production was at an all-time high of 1,364,000 metric tons. Mexico's general economic problems soon affected the fishing fleet's level of effort. By 1983, captures had fallen to 973,000 tons. Although production increased as the economy recovered, capture figures averaged 1,122,000 tons between 1980 and 1987 (see figure 1).

When Mexico's fishing sector is examined in greater detail, it is evident that this growth was not due to equivalent increments in yields among species exploited. The higher yields were achieved by widening the number of species targeted, intensifying their exploitation, and shifting to other species when catches dropped. The dynamics of this pattern are clearly illustrated in tuna, shrimp, sardines, and the industrial fish used to make animal feed and fertilizers.[7]

The tuna fishery represents a classical example of an overexploited species (figure 2). Tuna production that had been roughly 30,000 tons rose dramatically following World War Two. By 1948, some 48,000 metric tons were being caught, an average that was maintained for the next fourteen years. Despite signs in the mid-1950s that this level of exploitation could not be maintained, the Comisión Nacional Consultiva de Pesca—created during the administration of Adolfo López Mateos (1958–64)—attempted to expand seafood consumption, especially of tuna and sardines (Moctezuma-Hernández and Alvarez López 1989 : 129–30). Tuna populations were rapidly decimated, and in 1962 the tuna fishery collapsed. By 1965, only 2,000 tons of tuna were caught. As tuna populations take a long time to rebuild, production figures since 1962 have averaged only 17,000 tons (Instituto Nacional de Estadística, Geografía, e Informática 1990, I:432–33).[8]

Shrimp have a very high reproductive potential, so the dynamics of this fishery have been different (see figure 2). Since World War Two, shrimp production has been important, especially as an export, where it generated the much-needed hard currency required for payment of foreign debts. As a result, the Mexican government encouraged the expansion of the shrimping fleet. Production rose from an average of 24,000 metric tons in the 1950s to 40,000 during the 1960s. Despite fishery biologists' warnings as early as the mid-1960s that shrimp were being overexploited (Chavez and Lluch 1971 : 141; *Commercial Fisheries Review* 1964 26(3):100; McGoodwin 1979:59), government policies continued to encourage the expansion of the fleet. Newer, larger boats replaced older, smaller ones, and the number of shrimp boats plying the gulf increased in number and in capacity.[9] Although total shrimp production continued to climb, averaging 46,000 tons in the 1970s and 54,000 tons in the 1980s, the share of the catch per boat began to fall, making shrimping less and less profitable (Instituto Nacional de Estadstica, Geografía, e Informática 1990, 1:432–33). Although government policies that encouraged the expansion and modernization of the fleet did increase production, much of this increase came at the expense of fishermen, who saw their per-boat share of the total catch dwindle with each new boat added to the fleet.

During the Echeverría administration, national efforts were directed at expanding production of lower-priced, but more abundant, industrial fish such as sardines and anchovies. This was especially important because the effort to expand shrimp and tuna production had become increasingly counterproductive. Sardines were processed both for human consumption and to make

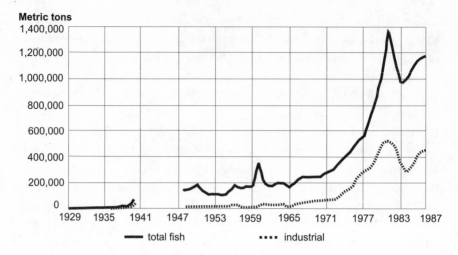

GREENBERG FIGURE 1. Total fish and industrial production in Mexico, 1929–87 (Source: Instituto Nacional de Estadística, Geografía, e Informática 1990, 1:432–33)

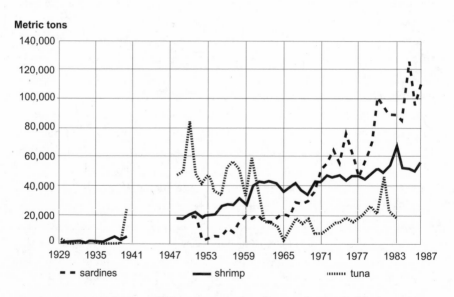

GREENBERG FIGURE 2. Shrimp, tuna, and sardine production in Mexico, 1929–87 (Source: Instituto Nacional de Estadística, Geografia, e Informática 1990, 1:432–33)

animal feed and fertilizers. Sardine production for human consumption grew steadily through the 1950s and 1960s, going from an average of 11,000 to 21,000 metric tons. During the 1960s, the Comisión Nacional Consultiva de Pesca began to push sardine consumption, and, as a result, in the 1970s and 1980s sardine production for consumption rose from an average of 57,000 to 99,000 metric tons. Industrial catches grew even faster. The National Fishing Program that encouraged the industrial processing of fish, especially sardines and anchovies to make animal feed and fertilizer, had an enormous effect on fish production (see figure 1, above). Fish processed for animal feed and fertilizers went from an average of 8,000 metric tons in the 1950s to 30,000 in the 1960s, to 176,000 in the 1970s, and to 416,000 tons in the 1980s. As this rapid growth proceeded, industrial uses of fish came to account for an ever-greater percentage of the total catch, spiraling upward from an average in the 1950s and 1960s of 5 to 13 percent of total fish production to an average of 35 percent of the total during the 1970s and 1980s (Instituto Nacional de Estadística, Geografía, e Informática 1990, 1:432–33).

When Mexico extended its waters to two hundred miles, the government not only gained control of the offshore fishery but also gave it greater priority. To administer its new territory, the Mexican government increasingly professionalized its fishery management. The organization of fisheries management is highly centralized. The Fisheries Ministry and the Instituto Nacional de la Pesca (INP), from its central offices in Mexico City, play a central role in the management of commercially important species and control all aspects of fishing law, enforcement, and research.[10] As administrative responsibilities were increasingly turned over to marine biologists and fisheries managers, the fishermen, fishing cooperatives, and other local interests lost control of local fisheries and also were marginalized from policy-making decisions.

Management of Inshore and Offshore Fisheries

Unfortunately, fisheries management has essentially been based on single-species methods that emphasize the maximum sustainable yield (MSY)—that is, exploitation of fish to the limit the species can bear without diminishing the population's reproductive power. Deplorably, production goals based on such calculations rested on assumptions that are deeply flawed. Methods of calculating allowable yields do not take such fundamental external factors into account as ecological fluctuations and the effects of other species in the biotic community. Most marine species live in perpetually changing and complex environments that cause chaotic fluctuations in their populations. Many species, as a result, experience boom-and-bust cycles that are entirely independent of fishing effort (McGoodwin 1990:72–74).[11] Moreover, rather than rationalizing fishing, such models help create the tragedy of commoditization by overestimating sustainable yields, often leading to overfishing of targeted species. Because estimates are arrived at separately for each species by holding the complex interactions among species as ceteris paribus constants, the recommendations for one species may not only have negative impacts on others, but may also profoundly change the structure of the biotic community. Because MSY and other similar models appear rational and scientific, they are often used despite their weaknesses to disguise highly political processes that place national interests over those of local fishermen. In Mexico, because government revenues and hard currency earned from exports are proportional to the total catch, models that encouraged the maximum sustainable utilization of resources quickly found state favor. As already noted, although these policies did increase total production and enhance national revenues, they did so by sacrificing the earnings and profits of local fishermen.

Conflicts with inshore fishermen increased as offshore fishing fleets expanded. When shrimp population began showing signs of overexploitation, the offshore sector blamed the problem on the fishing practices of inshore fishermen. They accused them of using damaging gear and fishing in offshore waters. The offshore sectors argued that harvesting shrimp in inshore waters is poor practice because it removes young shrimp from the fishery before they reach adult size and reduces the maximum potential shrimp biomass that can be harvested. They argued, moreover, that the larger shrimp caught offshore command a higher price, so that harvesting immature shrimp inshore makes little economic sense. Even though the entire capacity of the inshore fishing sector's *pangas* is equal to that of a few large shrimp trawlers, the government was swayed by such arguments. Since the 1970s, it has periodically attempted to curtail inshore shrimping by adjusting fishing seasons, regulating gear, and limiting access (McGoodwin 1979:57). Yet government efforts to diminish inshore shrimping have not been consistent. During the Echeverría administration, the same government programs that pushed the expansion of the offshore fleet also encouraged tremendous growth of the inshore sector by offering easy credit to *panga* cooperatives. Thousands of workers and peasants who knew nothing about fishing were attracted to the region and filled the coastal waters and estuaries with small boats. Between 1970 and 1980 the number of small boats in the gulf doubled from about fifteen hundred to three thousand. The government used the inshore cooperatives, as it did offshore ones, to concentrate its control over the fishery. Because fishing permits were issued to the cooperatives, in order to fish or obtain credit fishermen were forced to register their boats and motors as property of the cooperative.

The Mexican Crisis, Globalization, and Reterritorialization

In the 1970s, the underlying problems with the Mexican economy were already becoming apparent. The ISI policies that were supposed to foster domestic industries had led to an increasingly larger trade deficit. And, in 1976, faced with a balance of payments crisis, Mexico was forced to devalue its peso. In less than a year the peso slid from 12.50 to 22.70 pesos to the U.S. dollar. However, the discovery of huge oil deposits in Tabasco and Veracruz seemed to restore Mexico's prospects. Banking on oil revenues rather than undertake austerity measures, the new administration of President José López Portillo (1976–82) embarked on a massive program of fiscal expansion. Mexico borrowed heavily abroad to finance the expansion of its oil industry. And in an attempt to create jobs, the government poured massive sums into purchasing inefficient private-sector firms in order to set up parastatal companies. By 1982, the number of state-owned companies had increased from some 300 to 1,155. At first, these policies seemed to be successful. Mexico's economy enjoyed high rates of growth (Gould 1996:10–19). This prosperity, however, was premised on high oil prices. Because oil accounted for 78 percent of revenues from Mexico's exports, when oil prices began to fall and real U.S. interest rates rose, Mexico's boom turned to bust. The story of the crisis is told in exchange rates. Between 1981 and 1983, the peso–dollar exchange dropped from 26.2 to 143.9 (Gould 1996:20–21).

Despite these problems, because shrimp exports brought in notable sums of hard dollars needed for foreign exchange, the Mexican government continued not just to subsidize the shrimping industry, but also to encourage its rapid expansion. In 1982, the government enacted policies that entailed a massive reterritorialization of control over resources that forced the private shrimp boat owners to sell their boats to state-backed cooperatives. To compensate the private sector, the cooperatives were made to pay high prices for such boats and equipment, working or not. To finance the transfer of the fleet from the private to the public sector, Ban Pesca extended cooperatives special loans at rates far below those of commercial banks. During the mid-1980s, even as the crisis deepened and successive devaluations sent the peso plummeting to 2,281 to the dollar by 1988, Ban Pesca continued to offer trawler cooperatives easy credit to buy new boats and equipment. At the same time, however, because of rampant inflation, the costs of production also rose quickly. For example, in 1982, when the Mexican state cut many indirect subsidies it had provided, the price of diesel went through the ceiling. This might not have been problematic, but shrimp prices remained flat, or even dropped—partly because shrimp is an international commodity competing in a world market and partly because of competition from Mexico's own cultivated shrimp industry. As a result, by the end of the 1980s, most shrimp cooperatives were losing money and were deep in debt. As debt burdens and operation costs climbed, shrimpers were forced to intensify their fishing efforts just to meet their obligations.

In the late 1980s and early 1990s the problems in the fishing industry were compounded by the structural changes the Mexican state was forced to adopt to meet its debt obligations. Under President Miguel de la Madrid (1982–88), although Mexico began to reduce its public sector deficit, the fundamental problems underlying the crisis remained; for example, burdens of foreign debt and heavily subsidized state-owned enterprises. President Carlos Salinas de Gortari (1988–94), a Harvard-trained economist, essentially embraced the neoliberal, neoclassical policies of structural adjustment promoted by the World Bank and the International Monetary Fund, which were designed to help countries put their financial house in order and repay their foreign debts. This neoliberal package included opening Mexican markets to foreign capital, eliminating trade barriers, cutting back on government programs, ending subsidies, and deregulating and privatizing the economy. Moves to lower tariffs had already been made under President de la Madrid when Mexico joined the multilateral General Agreement on Tariffs and Trade (GATT). Under Salinas, following passage of the North American Free Trade Agreement (NAFTA), most import tariffs between Mexico, the United States, and Canada were eliminated. Mexico's efforts to privatize the economy, however, entailed the most profound reterritorialization of land and administrative control over resources since the Mexican Revolution. Most parastatal enterprises were sold, merged, or liquidated (so that by 1994 only 215 remained), and the new Agrarian Reform Law modified Article 27 of the Constitution to allow communities to lease or sell their *ejido* and communal lands.

In line with these policies, the Mexican state withdrew support from fishing cooperatives, and Ban Pesca ceased providing cooperatives credit after the 1988–89 season. Although private banks such as Bancomer and Banamex continued to lend to cooperatives, financing was at market rates and based on ability to pay. Economic conditions continued to deteriorate during the Salinas years. By 1994, the dollar sold for 5,080 pesos; and although inflation slowed, it still averaged 22.45 percent. Credit or no, unfortunately, shrimp prices remained flat, and cooperatives continued their slide deeper into debt. Eventually, even commercial banks were unwilling to lend to them, so by the 1991–92 season even private banks refused to extend them further credit. By the 1992–93 season, with no credit and burdened by debt, cooperatives began to default on their loans and were forced to sell their trawlers or had them seized by the banks. Many cooperatives simply went under. Inshore *panga* cooperatives faced similar problems and constraints and fared no better. Many failed, and when they did, the fishermen who had registered their boats and motors as cooperative property lost them.[12]

It is increasingly evident that the drop in shrimp production was not due to a tragedy of the commons, as environmentalists at the time alleged. Instead of seeing only shrimp production fall sharply (which is what one would expect if a targeted species is being overfished), during the early 1990s, we see the same pattern in the total fish production for the nation as a whole (figures 3 and 4). This suggests strongly that the sharp fall in production after 1990 was due not to a collapse of shrimp stock, but to a slackening of fishing effort as cooperatives were denied credit. Not only were fewer boats putting out to sea because they had been seized for debts, but those that did, being short of money, could do so for shorter lengths of time—days rather than weeks. Only after 1993–94, once privatization was well under way, do we see production figures recover. Yet, even if we were to give credence to the environmentalist argument that the drop in production was in part due to overfishing, the more general point to be made is that shrimp fishermen are hardly the independent actors posited in Hardin's model of the commons. Rather, their decisions and actions were overdetermined by the institutional matrix in which they are embedded—by state policies, agencies, banks, and companies. Because Mexico, in turn, is enmeshed in a global economy, decisions about exploitation of natural resources are apt to be based more on concerns about capital flows (e.g., foreign debt, state revenues, GNP) than on fish populations or the environment.

Conclusion and Discussion

Examining the historical development of Mexico's fisheries, one sees clearly that the ecological problems of the upper Gulf of California represent more of a

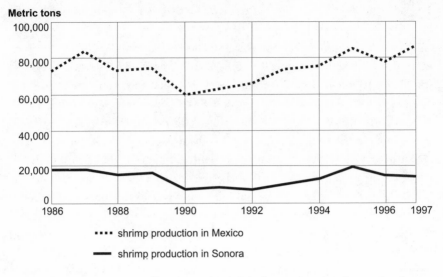

Metric tons

•••• shrimp production in Mexico

—— shrimp production in Sonora

GREENBERG FIGURE 3. Shrimp production in Sonora compared to national figures, 1986–97 (Source: Mexican Government, SEMARNP: Anuario Estadístico de Pesca, 1995, 1996, and 1997)

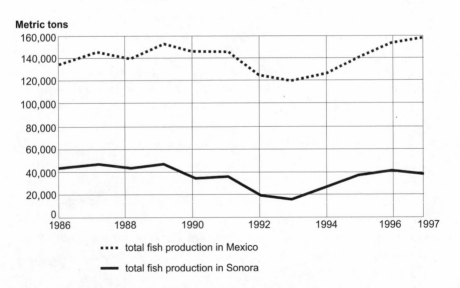

Metric tons

•••• total fish production in Mexico

—— total fish production in Sonora

GREENBERG FIGURE 4. Total fish production in Sonora compared to national figures, 1986–97 (Source: Instituto Nacional de Estadística, Geografía, e Informática 1990, 1:432–33; Mexican Government, SEMARNP: Anuario Estadístico de Pesca, 1995, 1996, and 1997) problem than that envisioned in the zero-sum game of the "tragedy of the commons" (Hardin 1968). While it may appear that Hardin's model fits this case, the tragedy here is not the result of decisions of individual fishermen, but is the outcome of Mexican policies that favored expansion of the shrimping fleet. As long as adding boats continued to increase overall production—hence, the exports that earned the hard currencies needed to pay off foreign debts—government policy supported fleet expansion, even at the expense of the profitability of individual trawlers. While the case for a collapse of the shrimp stock in the Gulf of California may be overstated, the evidence of collapse for tuna and totoaba is much stronger. When we look at the collapse of tuna historically, we see the same elements at work: an overcapitalized fleet being pushed by state policy to exploit this fishery. Again, the fishermen involved were hardly the independent decision makers of Hardin's model. While we might blame the state for the collapse of tuna, however, the complex case of totoaba would seem to point in the other direction—at local fishermen. Three factors seem to have been involved: overexploitation of the totoaba stock through the use of very destructive means; damming of the Colorado River, which seems to have affected the totoaba spawning areas at the mouth of the river (Greenberg 1998:145); and a continuing problem of the totoaba fry being killed in shrimping bi-catch. Here, despite the efforts of the state to declare the mouth of the river a reserve because of the high market price for totoaba, illegal poaching by local fishermen has pushed the species to near extinction.

The lesson is not that local fishermen are blameless, or that the state is the true villain, or that the private sector is a better manager than the public sector; rather, the lesson seems to be that the commoditization of natural resources inserts fishermen into alien logics, logics that arbitrarily value some resources while devaluing others. Seen in this light, the plight of these poor fishermen is not a tragedy of the commons but a tragedy of commoditization, and their troubles are an unhappy product of the complex processes by which natural resources are territorialized and reterritorialized as nation-states react to global capital as well as to their own internal political struggles and change strategies accordingly.

The tragedy of commoditization is not just that natural resources are managed as so many separate assets rather than as constituent parts of nature, but that commoditization is a deeply political process as well. The result of dividing the physical landscape both spatially, among local, state, and national entities, and conceptually, among various administrative hierarchies, is that the policies to which the physical landscape then falls subject are often poorly co-ordinated, frequently contradictory, and even incompatible. What seems rational use for one resource may harm another. If this were not calamity enough, as competing classes and interest groups vie for control and gain power or influence, policies change constantly. In Mexico, because each new administration is anxious to make its mark and pay off political debts, the turnover in programs and policies is high. If this were the best of all possible worlds, good policies would supplant bad ones. The world being what it is, more often the interests of the powerful are favored over those of the weak, the rich over the poor, the national over the local, and the short term over the long term, without much consideration of environmental consequences. These problems are further compounded as companies and nation-states vie in world markets, shifting investments, attempting to protect markets, and so on.

Transforming nature into commodities involves more than their coming to embody labor. Commodities are also embedded in hierarchies of territorializations through which bundles of jural rights over them—such as rights of ownership, means of transference, rights of regulation, and rights of consumption—are established. If territorializations define the rights that organize a means of production, then processes of globalization direct the fate of commodities. As they enter ever-larger spheres of circulation, they become subject to nonterritorial entities like multinational corporations, banks, and stock markets. This is the world of alienation in which the laborer is denied the product of his labor, and nature is stripped of its local meaning and importance: trees become lumber, shrimp are simply things that are bought and sold.

Although the tragedy of commoditization is driven by a logic that is very different from that which controls biotic relationships, it should be noted here that these management problems are not necessarily linked to monetary metrics. Often, as in the case of maximum sustainable yield, management models are based on what seem to be ecological criteria such as rates of reproduction. The real tragedy is that the management of the "valued" commodity is often at the expense of other, lesser-valued or nonvalued species or elements. Thus, for example, for each kilo of shrimp, a trawler may catch thirty kilograms of bi-catch. Because of the economics of freezing the catch, most of this bi-catch is dumped overboard, dead (McGuire and Greenberg 1993). The point is that commodity management, however scientific its methods may be, is not ecological management. Conversely, market participation is not governed by ecological considerations. Even if shrimp could be managed well scientifically, nonvalued species are not. And, in this case at least, one has no idea what effect pulling shrimp and bi-catch out of these seas may have on the stability of other species populations and food chains. In such cases, the price consumers pay when they buy a pound of shrimp does not measure their true ecological cost. Their cheap shrimp are subsidized by ecological destruction and by the devastation of hundreds of species dredged up with them.

Once commodities enter the market, they are subject to an alien logic in which price is a function not of biotic importance but of supply and demand. So where there is a world market for such commodities, prices depend on the average supply on the international market. This globalization of price fundamentally changes the relationship of the market to local ecologies. Because world market prices are not tied directly to local demand or supplies, they are fairly insensitive to local conditions. What this means for many developing countries is this: to pay foreign debts and buy goods on the international market, they must export their natural resources to earn the required hard currencies. Demand for such resources in world markets is seemingly inexhaustible, so when world prices are high, there are few incentives to conserve natural resources. The temptation is to make hay while the sun shines. Tragically, even when world prices are low, because the need for hard currencies is often paramount, developing countries may subsidize and even expand exploitation of natural resources, regardless of the costs to the environment. Unfortunately, as long as natural resources are treated as so many separate commodities rather than as integral parts of particular ecologies, tragedies of commoditization will remain commonplace.

Notes

1. Commenting on a similar situation in southern Sinaloa, McGoodwin argues that if its shrimp fishery has suffered a tragedy of the commons, it was not of its own making, but the result of federal "management policy over-emphasizing production for export" (McGoodwin 1987:229).

2. Bundles of rights are entailed in commodities over which the state may exercise control. In the process of territorialization and reterritorialization, the forms of ownership, rights of access, usufruct rights, modalities of transfer, and rights of consumption or destruction may be substantially redefined.

3. The "S.A." following the company name stands for Sociedad Anónima, meaning that it is incorporated and owned by anonymous shareholders.

4. The Chinese considered the totoaba's swim bladder, or *buche*, a great delicacy and used it in chop suey and other dishes (Craig 1926:166).

5. The totoaba have become an endangered species (Barrera Guevara 1992:56–57).

6. The fishing fleet in Guaymas was among the first to benefit. By 1954, cooperatives in Guaymas had 40 percent of the boats over one hundred tons in the country and nine of the thirty-four freezing plants in Mexico.

7. Although sardines and anchovies are the primary ingredients in industrial fish products, in the following discussion production figures for sardines are those for human consumption only; sardines processed as industrial fish are excluded.

8. This average is for the years 1962 through 1983, the last year for which these data are available.

9. The Gulf of California's fleet increased from an average of 263 trawlers between 1953 and 1979 to an average of 357 during the 1980s. By 1990 there were nearly 600 shrimp trawlers in the gulf (Vasquez et al. 1993).

10. Such control is extended to the local level through regional delegations that are responsible for the implementation and enforcement of national regulations and through Regional Fisheries Research Centers (CRIPs) located in coastal states that are in charge of monitoring particular species and advising central offices as to the need for closures (Vasquez Leon 1993:42).

11. The related notion, a sustainable maximum economic yield (MEY), is equally flawed in that it assumes a stable market for fish (McGoodwin 1990:72–73).

12. The upper gulf was declared a biosphere reserve in 1993 by the Mexican government. As a result, yet another reterritorialization is under way. Plans are being made to restrict or prohibit access to certain areas in the reserve and impose new fishing regulations.

"But the Young Men Don't Want to Farm Any More": Political Ecology and Consumer Culture in Belize

Richard Wilk

Introduction

In the recent past a recognizable anthropological subfield devoted to the ethnographic and cross-cultural study of consumer culture has emerged. Rich in detail and diverse in topics, this work ranges from McDonalds restaurants in Korea to the careful brewing of traditional banana beer in East Africa. But these studies are all very new; just thirty years ago there were virtually no anthropologists studying consumption. In 1982, when Eric Arnould and I sent a paper on the anthropology of consumption to the *American Anthropologist*, it was rejected on the grounds that the subject material was "not a topic of anthropological interest."

We had not been trained in or taught about consumer culture at any time during our graduate education in anthropology at the University of Arizona in the late 1970s (though Arnould later took some courses in the Marketing Department there). Both of us became interested in the topic because of what we had seen while doing our dissertation research, myself in Belize and Arnould in Niger. We had both gone to the field trained in political economy and cultural ecology, ready to do studies that would now be recognizable as political ecology. We wanted to do thorough ecological and economic studies of local communities and to show how those local relations were embedded in historically specific patterns of capitalist development, political power, and class or ethnic relations. What we found in the field fit very well with much we had been taught to expect, and we both returned with a strong sense that consumption was the missing piece of the puzzle.

In this essay I will use the example of my fieldwork in Belize as a starting point from which to critique the limitations of cultural ecology and also to argue that all the "new ecologies" need to incorporate the problem of consumption and consumer culture, not as an afterthought or addendum but at a fundamental level. Problems of consumption are found at every level of ecological analysis, from the local community to the management of the global commons. Therefore, no form of anthropological ecology—political, symbolic, or historical—can be a comprehensive tool for understanding change at either local or global levels until it incorporates consumption.

Learning Cultural Ecology

My training in cultural ecology began when I was studying to be an archaeologist, first as an undergraduate at New York University and then at Arizona. The New Archaeology included a healthy dose of cultural evolutionism, founded on the Sahlins and Service typology of political systems and types of subsistence. The work of ecologically oriented archaeologists like Sanders, Flannery, and Binford was deeply concerned with the sources of change, stability, and instability in human adaptive systems; their basic lesson from prehistory was that human-environmental relationships are rarely stable. They also argued persuasively that politics and cultural systems of meaning were integral parts of all subsistence systems and that past cultures were rarely isolated, so that intercultural relations could be a significant source of change in local adaptations.

Robert Netting became my advisor when I decided that for a dissertation project I wanted to work with live people instead of the dead. Netting advised many archaeology students, knew many archaeologists, and was often invited to archaeological conferences. His major interest in the mid-1970s was population growth and agricultural intensification, and he was writing up the results of his research on long-term population trends in an Alpine village (1983). In his ecological anthropology seminar he had students read Boserup and Malthus and histories of agriculture. He also had us working through Wallerstein's world systems theory, French Marxists like Meillasoux and Terray, and dependency theorists like Cardoso, Amin, and Gunder Frank. He wanted us to recognize that the sources of stability and instability in human ecosystems had to be understood at the level of global and regional historical and economic processes as well as in the individual household and in the community. His approach at this time, moving outward from Stewardian cultural ecology to recognize the importance of colonialism, unequal development, and local politics on production and property relations, marked out an intellectual territory that later became recognized as political ecology.

Netting agreed with Rappaport that many local communities had found social and cultural means to achieve some sort of balance in their subsistence system, so they were sustainable in the long run. He disagreed, however, on how that balance was achieved in both the short and long terms. Whereas Rappaport was concerned with ritual and belief and saw a separation between the cultural cognized and objective operational models of the ecosystem, Netting saw most people as pragmatic, reasonable actors whose depth of empirical knowledge about their environment and subsistence often exceeded that of the objective scientists. For Netting, people do not have perfect knowledge of the environment by any means, but they have worked out practical long-term solutions for most of the problems they face. Any sort of balance people achieved with nature was therefore the result of their own pragmatic action, rather than of ritual homeostatic devices operating without the knowledge of their operators (Netting 1965, 1981). This sort of reasonable, informed, pragmatic choice extended to people's relationships with political leaders, markets, neighboring communities, and other ethnic groups. But this pragmatism and knowledge did not always keep people from getting stuck with exploitative or self-serving leaders, poor terms of trade, or dramatically unequal relationships with neighbors.

While Rappaport and Netting agreed that many precapitalist societies were ecologically more benign and stable than those of recent times, they disagreed on many of the causes of both the prior stability and the subsequent instability. The most fundamental difference between Rappaport's and Netting's approaches is that Netting saw the distance between cognized and operational models as the main problem for sustainability, while Rappaport saw it as the best hope for a solution. At the risk of oversimplifying complex positions, I think Rappaport believed that religion and ritual were forces that preserved ecological stability, that the sustainability and coherence of non-Western subsistence systems was dependent on the "coherence, orderliness, and meaningfulness of the conceptual structures liturgy organizes" (1979:129). When Western economic logic replaces liturgical and ritual cosmology and money replaces meaning, the result is both social malaise and ecological instability (ibid.:179). Netting, on the other hand, believed that peoples' practical knowledge, skill, and social institutions were the key to long-term sustainable human adaptation (Netting 1993; Wilk and Stone 1998). Through long-term trial and error, creativity, and experience, people arrived at systems that work; in other words, the better they understood nature and each other, the better off they would be. In lectures Netting pointed out cases in which religion and ritual gave people incentives to overexploit or destabilize resources rather than to preserve them. Rather than loss of belief, Netting thought that the major causes of cultural ecological instability included particular kinds of markets for labor or produce (though some markets could actually have positive effects). But more often, Netting argued, the destruction of stable productive systems resulted from shortsighted and ignorant intervention by governments and elite classes that disrupted local social institutions and practices, often in the name of progress or reform (Netting 1993). There was nothing inherent in participation in a monetary economy or in changing religious beliefs that led directly to resource overuse or ecological destruction. Rappaport, in contrast, stressed the limitations of rational self-interest and cognition and argued that long-term adaptability depends on systems of morality and religion that can provide deeper and more important forms of knowledge about the world than practical reason can (1979:157).

The disagreements and differences in emphasis between Rappaport and Netting resonate with the formalist/substantivist debate in economic anthropology as well as with the broader division between idealism and materialism in anthropology at large (Biersack 1999c:3). Even more fundamental philosophical issues about human nature and the relationship between the individual and the group underlie and complicate their positions as well. I would like to be able to claim I was able to understand the theoretical complexities and the limitations of both versions of cultural ecology through careful reading and deep thought, but the fact is that I questioned what I had been taught only when I was forced to. I simply could not make sense out of what I saw during my fieldwork with the tools of cultural ecology, and it has taken years of further fieldwork and research in diverse fields to arrive at some idea of what exactly was wrong with the tools I was using.

Practicing Cultural Ecology

My research with Kekchi (Q'eqchi') Mayan farmers in the Toledo district of southern Belize began in 1978 and lasted fifteen months. I returned for short periods in 1982, 1984, 1990, and 1993.[1] My study was designed to test some of the classic issues of cultural ecology: the relationship between population size, social organization, and ecological stability. In particular I wanted to show how increasing population and intensification of agriculture led to changes in the domestic organization of labor and property, which in turn affected household formation and settlement patterns.

The Kekchi are tropical rain forest farmers. Today about five thousand Kekchi live in thirty villages scattered through an isolated southern district that still supports some areas of primary forest but that is dominated by anthropogenic secondary forests. They hunt, fish, gather food and other wild resources, raise livestock, and cultivate a mixture of subsistence and cash crops. Small but highly variable amounts of waged work is available in a nearby town, and there are a number of small enterprises, including retail shops, ecotourism lodges, trucking businesses, crafts, and other services. Present settlement, land use, and economy have been surveyed and portrayed graphically by teams of Kekchi and Mopan Maya in cooperation with geographers from the University of California (TMCC/TAA 1997).

In 1980, most Kekchi households still provided the bulk of their own subsistence, through swidden farming of maize in the wet season and short-fallow riverside cultivation in the brief dry season. They grew fifty-two other crops species in hundreds of varieties, including tubers, fruits, and vegetables. Pigs were the main domestic animal, supplemented by various kinds of fowl. In the villages with lower population density and more abundant forest resources, hunting was an important source of meat. In all communities wild plants were a regular part of the diet; the forest also provided tools, house materials, and raw materials for a variety of crafts.

The bulk of the daily diet consisted of corn cooked either in tortillas (*gwa*) or small steamed dumplings (*poch*). To arrive at a standard of consumption, I used a fairly standard anthropological method: weighing and counting the daily diet for samples of men, women, and children and then extrapolating to a minimum annual intake, which I could then use to compute the consumer/worker ratios in households and the adequacy of harvests to provide for household needs (Wilk 1997a). I also calculated how many pigs were being consumed per household per year. In conjunction with data I gathered on labor inputs and records of production from each field, I was able to work out a classic homeostatic model, which stated that a village producing corn entirely to feed itself and its pigs would require x number of hectares of forest, with a fallow period of fifteen years. Given the simple geometric problem of diminishing returns as fields get farther and farther from the village (because of increased travel time each day), I was able to show that a community could grow to a size of about twenty-five families before it would have to begin to cut fields on a shorter fallow cycle, beginning the process of degrading the land and reducing yields. Only at that point would the villagers begin to think about moving to pioneer new areas of forest, switching to higher yielding crops like cassava, or improving their productive technology.

Clearly this part of the study following Carneiro's and Chagnon's traditional cultural ecology was aimed at the issues of frontier colonization and the determinants of settlement size and community fission in tropical forests. I could have used the Kekchi case to build a general model of forest colonization and the levels of population pressure required to impel agricultural intensification. But because of Netting's influence and because he had made us read Gunder Frank and Wallerstein, there was no way I could pretend that the Kekchi were good examples of "living prehistory," whose way of life could represent something primordial and untouched. Gunder Frank (1969) argued that all the Indians of the Americas were products of a long-term encounter with capitalism and colonialism. Anthropologists, he implied, colluded with the state in portraying dispossessed peasants and serfs as untouched survivors of the distant past, the better to create them as objects for supposed development, ironically the very same project that had dispossessed and oppressed them.

One of the ways, I thought, in which anthropologists had perpetually constructed living Maya people as untouched survivors of the past was to reduce their economy to subsistence. All of the classic studies of Mayan farming had focused on corn and crops grown for home consumption, ignoring or minimizing the importance of crops and animals grown for trade and sale and of activities like hunting and gathering for the market. The goal, of course, was to abstract a model of what Mayan subsistence was like before the Spanish conquest, but the effect was a timeless suspension of Mayan people outside the present, what Fabian calls the "denial of coevalness" (1983). Finding "the real Maya" therefore meant cutting away the traces of a cash economy, treating subsistence production as ancient and authentic and everything else as foreign (Wilk 1987).

The Kekchi themselves were quite happy to help me along in this task. They also made sharp distinctions between activities and crops they considered sacred and those which were *caxlan* ("foreign").[2] Corn, for example, is treated with reverence and ritual throughout the growing season, and many people believe you cannot grow it successfully unless you have learned its mysteries and secrets and established a personal relationship with the deities of mountains and valleys. People do not like to sell or buy it. Rice, on the other hand can be grown by anyone. It is bought and sold as a spiritless commodity, and though it can fill the belly it cannot provide true nourishment. Additionally, a cultural ideal for many Kekchi farmers is being self-sufficient: living outside the market, untaxed and free, far from the anxieties of dealing with non-Kekchi-speaking middlemen, government officials, and surly shopkeepers. "We all used to live as one family, and we grew everything we needed," one elder said, after a farm extension agent visited the community to encourage them to plant more rice.

But despite being encouraged by both scholarly authorities and my informants to look the other way, that is, to ignore the cash economy or treat it as something new and disruptive, I kept noticing the appearance of dissonant facts that, like the biting black flies, would not go away. I could not miss the constant parade of commerce outside the door of my house: pigs and sacks of corn, rice, and beans from distant villages, sacks of flour and sugar, crates of beer and soft drinks on horse and mule headed in the other direction. Small troops of Kekchi traders from the highlands of Guatemala came by the house every few weeks selling plastic goods, clothing, toys, and salt from sacred and medicinal springs, while buying shotgun shells, cacao beans, and copal incense.

My agricultural records revealed that almost a third of all agricultural labor was devoted to cash crops. The local government marketing board was buying more than three million pounds of rice a year from fewer than seven hundred Kekchi households, and butchers were buying well over three thousand hogs a year. This cash economy brought a steady flow of manufactured goods into Kekchi households. All but the oldest and poorest had given up making their own pottery and sugar, and everyone used flashlights, kerosene lamps, metal pots, laundry soap, and plastic dishes. Canned foods like mackerel, corned beef, tomato paste, and soup were used occasionally in many households, and while people much preferred to eat their own corn, they did buy corn, rice, and flour when supplies ran short in the wet season. While many households still grew their own coffee or traded with neighbors, most kept a jar of Nescafé instant coffee to serve to guests or on special occasions.

Older people lamented the shift away from home production of foods and crafts and the growing dependence on things from stores. But young men, still living with their parents, were particularly avid producers of cash crops and were the most likely to spend money on clothing, musical instruments, watches, liquor, cigarettes, and jewelry, while their sisters would wring every penny they could from selling eggs and small crafts to buy cosmetics, jewelry, and clothes. Mature families with a number of older working children bought the village's "big ticket" items: a corrugated iron roof for a small shop, a bicycle or a horse, a radio, a cement floor, a chainsaw. Some dreamed of owning a motorbike or a used pickup or of sending their children to high school. Many people were intensifying their agricultural production and clearing larger swidden farms each year to produce more rice and pigs to sell to increase their cash incomes. People were migrating from remote areas to new settlements near the roads, where they had better access to markets for their crops and to shops and schools. But the increased population density in these areas led to conflict over land and degradation of the forest as fallow cycles were progressively shortened. In some roadside communities farmers were already on a "bush-fallow" cycle where regrowth was cut after only four or five years. To maintain production they were using more and more pesticide and fertilizer.

In the village where I lived the longest, there was one young man who had stopped farming altogether. As he explained, he had never liked going to the fields as a boy, so he had decided to open a shop. Much to the displeasure of his elders, who were scandalized by his actions, he paid another young man to clear and plant a cornfield for him, while he spent his days expanding his mercantile enterprise, making small loans, wholesaling hogs, and serving cold drinks. I suspected he was also involved in a small way in selling illegal alcohol, and later I heard he had also been involved in the marijuana trade that was then just beginning.

All of these observations about commerce and the cash economy were difficult to reconcile with the kinds of accounts of subsistence I had been reading in the classics of cultural ecology and archaeology. There was nothing remotely closed or homeostatic about this dynamic mix of subsistence and commercial production. The easy thing to do would have been to follow many other Mayan ethnographers and argue that the cash economy was something new, a recent disruption. Then I could have written a dissertation that told the familiar story of how the ancient and primeval self-sufficient subsistence economy was disappearing under the onrushing flood of modernization and market. I could have then linked the arrival of a commodity economy to the breakdown of traditional religion, ritual, and cosmology, as other Mayan ethnographers had done. And there would be my explanation for ecological destruction.

The only problem was a host of obtrusive facts I would never have noticed if Netting had not taught me to place my local case within a wider historical and political economic framework. I began to read more colonial history, and I took some time away from the villages to dig into colonial administrative records in the National Archives. What I found was disturbing and could not be reconciled with the idea that the Kekchi subsistence system was a survival of ancient times, nor did it allow the possibility that commercial production was new. It turned out that the Kekchi had a unique colonial history. Before the conquest they lived mostly in the temperate highlands of eastern Guatemala. Under their own kings they had large urban settlements, a good deal of commerce, and intensive (rather than swidden) farming. They were not conquered, but rather successfully fought off the Spanish and then accepted conversion in exchange for control of their land and exclusion of settlers. Their region remained under the rule of the Roman Catholic Church until the end of Spanish colonialism, at which point the state began to modernize by allowing colonists to enter the region and expropriate Kekchi lands.

The colonial regime had forced the Kekchi to trade within a system called *repartimiento*, through which they were forced to sell certain goods like cotton and wax at artificially low prices and in exchange were sold inferior manufactured goods at elevated prices. As elsewhere in Latin America, a good deal of their hesitant attitude about consumer goods and the cash economy was probably learned from this experience (Krüggeler 1997:49). After the colonial regime, their region of the highlands was flooded by Guatemalan, British, and German coffee planters, who entrapped rural Kekchi in plantation debt-servitude. While the urban population concentrated on handicrafts and petty trading, independent farming became untenable in the countryside as the best land was expropriated and coerced plantation work grew commonplace. Some Kekchi fled into the lowland rain forest, and some of those ended up in Belize. Other Kekchi were taken to southern Belize as a captive labor force on an Anglo-German plantation there. It was clear there was nothing primordial about the Kekchi swidden system I was studying in 1980; to portray it as an ancient survival was clearly in error (though the skills, rituals, and knowledge the Kekchi used in it certainly had deep roots in the past).

As I looked at the twentieth-century history of southern Belize in the colonial archives, I found that instead of a gradual transition from subsistence to a cash economy, there had been a number of boom and bust cycles in different kinds of capitalist development. When the coffee and cocoa plantation closed in 1914, people moved back to subsistence farming. But then there had been a banana boom, and Kekchi had produced thousands of tons of bananas for the Standard Fruit Company. When that crashed there was a logging boom. Then during World War Two, Kekchi farmers sold large amounts of corn and beans to the colonial authorities, who exported them to other colonies in the Caribbean. Given an opportunity and a market, Kekchi people repeatedly entered the cash economy, bought consumer goods and staples, and cut back on subsistence production. In times of recession and market collapse, they went back to self-sufficiency. And in each cycle of development, outsiders portrayed the Kekchi as primitive Indians emerging for the first time into civilization.

A little historical archaeology confirmed that there had been earlier periods of participation in a consumer economy. Surface collections in several villages revealed substantial amounts of china, patent medicine bottles, and liquor bottles dating to the end of the nineteenth century and the early twentieth (Staski and Wilk 1985). In high rain forest I found traces of old barbed wire fences used to keep cattle and old abandoned groves of nutmeg, cacao, and coffee.

Interpretation

All of these facts and bits of knowledge led me to write a dissertation that combined various aspects of cultural ecology and political economy. I worked out the details of the subsistence system and showed how the population was well below carrying capacity as long as they were producing for their own use. Only when they intensified production to sell more products on the market, which often entailed moving to large roadside villages, did they begin to face declining returns and the need to intensify their farming methods. I detailed some of the characteristics of capitalist development in Belize (not in the detail of later work like Moburg 1992) and showed how it created markets for particular products, for labor, and for other resources at different times. I felt that the historical view and the broader perspective offered by political economy made the household- and community-level ecological analysis a lot more accurate and relevant. But I was deeply frustrated as well because neither the ecology nor political economy explained the really fundamental changes that were taking place in Kekchi life. Let me explain why.

The story about change told by classic cultural ecology is about balance and functional adaptation. People respond to environmental problems by crafting sustainable solutions. In the long run things can change because of population growth, climatic change, or the growth of internal social stratification or inequality. The underlying assumption is that, if left to themselves, people will try to find ways to live within their means, and their particular culture defines a common standard of living that all can attain. So, if they had enough land, the Kekchi would try to find some combination of subsistence and trade that gave them a stable livelihood and high returns for their labor. In other words, they would act like the Russian peasants described by the economist A. V. Chayanov (1966): they would produce enough to satisfy their socially defined needs, and then they would stop. If you know what people need, then you can figure out what level of population they can support with a given technology in a particular environment: that's basic ecology.

But the Kekchi were not acting like Chayanov's peasants. They weren't like an organism in a natural ecosystem either; they did not have biologically limited needs. Instead, their consumption seemed to expand whenever they could find a good opportunity to convert labor into products. They were expanding production, intensifying, and working harder not to feed more people but to have more things. The story of functional adaptation makes sense only if you hold needs constant; if needs expand and contract unpredictably, there can be no balance in the system. At this point, an ecological model has to become an economic one, for we have to begin to think about how people decide when to stop working, how they can convert things they have into other things they want, and so on.

Did a political economic approach provide a better explanation? The kinds of stories about change told by political economists at that time portrayed rural people, especially Indians, as the victims of powerful interests. Inevitable pressure would drive independent subsistence farmers like the Kekchi off their land and out of their traditional communities. The Indians would become "proletarianized," and without land they would have to work for starvation wages on large estates and farms or be driven into the cities to become poor factory workers. Sometimes this was done by governments in order to seize Indian land for farming, logging, or mining. Other Indians would be allowed to stay on small, marginal farms and remain in their communities, working seasonally in plantations, forests, and mines. If their labor was needed for a small part of the year, it was cheaper to let them feed themselves the rest of the year. Other political economists saw other forms of exploitation in the ways markets were organized, in the growing dependence of small farmers on expensive agricultural chemicals and machinery, and in rigid class hierarchies that excluded the poor from education and political participation.

There is no question that Mayan groups in parts of neighboring Guatemala and Mexico were indeed exploited and dispossessed in all of these ways. Yet anthropologists have been divided on the degree to which Mayan people have effectively resisted, accommodated, or even collaborated with various forms of capitalist development. We have also come to realize that far from being a monolithic conspiracy, the various public, corporate, and private interests pursuing economic change in the Latin American countryside are themselves divided, competing with each other.

I was able to identify a number of ways Kekchi people in Belize were exploited through unequal trade. They certainly paid very high prices for basic goods and received the worst health care and education of any Belizean population. On the other hand, the government marketing board bought their rice every year at prices considerably above the world market price, which amounted to a form of subsidy, though one that did not provide anything close to a living wage for farmers (cf. Moberg 1991). In the 1970s, a few foreigners had bought large chunks of land in southern Belize, but most were losing money trying to find a suitable export crop, and there seemed to be little threat to the Kekchi reservation lands. There was very little demand for farm labor at the time. Most Kekchi complained that there was not enough wage labor, and they wished there were more foreign businesses around. In short, there was not much evidence that Kekchi people were being coerced or forced into giving up their self-sufficient way of life.

So if there was no imbalance within the system, like population pressure, squeezing them out of subsistence farming, and if there were no powerful capitalist interests driving them off their land or forcing them into factory labor, why were so many fleeing the forest villages and heading out to the roadside to farm cash crops? If they had not been driven or forced out of their self-reliant way of life, had they perhaps been seduced, persuaded, or otherwise drawn away? Or were they simply looking for something better than the living provided by shifting cultivation?

In my own writing I defined a process I called the "crunch and ratchet" to explain the long-term changes taking place (1991:140). The crunch is a sudden drop in the price of a cash crop. The ratchet is the rise in accepted standards of living that occurs when incomes go up for a while. So when the next crunch comes, people are driven further into a cash economy in an attempt to maintain their new standard of living. But why and how do living standards rise, and why don't people simply let them fall again when their incomes fall? Neither Rappaport's nor Netting's cultural ecology answered this question, nor did the political economy of the early 1980s.

Return to Belize

While I had been running around villages asking people about their diet and farm labor, the missing pieces of my argument were right under my nose. Or should I say, in my face? Because most people did not want to talk about crops or kinship. The young people in particular thought I was a terrible bore. What they were really fascinated with were my watch, clothes, compass, pencils, typewriter, glasses, and kerosene lantern. People never tired of talking about tools, gadgets, and consumer goods of all kinds. They loved following British soldiers around for just this reason—it was a chance to see all kinds of new objects and tools. They even went through the garbage left behind by soldiers on patrol. Hundreds of times a day people asked me where I had bought something and how much I had paid. On weekends groups from the village would pay a substantial sum to travel to town, where the favorite activity was window shopping and watching people from other places. On their return they would talk at great length about styles and fashions, prices, and the new goods they had seen.

In the village people experimented with consumer goods of various kinds, but there was also a good deal of fear associated with trying new things. As in many Mesoamerican cultures, community opinion has a powerfully restraining effect on behavior. People are afraid of arousing envy, often with good reason. The person who displays newer or finer things can be the object of gossip or even revenge. People thought to be enriching themselves at the expense of others were suspected of malign sorcery. In some communities people who had tried to build houses with tin roofs instead of thatch had their houses burned down (Wilk 1983). But fear of envy did not deter all kinds of experiments with new goods. One of the alluring things about the new Protestant sects that were spreading through Toledo district at this time was that belonging to one legitimized new forms of goods and recreations. Churches eager for converts distributed musical instruments, chainsaws, religious books, and radios, and they held frequent meetings, gatherings, and celebrations at which new foods were introduced (Schackt 1986).

During my original fieldwork, I talked to many Kekchi who had moved from forest villages to the roadside, an area many described as being bright. They recognized the disadvantages of living there: more competition for land, less cooperation between neighbors, more crime and physical danger. But they were still drawn, not just by the physical conveniences like better transportation, schools, churches, health care, and lower prices, but by the sense that this was a place where there were opportunities and possibilities. The roadside beckoned strongest to young people, to religious converts who no longer felt welcome in Catholic villages, and to people who had been losers in political struggles for land or power in other parts of the district.

A surprising number of families moved in the opposite direction, or spent some time by the road and then went back to the bush. Life in the villages away from the roads was peaceful and more secure. Anyone who was willing to work hard could feed his or her family. People might go to town once or twice a year, but generally they avoided the prying eyes of government officials, depended on each other, and paid the price in poor access to health care, education, and other services and in very limited access to the market. In remote villages people often complained about life by the roadside, where "you need money for everything." Contesting the value of the cash economy, a common saying went roughly, "Here we may not have money, but we are rich in food, and our children are our wealth."

I finished my dissertation uncertain if the economic changes I had been seeing were going to continue, or if it was just another cycle of market expansion that would be followed by a bust and a return to subsistence farming. But while I was finding a job in the early 1980s new forms of expansion began. Farmers in several Kekchi villages made unprecedented wealth growing marijuana, before the government crackdown and aerial herbicide spraying in 1984 and 1985 squashed that trade. Cacao prices rose dramatically in the mid-1980s, triggering another boom, followed by some excellent years for citrus production. Jobs opened up in bananas, citrus, urban construction, and shrimp farming, and many young Kekchi men and a few women found their way into these industries by the end of the 1980s. As some of these industries declined in the 1990s, tourism began to grow in the district, and various kinds of small lodges and associated craft and guide services emerged. Yet despite the commercial growth, the agricultural base of the district has been stagnant, and production of rice, corn, beans, and hogs has not increased substantially.

On each visit I see more shops, new kinds of consumer goods, an almost incredible rush of new ideas and practices. Housing has evolved from thatch houses to cottages made from boards with galvanized roofing, and then to concrete block. Bicycles, motorbikes, and pickup trucks, boom boxes and TV sets, frozen chicken and boxed pasta are ubiquitous. Village shops grow into markets and supermarkets; all mirror a general flowering of consumer culture in Belize, transforming the whole country. Toledo is still poor and rustic compared to the more northern parts of the country (where I have done my fieldwork since 1986), but it has a far more elaborate consumer culture today than it did in 1978.

How do Kekchi people interpret the changes in the local economy? The people I spoke to in 1990 saw most of it in intergenerational terms. Under the mixed subsistence–cash economy of the 1970s and 1980s, the ideal of wealth was to marry and raise a large family, so that as a couple got older they could look forward to having several grown sons and daughters helping with farm and household. The wealthy and powerful households in each village had married sons and daughters living close by, sharing labor and produce and enjoying the benefits of many economies of scale. But when all kinds of economic opportunities opened up for young men, especially those who could speak some English (unlike the older generation), it became harder to keep them tied to their parents' households. They wanted to grow cash crops and find wage work, and they wanted to spend more of their cash on clothes and other consumer goods, instead of spending their time and money on village festivals or serving in the cargos (offices) of village government.

As one scandalized man told me in 1990, "It's the young men. Some of them don't even want to farm anymore!" At the same time, few opportunities were available for young women, who were discouraged from education or any sort of work outside of the domestic. As young men acquired experience with the world and independent sources of wealth, they tended to delay marriage. This in turn changed the balance in Kekchi marriages in subtle ways, often to the disadvantage of the female partner.

In 1999, I met a young Kekchi man at a tourist resort in northern Belize. Along with two of his brothers he had migrated from Toledo, learned scuba diving, spearfishing, and boat handling, and had a steady job as a tour guide. He said he did go home now and then to help his father back on the farm, and sometimes he did miss Kekchi food and his friends, but there was no money or future in farming, only a lot of hard and dangerous work. I doubt if he will ever go back to live in Toledo.

One way to think about the fate of the Kekchi is to put them in a broader context. In many respects they are simply becoming more integrated into a national economy that is increasingly open to foreign capital, business, and consumer goods. My work on the history of Belize's consumer culture shows a dramatic growth in the consumption of all kinds of consumer goods, beginning after World War Two and then increasing more rapidly starting in 1975. The dollar value of imported foods, for example, went from US$51 per person in 1970 to US$131 in 1975, then to US$166 in 1980 and US$371 in 1988. By 1990, almost half of the average household's annual income was spent on a bewildering variety of imported goods, a lifestyle that was supported by an overvalued currency and the massive inflow of remittances from émigrés to the United States.

In a sense, then, the growth of a consumer culture among the Kekchi is part of much larger trends toward economic and cultural globalization during the late twentieth century. They are a microcosm of the kinds of changes that have swept through the rest of Belize and indeed many parts of the developing world (see Jackson 2002; Miller 1990). As I will explain below, the growing participation of people like the Kekchi in global consumer culture and the continuing growth in standards of living in wealthy countries are two of the fundamental environmental and ecological issues we face today. Ecological anthropologies must therefore find the tools to understand more than the direct management or use of resources in circumscribed areas. First, they must show how distant consumers, through specific market connections, put pressure on those resources (as Mintz has already done in his work on the sugar trade [1985]). The Atlantic cod, for example, would never have been wiped out if there had not been consumers all over the world who considered it a choice dish. But, second, ecological anthropologies must anticipate the ways in which the people who exploit natural resources on a daily basis are going to intensify and change their demands on nature as their standards of consumption change through time. It is no use modeling the sustainable yield from a forest, for example, holding annual income or consumption constant, if people are going to increase their demands on that resource. Increasing consumption is the wild card in any ecological analysis. But very few ecological anthropologists take this key variable into account. Why?

Better Explanations?

Some ecological anthropologists, faced with changes in people's needs and standards of living, tried to salvage functional explanations. For example, when

Gross et al. (1979) found Amazonian indigenes buying jewelry, watches, and guns as well as cooking pots and steel tools, they suggested that people wanted these items because they were an effective way to store value in a tropical environment. In other words, buying these items was a way to convert perishable goods into permanent ones, which could make some sense. Many people justify buying jewelry on the grounds that it can always be sold in the future. But the functional explanation is hardly the full reason they want jewelry (one suspects there are other reasons to want guns too). This form of functional explanation is closely related to generations of economic anthropology that have explained the cattle complex, feather and stone money, *kula* exchange, and potlatches as rational competition for status or as a latent means of leveling out surplus (or sometimes, confusingly, as both at the same time). Functional explanations of this type never consider alternative allocations of resources that might make a good deal more sense. The goal seems to be to find material reasons why people might devote such great time and energy to acquiring objects that make little overt contribution to their survival or the provision of their basic needs.

There are, of course, often very good economic reasons to buy something in the marketplace instead of producing it yourself. As generations of anthropologists have noted, items like steel tools and cook pots are functionally superior in many respects to their homemade equivalents, and most people find it worth a lot of effort to obtain them. Heyman (1997) points out that when people can put a cash value on their own labor time, they start to find that it makes economic sense to buy many things that take a lot of time to make. As the value of labor goes up, the range of purchases also goes up.

But people also resist some aspects of commoditization and refuse to buy market equivalents. They prefer homemade, hand-ground corn tortillas, even when rice is cheaper, or they prefer homespun textiles to those they could buy in the store (Wilk 1991:160). And, of course, a large amount of human consumption has little to do with utility at all. Economic logic tells us little about why some Kekchi spend all their money on liquor and others sell eggs from the family's chickens to get money for Coca-Cola, while their children clearly need protein more than sugar. I saw men sell their pigs to get money for a boom box or a carton of cigarettes, when they could have been sending their kids to school or building a latrine or improving their corn storage or planting some cocoa. At the same time, coming from a society in which people spend huge amounts of money on totally useless items and unimaginable luxury, I asked what gave me the moral authority to judge the rationality of *any* kind of consumer choice? Could I really say it was wrong to want to wear better clothes or drink a cold beer and listen to music rather than invest the money for an uncertain future?[3]

Rather than try to answer these questions directly, anthropologists since Malinowski have tried to explain how and why noncapitalist cultures *do not* suffer from the seemingly endless, insatiable desires for more goods they attributed to the West. Much of classical economic anthropology can be read as accounts of the means that different cultures have developed to limit needs, to channel or restrict competition within accepted boundaries. Godelier's work on Baruya economy (1986), for example, argues that rules and ritual sanctions enforce a nonequivalence of different kinds of goods and power, keeping any competition within a narrow field. A "great gardener" cannot exchange his surplus for trade goods or use it to develop a political following. Restricted spheres of exchange like the *kula*, in which various kinds of feather, shell, bead, and stone money circulate, keep people from converting one kind of valuable into others and therefore restrict the kinds of accumulation that are possible. Economic anthropology also offers insights into the operation of envy, fear of envy, and witchcraft in restraining consumption through means often lumped under terms like "image of limited good" or "leveling mechanisms" (Dow 1981).

Traditional anthropology, then, uses a theory of constraint: once the cultural barriers to unlimited desire break down or disappear under the impact of the West, the floodgates are open, and everyone becomes a modern consumer with no limits on their needs and desires. But as anthropology belatedly began to study consumption in a more systematic way in the 1980s, this idea began to fall apart. Culture does not disappear as people enter a cash and commodity economy; instead, new forms of *consumer culture* appear. In a wealth of new studies (see Miller 1995a, 1995b), anthropologists have shown how new patterns of consumption can help preserve existing cultural institutions, cause radical change and abandonment of cultural practices, or forge new "creolized," hybrid, or complex mixtures that are simultaneously new and old, local and global. At the same time, research in developed countries has challenged the idea that culture is no longer important to *modern* consumers. We now recognize that instead of being out of control, consumption is still everywhere highly cultural and specific to particular times and places (Holbrook 1991; McCracken 1988).

Confronted with the rich, meaningful quality of consumer goods, many anthropologists have dropped the tools of social, ecological, or economic analysis and have embraced cultural studies and tools borrowed from semiotics, critical theory, and the politics of knowledge. Much of their work struggles to acknowledge the power of the media, advertising, and multinational corporations to shape consumption at the same time that they recognize the ways people use consumer goods to build a unique identity and to forge collective bonds of family, ethnicity, and nationality. Carrier and Heyman, in a recent survey, find most of this work to be "synchronic and psycho-cultural," and largely neglectful of political economy (1997:355). But this may be partially due to the failings of political economists to take the cultural and meaningful aspects of consumption more seriously.

This is not the place to survey a large and growing literature on consumption. Elsewhere, in work which focuses on the importance of gender, authority, and household organization (1989), I have analyzed Kekchi choices about how to spend money, and I have written a number of pieces about the influence of television and of other factors on consumption in Belize (e.g., 1993, 1994). In these papers I try to find effective ways to connect the globalizing aspects of the modern world economic system to the very local level where real people make choices on a daily basis and within very particular circumstances.[4] I would argue that finding these connections between the local and the global, and especially between political economy, culture, and local systems of production, is an absolutely essential task, not just for the future of our discipline, but also because consumption is now one of the central issues in global environmental change. Building a global cultural ecology may require expeditions into territories of analysis that have been colonized largely by cultural studies and political science, on issues of transnationalism and nationalism, identity, and new cultural and political phenomena that are of fundamental importance to the way environmental issues are perceived, formulated, constructed, and institutionalized (see Mittelman 1997; Wilson and Dissanayake 1996; Root 1996).

The Global Difference

Consumption has been a key issue, both in the foreground and background, at every major world conference on environmental issues from 1972 in Stockholm through 1997 at Kyoto. All parties at the table begin with a recognition that the affluence of the North has been based largely on the consumption of huge quantities of nonrenewable resources and the consequent emission of equally vast quantities of waste. Questions of "carbon guilt" and the equity of various kinds of solution are debated largely within a framework that recognizes a linkage between wealth, high rates of consumption, and ecological impact; the arguments revolve around how these variables are related to each other and who is going to pay the price of change. Inequity is the stumbling block in every aspect of global environmental discussion as well as in the debate about sustainability (Timmerman 1996:228). From the economists' and Western perspective, consumption is a reflection of prosperity and productivity, while for developing countries high consumption represents profligacy, luxury, and the destruction of valuable common resources. Recognition of the close relationship between consumption and sustainability of global climate is attested in Agenda 21, in which chapter 4 addresses consumption patterns, coining the term "sustainable consumption."[5]

The global inequalities in levels of resource consumption are striking. Kennedy (1993) estimates that an average American baby at birth represents 280 times the environmental damage of a Haitian or Chadian baby. Estimates of daily per capita consumption of materials and energy in developed countries suggest levels 30 to 50 times those in low-income countries, and the resulting emissions of greenhouse gases are equally disparate. North American carbon dioxide emissions are 5 tons per capita, compared to .19 ton per capita in Southeast and South Asia (OECD 1997a; Redclift 1996). Yet, while consumption is increasingly being identified as a key component of global environmental problems, there is very little consensus on the forces that impel and maintain high levels of consumption, on what kinds of policy making can be effective in restricting the impact of consumption, or on finding ways to persuade or force people to limit their consumption (OECD 1997b; NRC 1997).

At the global level overconsumption is tendentious, but it remains abstract and hard to distinguish from concepts like affluence or standard of living. Do wealth and high consumption always go together? (The best answer seems to be, not necessarily.) Do increased levels of consumption make people happier? (Scitovsky [1992] says it makes them *less* happy.) Are human needs and wants infinite, or are their limits? (Nobody seems to know.)

The continual growth of humanity's culturally defined needs is one of the most conspicuous trends of the past five thousand years. While scholars and priests may doubt if all the abundance has really made people any happier or better off, all over the world people have enthusiastically pursued a path of material abundance. In many places, while anthropologists are out praising the wisdom and sustainability of local agroecosystems, the children of farmers are heading off to the city to get some consumer culture. I once worked on a USAID project in Belize that sent hundreds of bright rural kids off to agricultural schools to learn to be better farmers; almost all of them now work in an air-conditioned urban office, many in the United States.

Conclusions

There are, of course, many places in the world where rural people face declining standards of living, ruined environments, and increasing levels of exploitation, conflict, and misery. In the same societies, however, new middle classes pursue the "good life," building new towns and suburbs filled with appliances and other new products. The consumers and the destitute are indeed part of the same phenomenon, tied together in a single system, with equally important impacts on the natural environment. And even among the victims, we should recognize that rising levels of discontent as well as pressures on resources may be due as much to increased standards of living, greater expectations as well as population growth or absolute economic decline.

I am not in any way suggesting that the legitimate aspirations of rural people to improved water, medical care, and diet should be seen as somehow being to blame for ecological problems (though I have heard this in unguarded moments from government officials and development workers). But what aspirations are legitimate? A bicycle? A few beers every week? A car for every Chinese peasant? A gallon of beer a day? We have to recognize that the basic ethical and moral problems of people's economic goals are a part of political ecology. We cannot say we trust rural people to make their own choices and choose their own path, but then change our minds when their choice ends up being spending their money on cigarettes instead of on integrated pest management.

Notes

My research in Belize has been generously funded by the National Science Foundation, a Fulbright research fellowship, two grants-in-aid from the Wenner-Gren Foundation, and small research grants from The University of Arizona, New Mexico State University, and Indiana University. This research has been a continuing collaboration with Anne Pyburn. It has benefited from insights and comments from others far too numerous to mention here. This paper owes something to conversation with Thomas Princen, Melissa Johnson, Danny Miller, James Carrier, and especially Robert Netting, though none should be held responsible for the final result (unless they wish to claim it). A number of connections to literature and resources on consumer culture and global environmental problems can be found at http://www.indiana.edu/~wanthro/consum.htm.

1. In Guatemala the orthography "Q'eqchi'" is now preferred, while various different spellings are in use in Belize. My monograph on Kekchi agriculture and households is Wilk 1997a; there are also several papers addressing different aspects of Kekchi consumption, particularly houses (Wilk 1989).

2. The word *caxlan* literally translates as "chicken." Chickens are themselves nonnative to the Americas, but most Kekchi say the word refers to the similarity in skin color and texture between white people and chickens! The word is a common modifier of nouns, to denote something recently introduced (e.g., *caxlan puub*, literally "foreigner-blowgun" for a shotgun).

3. On the morality of consumption, see Horowitz (1988), Illich (1977), and Belk (1983). The way farmers spend their money should have an obvious effect on their farming success and the sustainability of their farming methods, though few anthropologists have studied this relationship. In Belize, the Mennonite colonies have been tremendously successful, partially because so much of their earnings is directly reinvested back into farming or food-processing and marketing enterprises.

4. On the excesses of globalism, see cautionary tales from Miller (1997), Wilk (1995), and Abu-Lughod (1997). The strongest proponents of global transformation may be Appadurai and Hannerz, though each tempers his statements with a strong appreciation for the continuity of local social relations and cultural boundaries. A fair middle ground state-of-the art can be found in a collection edited by Arizpe (1996) and another by King (1997). Morley and Robbins (1995) provide an excellent and moderate summary of developments in global media and communications.

5. Here is an example of the kinds of insights many derived from the Rio conference: "Paradoxically, the North is viewed as more conscious and respectful of environmental limits than is the South, when all available evidence shows that the environmental crisis has been precipitated almost exclusively by the North's wasteful and excessive consumption. Indeed, roughly 80 percent of the planet's resources, as well as its sinks, are being utilized by the 20 percent of the population living in Europe, North America, Oceania, and Japan. If the South disappeared tomorrow, the environmental crisis would be still with us, but not if the North disappeared" (Banuri 1993:51).

Properties of Nature, Properties of Culture: Ownership, Recognition, and the Politics of Nature in a Papua New Guinea Society

Joel Robbins

The study of ecology today attracts anthropologists working in an extraordinarily wide variety of theoretical traditions. As Biersack (1999c:11–12) has recently pointed out, the fact that this is so offers hope that within contemporary ecological anthropology the persistent gaps that separate symbolic and political approaches to social life, along with the broader idealist and materialist ones that underwrite them, might finally be closed. Indeed, much of the energy that marks contemporary ecological anthropology derives from the way it is founded on a movement in which approaches drawn from both symbolic and political anthropology have come to take up issues once considered by the older ecological anthropology that these two schools edged out of the disciplinary limelight in the late 1970s and the 1980s (cf. Brosius 1999c:278; Dove 1999:290). We can take, broadly speaking, symbolic approaches to be those concerned with the cultural construction of the environment and its meaning and political approaches to be those that ask who exercises power over, and whose interests are being served by, the ways human beings are relating to the environment in specific cases. Given these definitions, it is clear that there has recently been an efflorescence both of symbolic work detailing how the environment is understood in various cultures (e.g., Bird-David 1990, 1992, 1993; Descola 1994) and of political-economic research on how the environment and development figure in the construction of political relations within and between cultures (e.g., Ferguson 1990; Escobar 1995; Brosius 1999c). Having found in the environment an aspect of social life that registers as important in both theoretical traditions, symbolic and political anthropologists have at the very least found a terrain on which they can meet to consider what unites and divides them.

Yet the fact that representatives of both symbolic and political anthropology now converge in the opinion that nature and ecology are important areas of study provides no guarantee that these two approaches will be synthesized within this new domain any more fully than they have been within others.[1] I argue here that a focus on property might help effect such a synthesis. The first basis for this claim is the fact that in very many cases it is as property that nature is socialized (Hanna et al. 1996). That is to say, many aspects of nature enter social process only through the grid of a system of property rights. Notions of property thus mediate between nature and culture, and the study of such notions ought to figure importantly in analyses both of the symbolic conceptualization of these two domains and of the political negotiations that surround the relationship between them. The second basis for this claim follows from the fact that, as Hann (1998:34) has recently been at some pains to point out, property, bearing as it does on questions of distribution, is always a matter not only of "cultural sense" but also of "power relations"; it is always, that is to say, at once symbolic and political (cf. Carney 1996). Participating centrally in both realms, it is well placed to mediate between them.

In this chapter, I take advantage of the way property mediates both nature and culture at the level of ethnography, and symbolic and political approaches at the level of theory, to construct an ethnographically grounded critique of the separation between symbolic and political analyses within the new ecological anthropology. The ethnography I use here draws on understandings of property and ownership, nature and culture, and politics among the Urapmin of Papua New Guinea. Through an analysis that begins in terms familiar from symbolic ecology, I demonstrate both that property mediates between nature and culture and that the symbolic ecology of the Urapmin has always taken up essentially political themes. At the heart of this argument is a plea for a shift from looking at property through our established categories to looking at it through the multidimensional lens provided by Hegel's discussion of it in his *Philosophy of Right* (1942). In that work and others, Hegel argues contra Hobbes that politics is a matter of the pursuit of mutual recognition, not of the struggle for self-aggrandizement or self-protection. For Hegel, property functions in this scheme not only as material goods to be possessed, but also as symbolic ones to be given away in order to create communities of recognition. If we look at property in Hegelian terms, I argue, we can begin to examine in ethnographically sensitive terms places where politics centers on attempts not to possess property as something material but rather to exchange it as something meaningful. This is the sort of politics through which the Urapmin approach nature, and this essay seeks to demonstrate that an understanding of that politics requires an analysis that attends at once to the symbolic and the political aspects of Urapmin life.

The Owned World of the Urapmin

The Urapmin are a group of approximately 350 swidden horticulturists living in the West Sepik Province of Papua New Guinea. A striking aspect of Urapmin culture is the extent to which its members live in what we might call an owned world. As the Urapmin frequently say, from their point of view "everything [in the world] has an owner."[2] In putting the matter in these bald terms, the Urapmin do not exaggerate either the extent to which ownership pervades the world around them or the important ramifications that such widespread ownership has on the way they lead their lives.

The landscape the Urapmin inhabit is an extensively owned one in a double sense. First of all, almost all of the striking features of that landscape—the streams (*ok*), caves (*tomb tem*), and large trees (*at dawomb*) and rocks (*tomb dawomb*)—belong to the nature spirits (*motobil*).[3] These spirits also own many of the mundane features of the landscape, including some large and important stretches of ground (*bokon*) and the marsupials (*nuk*) and wild pigs (*samin*) the Urapmin hunt. As the Urapmin make their way through this spirit-owned landscape, they have in the past had to be careful not to use the taboo (*awem*) ground that the spirits forbid them to use and to use respectfully (which usually means without undue noise or other disturbance) that ground that the spirits do let them use (Robbins 1995). When the Urapmin break these taboos or offend the spirits through a lack of respect, the spirits make them sick. Many illnesses are diagnosed as having been caused by offended spirits, and hence the Urapmin see themselves as being in constant negotiation with the spirits over the right to use the resources that belong to these spirits.

The second sense in which the Urapmin confront a world of ownership follows from the widely applied principle that individual human beings can own things. Only against the background of claims held by the spirits, claims that the Urapmin take to be prior to human ones, can the Urapmin fashion their own claims to hold resources over against one another. Yet in the human realm, too, everything has an owner. Urapmin reckon human ownership on the basis of a labor theory of property that is familiar throughout Papua New Guinea: whoever first works a piece of land or creates an object owns that land or object. While landownership receives the greatest public play in arguments and court cases, in a more quiet way the Urapmin are aware at all times of who owns every object they encounter. Although sharing is constant, no one ever imagines that things are held in common beyond the household. And even within the household, members recognize that everything, even a seemingly abandoned taro or sweet potato sitting at the edge of the fire, belongs to a particular person. Some household work groups, including the most successful one during the period of my research, go so far as to divide the gardens they make together into individually owned plots, such that a husband cannot harvest from his wife's side of the garden without her permission and vice versa. In general, it is fair to say that Urapmin never in the course of their lives encounter any object they cannot assume is owned by someone.

Given this developed concern with property, it is not surprising that the Urapmin see theft as an ever-present threat. An impressive corpus of traditional magic (*selap*) allowed people to protect their possessions against thieves and to force those who did have the temerity to steal things to confess and return them. Today the Urapmin affix padlocks to the doors of their houses, consult Christian spirit mediums (*spirit meri*) about the identity of those who have stolen from them, and regularly charge one another in conversation and in local courts with violations of property rights.[4] Like spiritual ownership, then, human ownership leads to struggles that very much mark everyday life in Urapmin. Both kinds of struggle serve to keep the image of the owned world in the forefront of Urapmin consciousness.

Nature, Culture, Property

The centrality of property in Urapmin life, and the sense in which its importance appears to the Urapmin as inevitable, follows from the fact that it is an institution that spans the realms of nature and culture. In order to demonstrate this point at present, a time when most major binary oppositions on the order of nature and culture are suspect, it is necessary first to argue for the value of using these terms in the Urapmin context. This section makes that argument while also showing how property spans both sides of the nature/culture opposition as the Urapmin conceive it.

In one of the first papers to employ what she would later call a "negative strategy" (Strathern 1990), Strathern (1980) argued that the nature/culture opposition as understood in the West is not present among the Hagen people of Highland Papua New Guinea. While some aspects of the nature/culture contrast seem to figure in a contrast Hageners do make between the wild and the domestic, important aspects of it do not. In particular, notions of the cultural control of nature, of a clear spatial separation of nature and culture, of natural law, and of a connection of nature with domesticity are not present in Hagen. Crucially for Strathern, since this piece, entitled "No Nature, No Culture," is among other things a critique of Ortner's (1974) "Is Female to Male as Nature Is to Culture?," these differences between the Hagen wild/domestic opposition and the Western nature/culture one ensure that the former opposition does not link up with gender ideas in Hagen in the same way the latter does with gender ideas in the West. Strathern's piece has been important not only to the anthropology of gender, however, but also to the anthropological study of nature; it has succeeded in raising the bar for those who want to claim that the people whom they study have an indigenous idea that might be glossed as nature (or, for that matter, as culture). Indeed, ten years after it was published, Valeri (1990:264–65) would claim that Strathern's argument against any easy use of the contrast represented "the present anthropological wisdom on the nature/culture opposition" (see also Escobar 1999a:8).

Strathern's article raises two kinds of issues for those who would continue to employ the notion of nature in cross-cultural research. The first of these is a theoretical one concerning the very possibility of such research. The second one is ethnographic and has to do with whether a focus on nature allows one to trace an interesting and complex set of linkages between elements of the culture one is discussing. The correct solution to the theoretical problem, I think, leads on to the ethnographic one, so I will begin with the theoretical issue here.

As Valeri (1990) has argued, Strathern in the end sets the bar too high in arguing that, unless another culture's ideas are congruent with Western ones in every respect, it makes no sense to speak of a nature/culture opposition among them. Instead of taking Western ideas as fundamental in this way, he argues that we should see nature and culture as terms in a metalanguage of our own creation, a metalanguage in which these terms "need not have any other meanings besides those we decide to give them on the basis of what we know about the cultural notions we want to compare" (Valeri 1990:265). The point here is to find an area of productive overlap between usages in two or more cultures and to build this overlap into the metalanguage. But when an anthropologist identifies an area of overlap in this way, he or she does not assume there are no differences between the cultural conceptions involved. In fact, if the overlap is complete, as Strathern seems to demand, the comparison is pointless, since in all respects the two cultures would not differ. What is required is enough overlap to make the comparison productive on both ends, but not so much overlap as to obviate the need for it.[5] Of course, finding such an area of overlap requires that one start with some ethnographic material, and thus it makes sense to turn to ethnography at this point.

Soper (1995:40–41) has argued that at the heart of the Western understanding of nature is "the idea of human distinctiveness." It is by tracing and defending the borders of human uniqueness that we come to define the natural. In some respects, the differences between humans and nature are differences of degree (such that in the West humans have some nature in them) while in others they are differences of kind (in the West, it is widely held that only humans use language). But in all cases our talk of nature makes sense only against the background of our ideas of human distinctiveness (Soper 1995:40–41).[6]

In Urapmin, too, notions of nature emerge quite clearly against the background of ideas about human distinctiveness, and this constitutes the area of overlap that allows us to use the nature/culture distinction productively in discussing Urapmin culture. The Urapmin make a distinction between human beings (*unangtanum*, literally "men and women") and the rest of what exists in the world. They make this distinction in both spatial and temporal terms. In their everyday speech, the Urapmin constantly distinguish between villages (*abiip*) and the bush (*sep*). Villages are spaces made and controlled by humans (Robbins n.d.). Like the neighboring Teleform described by Jorgensen (1998:102), Urapmin keep their village free of all grass and other plant matter that belongs in the bush. They also react with fear whenever animals of the bush appear in the village, for they assume the animals must be shape-shifting sorcerers. The spatial boundary between the human village and the forest is thus one they are eager to keep in place.[7]

Complementing this spatial distinction between the human and the non-human, the Urapmin also have a view of their history that serves to set humans apart in temporal terms from the rest of the living things that exist in the world. In Urapmin mythology, all beings that existed before the creation of human beings were spirits. Once humans were born, no further spirits came into the world. It is as if the birth of humans introduced a new principle into the world that put an end to the production of spirits. The break was not only total, it was also sharp: the first human being was born last in a multiple birth in which the first dog (*kyam*) was also born. Having been created as a species immediately before the creation of humans, all dogs are spirits. But dogs were also the last spirits to be born. With the birth of humans, the temporal divide had been crossed.

The way the Urapmin treat dogs indicates the extent of the difference that separates spirit beings from humans. Because all dogs are spirits, humans obey several stringent taboos in relation to them, just as they have in the recent past in relation to all of those spirits or spirit-owned things that constitute nature. Urapmin can neither kill dogs nor eat them (despite the fact that some of their neighbors do). They also have to keep dogs from breathing on their food. No such taboos apply to interaction with humans: in the past there was no Urapmin taboo on killing and eating other human beings, yet they were and still are able to share food with them. Taboos in relation to dogs and other spirits serve to regulate contact between things that are different by virtue of their temporal origins.[8] These practices of separation along the temporal boundary, like the methods of defending the spatial one discussed above, serve to emphasize the distinction between that which is human and everything else.

The Urapmin understanding of nature as the realm of the nonhuman is crucially bound up with the idea that nonhuman spirits are parts of nature. This is true in at least three respects. First, it follows from the spatial distinction between village and bush, for spirits are preeminently beings of the bush. Except in the rare cases in which a huge and ancient tree that harbors a spirit has been left standing on the outskirts of a village, spirits do not live near man-made settlements. Second, the placement of spirits on the side of nature follows from the temporal division that defines humans as distinct. Like other parts of the bush—trees, animals, stones, etc.—the spirits were all created before humans were born. Third and finally, the spirits are identified with nature because, as we have seen, they own it. As Urapmin tell it, humans, like many of the nature spirits as well as most animal species and food crops, were created by a culture heroine named Afek. It was she who gave birth both to the dog and other spirits and to the human being. But before she gave birth to humans, she gave the bush to the spirits as their home and their possession. She did this so she could clear the spirits out of the villages in which she wanted to put the human children she planned to create. This move of Afek's to establish the spirits in the bush and her human children in the villages set up the spatial register of the nature/culture opposition that is still in force in contemporary Urapmin.

The temporal aspect of Afek's creativity, that she settled the spirits in the bush even before the birth of human beings, figures importantly in Urapmin ideas about property and its relation to nature. Indeed, it is this matter of timing that ensures that property spans the realms of nature and culture. For in giving the things of nature to the spirits as their own, Afek either created or assumed the existence of the institution of property and of individual ownership (for individual spirits were given specific parts of nature). As part of the prehuman world of the spirits, the institution of ownership predates human culture and is thus a part of nature. Human claims on nature come only later and are for this reason weaker than spiritual ones. This is why the claims to ownership that humans make vis-à-vis other humans are no protection against the illnesses that spirit owners send; one can never claim that a spirit has less right than oneself to a particular resource because the spirit always got there first. But even as the natural origin of property renders human claims weak in comparison to those of the spirits, it also completely naturalizes the claims humans make vis-à-vis one another, and thus this prehuman origin of property accounts in large measure for why the language of ownership is so rhetorically powerful in Urapmin. Ownership saturates the world, its existence as an institution is beyond question; there is no state of nature from which it is absent and from the point of view of which it might appear to be artificial. In socializing nature as an original regime of property relations, then, the Urapmin have also naturalized their society as a similarly constituted regime.

With this idea that parts of nature (i.e., spirits) can own other parts of nature (land, animals, etc.), we leave the realm of productive overlap between Western and Urapmin views of nature and enter the one in which the differences between them make comparison valuable. The rest of this essay thus focuses not on exploring similarities between the two views but rather on looking at what makes Urapmin views distinct. Toward this end, I turn to a consideration of how the Urapmin understand property ownership as an institution and how this understanding shapes their political life.

Possession and Exchange

There is as yet no well-developed account of the nature of personal property in Melanesia. In fact, it would not be surprising if one came away from the

Melanesian literature convinced that the institution of personal property did not exist in the region. Worsley some time ago accurately glossed the general anthropological wisdom on this issue: socialist aspirations to create a system in which property is socially produced but privately appropriated do not at all square with Melanesian ones, he argued. In Melanesia, "to exaggerate somewhat, deliberately, one might say that the product is privately produced but socially appropriated. In a kinbound society . . . where most social relations are face-to-face, private property is subject to many more over-claims by kin and relatives than in our society" (Worsley 1968:246–47). While the reference to "private property" is intriguing, the emphasis here is on the way almost every object produced by a household or an individual has multiple claims on it and is as such ultimately destined for exchange. Socially appropriated in this way, objects begin to appear as if they are not personal property at all.

Making a similar point in the context of a philosophical analysis of Melanesian land tenure, Lea (1997) deploys a distinction between exclusive and inclusive rights to property. Exclusive rights, which form the basis of Western notions of property, are those that empower persons to exclude others from the use of their property. Inclusive rights, in contrast, empower persons to claim a share of property belonging to a communal group of which they are a part. For Lea, inclusive rights characterize Melanesian understandings of property. People see themselves as having inclusive rights to things that belong to their kin or affines. There is much less emphasis on personal rights to exclusive possession.

In these standard Melanesianist accounts, individual, exclusive ownership of the kind that is so important in Urapmin is relegated to the background. One might hope to find a more applicable model in the broader anthropological literature on property. Here, too, however, there is little that is of help. When one looks at how anthropologists have defined the content of property, one cannot help but be struck by the extent to which in this one case Western models of a key social phenomenon have slipped into our discourse seemingly without resistance. In large part this is due to the fact that Western legal models of property look very sociological, having long ago ceased to define property as a simple relationship between persons and things and reconstituted it as a social relationship, most famously as a bundle of rights people hold vis-à-vis others in regard to things.[9] While the anthropological adoption of this definition has been useful in some cases, it has tended to direct attention away from the person–thing relationship itself. The very fact of individual possession of the thing, figured in Urapmin in the sensual terms of having something in one's grasp, does not find relevance in the arguments that follow from these models. But if, as Biersack (1996c) has recently reminded us in a paper central to the argument developed here, Melanesians are "materialists" in complex ways, then this relationship probably should not be ignored.

Let me begin to unpack this statement about Melanesian materialism by laying out an alternative understanding of property, one based on Hegel's analysis of it. For Hegel (1942), property is made up of three elements: possession, use, and alienation. If we take alienation to be the element of property that allows for exchange and use to be that which allows for consumption, then clearly it is these two elements of property that have received the most attention, both implicit and explicit, in Melanesianist anthropology.[10] Use figures prominently in cultural ecological accounts (e.g., Rappaport 1984) and in discussions of the importance of consumption in Melanesian cultures (e.g., Munn 1986), while alienation is at least implicitly a feature of every account of exchange. The element of possession, however, the fact of holding something as one's own, has been largely ignored. Indeed, as the discussion of Worsley and Lea above would lead one to expect, the very idea of possession has recently come under attack by those who suggest it may not exist in Melanesia or may not be present in the cases of important kinds of property such as exchange of valuables (Sillitoe 1986; Battaglia 1994; Strathern 1998).[11] This sense that one never truly holds something as one's own, but instead always already owes it to others with whom one has exchange relations, fuels the argument that there is no such thing as individual property in Melanesia. But in the Hegelian system, at least, possession is logically fundamental to the existence of property (Schroeder 1998:38); it is the element on which the others rest. Perhaps, then, it is there in Melanesia if only we look for it under the welter of exchange practices that to this point have diverted our attention from it.

In Urapmin, possession is foregrounded in accounts of the way spirits own property. That the nature spirits possess property is the fundamental fact about them. The imagery surrounding them is all that of grasping possession. They hold (*kutalfugu*) their resources, and when their rights are violated they hold the violators. It is the grasp of the spirits that brings illness to humans. Spells said to heal these illnesses dwell on the spirits' prehensile arms and legs, demanding that the spirits unhand their victim. Contemporary Christian prayers to God ask him to bind these same clutching hands and feet so that they no longer can possess parts of the world by holding them. When prayers fail, the

Urapmin turn to sacrifices to entreat the spirits to take the smell (*tang*) of the sacrificial pig as their own possession and in return to give up possession of the victim. This may look like an exchange, but it has much more the character of what we (and the Urapmin) do when we give babies one thing to hold so that they will relinquish what they are already holding.[12] It is an attempt to create a moment of distraction from the spirit's ongoing effort of possession.

In general, spirits never alienate those parts of the landscape that they possess. At best, they sometimes disregard Urapmin use of their property provided certain conditions are met. In doing so, however, they do not relinquish the right to defend their ownership of that property in the future; this is why they have remained dangerous generation after generation.

The one case in which a nature spirit does alienate its property to human beings turns out to be the exception that proves the rule that spirits are interested in possession rather than in exchange. The *nuk wanang* are marsupial spirit women who are guardians of the marsupials that humans hunt and eat. Sometimes these women involve themselves with men who hunt frequently. As a marsupial woman begins to have sexual relations with such a man and eventually marries him, she also gives him dreams telling him where to find game. He then becomes a spectacularly successful hunter. At this point, this is a case of a spirit giving marsupials to a human being. But this moment of spiritual alienation does not lead to a happy ending. For in all cases the *nuk wanang* will eventually become jealous of a hunter's human wife, feeling that she is giving up too much in return for something less than complete possession of the hunter. In response, she will cause the hunter to have accidents, and eventually she will kill him. Here then is a case in which a spirit's drive for possession ultimately encompasses any efforts it might make toward alienation in the Hegelian sense.

Cultural notions of property do not, like the natural ones we have been reviewing, dwell on possession. They focus instead on alienation, on the ability of those who own property to give it away. It is in the form of the gift that human property becomes socially effective. The hands (*sigil*) that in the case of spirits only serve to hold things are in the human case open, and the Urapmin speak of a person's hands as a way of speaking metonymically of their generosity. The person devoted to possession or, even worse, to consumption is roundly condemned.[13] All of this is familiar in Melanesianist ethnography. In the context of the argument of this essay, it is important only that we remember that exchange is not a negation of the idea of property but is rather an aspect of the property relation (see also Carrier 1998:86; Dwyer and Minnegal 1999), albeit one that plays down possession and use.

Having established that nature reckons property from a point of view that foregrounds possession while culture reckons it from one that foregrounds alienation, we now have to ask what these differences amount to in Urapmin life. The argument of the next section is that these ideas of ownership profoundly shape the Urapmin conception of politics in general and of the politics of nature more specifically.

Property and the Politics of Recognition

For Hegel, the institution of property exists to allow human persons to constitute themselves as self-conscious subjects through the process of mutual regard that he calls recognition. As Haddock (1994:155–56) notes, Hegel's discussion of property in the *Philosophy of Right* should "be read in conjunction with his discussion of the emergence of self-consciousness in the *Phenomenology of Spirit*." As is well known, the struggle for recognition is a central part of that discussion. Laying out the development of self-consciousness in overly simplified terms and setting aside the rather fanciful origin tale that is the infamous master–slave story literally understood, we can say that for Hegel people take possession of objects in order to embody their wills and thus create themselves in objective terms. This process of self-creation reaches its highest point when the person is able to exchange the object he or she has taken possession of with another person, who through this exchange recognizes him or her as a full person capable of ownership and thus of entering into exchange. In this respect, possession initiates the process of self-creation, while alienation is "the most complete *actualization* of ownership" and of the selfhood it creates (Arthur 1985:52).

The result of this process of recognition in social terms is a community of people who recognize one another as persons capable of exercising their wills in socially meaningful ways. The institution of ownership—involving the possibility of possession, use, and alienation—is crucial to the construction of such communities. Benhabib (1984:172) puts it in the following terms: "For individuals who constitute a community of reciprocal recognition, the object of property serves as a medium in and through which such recognition is manifested and given presence." Through the possession and exchange of objects, people come to recognize themselves as social beings, as subjects with whatever rights and capacities their society imagines such social beings to have (Schroeder 1998:34; Honneth 1995:51; Biersack 1996c).

This argument accords well with Urapmin understandings of their own society. It is through the objects they own that people meaningfully impinge on one another and appear to each other as social persons. This is even more emphatically true in Urapmin than it would be in other societies in which exchange is fundamental, for the Urapmin do not trust language to convey intention or demonstrate individual will (Robbins 1996). Instead, the Urapmin rely on communication through the exchange of objects and hold this to be far more meaningful and revealing of a person's heart (*aget*, here in the sense of "mind") than communication conducted through verbal channels. To fully recognize a person in Urapmin is to give to that person and receive from that person. Personhood is, in Knauft's (n.d.) felicitous phrasing, "a transacted process."

This discussion of the formation of a community of recognition brings us to the matter of politics. Honneth (1995), in a discussion of Hegel's account of recognition, has argued that Hegel developed this theory in critical dialogue with Hobbes (see also Haddock 1994; Siep 1996). At issue was how to characterize human beings in the state of nature. For Hobbes, such beings are egocentrically concerned only with self-assertion and self-preservation, while for Hegel they are concerned with gaining recognition from others (Honneth 1995:43; cf. Benhabib 1984). This concern leads not to the formation of a social contract, but rather to a struggle for recognition that creates the bonds of mutuality that constitute society. In an argument that strikingly foreshadows Durkheim's (1984) demonstration of the noncontractual basis of contract, Hegel claims it is only after the social bonds of recognition have been created that contract is possible.

Given that Hegel was in dialogue with Hobbes, it is not difficult to arrive at the conclusion that recognition is for him about politics. In fact, the theory of recognition is another way of conceiving of politics, one in which mutual regard replaces personal material gain as the key value toward which political struggle orients itself. Our fundamental interests, in this scheme, are not those of simple material reward or autonomy understood in the asocial, Western individualist sense, but rather those of relatedness and human community (cf. Siep 1996:285; Biersack 1996c). Given that people realize these relational interests through the possession and exchange of property, at least in places like Urapmin, then property is also fundamentally political (Biersack 1996c).

In the terms of this argument, the foundation of Urapmin political life is built on practices of exchange and sharing through which the Urapmin accord mutual recognition to one another. When this mutual recognition breaks down, people work to organize reconciliation rituals that consist of simultaneous, equivalent exchanges that restore it (Robbins 1996). Although the various modalities of exchange are too complex to lay out here (see Robbins 1999), suffice it to say that Urapmin political life centers either on giving and receiving when things are going well or on arranging redressive exchanges when they are not. Because exchange defines the realm of the political in this way, in Urapmin one's property allows one to enter that realm. It is by virtue of their property that Urapmin people appear to one another not just as human beings, but also as political subjects (Arendt 1998). This is what Melanesian materialism amounts to, at least in the Urapmin case (cf. Biersack 1996c).

Given that the world of exchange in Melanesia is often understood as one dominated by men (e.g., Strathern 1972), it is important to examine the way women relate to the politics of recognition in Urapmin. The place of women in this community of recognition is at one level straightforward. This level is that of the everyday construction of social personhood through exchange. Urapmin women are involved in virtually all of the kinds of exchanges that men take part in. They give cooked food, string bags, and uncooked food crops that they own to a wide range of people, and in turn they receive these sorts of things from an equally wide range of people. While it is true that men tend to be more involved than women in ritual exchanges involving shell money, some women take part in these exchanges as well. Furthermore, there are no major pig exchanges in Urapmin that would serve to dramatize men's roles as exchangers over against women's as producers (ibid.). At a less quotidian level, however, there are hints in Urapmin culture that women can, in at least one crucial instance, bestow socially effective recognition without the mediation of property. This happens when a woman "calls the name" (*win bakamin*) of the man she wishes to marry. This is the one case in Urapmin in which speech alone can confer recognition in a way that is itself recognized by others rather than dismissed as "mere talk" (*weng katagup*). This peculiarity of the woman's voice hints at a model of essential, as opposed to relational, personhood that exists alongside the more prevalent recognition-based model. But seeing as the latter model dominates the everyday life of both men and women, this is the one I will focus on here.[14]

The question that follows from the close accord between the Hegelian account of the role of property in the political creation of a community of recognition and Urapmin ideas about the human realm is the one that asks what this way of looking at the world means for Urapmin relations with nature. Given that property ownership proves central to the politics of recognition, we can reexamine the symbolic ecology that constitutes the owned world of the Urapmin as a political ecology as well. The most important fact about nature in this regard, especially as it is figured through the spirits that own it, is that while it possesses things it does not give them.

In the Hegelian scheme, simply possessing and using an object is enough to begin to define the self, but it does not create a social world of recognition in which beings become subjects in the social sense. Nature in Urapmin is stuck at just this point where it has defined itself but has not put itself into relation with other subjects (that is, human beings). Nature limits itself to defining itself through possession and refuses to relinquish its property in order to form the relationships that would make it a subject that would be recognized as such by the Urapmin. For Hegel, this dependency on the object and unwillingness to give it up robs a subject of its own freedom. In Urapmin terms, this single-minded possessiveness on the part of the nature spirits leads people to treat those spirits as less than full subjects. That is to say, while they recognize that nature spirits have identities (their possession of things is enough to establish this), they do not feel compelled to deal with nature spirits in terms of the strict reciprocity that governs relations between human beings.

There is in Urapmin, then, what we might call a primordial political ecology that involves the relationship between human beings and the nature spirits. In general, the spirits, focused as they are on possession, seek recognition from the Urapmin but do not offer reciprocal recognition in return. That is to say, the spirits want to be recognized as owners but refuse to recognize the Urapmin in similar terms. This is why the Urapmin will not exchange with the spirits but will only attempt to distract them through sacrifice when necessary. A dialogue of fractured exchange—one whose elements are avoidance, sickness, and sacrifice—is all that this primordial politics is able to produce. Because this is so, the Urapmin attempt to use as much of the spirits' property as possible, in fact to build their own human system of property relations on top of the spirit's claims as if the latter did not exist, and they explicitly recognize spiritual claims only when they are forced by sickness to do so. Furthermore, as I have discussed in some detail elsewhere, since their conversion to Christianity in 1977, the Urapmin have hoped that God will vanquish these spirits and banish them to some place where they will never bother the Urapmin again, leaving the Urapmin free to use nature as they wish (Robbins 1995, n.d.). The Urapmin do not imagine that their community would be at all diminished were the spirits to be removed from it in this way. This is so because, through their failure to give, the nature spirits have effectively shunned the political arena as it is constituted in Urapmin. There is thus no reason to hope that relationships with them can be sustained in the future.

For people who reckon politics as a matter of struggles for recognition carried out through the mediation of the exchange of material things, the primary roads to political failure are those one takes by not giving or, even worse, by having nothing to give (possessing nothing of value). The spirits fail in the former way. Because they do not give and thus are not political actors, the Urapmin try not to recognize them. We have registered the effects of this failure in the previous paragraph. The second form of failure, that which comes from having nothing to give, is one the Urapmin find themselves in currently vis-à-vis the Western, in their terms white, world. The Urapmin would like to be recognized in the wider political arena that has encompassed their own over the past fifty years. But as Burridge (1960) pointed out some time ago, when confronted with whites, Melanesians find themselves with nothing to give that whites will receive. The dialectic of recognition is thus stalled—without taking from them, whites can never recognize Melanesians as people. And this situation remains in force no matter how much or how little the whites give to the Urapmin. For recognition to occur, it must be reciprocal. Without property capable of representing themselves to whites, the Urapmin do not appear as subjects in the political sphere of the white world.

Resource-rich environments are the one exception to the generalization that the Urapmin have nothing to give to whites. The white world is willing to receive land rich in mineral resources. Ballard (1997:48) understands something like this when he notes that in modern Papua New Guinea "landowner-ship confers 'voice'—the right to speak and the ability to influence the flow of benefits from the land and its resources." Having land to give, the Urapmin could successfully garner the recognition that would make them subjects in the world the whites have created. But what is missing from Ballard's formulation is the fact that land warrants recognition or confers voice only when one is prepared to give it away either through outright alienation or through a lease arrangement that will in effect lead in most cases to its destruction. The Urapmin know this, and thus have come to the point where they quite chillingly tell mineral prospectors they want to give their land to a mining company so that the company can destroy (*destroim*) it and move them to a specially built town somewhere else (Robbins n.d.).

The Urapmin feel they must give up their land because the parameters of the struggle for recognition have now changed, and they cannot enter this new struggle on the basis of the property they are able to seize from their land. Their land no longer allows them to appear as subjects in all of the arenas in which they want to do so, and as such its destruction figures not as a tragedy for them, but rather an opportunity. And since the spirits have never entered a community of recognition with the Urapmin, their claims provide no brake on this desire: the Urapmin simply attempt to distract them with larger than usual, and in some cases prophylactic, sacrifices so that they can wrest the land from them without becoming ill (Robbins 1995). Caught between spirits who have never recognized them in the past and a white world they dearly hope will recognize them in the future, the Urapmin have no doubts about how they want to expand their community of recognition in the present.

Conclusion

Although there is much talk these days about topics that would appear to be at the heart of political anthropology—topics like power, domination, and resistance—Spencer (1997) has recently argued that this subdiscipline is not a healthy one. Although Spencer does not claim so directly, I think it is in keeping with his argument to say that an important part of the problem with political anthropology stems from the fact that it never had its own equivalent of the formalist/substantivist debate that so profoundly shaped economic anthropology (cf. ibid.:5). Power, domination, resistance, and the rest look in contemporary ethnographic accounts suspiciously similar to Western notions of these things, and new, more nuanced models of these phenomena are not in great supply (Robbins 1994). Essentially, Western commonsense notions of the nature of power and of political struggle still dominate anthropological analyses of these phenomena around the world. The argument of this essay is that the model of politics we have exported is largely a Hobbesian one in which people who are looking only to increase private material gain or individual autonomy are willing to suffer a little bit of society but only in order to protect themselves from their fellows. I want to counterpose to this model a Hegelian one in which political struggles center on forming relationships rather than on limiting them; a model in which liberation might be more a matter of getting into the right kind of relationships than of getting out of the wrong kind of relationships. The Hegelian model at least has the virtue of letting us get closer to understanding the way people like the Urapmin conceive their political life, and recent discussions of the way the politics of recognition has come to rival the politics of redistribution in the West suggest that it may have value even in some unexpected locales (Fraser 1997; see also Honneth 1995; Taylor 1994).

In this essay, the crucial role recognition plays in Urapmin political ecology became evident only when attention was paid to the way Urapmin symbolically construct nature. One must understand how the Urapmin differentiate nature from culture and how they think about spirits and their clutching, possessive ways before one can adequately assess what the politics of nature amounts to in their community. At the same time, however, one cannot lay out Urapmin symbolic ecology as nothing more than a set of inert conceptions with no connection to the strenuous politics of recognition it helps shape. For these reasons I argue that we must continue our efforts to bring symbolic and political approaches together within contemporary ecological anthropology.

This essay has argued that the study of property is an especially promising area in which to try to effect a synthesis of these two approaches. In closing, I want to point out that property is crucial to both the Hegelian and the Hobbesian models of politics discussed here, but differently so. In the former it is a means to a relational end; in the latter it is the end toward which relations are entered into. If we take the full measure of this difference, we can recognize the powerful point on which Jorgensen concludes a very careful article about landownership and resource development among some neighbors of the Urapmin. In that article, Jorgensen (1997) points out the futility, in contexts of impending resource development, of trying strictly to determine who owns what land. As he puts it elsewhere, in such contexts "discussions which at first sight appear to be about property must be understood to be at least as much about the broad political relationship between the state and its disgruntled citizens" (Jorgensen 1999:5–6). Given that this is so, the real task in areas of imminent development should not be the simple registration of land claims but rather the establishment of a political process in which people can work out an approach to the cascading changes resource development threatens to bring. This process may begin by considering claims to ownership, but it will not end with them. It will end with an expanded political community of mutual recognition in which future difficulties can be addressed. The Urapmin are still waiting for this expanded community of recognition to take shape. They want it so desperately they are willing to destroy their land to get it. But this should not be the only way it can come about. Rather than forcing people like the Urapmin to give up nature in order to participate in the modern political sphere, we must find ways to let that sphere form while there is still a politics of nature that can unfold within it.

Notes

I have presented this paper at the American Ethnological Society meetings and at the CREDO Centre in Marseilles. I thank those who offered comments on those occasions as well as those who have read drafts of the manuscript. In particular, I want to thank Chris Ballard, Sandra Bamford, Pascale Bonnemère, Roy D'Andrade, Don Gardner, Timothy Knickerbocker, Pierre Lemonnier, Jim Moore, Julie Polkrandt, Rupert Stasch, Karen Sykes, and Don Tuzin for their comments. I also presented a related paper, since published as Robbins 2003, at the University of Helsinki. I thank those who offered comments on that paper, particularly Jukka Siikala and Karen Armstrong. Finally, I thank Aletta Biersack for several very close and constructive readings of this paper that very much improved it and for letting me work with her unpublished paper "The Human Condition and Its Transformations," which provided an early impetus for me to pull together the ideas that appear here.

1. Brosius's recent review, "Anthropological Engagements with Environmentalism" (1999c), provides one example of the difficulty of effecting this synthesis. This is an exemplary discussion of the range of politically focused work that anthropologists have done in relation to the environment from which symbolic studies are completely left out. Escobar (1999a:291) and Hornborg (1999:294) point this out in their commentaries on the article, and Brosius (1999c:300) acknowledges their point in his response.

2. The term the Urapmin use to mean owner here is "father" (*alap*). Father is used here more in the sense of caretaker than of progenitor (Robbins 1995; also see Strathern 1998 on procreative metaphors of property).

3. As will become clear in a later section of this chapter, *motobil* are spirits that have never been human. The spirits of humans who have died (*sakbal*) are not important in the Urapmin scheme of ownership. In this essay, I use the term *spirit* only to refer to *motobil*.

4. This term is in Tok Pisin, the main lingua franca of Papua New Guinea. With few exceptions, most foreign terms in this chapter are in the Urap language.

5. Strathern's approach to comparison has developed in important ways since her "No Nature, No Culture" discussion was published (e.g., 1988, 1998). That discussion

has been so influential, however, that it needs to be dealt with in its own terms when the topic of comparison is the nature/culture distinction.

6. Even radical environmentalists who argue that we should see human beings only as parts of nature assume that humans are unique, according to Soper (1995:40ff.), for their arguments depend upon the idea that only humans can become conscious of their embeddedness in nature and change their behavior accordingly.

7. Strathern (1980:193) points out that the Hagen people do not live in villages but in scattered "homesteads and settlement clusters." This perhaps in part accounts for why the wild/domestic distinction in Hagen does not ramify into something like the kind of nature/culture distinction discussed here.

8. Interestingly, the taboo on eating dogs is one of the few that is still strongly observed in Urapmin. In terms of the argument developed here, the taboo on dogs would be particularly important because as the final spirit created before the birth of humans, and hence as their "older brother" (as the Urapmin say), the dog stands as that part of the nonhuman which is closest to humans and thus as the being in regard to which the difference must be defended most strenuously. As domestic animals, they also challenge the nature/culture distinction in its spatial coding. Here again, as the closest representative of the nonhuman, it is crucial to enforce some spatial boundaries with dogs (as is done by keeping them away from human food). (See Valeri 1990 for a general discussion of taboo in terms similar to that adopted here.)

9. Hunt (1998) details how Hallowell brought this conception into anthropology, having borrowed it from the legal theorist Hohfeld. Schroeder (1998) provides a partial historical account from the legal side.

10. I use the term *alienation* here in the sense of disposal, not in the Marxist sense in which it has been debated in Melanesianist anthropology (see Thomas 1991 for a discussion of this debate). In this Hegelian sense, it can be used to refer to what anthropologists call prestation as well as to other kinds of disposal.

11. Weiner (1992) offers the best known defense of the importance of possession in Melanesia. In the context of the present argument, however, her approach in its complementary one-sidedness reproduces the problems of the approaches I have been considering: it does not allow us to give alienation its due as a crucial part of Melanesian systems. Furthermore, her interest is primarily in valuables owned by social groups, not by individual people. Her model is of little help when it comes to analyzing the broad spectrum of individual ownership seen in Urapmin.

12. The claim that these sacrifices are not first and foremost exchanges is supported by several kinds of evidence. Exchanges in Urapmin generally involve both parties giving material objects to one another; they are not payments so that one party will desist from something they are doing. As I will discuss below, Urapmin use exchange of exactly equivalent objects to settle disputes among themselves. It seems important in this context that no one ever confuses these exchanges with pig sacrifices, although both serve

to redress wrongs. Furthermore, the term that designates human dispute resolution exchanges (*tisol dalamin*) and that which designates sacrifice to the spirits (*kang anfukeling*) are unrelated, and the term that designates sacrifice is not used to refer to exchanges of any sort.

13. I have not focused on consumption here. In Urapmin, those pathetic characters who eat alone (*feg inin*) provide the primary image of those who treat enjoyment as the primary element of property (see also Munn 1986).

14. There are several ways one might go in expanding on this peculiarity of woman's voice in the calling of a marriage partner. One could examine it as an example of the common Melanesian perception of women as "sufficient" and men as "contingent" (Wagner 1977:628). The creativity of Afek would figure importantly in such an analysis. One could also relate it to the importance of the mother in supplying the infant with their first experiences of recognition. This would accord with the psychoanalytic reading of Hegel's theory of recognition that has been very suggestively applied to a Melanesian case in a paper by Barlow (2001). A more general discussion of how women and men engage in the politics of recognition could also lead to a consideration of how this politics unfolds within households. Schroeder (1999) provides a stimulating analysis of related issues in a West African context that is particularly germane to my concerns by virtue of its focus on how people's productive engagement with nature is central to household politics.

Ethnographies of Nature

Progress of the Victims:
Political Ecology in the Peruvian Amazon

Søren Hvalkof

Introduction

Through the 1970s, a renewed interest in ecological anthropology was evident, especially in the United States, paralleled by the development of new Marxist theorizing, mainly in European academia. This reflected an increasing questioning by intellectuals of the grand developmentalist narratives and a growing criticism of hegemonic political systems on a global scale. Advocacy became a new and resourceful political phenomenon altering students' interest and academic priorities. Among the new political issues was the environmentalist's concern for the rain forest and the indigenist's concern for autochthonous populations. An obvious space where both interests could be cultivated and even combined was the Amazon region, and a number of studies addressed a broad spectrum of approaches and issues within this ecoethnological framework. The theoretical instruments at hand, however, were still dominated by more or less neofunctionalist interpretations, and the refreshing attempts in ecological anthropology to adopt a systems theory approach were still marked by circular logics and tautological arguments. Although the systems were open, the minds were still not, and most of these studies lacked a broader integrated historical and political contextualization.

This was to a certain degree compensated for by more politicized, advocacy-oriented studies aimed at documenting the then-current situation of specific indigenous groups. New support groups and organizations were founded, documenting atrocities and abuses committed by the expanding national state societies against indigenous peoples and calling for international action.

The general situational image of indigenous third world populations conveyed in this period was that of relatively isolated tribal groups victimized by
the cruel and genocidal expansion of Western civilization threatening their
very existence. A number of books and articles addressing this urgent issue
were published, with titles like *Victims of the Miracle* (Davis 1977) and *Victims
of Progress* (Bodley 1975) epitomizing the message. These two works are not
singled out to argue that their presentations were unreflective. Rather they
were among the most important contributions at the time. Indigenous groups
were indeed being deliberately exterminated, thrown off their lands and territories, decimated through epidemics, enslaved, and even hunted down for
sport, all of it sanctioned by uncomprehending and unsympathetic national
societies. But the general portrayal of indigenous groups as having precarious
existences, objectified in the historical process as mere victims with no influence on their own situation, reinscribed them into the dominant modernist
discourse as essentialized cultural isolates, prone to measures of protection by
the liberal state, leaving little options for their political agency. Such an objectified image of native Amazonians was simultaneously reinforced by the so-
called rain forest movement's global campaign, which drew parallels between
the indigenous situation and that of endangered species. (See Brosius 1999c
for an excellent review of the development of environmentalist agency and its
relations with anthropology.) Up through the 1970s and 1980s advocacy of indigenous self-determination was left with inadequate theoretical and analytic
instruments to cope with the ever-changing situation and in many ways found
itself in a catch-22. The more it essentialized stereotyped images of the noble
and environmentally correct savage, the more it undermined its aim, which was
to realize the political agency of indigenous peoples. The systems-ecological
approach in anthropology, which had often focused on the same ethnic groups
as the activists, was unable to deal with the complexities of state society and increasing global integration and politicization. Instead, in conformity with the
governing paradigms, the approach reproduced the illusion of relatively static
systems seeking social and ecological equilibrium. Marxists, on the other hand,
generally regarded the issue of indigenous peoples as politically irrelevant and
odd, and insofar as they recognized the existence of such social groups at all,
Marxists viewed them as merely a residual category of historical relics doomed
to rapid extinction in the self-driven machinery of evolutionary schemata.

As we know, however, the indigenous peoples did not vanish or assimilate as anticipated—on the contrary, many of them created their own politi-

cal spaces for agency in the reconfiguring modern states, gradually taking the form up through the 1980s and 1990s of a social movement of ethnopolitical orientation, a process which was particularly conspicuous in Latin America. Accelerating globalization had created a number of new political constellations and dynamics, compelling indigenous groups to redefine their political and social identity, altering their consciousness of what indigenousness means in the remodeled architecture of national and transnational dependency and domination (e.g., Turner 1993, 2003). As usual, theory was overtaken by historical reality, while we as academics attempted to keep up, trying to tidy up after the runaway elephant. After a period dominated by deconstructionist positions, diffuse theorizing, and disciplinary depoliticization in the 1980s, a myriad of inventive contributions has seen the light of day during the past decade, attempting to combine the global perspective with local dynamics, merge ecology with economics and relations of power, opening the systems and repoliticizing the endeavor. Political ecology is but one expression of this creation of new discursive regimes and although "political ecology has no settled paradigms" (Biersack 1999c:11), it could tentatively be defined as "the study of manifold constructions of nature in contexts of power" (Hvalkof and Escobar 1998:426; emphasis removed) aiming at understanding and participating "in the ensemble of forces linking social change, environment, and development" (Escobar 1999a:15).

Within such a general framework of political ecology, an "ecology of practice" has recently been proposed by Nyerges and Green (2000:273–74) as an explicitly sociocentric focus "on local social relationships and regional sociocultural patterns as basic determinants of resource management practices, and, consequently, the processes of ecological change occurring both now and in the past."

The present case study is an attempt to present such an analysis and demonstrate how a specific indigenous group in the rain forest of the Peruvian montaña, the Ashéninka of Gran Pajonal, underwent a metamorphosis. From being seen in a national perspective as objectified, extrasocial labor subjected to grand cattle ranching schemes and colonist exploitation, the Ashéninka themselves became active political agents of social change and democratization, an unexpected and hitherto unseen transformation in the long, depressing history of Amazonian colonization. The catalyst for this process of radical change in the relations of power was an indigenous land titling project resulting in the reappropriation by the Ashéninka of large portions of their former territory. The

case and the analysis basically follow the historical trajectory of indigenous–
colonist relations, identifying the specific historical circumstances and changing political constellations on the local and national level that conditioned and
enabled the alterations in power relations and the production of new social
identities. A special emphasis is put on the interethnic relationship between
the local population of settlers and the Amerindians, the pivotal point of the
social dynamic of the zone, and how their respective positioning in the social hierarchy is related to their respective exploitation of their shared natural
resources. Finally, the chapter explores how the cultural values and goals conditioning their different ways of resource use and their respective ideologies
and cosmologies (a distinction that will be discussed in the concluding section) shape their shared and contested landscape, conditioning both their productive and economic possibilities, the ecology of the area, and their political
options.

To support the analysis and help readers visualize these ecological, spatial,
and social processes in a broader synoptic context (ibid.), a series of six comparative thematic maps produced through GIS and remote sensing are presented to demonstrate changes in the vegetation cover over a fifty-year sequence. The analytic maps are based on digitized detailed aerial photos taken
from 1953 through 1984 and new SPOT satellite images from August 1996.
These data were corroborated through fieldwork and GPS readings in situ by
the author while at the Office of Geographical Information Analysis, the University of Massachusetts at Amherst, and working with Mark Goodwin and
John McGee, my research assistants. The resulting maps (color plates 2–7)
compare indigenous land use patterns with the use patterns of the colonists,
demonstrating the incompatibility of the two production systems and their almost antagonistic effects on the same environment. The data are summarized
in tables 1 to 3.

The case study also shows how the Ashéninka radically empowered themselves by exploiting the changing nature of the national state. Hitherto the state
had been represented by local hierarchies headed by colonists, but in the increasingly globalized contexts these lost their legitimacy and maneuverability
and basically transmuted from local agents of modern progress into anachronistic social relics. As they were unable to alter the developmentalist ideology
on which their social identity depended, the modernist paradigm increasingly
proved obsolete. Contrary to this stood the former victims of modernization,
the Ashéninka, now prepared to buy into the new postmodern, neoliberal, and

globalized discourse of which they appropriated exactly the parts they found suitable, without petty-minded concerns with ideological positions, and pragmatically reproduced their cosmological ideals within the Peruvian state in a new globalized setting. This may confirm claims by systems theory that all systems must change (be open) to survive and that "every closed system will tend toward its most statistically probable state, i.e., chaos (the definition of entropy). In order to retain its state of organization and differentiation, an open system is continuously sucking orderliness from its environment" (Lewellen 1978:4). In this light the progress of the victims seems explicable.

Facts and Fiction

Some Facts

The Gran Pajonal is an interfluvial plateau of approximately 360,000 hectares situated in the eastern part of the central Peruvian Amazon, where the Andean foothills stretch into the lower Amazon Basin (map 1). It rises like a rocky block from the surrounding landscape—a dramatic landscape nurturing the imagination of the spectator. But inside the rock barrier one finds a much more friendly plateau characterized by a combination of rolling hills and steep slopes averaging an elevation of approximately three thousand to five thousand feet and crisscrossed by numerous streams and smaller spate rivers cutting deep ravines (maps 1 and 2).

The area is covered by lush forest vegetation classified according to eco-climatic parameters as Humid and Very Humid Montane subtropical forest (ONERN 1968:72–73). It combines primary forest intermixed with secondary forest growth most predominant around the populated centers. The most distinctive feature of this landscape, however, is the *pajonales*—the hill savannas—open, grass-covered areas that are scattered all over the inhabited inner zone of the Gran Pajonal. Numbering in the hundreds, these patches of grassland range from small glades the size of a backyard to large savannas covering hundreds of hectares.

The indigenous population living in Gran Pajonal are the Ashéninka, a subgroup of a larger conglomerate of Arawakan-speaking groups, including the Asháninka, Yíne, Yánesha, Matsigenka, and Nomatsigenka.[1] Approximately 6,000 Ashéninka are currently living here in some 39 native communities surrounding the small settler community of Oventeni, which is inhabited by some 120 colonist families (roughly 600 persons), mostly of Andean descent. Over-

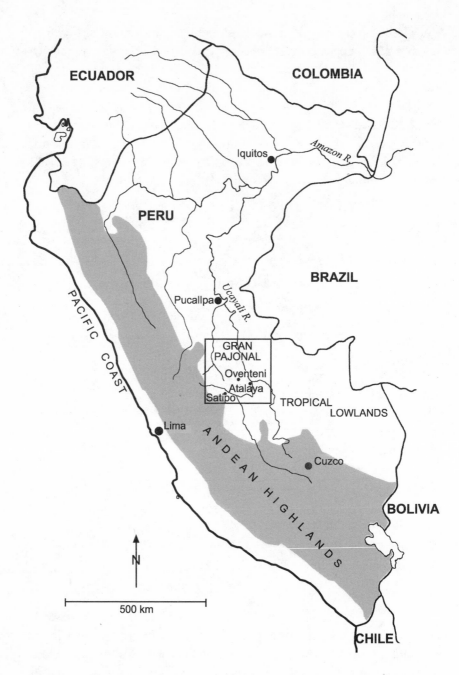

HVALKOF MAP 1. Location of Gran Pajonal in Peru (Source: author 1997 and 2004; © 2004 by S. Hvalkof)

HVALKOF MAP 2. General site map of Gran Pajonal (Source: author 1997 and 2004; © 2004 by S. Hvalkof)

land access is possible only on foot or by beast over small trails. The alternative is flying in in small one-engine aircraft. Currently such aircraft are assuming the bulk of transport to and from the Oventeni colony and the neighboring indigenous community of Ponchoni, the base of the Ashéninka organization. The colonists mostly raise cattle on cleared forest ground, whereas the Ashéninka are subsistence swidden horticulturists par excellence who increasingly produce organic coffee as an integrated part of their cropping system. Their horticulture is supplemented with hunting and forest gathering.

During the past two decades the natural grass areas have been joined by pastures for cattle grazing planted by the local colonists in cleared forest. The two types of grass areas are, however, quite distinguishable. Whereas the natural grassland, the *pajonal*, is a nonproductive zone maintained by indigenous burning and is a preferred location for settlements, the cattle pastures are quite the opposite, designated for production and maintained through cultivation. The two types of grass areas, although often adjacent, look conspicuously different to the field observer and connote two very different systems of meaning and value, as we shall see.

What's in a Name?

The Gran Pajonal means the "great grassland" or "savanna."[2] Although the name of the place suggests an extensive savanna area, the total area of natural grass covers only some ten thousand hectares, or less than 3 percent of the entire Gran Pajonal. The origins of such savanna landscapes have always been disputed (cf. Fairhead and Leach 1996; Nyerges and Green 2000), but in this case there seems to be agreement that they are the combined result of anthropic activities with climatic, soil, and edaphic conditioning—however, with a clear anthropogenic dominance (Denevan and Chrostowski 1970; Scott 1979; ONERN 1968). Denevan and Chrostowski mention historical factors such as indigenous trading routes and much higher population densities in past centuries (1970:58), and we could add early cattle-raising programs by eighteenth-century missionaries. But the local indigenous population not only have produced the *pajonal* landscape through centuries of use; they have deliberately formed and maintained it through fire management of the open grass areas. Burning the pajonales has been and still is a general practice by the Ashéninka and a favorite sport of the children, who will burn any *pajonal* as soon as it is dry enough. The Gran Pajonal's savanna-forest landscape is a dynamic anthropogenic system—a human creation.

But Gran Pajonal does not refer simply to the geographical characteristics of the zone. It is a loaded ontological metaphor of multiple signification (cf. Lakoff and Johnson 1980) — an allegorical construct saturated with meaning both for the settler population and for the indigenous Ashéninka living there, although the meaning conveyed and captured is very different for the two groups.

To the Andean colonists, the *colonos*, the term is emblematic of modern progress, the very reason for their existence and presence in this remote forest area. Grassland means pasture, and pasture is the basis of their cattle-ranching venture, the prime motivator and historical mover for colonizing the zone and civilizing the savages. Although cattle raising in the Gran Pajonal has failed repeatedly over the course of modern history, the great grasslands still symbolize the colonists' millennial dream of success, wealth, and greatness: the vast space where development freely unfolds, the eternal grazing grounds where the cattle, the value, will multiply in an ever-accumulating process. This idea of pasture as an expression of one's success as a "settler in the jungle" has been reinforced by small government loans given exclusively to cattle raisers and administered according to numbers of hectares sown. No matter the actual disappointing productivity in economic terms, cattle are more prestigious in the Andean peasant system than any agricultural produce. They are a token of civilization and progress; thus, the Gran Pajonal conveys the entire modern developmentalist paradigm, with which these colonists wholeheartedly have identified.

The Ashéninka, on the other hand, also strongly identify with the grasslands. They produced the Pajonal landscape through centuries of use, as mentioned, and still maintain it. The reasons they give for burning the grass are various: pest control, killing or scaring off snakes, maintaining open spaces for security reasons, customs, and fun, or simply for the aesthetic value of the open savannas. The pajonales are nearly always situated along the ridges and on hillcrests, following traditional Ashéninka trail systems; they are preferred settlement sites, provided there is water available in the immediate vicinity.[3]

However important the pajonales are as a discernible feature giving identity to the place and the people, it should not be forgotten that the surrounding and dominating rain forest is still the soul of the Ashéninka livelihood and existence. All material production takes place in the forest, without which there would be no Ashéninka. It could be said that the presence of the many small and large grass areas that appear barren from a horticultural perspective actually bears out the importance of the forest from a cultural perspective. The Ashéninka forest is a fully socialized universe, and by ascribing symbolic significance to the pajonal areas, these are incorporated in both a symbolic and functional way. Pajonales are among the two most commonly named features in the indigenous landscape, the other being watercourses. Pajonales are used as spatial orientation indicators in an otherwise undifferentiated forest environment, and a number of them bear place-names that recur as specific sites in Ashéninka mythology, referring to specific primordial events. Thus, the grassland dwellers have written their cosmology and identity out in the culturally affirmative landscape, which they then obviously have to maintain. Every youngster walking the trails to school, to their gardens, or elsewhere is reminded of the mythological past and of his or her place in the universe by these named sites. These refer to known legends and mythical events and point toward the existence of the ultimate sacred, thus recreating order and meaning in a world that has been perverted by colonists' encroachment.

For the Ashéninka the landscape is, among other things, a referential model, alluding to their cosmology and the various other levels of the grand Ashéninka narrative as presented in their mythology. Whereas the colonists terminate the forest, incessantly expanding cattle pasture, the Ashéninka strive to regulate the balance between the grasslands and the forest. Thus, there are two rather strong and incompatible identifications with the Gran Pajonal, creating a contested space that evidently holds the potential for latent social conflict, a conflict that increasingly has been articulated vis-à-vis the Peruvian state and its changing policies on land and development.

History of Progress

The Early Colonization

The central Peruvian Amazon was colonized relatively early in the colonial period, with the establishment of a Spanish mission among the Ashéninka in 1635. The initial motivation was minerals, slaves, and extractive products, but it soon evolved into a complex quest for agricultural development and logistical access to the main Amazon River system, accompanied by a desire for social and economic control in the face of increasingly rebellious indigenous societies. Within the first century of colonial rule, the unfolding modernist paradigm was on track and operationalized in the colonizing venture, led by the Franciscan mission, to whom the irksome chore of penetrating, concentrating, pacifying, and colonizing the obstinate "Campa Indians" had fallen. The rumors of the Great Grassland fostered the dreams of establishing a center of cattle ranching, European settlements, and modern development, converting the area into a civilizing dynamo in this part of the upper Amazon. The Franciscan mission established itself in the grasslands with a series of cattle stations, agricultural initiatives, specialized personnel, and overseers.

The missionary venture, however, came to a sudden halt with the outbreak of a large-scale indigenous insurrection headed by the charismatic and legendary Juan Santos Atahualpa, an Andean mestizo claiming to be of Inka descent and schooled by the Jesuits. The rebellion that soon embraced all indigenous groups in the central Peruvian Amazon cleared the central forest of Franciscan missions and Spanish colonies. An active indigenous ad hoc militia was maintained for more than fifteen years with far-reaching effects on the development of the region, which remained largely uncolonized until the late nineteenth century.[4] In the Gran Pajonal the effect lasted much longer, and a recolonizing effort was not initiated until well into the twentieth century.

In the intervening period no new colonization efforts were launched. Because of the political turmoil surrounding Peruvian independence and the creation of the new republic, civilizing the Amazon was taken off the national agenda. But other forces were now at play. The rubber boom at the end of the nineteenth century and the expansion of the extractivist frontier had a devastating effect on the Ashéninka of the Gran Pajonal. Although the area did not contain any rubber, it was rich in another extractive resource: native labor. Extensive slave raids into the Gran Pajonal, so-called *correrías*, were organized by the European rubber patrons along the neighboring Ucayali River, and large areas of the Gran Pajonal were devastated and depopulated during the peak period of slave hunts (cf. Sala 1897). The terror of the *correrías* was accompanied by recurrent measles epidemics continuing through the first half of the twentieth century, resulting in a drastic population decline. The *correrías* gradually ended after the collapse of the rubber economy around 1915, but they were still taking place well beyond World War Two, and apparently the practice was occurring up until the 1960s in certain areas.[5]

Reintroducing Modernity

In 1934, the Franciscan mission resumed the development and colonization project it had aborted nearly two hundred years earlier. Contracted peasants and artisans from the Andean highland were settled to raise cattle, grow coffee, and build the new mission in Oventeni, right in the center of the Gran Pajonal. The small colony barely survived by growing coffee and grazing a little cattle, supplemented with some income from the privately subsidized orphanage and boarding school for the Indians the Franciscans set up. But in the late 1940s the mission succeeded in attracting the interest of major investors, and in the 1950s a modern cattle-ranching enterprise covering all of the larger savanna areas was set up at Shumahuani in the interior of the Gran Pajonal. Despite enjoying the benefits of aerial surveys, resource mapping, haciendas, workers, veterinarians, skilled specialists, imported cattle, and large investments, the project never generated the economic boom that its promoters had envisioned. The economy was ailing, and cattle diseases flourished. The natural grass of the pajonales had a low nutritional value and proved worthless for intensive cattle raising. Logistical problems prevailed, and management problems increased up through the 1960s.

The fatal blow was dealt in early 1966 by the leftist MIR guerrillas, led by another legendary figure, Guillermo Lobatón. Fleeing counterinsurgency forces in the highlands, Lobatón's guerrillas passed through Oventeni and the Gran Pajonal. The cattle hacienda was an obvious target, but as the administrator in charge was not present, the guerrillas had to be content with liquidating the best breeding bulls. Shortly thereafter special counterinsurgency forces led by U.S. specialists caught up with the group, and one of the last brutal encounters with the guerrillas ensued (cf. Brown and Fernández 1991).[6] The incident shook the whole Oventeni colony. The nuns were evacuated, and the mission together with its boarding school was closed; only one priest stayed behind. A temporary military post was established in Oventeni for a couple of years. Eventually the cattle ranch also closed down, and all its workers were dismissed. For the second time in history, the dream of the great development had disintegrated.

Epidemics and Land Use

The cattle ranching venture in the Gran Pajonal had profound effects on the indigenous population. The Ashéninka were still marked by depopulation, and their organizational abilities were weak owing to factionalism caused by the slave raiding. With the new influx of hacienda workers and colonists, violent measles epidemics broke out and swept the area in several waves through the 1950s and 1960s, when entire Ashéninka communities were destroyed. Many fled their settlements and sought refuge in isolated areas in the mountain forest, where they usually stayed until the epidemic was over, shunning further contact for long periods of time. Besides measles and other viral epidemics introduced through the colonization, tuberculosis and other poverty-related diseases also took their toll. The result was a precipitous population decline. Denevan and Chrostowski, who visited the hacienda in the mid-1960s, noted that the "present Campa [Ashéninka] population is only about 20 per cent of the number residing on or near the pajonales before 1950" (1970:58). We have no accurate information on the size of the indigenous population prior to the recolonization, but the American anthropologist John Bodley, who surveyed eighty households in the Gran Pajonal in 1969, estimates the precolony population at some six thousand Ashéninka, based on comparative data from neighboring areas, and a maximum of fifteen hundred at the time of the survey (1972:8); these figures suggest a decrease of around 75 percent in a relatively short time span, an estimate that nearly coincides with the estimate of the geographers. In a study carried out by the national office of natural resource evaluation (ONERN) in the mid-1960s, the population in the Oventeni colony was calculated to be three hundred (predominantly colonists), with around two thousand Ashéninka in the rest of the Gran Pajonal (ONERN 1968:34).[7] This sharp population decline obviously made the process of colonizing the area relatively easy, but it also affected the availability of indigenous labor on which the *colono* economy was based. The colonists increasingly secured Ashéninka labor through debt bondage and chattel slavery. Although there were occasional protests and sporadic attempts to counter the colonist expansion, conditions did not favor indigenous organizing.

The production of the colonists and that of the Ashéninka did not differ much at this point, apart from the cattle raising, which took place on the natural pajonales around Oventeni and in Shumahuani. (For Oventeni, see colonist case study area, and for Shumahuani, see indigenous study area, both on map 3.) Most food was produced by the indigenous peons, either in their own gardens or from working special plots for the colonists. Some coffee was grown, but generally it was integrated in the subsistence gardens and followed the traditional fallow cycles. The indigenous population was still scattered, and the colonos resided mostly in the Oventeni settlement or as workers on the Shumahuani cattle hacienda.

This situation is clearly reflected in the land use pattern. Comparing the land use patterns in the mid-1950s in the Shumahuani cattle ranch area with the area around the Oventeni colony (through a GIS analysis of aerial surveys of 1953–

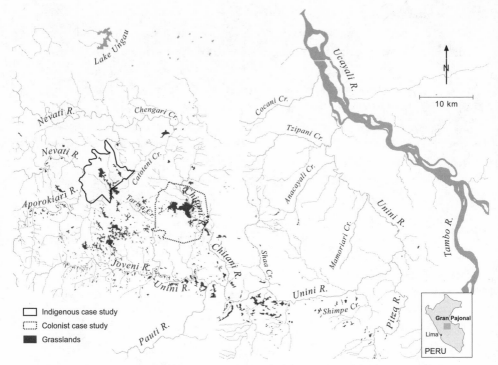

HVALKOF MAP 3. GIS projection of natural grassland based on 1958 air photo data and showing the two study areas (Source: author 1997 and 2004; copyright S. Hvalkof 2004)

54 and 1958) (see table 1 and color plates 2 and 3),[8] one can see the area is about evenly divided among grasslands, land used for primary horticultural production (including new swiddens), and land used for secondary production and new fallow gardens.[9]

Many colonists left the area after the collapse of the cattle project. Others stayed and tried to make it on their own, while the Ashéninka, who had fled the epidemics, gradually moved back into their old territories. Still, everything that happened in the Gran Pajonal was revolving around a modern developmentalist ideology and discourse, and social control was in the hands of the colonist society.

Accelerating Development

The scenario of an indolent colonization and exploitation of indigenous labor in the Gran Pajonal changed drastically during the 1980s, when a new wave

HVALKOF TABLE 1. Land use, 1954

	Shumahuani (%)	Oventeni (%)
Forest	87	87
Grassland	7	7
Garden (Primary Production)	3	2
Garden (Secondary Production)	3	4
Settlement Center	—	<1

of grand development schemes in the Amazon region was introduced by the international development establishment represented by the World Bank, the Inter-American Development Bank, USAID, and some European agencies. Although initially no project was directly involved in the Gran Pajonal, such programs caused an intense colonization pressure on all surrounding areas, which obviously increased the influx of new colonists into the Gran Pajonal. The Oventeni colonization was growing fast, and so were the conflicts with the Ashéninka of the zone. Falling coffee prices in the late 1970s had motivated the Oventeni colonists to experiment with cattle grazing on planted pastures. The combination of cultivated pasture and new generous credits made available to small-scale cattle raisers proved to be an explosive cocktail (Hvalkof 1986). The only investment possible in the Gran Pajonal was in Indian labor, which was procured through debt bondage and a form of chattel slavery known as *enganche*, a feudal system of exploitation known from the Andean haciendas. Through the 1980s forest was cleared at an alarming rate to make room for planted pastures. All work was done by indigenous labor, and compliance with labor "contracts" was secured through institutionalized violence meted out by the civil authorities in Oventeni. Punishments included imprisonment without food or water for several days, flogging with the dried penis of a bull (a so-called *chicote*) on Sunday mornings in Oventeni, in addition to regular beatings. Sentences also included punitive labor on the colonist's farms (e.g., Hvalkof 1986, 1987, 1998; Schäfer 1988).[10]

The (over)exploitation of indigenous labor eventually threatened the social reproduction of the Ashéninka. Their subsistence production declined rapidly as an increasing number of people were being contracted for clearing forest and planting pasture, leaving them no time or opportunity for preparing their own new garden plots, which must follow the cycle of seasonal fluctuations. Returning to their settlements after completing their work contracts with the colonos, they had to be provided for by the local kin group until they had a garden of their own in full production. This not only caused annoyance and friction within the local groups (sometimes forcing the peon to accept another colonist contract), but also put pressure on the colonist economy and production. Hitherto the colonists had procured the bulk of their staples and other daily provisions from the Ashéninka at a very low price or through barter. Now the colonos complained that it was nearly impossible to find anything to buy and that the Ashéninka simply had ceased to offer their produce to the Oventeni settlers (a reluctance they attributed to the rebellious and obdurate character of the Ashéninka). The decrease in Ashéninka surplus production that had been important in colonist–indigenous interactions was now causing the disintegration of the economic relationship. The settlers had to import provisions from the outside by air, causing a dramatic rise in the general price level in Oventeni, again putting extra pressure on the cattle-raising effort. The production costs were skyrocketing but were not followed by corresponding economic output.

Complex ecological problems associated with increased overgrazing, cattle diseases, shrub and weed invasions of pastures, acid soils, and erosion were beginning to impact negatively on productivity, and the latent logistical problem of getting the beef to market made cattle raising a risky living.[11] The colonists responded the only way they knew how: by increasing the exploitation of the indigenous labor to get more land cleared.

Land Titling and Transformation

Introducing the Native Community

The Ashéninka society of the Gran Pajonal underwent conspicuous structural transformations during the 1970s and 1980s. Evangelical missions operating in the area since the late 1960s had launched vaccination campaigns during the 1970s and repeated them in the 1980s.[12] The immunization against viral killers, especially measles, had a noticeable effect, and the Ashéninka population increased rapidly. There is little doubt that, had it not been for these vaccinations, the Ashéninka population would not have grown quickly enough to fill in both the spatial and political gap created by the collapse of the cattle project. This demographic change became a crucial factor in the reorganizational process that was about to begin. It affected land occupancy, production, labor relations, and political potency.

At the same time, a new system of indigenous bilingual schools was being established by the evangelical Summer Institute of Linguistics (SIL), forming new social foci that greatly lifted the organizational capacity of the indigenous population, regardless of the ideological motive and proselytizing effort of the mission (Veber 1991, 1998). Indigenous organizations had been established elsewhere in the Amazon since the late 1960s, and in Peru a whole new institutional structure of indigenous Amazonian organizations was taking shape. Inspired by such organizations, the Ashéninka began organizing themselves in the 1980s, holding yearly assemblies supported by a few sympathetic SIL missionaries.[13] The first officially registered Native Communities in Gran Pajonal were formed in 1983.

The Peruvian idea of community is derived from the peasant societies of the Andes, where indigenous communities were established during the colonial period in order to control labor and regulate land tenure. During the agrarian reform period of the 1960s and 1970s, all "indigenous" connotations were eliminated, in keeping with the nationalist zeal and development policy aiming at creating a modern, ethnically uniform mestizo nation and state. Terms like *Indian* and *indigenous* were replaced by *peasant* in the official idiom. New agrarian legislation favored the establishment of collectively titled areas for peasant communities, irrespective of ethnic composition. Privately owned estates and haciendas were expropriated, however, not to be redistributed to the indigenous peasant population but to be nationalized and converted into state cooperatives of various kinds, a process that, after a few years of public enthusiasm, turned into a complete economic disaster. Thus, the legalization of collective land tenure through community titles was not an attempt to recognize indigenous territories but to secure land as a means of production, as part of a nationalist, populist, and integrationist political discourse aiming at modernizing and streamlining the Peruvian society (cf. Hvalkof 1999; Plant and Hvalkof 1999).

Special legislation granting rights to community titles to the native inhabitants of the Amazon region soon followed. The legal and technical model for establishing *comunidades nativas* ("native communities") in the Peruvian Amazon was copied from the Andean peasant community model—understood as a corporate peasant community with a high degree of structural and economic integration—and featured a residence pattern characterized by territorial centers of hamlets and villages. Ashéninka society in no way conforms to this organizational model, its social organization being characterized by a loosely knit network of scattered residential groups with high flexibility and individual mobility. In spite of whatever expectations official Peru may have had as to the social functioning of a community in the Amazon, the Ashéninka redefined the concept to be synonymous with a demarcated land area, a piece of guaranteed territory, with some additional benefits tagged to it, such as an Ashéninka school and possibly their own landing strip. A community and its boundaries were defined by the local territorial group, often organized around a local headman or charismatic leader, thus adapting a managerial concept born in the discourse of national integration and development to conventional Ashéninka patterns of organization and settlement. Still, the whole idea of establishing bounded territorial units with formal status in the nonindigenous world was utterly alien and dubious to many Ashéninka in the initial phase of this development.

The first four communities demarcated and titled in 1984 were adjacent to and covered most of the old concession area of the cattle hacienda in Shumahuani. The symbolic value in demarcating and titling exactly these areas was important. When the colonists realized what had happened, they did everything possible to reverse or halt the process, including threatening the emerging indigenous leadership, which ironically helped to define and politicize the role of the new leaders and their organization.

Deforestation and Land Use

To illustrate this development we can compare the land use patterns mapped in the colonist zone of Oventeni and Shumahuani in the 1950s (color plates 2 and 3) with the land use patterns as they appeared in the same two areas in the 1983–84 period (color plates 4 and 5). In the Oventeni colony the population had reached its maximum, with some 120 colonist families totaling about 600 persons registered as residents. Their pastures and crops were scattered about in the vicinity of the village. The population in Oventeni had more than doubled since the 1950s, when the estimated colonist population was below 300. The distribution of land among gardens in production, fallows, pastures, and natural grassland is shown in table 2.

As of the 1983–84 period, the increase in deforestation around the Oventeni colony had reached over 20 percent. The expansion of pastures accounts for 15 percent of this, the rest being new swidden gardens for colonist food production. Most of the colonists were (and are) living in very poor conditions, owning only a few head of cattle; some of them had none at all. All larger cattle

COLOR PLATE 1. Cover drawing 1997 *The New Yorker Magazine*, Inc., "Lobsterman's Special," by Bruce McCall. Permission granted by artist

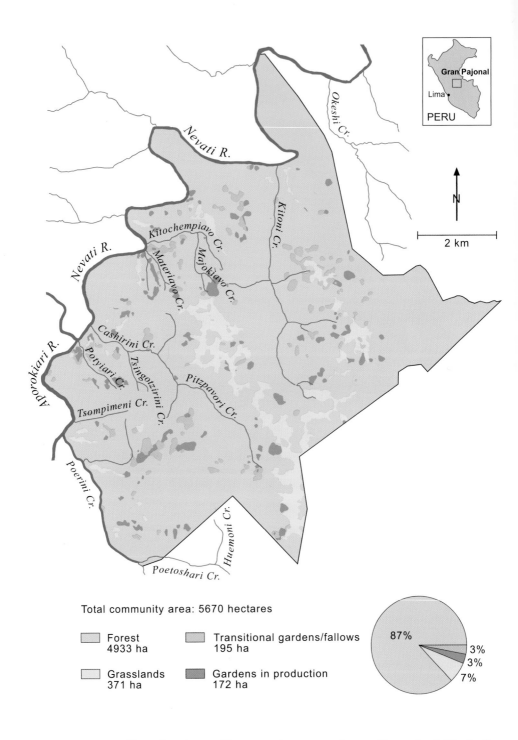

Total community area: 5670 hectares

Forest
4933 ha

Grasslands
371 ha

Transitional gardens/fallows
195 ha

Gardens in production
172 ha

87%

3%

3%

7%

COLOR PLATE 2. Shumahuani, 1954 (Source: author 1997 and 2004; © 2004 by S. Hvalkof)

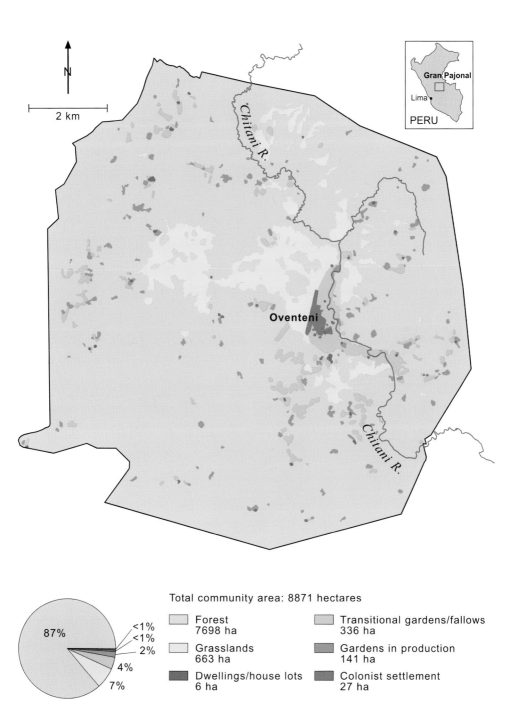

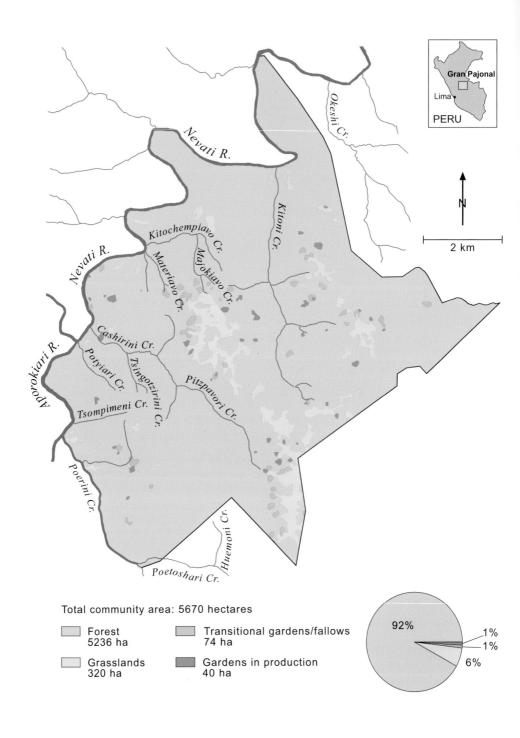

Total community area: 5670 hectares

Forest
5236 ha

Transitional gardens/fallows
74 ha

Grasslands
320 ha

Gardens in production
40 ha

92%

1%

1%

6%

COLOR PLATE 4. Shumahuani, 1983 (source: author 1997 and 2004; © 2004 by S. Hvalkof)

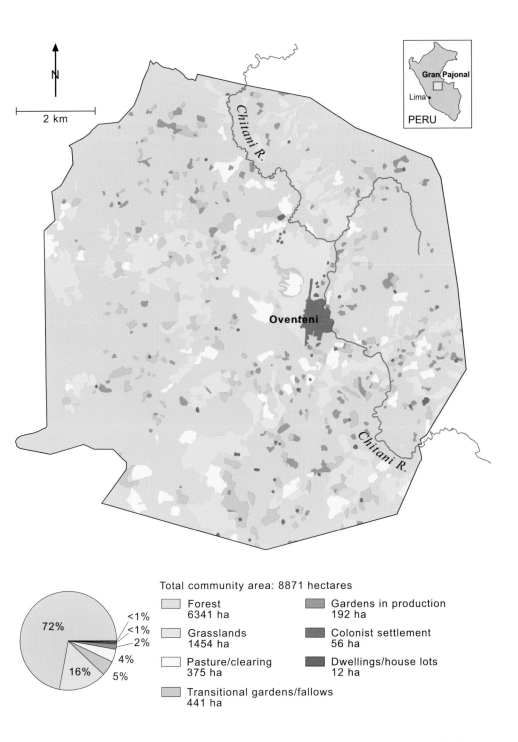

Total community area: 8871 hectares

Forest 6341 ha	Gardens in production 192 ha	
Grasslands 1454 ha	Colonist settlement 56 ha	
Pasture/clearing 375 ha	Dwellings/house lots 12 ha	
Transitional gardens/fallows 441 ha		

COLOR PLATE 5. Oventeni, 1984 (Source: author 1997 and 2004; © 2004 by S. Hvalkof)

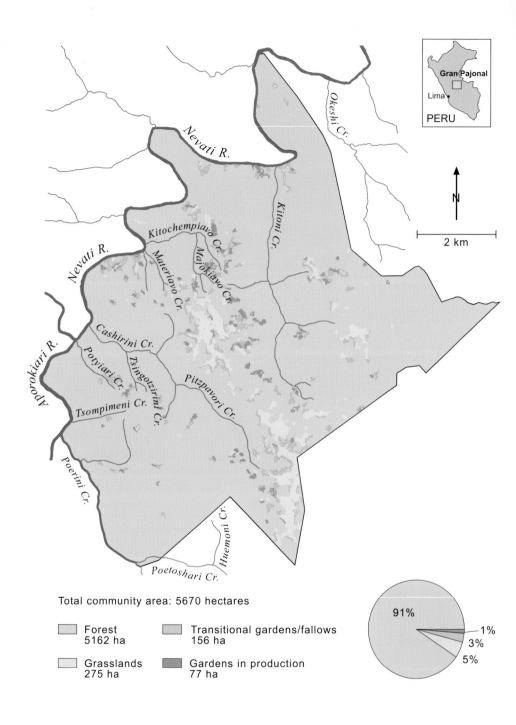

Total community area: 5670 hectares

- ▢ Forest
  5162 ha
- ▢ Grasslands
  275 ha
- ▢ Transitional gardens/fallows
  156 ha
- ▢ Gardens in production
  77 ha

91%   1%   3%   5%

COLOR PLATE 6. Shumahuani, 1996 (Source: author 1997 and 2004; © 2004 by S. Hvalkof)

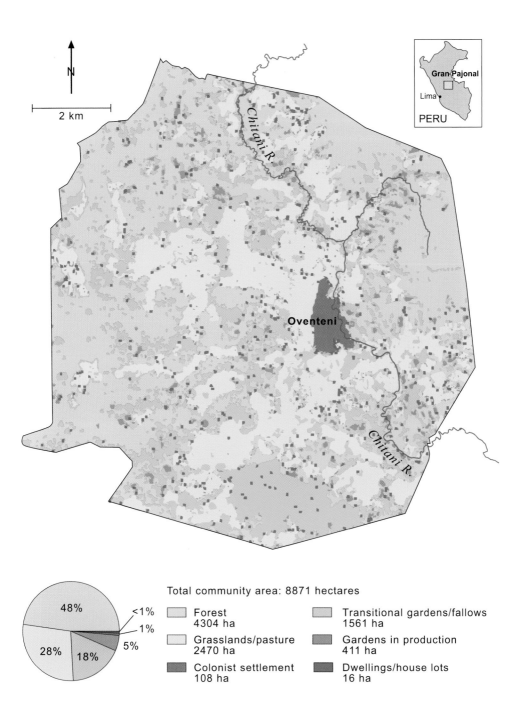

COLOR PLATE 7. Oventeni, 1996 (Source: author 1997 and 2004; © 2004 by S. Hvalkof)

COLOR PLATE 8. Kantu' man seeking auspicious bird omen at possible swidden site (photo by author)

HVALKOF TABLE 2. Land use, 1983–84

	Shumahuani (%)	Oventeni (%)
Forest	92	71
Grassland	6	21
Garden (Primary Production)	1	2
Garden (Secondary Production)	1	5
Settlement Center	—	<1

herds and pastures were owned by around ten family groups, and of these only a few could be classified as relatively wealthy in a settler context. Still, the effects on the local environment are conspicuous (see color plates 4 and 5).

Shumahuani, the former grazing area of the hacienda, had now been titled as a Native Community, and only Ashéninka resided there. From 1985 to 1986, the Shumahuani population was made up of some 10 to 20 family groups with a total population of 100 to 120 persons. This appears to be a considerable population increase from the 1950s, when the indigenous population had reached its nadir. Although no demographic surveys or statistics on the Ashéninka population are available from this period, I have made a rough estimate (based on settlement plots revealed in aerial photographs 1:10,000 and 1:15,000 of the area) that no more than 10 to 12 families lived or had been living there recently. The doubled population apparently had not expanded the area used for subsistence garden plots integrated with coffee; on the contrary, there were fewer hectares in use in the 1980s than in the 1950s. The notable increase in forest growth in the Shumahuani community and decrease in gardens over this thirty-year period are owing to the presence of the cattle hacienda in the 1950s, which cleared forest for food production for its workers. It illustrates, however, the potential of the Ashéninka production system to sustain a viable economy and forest regrowth. The colonist production, on the other hand, seems problematic in terms of forest reduction and expansion of grazing ground, which eventually will reach its limit when no more forest is available to convert into pasture or when it is no longer possible to secure the cheap indigenous labor on which it is based.

Titling the Rest

The initial titling did not stop the overall expansion of the colonist cattle economy in the rest of the Gran Pajonal. On the contrary, it seemed to accelerate it, and conflicts between colonos and Ashéninka grew disturbingly, as more local Ashéninka neighborhoods realized they also had the legal right to form communities, define their borders, and have them demarcated. A general quest for land titling emerged (Hvalkof 1986).

In 1985, the up-and-coming indigenous leaders decided to organize a general land titling process in the Gran Pajonal to counteract the developing colonist cattle frenzy. Mobilizing all human resources available, they succeeded in lobbying the World Bank and its special development program operating in adjacent areas, making these leaders responsible for the colonist expansion and escalating conflict in the Gran Pajonal. They also solicited the continuation of the land titling process as a means to stop the social, economic, and ecological destruction. The World Bank responded positively and sent a consultant, who confirmed the allegations and obliged the bank's Peruvian counterpart to carry through a demarcation and land titling process for all the indigenous communities in the Gran Pajonal (cf. Hvalkof 1998a:104–12).[14] Despite fierce resistance from the colonists and their allies in the regional administration, the indigenous Organización Ashaninka del Gran Pajonal (OAGP), and the international development program completed the land titling process in the following years.

By 1988, as many as twenty-seven new adjacent indigenous communities (Comunidades Nativas — C.N.) had been demarcated and titled, forming an almost continuous indigenous territory that circumscribed the settler zone.[15] The community structure did not alter the Ashéninka communities' internal function in any significant way at this point, but the adaptation of the concept of community to the Ashéninka context had created a new organizational platform for the indigenous population, who enthusiastically participated in civic decision-making processes and political initiatives regarding the Gran Pajonal.[16] The Ashéninka were no longer just a cheap, commodified labor resource. They were owners of land and had become a political factor. A new democratic reality was forming.

Postmodernity: Territory and Terror

Shortly after the Gran Pajonal demarcation and titling were completed, the strengths of the new organization and its leadership were seriously challenged. The generalized social chaos following the deep economic and political crisis in Peru in the 1980s had led to the emergence of the Shining Path (Sendero Luminoso) and MRTA (Movimiento Revolucionario Túpac Amaru) guerrillas in neighboring Ashéninka territory (cf. Benavides 1992, 1993; Hvalkof 1994a; García et al. 1998). A nexus of illegal cocaine production and drug trafficking created a disastrous state of latent violence in the central Peruvian Amazon. Both guerrilla organizations were founded on a modernist ideology embracing visions of progress with absolutely no room for indigenous special interests or politics. In the areas surrounding the Gran Pajonal, the Shining Path secured a foothold through forced recruitment and deadly terror against the native communities. From the indigenous point of view, Sendero was "yet another patron," as one Ashéninka expressed it, a patron indistinguishable from colonists. The Sendero Luminoso appears to have intended to establish a strategic center of food production in the Gran Pajonal, a plan that was emphatically opposed by the Ashéninka. This put the indigenous leadership in the Gran Pajonal on a collision course with the Sendero Luminoso, who put a price on the heads of the Ashéninka leaders. Alarmed by the guerrillas' targeting of indigenous leaders and sparked by an Ashéninka uprising in the neighboring Pichis valley following the murder of one of their leaders, the Pajonal Ashéninka decided to take control of the Gran Pajonal before the military intervened. One early February morning in 1990, a couple of hundred Ashéninka armed with shotguns and bows and arrows occupied Oventeni and declared it to be under the control of the Ashéninka Army (*El Ejército Ashéninka*). The Ashéninka had taken full control of the Gran Pajonal. They declared the establishment of the Ashéninka Army a fact and set up a comprehensive defense and surveillance system in the periphery of the Gran Pajonal. None of the guerrilla organizations ever succeeded in establishing itself in the area, and, following the general decline of their movements in the late 1990s, the guerrilla units gradually withdrew from those Ashéninka areas bordering the Gran Pajonal where they had sustained a terror regime since 1987. The Ashéninka had succeeded in pacifying the zone, a great accomplishment in the violent Peruvian reality, where "pacification" normally has been a military metaphor for death and destruction (cf. Hvalkof 1998:145–47).

The colonists maintained a low profile during most of the turbulent years from 1988 to 1995, intimidated by the unexpected organizational capacity, reaction, and success of the Ashéninka and their militia. The cattle-grazing zone had not been directly affected by the titling process, but it had been enclosed by the indigenous communities. Recognizing that all future cattle ranching had to take place inside this area and that there was no immediate possibility of expanding beyond it, the colonists remaining in Oventeni also had their

HVALKOF TABLE 3. Land use, 1996

	Shumahuani (%)	Oventeni (%)
Forest	90	48
Grassland	5	28
Garden (Primary Production)	2	5
Garden (Secondary Production)	3	18
Settlement Center	—	1

individual properties demarcated. This resulted in a drastically declining motivation for further colono immigration. Cattle were still produced and new pastures established, but they were slowly eating up their own economic basis. The new situation had also accentuated ethnic and class differences within the colonist population, which had now become conspicuous. An increasing number of poor colonos and the new generation of mixed ethnic background had sided with the Ashéninka and their organization.

If we look at the land use patterns in 1996 for the same two areas compared above (color plates 2 and 3 compared to color plates 4 and 5), we find in the Oventeni area a drastic reduction of forest to 48 percent, an increase in ten years of 23 percent in the colonist production zone. There is also a notable increase of 13 percent in fields of secondary production (table 3). The total population in Oventeni decreased somewhat since its zenith in 1985 to around one hundred families by 1996. Several cattlemen are still producing in the Gran Pajonal, although they reside outside of the area. Basically this means that just to maintain the same colonist population on very much the same standard of living over the past ten years, the colonos have had to deforest an additional 21 percent, of which 14 percent has been used for purposes other than pasturing.[17] The increased deforestation in the colonist zone is partly a result of the land titling process, as the circumscription has constrained the expansion of new clearings, concentrating cattle raising within the colonist zone. Without entering into the intricacies of cattle raising in tropical forest habitats (for example, Hecht et al. 1988), it is evident that the cattle-raising system of the Oventeni colonists is self-destructive and needs to be changed. Unfortunately, there are no signs yet that this is going to happen (see color plates 6 and 7).

The land use pattern in the Shumahuani community in 1996 shows a very different tendency. The indigenous population has more than tripled since the 1950s, and during the past decade it has concentrated around the larger pajonal areas where community infrastructure—such as the bilingual school, health service, and landing strip—is located, but this demographic change appears to have had no impact on the amount of grassland. In fact, there has been a slight decrease in pajonal during the past decade from 6 percent in 1985 to 5 percent in 1996. On the SPOT images I cannot distinguish between older secondary forest and primary forest, but most forestland with arable potential has been cultivated before and is in some state of regeneration. Because of the population increase, interestingly, the cultivation pattern close to the edges of the grassland has produced more secondary growth in the pajonal areas rather than the deforestation and spread of the savannas that might have been expected. It is evident that the forest destruction is solely a result of the colonist cattle economy and that the Ashéninka have developed a contemporary indigenous "agroforestry system" (cf. Denevan and Padoch 1988) that so far has been able to sustain both an increasing population and the forest simultaneously.

One of the new and expanding cultigens reflected in the present land use pattern is coffee. The Ashéninka have been cultivating coffee for the colonists for decades and have now themselves successfully adopted coffee as a favorite cash crop, developing their own system of plant improvement. Coffee is an excellent product for the Pajonal Ashéninka. They love the plant, which they successfully have integrated into the cropping cycles of their subsistence plots, keeping their production costs considerably lower than those of the colonists. This is possible because the social reproduction of Ashéninka society is being guaranteed through their subsistence production, implying that they are impervious to market fluctuations. Presently, the OAGP is trying to get the Pajonal Ashéninka registered as organic coffee producers in an attempt to get a better price and direct access to alternative markets overseas. A novel indigenous economy seems to be forming.

The New Ashéninka

The catalyst for the metamorphosis of the Ashéninka from an extrasocial labor commodity to active political operators in the civil Peruvian system was the land titling process. It entailed a parallel organizational process, creating a de-ideologized political space in which intercultural and cross-sector communication among national public authorities, regional officials, technical personnel, colonists, and Ashéninka could take place devoid of the political rhetoric of identity politics. The success of their pragmatic maneuvers to defend and consolidate their territorial integrity encouraged the Ashéninka to seek access to and control over political resources, too. With support from lower sections of the settler society, the OAGP succeeded in winning the local elections, and today, remarkably, the Ashéninka militia leader is mayor of the settler colony of Oventeni. Formal political power today is in the hands of the Ashéninka organization, the members of which dominate even the village council of Oventeni and occupy all the posts in the local civil hierarchy, much to the annoyance of the cattlemen.

The indigenous organization has used this new political power to get public support for their district. Most communities now have their own bilingual (Ashéninka–Spanish) elementary school. A secondary vocational school is located in the OAGP base community. To the benefit of both colonists and indigenes, the organization has secured a staffed health center and potable water in Oventeni, and they also run an alternative indigenous health program. The colonist society is split in their attitude toward the Ashéninka organization, but there is increasing support and participation from broader sections of the colonos.

A recent development demonstrates the rapprochement between the Ashéninka and the colonos. The OAGP is supporting the construction of a road through the Gran Pajonal, a road that has been planned since the 1960s as part of the colonizing effort and that until recently had been vehemently opposed by the indigenous organization. The reason for the indigenous U-turn is that, being assured that further colonist encroachment is no longer a threat now that they control the zone and own most of the land, the Ashéninka now want to improve the commercialization of their organic coffee, their new cash crop. It may very well turn out be a disastrous decision, but the colonists are impressed. It is doubtful, however, whether it will ever be completed due to the costs, the topography, and the climate.

However, we may conclude without exaggeration that the completely underestimated Ashéninka of the Gran Pajonal have succeeded not only in liberating themselves, but also in initiating a genuine process of democratization in a Latin American locale that hitherto has failed completely to fulfill its own liberal aspirations. The Ashéninka have written themselves into the discourse of Peruvian civil society with a fearless pragmatism, aiming at consolidating their territoriality and identity as Ashéninka of the Great Grasslands. But how do we explain this extraordinary transformation in power relations? and which ontological configurations are framing the political parameters, discursive elements, and practices conditioning this unexpected "progress of the victims" (Veber 1998)?

Peoples and Power

Ideology and Cosmology

Power is "not an institution and not a structure, neither is it a certain strength we are endowed with; it is the name that one attributes to a complex strategical situation in a particular society" (Foucault 1978:93). To understand the dynamics of the specific "complex strategical situation" in the historical context of Ashéninka and colono relations and interactions with their common space, the Gran Pajonal, I will look at the different operational models of identity and space that each of these two principal actors is operating within.

It seems relevant here to differentiate between ideology and cosmology, a distinction drawn by Terence Turner in his analysis of Kayapó interethnic conflicts and ethnopolitical struggles and success in contemporary Brazil (Turner 1993:8–11). In many ways the process resembles the one the Ashéninka are undergoing. Turner shows how the Kayapó assimilate new situations in terms of traditional structures, but also how this assimilation simultaneously modifies these structures as a transformation "from cosmology to ideology" (ibid.:12). The cosmological system of the Ashéninka is ontological and spiritual: it has no goals, no direction, no specificity, no logical time, and no sequence. It is upheld by ritual, the structure of the physical space and the landscape, and the performing of Ashéninkaness. It is basically a nonhierarchical system, but nevertheless refers all meaning and reason to the "ultimate sacred," in which the existence of God and the godly above merge.

In opposition to this stands the colonist system, which is almost exclusively based on an ideology of modern progress. Ideological systems are goal seeking and specific, have a direction and a sequential time dimension, and explicitly refer meaning and reason to well-defined logics, tautological though they may be. Colonist ideology is dependent on economic performance, production, accumulation, and secular qualities embedded in the Peruvian state.

Other colleagues have addressed the same distinction. Maurice Bloch (1986) sees ideology as a particular form of knowledge resulting from a historical process related to the formation of the modern capitalist state and constantly propagated by the "ideological state apparatuses" (Althusser 1977), which, in this case, would be the colono school, the church, the agrarian credit institutions, the ministry of agriculture, etc. What we call Ashéninka cosmology is almost identical with Maurice Godelier's "non-ideologized consciousness" (1984), which he sees as a political potential of resistance to ideology, given the right circumstances (Bloch 1997:294). Also, the late Eric Wolf makes a parallel distinction in his discussion of Rappaport's (1979) cognized models, arguing that "cognition that is close to experience—and learned through contact with it—needs to be distinguished from ideology, discourses and performances that resemble cognition but in fact deny it and subsume it under the aegis of untestable transcendental schemata" (Wolf 1999b:20). Although the philosophical dimensions of furthering this discussion are overwhelming, I will simply apply the distinction here for heuristic purposes.

Spatial Identity Models

Let us first take a look at colono identity, self-conception, and motivation. The colonist population in Oventeni is not undifferentiated but forms a stratified group of people with diverse economic abilities who are organized in a hierarchy of prestige and influence. A few cattle-raising families are rather wealthy by local standards, and some own property outside of the Gran Pajonal. The majority, however, are poor peasants, living close to a subsistence economy supplemented by the selling of a little coffee, a little beef, and a few other agricultural products. Several households run small shops that sell and buy anything possible, including barter business with the Ashéninka. But despite these differences, colonists have a rather uniform identity as *serranos*—that is, highlanders from the Andean sierra, or *chóri*, as the Ashéninka call them. To the outsider they appear to belong in the special social and ethnic category of the *cholo*, an ambiguous term that they only occasionally would use themselves.

The term *cholo* has changed significantly through colonial history and holds several meanings and connotations in contemporary Peru, depending on the context.[18] Generally, *cholo* has become the term for the deindigenized peasantry, a growing population with roots deep in the Quechua-speaking communities of the Andes and now seeking a life as individuals or individual families outside the constraints of the traditional indigenous Andean communality. *Cholo* is not synonymous with *mestizo*, although the two categories may be overlapping.[19] The cholos mark their "defection" from the indigenous background by adherence to the national progress-ideology characterized by highly individualistic and entrepreneurial behavior.

Most of the Oventeni colonists, irrespective of their individual status and wealth, could be classified as cholos. They are identifying enthusiastically with the most conventional modernist progress ideology, an ideology that was retailed to the Andean peasantry during the three decades after World War Two as part of the developmentalist millennial fantasies vehemently propagated in the third world by the industrialized countries. In the national Peruvian tradition this development discourse was expressed through the great nationalist project: the creation of a unified mestizo nation and state. To this end a deindigenization and cultural mestization process was launched in the agrarian reforms of the 1960 and 1970s (cf. Hvalkof 1999; Plant and Hvalkof 1999). The cholos of the highlands were absorbed by this discourse to the point of being the embodiment of it.

The colonos and their society in Oventeni are of this construct. They are not only deindigenized Indians, they are distinctly *nonindigenous*, which is their identity marker. Because they are historically situated so closely to the indigenous and placed so close to the bottom in the national hierarchy of ethnosocial classes, it is of the utmost importance to them to distance themselves from everything "Indian," especially since the dynamo of progress is individual social climbing. Seeing themselves as agents of civilization, they have appropriated the national developmentalist zeal, reified in their expanding pastures and grazing cattle. Figure 1 illustrates a simplified spatial, two-dimensional model of the space within which the colono operates.[20] The concentric circles represent the main social and ethnic categories in the national context, with value attached to placement. Thus, the closer to the white center, the higher the probability of getting a larger share of wealth, prosperity, and happiness. Upward social mobility also means getting closer to the center—that is, Lima or, ultimately, New York. The closer to the center, the more culture and civilization; and the more peripheral, the more nature and savagery. Colonists are operating within the conventional nature–culture dichotomy, and I have added the classic dualistic paradigm, the Cartesian scheme, as a tangent to the circle to situate "development" as a directed motion and modernist idea.

Oventeni is situated closer to the periphery than to the center, but through the establishment of symbols of civilization and progress (pastures and livestock, church, plaza, concrete house, airstrip, roads, satellite dishes, etc., *in perpetuum*)—an almost ritual gesture—Oventeni and the Gran Pajonal will move closer to the center of civilization and wealth, improving opportunities for a prosperous life. Subduing and civilizing Nature and the Indians, of which there

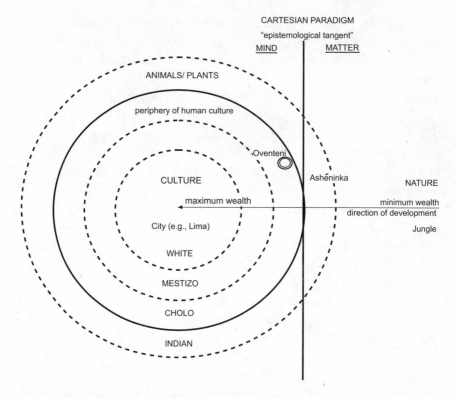

HVALKOF FIGURE 1. Model from the perspective of the colonists. Created by author

are plenty, is part and parcel of this Peruvian version of manifest destiny. Rational arguments for changing the way settlers raise cattle in order to prevent the ecological and economic collapse they are heading toward do not count here. Thus, it could be argued that we are dealing with a mimicry of a modernist universe, where it is the symbolic simulation that counts, not productivity or output, which are clear ideological constructs.

The colono model sketched here seems *in grosso modo* to fit the category of ideology and discourse. The tragedy in this is that the colonist society has been taken in by such developmentalist schemata, and just as the great metanarratives are declining on a global scale and the remodeling of the global structures of capitalism is forming, Oventeni colonos are left with only profaned and worn-out caricatures of Western society, which they desperately try to keep alive through exercises in simulation on the Great Grasslands. Their caricature

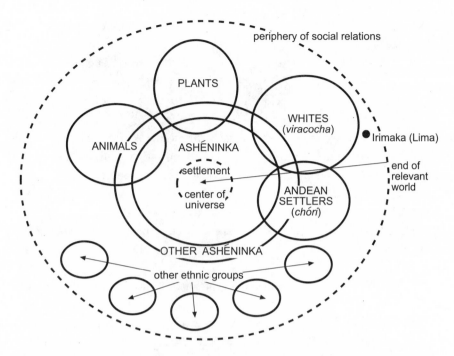

HVALKOF FIGURE 2. Model from the perspective of the Ashéninka. Created by author

of development does not facilitate the invention or implementation of alternatives to the status quo.

The Ashéninka model (figure 2) is of a different construct altogether, belonging to the realm of the cosmological. In the same design of concentric spheres in two-dimensional layout, the Ashéninka of the Gran Pajonal are placed right in the center of the universe, surrounded by other closely related Ashéninka, forming a relatively uniform cultural and societal unit. Beyond that identity sphere there is a sphere of potential and blurred social relations, which gradually fades with the distance from the center toward the periphery of social relations. Within this sphere, other peoples and classes of social beings exist, some of them named, some of them not, and some of them interacting with the Ashéninka in different ways. They are all regarded as having their own logic and their own autonomous sphere of social relations, the quality and composition of which are highly irrelevant to the ethnocentric Ashéninka.

The Ashéninka universe is absolutely socialized, implying that there is no explicit concept of nature as external to the social reality. Beyond, the social does not exist. According to Ashéninka mythology, the world and the sky were once united, and in this primordial setting lived the proto-Ashéninka, living with God on earth. But owing to a series of conflicts and ensuing enigmatic events, God got upset and decided to depart from the earth, ascending to the sky. He invited all his Ashéninka kin to join him, but most of them decided to remain on earth. From this point on, the earth and the sky parted, and the distance kept increasing. Then followed a period of mystic metamorphoses. The remaining proto-Ashéninka were transformed into the different animals and some plants and those who remained unchanged ancestors to the present Ashéninka. Thus, all Ashéninka are related as kin to all animals and living species as a matter of primal and creational imperative. Even certain features in the landscape are transformed proto-Ashéninka, features that still are seen as living and acting.

As I have pointed out elsewhere (Hvalkof 1989), the absence of a concept of nature in the Cartesian sense of the term also inhibits the cognizance of the development concept in the modernist sense, as the existence of a nonsocialized space, "nature," is a prerequisite for the civilizing "development" process. Teleological conceptions of modern development along such lines appear to be foreign to the Ashéninka universe.[21] To the extent this universe implicates a sense of coherence, it is also a particularistic universe, as sketched in the figure. This universe appears to picture the various categories of known social beings, be they human or animal, as separate, mutually unmergeable groups. Transfer or transcendence between such groups takes place only via spiritual and sacred intervention. Accordingly, the Ashéninka are hardly disposed toward imagining any possibility that they might ever become white/*viracocha* (they have never expressed such ambitions to me) or colonos/*chóri*, both of which are basically regarded as socially perverted usurpers of their space. Unlike the colonos, who explain their poverty as a result of their marginal position in relation to the civilized urban center, the Ashéninka tend to regard themselves as marginal but as right at the center of the relevant world. Lack of access to resources is due to the wrongful arrogation of power by the *chóri*, a fact they have had to live with for decades, but one they eventually will overcome. Absolute marginality does not exist in the decentralized indigenous universe, as each category of people is supposed to have created its own concentric and meaningful world, each with its own center. Whereas the colonist universe is a hierarchical, taxonomic, and monocentric construct, the indigenous universe is a paradigmatic, relativist, and polycentric design, and the Ashéninka do not consider themselves as being in any way situated at the bottom of a national social or class hierarchy or as subordinated to other ethnic groups.

Thus, colonists and Ashéninka do not communicate from the same cognitive platforms or with identical sets of ontological axioms. Yet, the colonists presume that they do and that the Ashéninka acknowledge the universal hierarchical organization of power and meaning and situate themselves accordingly—that is, at the bottom. The Ashéninka, however, do not recognize this at all, and they do not behave like the humble servants they are supposed to be; they behave rather as pragmatic operators in a universe of multiple opportunities for resource access. This appears to be a tremendous advantage in an increasingly globalized setting.

A Conclusion

The New Globalized Setting

Through the accelerating process of international integration, the power relation hitherto expressed in the Amazonian patron–peon nexus, which for centuries has characterized colonist–indigenous relations, has been subverted by indigenous linkages with wider systems, eventually overruling the significance of local colono patrons.

The American-Brazilian anthropologist Paul E. Little uses the fractal analogy to describe such cross-scale social relationships, in which local actors link directly to a larger international system, skipping over scales to promote their specific local interests. He writes,

> These connections are rarely neatly organized and mechanically mobilized but rather are highly volatile and irregular and vary according to the historical moment, the strength and density of the cross-scale contacts, and the specific issues at hand, . . . I call these fractal power relationships since they are, on one hand, highly irregular and unpredictable, yet on the other, they seek and partially achieve the furthering of common interests of the social groups operating at different social scales. (Little 1998:13)

The process of increasing global integration has produced an international discourse favoring indigenous self-development in the Amazon. Some of the actual topics supporting this are human rights, sustainable development, biodiversity, democracy, privatization, and participation (Hvalkof 1998). By establishing new "fractal" partnerships with international organizations of various origin, the Ashéninka have now been able to change and consolidate their position in both the regional and national contexts.

Ironically, the new resources for an alternative power nexus were found in the grand development programs kept in place by an international developmentalist discourse and its institutional manifestation, in this case the World Bank. In this context the new, fractal relations were established between the Ashéninka and governmental institutions whose function has been to implement the structures of civil society as part of the modernist endeavor.

The specific field of articulation for new relations between the Ashéninka and the national society became the process of indigenous territorial legalization and titling. In the international institutional contexts it echoed the "greening" in discourse and policy in which the "rainforest debate" has been a prime mover (cf. Brosius 1999c). The process of land titling introduced a new social institution in the Ashéninka reality: the native community (*la comunidad nativa*). This construct was foreign both to the dispersed settlement pattern and to functional relationships in Ashéninka society. But the idea of a local territorial group or agglomerations of such groups under the leadership of a headman fit very well with the existing pattern of social organization in the Gran Pajonal. In this way a strange interface emerged between two different conceptual constructions, "a working misunderstanding," to paraphrase Marshall Sahlins's description elsewhere of such phenomena (1981, 1985).[22]

The Profane and the Sacred

The Ashéninka have been able to maintain and reproduce their identity, their Ashéninkaness and cosmological order, while simultaneously taking part on unequal terms in the same development discourse as the colonists, for whom the discourse has been absolute, identity absorbing, constitutive, and in the last resort devastating for both their material production and their identity as colonos.

The Ashéninka cosmological reason tends to be cryptic, ambiguous, and remote from social life or couched in a language that is, in Rappaport's words, "devoid of material terms . . . not fully of this mortal world and can be regarded as eternal verities. Being devoid of explicit social content they can sanctify everything, including change, while remaining irrevocably committed to nothing" (Rappaport 1979:119). The omnipresence of the "ultimate sacred" as guarantor of ultimate meaningfulness is not only witnessed and maintained through ritual but also in the metaphorical landscape of the Gran Pajonal, which, as mentioned earlier, constantly reminds any Ashéninka of the cosmology and order of meaning, constantly reaffirming the "self-centeredness" of the Ashéninka world. It does not matter whether this is done vis-à-vis a World Bank official or the local shaman.

It seems that when the Ashéninka engage in political power strategies related to the non-Ashéninka world, they connect, enter into, manipulate, and articulate with already existing discourses, rather than aiming for something constituted solely from within their own cognized system. The remarkable thing is that they seem to be able to do this without getting co-opted by the system that produced the discourse they so openly dig into (see Turner 1993 for an analysis of similar Kayapó strategies).

Their practice is not guided by a goal-seeking system. There is no ulterior motive in living; the meaning of life is simply being Ashéninka, but in order to maximize their options and access to whatever resources are at hand, they will log into any discourse they find "close," interesting, or just accessible. Their multicentered, particularistic worldview leaves them with no ideological, ethical, or moral preferences as to whom or which world they want to cooperate with, as the symbolic and moral values pertaining to them apply only to themselves. It is in principle a nonessentialist and nonhierarchical construction, one that gives the indigenous society a remarkable strategic maneuverability on the local and global scale, as the cultural content of the non-Ashéninka is irrelevant and not a prerequisite for relating to it as resources.[23]

Contrary to this stands the colonist system as an ideologically informed paradigm, an episteme. The colonists' binary model does not resort to ultimate sacred propositions. It operates in a stratified, unidirectional, moralist universe, narrowly seeking a specific goal, the accumulation of material capital. By definition the colonist system has to be ever expanding, ever civilizing, and never structurally changing, the movement itself being a prerequisite of its existence. Thus, the colonist cannot take advantage of the new global tendency and relate fractally in the postmodern, pluralist reality, precisely because they relate only to one discourse, an outmoded discourse, and their system is not geared to anything else. They have literally been absorbed by the paradigm and subsumed under the developmentalist schemata. They have only one tune to play, which unfortunately for them has stopped resonating in the world surrounding them. They desperately try to revoke the golden times of the great cattle frenzy and hope for progress, but their performance becomes increasingly anachronistic.

Summing Up

The indigenous–colonist struggle for livelihood, space, and meaning stems from a conjunctural constellation of different ontological systems that articulate with social and economic factors external to both locality and peoples. The facilitation of the sudden Ashéninka access to political power and success has been conditioned by several external determinants, such as the enforcement of indigenous land titling legislation in Peru, a particular historical situation of the Peruvian state creating an operational space for indigenous groups, favorable international discourses, a changing global scenario facilitating political alliances between unequal and otherwise unrelated partners (like the Ashéninka–World Bank connection), and a demographic resurgence brought about by immunization campaigns conducted by the evangelical missions. The surprisingly rapid change in the role of institutions that hitherto has been regarded as the problem rather than the solution recalls Foucault's definition of power as strategical positioning in relation to multiple factors, a strategical positioning the Ashéninka seem to master.

It is paradoxical that the Ashéninka access power from the very same social system that less than a decade earlier was seriously threatening to destroy the forest environment and a landscape so intimately linked to Ashéninka identity and livelihood. They now operate with all the ideological "state apparatus instruments" at hand, which so far seem to be reinforcing Ashéninka identity, culture, and the reproduction of the forest–savanna environment.

Their nonideologized consciousness has furnished the Ashéninka with an instrumental pragmatism, enabling them to enter into whatever partnership and alliance they may find useful for whatever strategic purpose they can agree upon. The potential of this relative freedom may have been present all through the history, but it could not be realized without a state mature enough to guarantee and enforce, although reluctantly, the Ashéninka's rights as an indigenous minority and without a new globalized order providing them with alternative alliances and empowerment to assure them such progress. Their choice of adopting coffee as a cash crop and rejecting cattle as a realistic viable produce is equally pragmatic, reflecting the immediate suitability of coffee to their existing system of production rather than direct cosmological functionality of environmental sustainability, a point underscored by the indigenous endorsement of the road project.

It remains to be seen whether this development is an expression of a cosmological consciousness able to resist ideology under the present circumstances (Godelier 1984; Bloch 1997) or whether these circumstances, accelerating globalization and the formation of new capitalist structures and social identities, eventually will ideologize the indigenous Gran Pajonal and finally subsume them under the aegis of the grand schemata.[24] Whatever the outcome, the "progress of the victims" is a fact for the globalized, postmodern, sustainable, and coffee-exporting Ashéninka.

Notes

The research on which this chapter is based was undertaken at the Department of Anthropology, University of Massachusetts at Amherst, where I was associated as adjunct researcher from September 1994 to July 1997. This postdoctoral fellowship and its research project, "Rainforest Political Ecology: An Anthropological Approach to the Social Construction of Space, Territory and Economy in Gran Pajonal, Peruvian Amazon," was generously funded by the Danish Council for Development Research. The period was, without doubt, the best and most productive in my academic life, and I want to express my warmest thanks to the colleagues and students in the Anthropology Department at the University of Massachusetts for making it such a positive experience for me and my family. My gratitude also extends to colleagues at Hampshire College, Smith College, and Mount Holyoke College. A special thanks to my two research assistants, Mark Goodwin and John McGee, University of Massachusetts at Amherst, who initiated me in the mysteries of UNIX-based GIS analysis and Remote Sensing and who stayed up long nights at the Office of Geographical Information Analysis (OGIA) and at the LARP/METLAND labs, to finish our work. Color plates 2 through 7 and tables 1 through 3, which further report on the data, owe much to Goodwin's and McGee's assistance.

Also my reverence to the editors of this volume, Dr. James Greenberg and Dr. Aletta Biersack, whose encouragement and momentous editing jobs made my contribution a reality. Finally, I want to thank my wife, Dr. Hanne Veber, for her continuous support and as usual for helping identify lost references and quotations. My thanks to her also for the title of my chapter. Dr. Veber used the phrase "Progress of the Victims" as a section subtitle in her paper "The Salt of the Montaña: Interpreting Indigenous Activism in the Rain Forest" (1998) and generously allowed me to borrow it.

1. This ethnolinguistic conglomerate, excluding the Yíne (Piro), was formerly referred to as Campa Indians in the historical and ethnographic literature.

2. *Pajonal* is defined as "a tall grass community with very scattered woody growth (subshrubs, shrubs and low trees)" (Denevan and Chrostowski 1970:18).

3. Although such a settlement location is preferred, only a portion of the Ashéninka population is actually residing directly on a pajonal. Most are settled in the forested areas close to or between pajonales, and many families have always been settled inside the forest. There are various practical reasons for this, water access being one. Still, all communities are close to a pajonal somewhere within their local territory, and most communities are named after a pajonal, as are bilingual schools commonly being located there.

4. The intricacies of the rebellion of Juan Santos and its historical context have been exhaustively analyzed by several scholars (e.g., Castro-Arenas 1973; Lehnertz 1972; Loyaza 1942; Metraux 1944; Santos-Granero 1987, 1992; Tibesar 1952; Varese 1973; Veber 2003).

5. Slavery and slave trade continued in the neighboring area of Upper Ucayali up till around 1988 (García 1998; Gray 1997, 1998; Gray and Hvalkof 1990; Hvalkof 1998; Renard-Casevitz 1980:252).

6. The Ashéninka claim that both Lobatón and his second in command, Jaime Martinez, were captured and executed. I spoke with two persons who were present at the execution and who pointed out where the corpses had been buried. Brown and Fernandez has another version of the events in their *War of Shadows* (1991). A couple of people who were immediate neighbors of the ranch were upset at the behavior of the hacienda administrator, but in general the Ashéninka were not supportive of the guerrillas, and no major punitive action was taken against them.

7. The estimate is based on the 5. National Census 1960 and data from the Peruvian malaria eradication agency 1965.

8. The areas and extensions used for this comparison are not arbitrary but coincide with the exact demarcated areas of the Shumahuani Native Community and the Oventeni colonist zone, demarcated and titled in the late 1980s. This makes it possible to compare changes in land use patterns over time, following the changes in development policy, managerial forms, and landownership for the areas dominated by colonists' production and Ashéninka swidden horticulture, respectively.

9. The technical details in relation to the GIS analysis, the data generation, and other aspects of this complicated process have not been commented on here, partly because of the character of the chapter and partly because of the limitation of space. The two cases selected are typical for the area, but obviously more variation would be present if all communities and settlements had been included. The spatial GIS-supported analysis eventually needs to be expanded to cover the Gran Pajonal, but generating the data for a similar detailed comparison covering the entire zone is an enormous task, one that has not been possible hitherto within the limited research resources available.

10. In 1985, an entire Ashéninka family of fourteen persons resorted to a collective

suicide attempt by drinking fish poison (*barbasco*) because of such humiliating treatment in Oventeni. Nine died, most of them children.

11. The type of traditional cattle ranching described here is well known all over the Amazon basin. It is characterized by a low animal productivity rate, limited sustainability of pastures due to soil deficiencies and weeds, and subsidized credits (Hecht et al. 1988).

12. The most active of these was the Summer Institute of Linguistics (SIL); but missionaries from the South American Mission (SAM), Swiss Indian Mission (SIM), and, at an early stage, the Seventh Day Adventist mission also took part in these campaigns.

13. The SIL missionaries invited officials from the educational sector and other selected friends, mostly with the aim of promoting their Ashéninka initiatives and establishing an evangelical organization or even a native church. They did not succeed in the latter, but definitely made the problems and interests of the Ashéninka of the Pajonal known to sectors of the public administration.

14. The counterpart Peruvian institution was the Chanchamayo-Satipo Special Project, accountable to the Ministry of the Presidency of the Republic.

15. Today the indigenous organization of Gran Pajonal, the OAGP, includes thirty-four associated communities, and several of the communities first titled have subsequently had their land bases extended.

16. The response from the colonist establishment was one of constantly attempting to delegitimize and undermine the new Ashéninka leadership and its organization, OAGP. But the circumstances eventually forced them to accept its existence (cf. Hvalkof 1997 and Veber 1998 for a detailed analysis of the extraordinary organizational process leading to this).

17. The 1996 classification is a little different from the two prior mappings in that the 1996 map is based on a digital analysis of two French SPOT satellite images, which, due to its spectral bandwidth, cannot distinguish between natural grass areas and pasture. Thus, in the Ovenenti land use classification from 1996, both natural grassland and planted pasture have the same digital signature. This could be corrected by comparing the maps with the earlier vegetation classification as shown in color plates 3 and 4, but this has not been done in this graphic presentation.

18. During the Spanish colonial regime a series of ethnoracial categories were part of the feudal system of exploitation, and *Indios* and *Indígenas* were subject to tribute collection and forced labor. Many opted for getting themselves recategorized as *cholos* in order to avoid such abuses.

19. The mestizo category is based on notions of racial merge—an almost genetic concept of Indian–white mix on the one side, but with a cultural dimension attached, locating it on the side of European descent and identifying it with mainstream Latin American culture and national identity and civilization. The cholo is not identified as a racial mix but is clearly seen as a person of Indian descent, only with a special cul-

tural identity as *serrano*, "highlander"; cholos have adopted cultural characteristics of the national society without really being qualified for them from a mestizo point of view. Most cholos, however, will probably classify themselves as mestizos or just *serranos*, or even more neutrally as Peruvians to avoid being classified low in the national ethnoracist hierarchy.

20. The models drafted here were originally used in a small article on nature concepts in the development process of Gran Pajonal, an article with rather limited distribution (Hvalkof 1989). The specific Ashéninka model (figure 2) is elaborated on the basis of a model of interethnic relations presented by Stefano Varese in his excellent ethnohistorical monograph *La Sal de los Cerros: Una aproximación al mundo Campa* (1972).

21. This two-dimensional graphic presentation precludes depicting the other dimensions of the Ashéninka cosmos, but there is a corresponding hierarchy of heavenly spheres.

22. Thanks to Hanne Veber for pointing out Sahlins's description to me.

23. As Eric Wolf points out, "Culturally cognized models may be adaptive or humanly constructive (the two are not isomorphic), but they can also be or become grossly nonadaptive as well as humanly destructive" (1999b:20). The very same ability to enter into the other's discourse and into fractal power relations without moralistic criteria nearly destroyed the Ashéninka during the rubber boom as both victims of and partakers in the slave-raiding practice.

24. The effect of these adjustments will rapidly be reflected in changes in the landscape and vegetation patterns, which can be followed through remote sensing and GIS-assisted analyses. This may be of interest both to researchers and to the indigenous organization.

Red River, Green War: The Politics of Place along the Porgera River

Aletta Biersack

The Porgera valley is one of two valleys in the southwest corner of Enga Province, Papua New Guinea, to host Ipili speakers. Directly west is the Ipili-speaking Paiela valley, a valley that has recently acquired unprecedented national and international presence, even notoriety, in light of its own Mount Kare source of gold (Biersack 1995a:31–43, 1999a, 2004a; Clark 1993, 1995; Ryan 1991; Vail 1995). From the 1940s onward, alluvial gold has been mined in the Porgera River valley. High-grade ore was not discovered until the period 1982 to 1984 (Jackson and Banks 2002:63–66).[1] In May 1989 (CSIRO 1996:2–1), Porgera Joint Venture (hereafter PJV) — presently owned by transnational corporations as well as by the State of Papua New Guinea, Enga Provincial Government, and the descent lines[2] recognized as owning land within the mining area[3] — obtained a Special Mining Lease (SML). An underground mine was launched in 1990, with plans to add an open-pit mine later on (Handley 1987; Handley and Henry 1990:1717).[4] In 1992, the Porgera gold mine was the third most productive gold mine in the world, and ten years later it was still reckoned in the top ten gold mines worldwide (*Post-Courier* [hereafter PC] 7/15/02/39;[5] see also Banks 2002:45). From 1990 to 1997, the mine accounted for "15.7 percent of [Papua New Guinea's] total export earnings" (Nita 2001:158).

The most conspicuous penalty for Porgera gold mining has been environmental, for the Porgera River has been discolored. In 1992, a consultancy team referred to the redness of the river as "vivid" and "intense" (Sullivan et al. 1992:5), and, while the redness has noticeably faded as the years have passed, the color red carries a heavy symbolic load, and the discoloration has set off alarm bells in the minds of many Porgerans as well as of those living west of the

Porgera valley, in the Paiela valley. Waste products from the mining—a combination of waste rock (rock with no economically valuable metal content)
(Jackson and Banks 2002:2) and tailings ("very finely crushed ore from which
the bulk of the gold has been removed but which also contains remnants of the
chemicals used to treat the ore [including cynanides]" [ibid.:241] along with
"metals contained in the original ore but not extracted in the mill" [ibid.])—
are deposited in local streams and rivers that ultimately feed the Porgera River
(ibid.:240). The Porgera River empties into the Lagaip River, which empties
into the Ok Om River, and thence to the Strickland River and the Fly River
(CSIRO 1996:4–2). The negative effects are far-reaching, involving portions
of Enga Province, Southern Highlands Province, West Sepik Province, and
Western Province (see map 1).[6] Australian NGOs monitoring the situation have
made doomsday predictions (MPI 1995:7), and PJV has come under sustained
attack in a series of impact studies, position papers, an undergraduate thesis,
and a documentary on the Australian television station SBS (see CSIRO 1996;
Jackson and Banks 2002:ch. 10; Kennedy 1996; MPI 1995; Nita 2001; Papo 1992;
PJV 1997; Shearman 2001; Sullivan et al. 1992).

Waste rock and tailings have had their highest impact on the area downstream from the mine, in what has become known as the Lower Porgera.[7] Historically this area has been known for its alluvial gold. Discovered in the late
1930s, alluvial gold was first mined by expatriates in the 1940s. By the 1950s,
local people began to mine alluvial gold as well, and they continued to mine
through the start-up of intensive hard rock mining in 1990. Even today, alluvial
mining continues, although most alluvial miners have abandoned the enterprise because the waste rock from hard rock mining has buried the alluvial gold.
The color of the river—red, like menstrual blood, which men find threatening and women find disgusting (Biersack 1987)—has made the Porgera River
noxious to local sensibilities. Many consider contact with the river lethal.

As the damage caused by the waste rock and tailings became clear, those
living downstream from the mine and north of the SML boundary (map 2)
organized themselves into the Porgera River Alluvial Miners Association, or
PRAMA, to press for compensation. When PRAMA and PJV could not agree
on compensation, a determination of the extent of the damage and the level
of just compensation for it was sought from Minister for Environment and
Conservation Paul Mambei. On February 7, 1996, Mambei awarded a compensation package estimated at 15.2 million *kinas* (the *kina*, or PNG dollar, was
then worth between US$.76 and US$.78, making the package equal to about

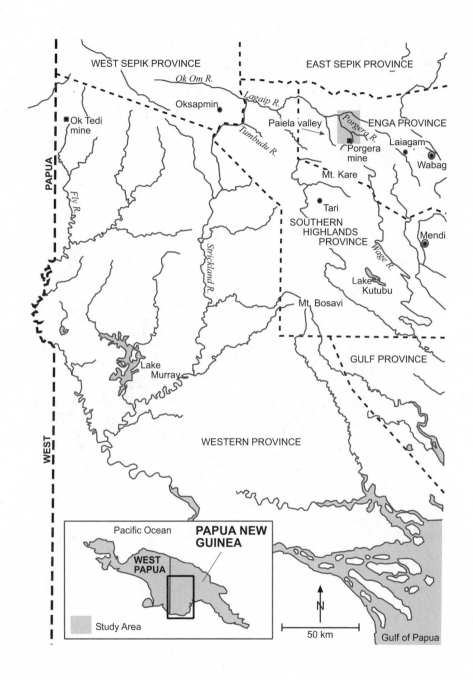

BIERSACK MAP 1. The Lagaip-Strickland river system

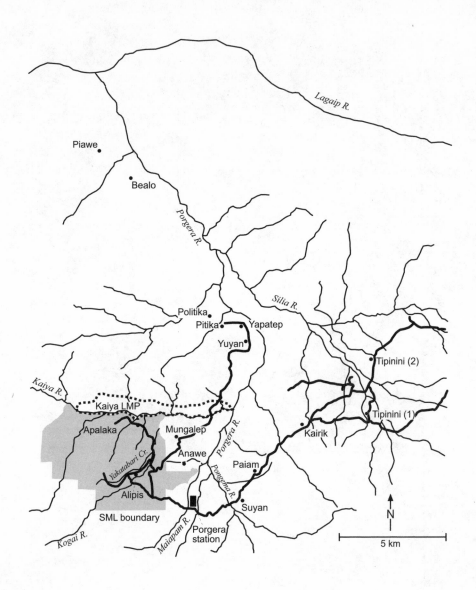

BIERSACK MAP 2. The Porgera valley

US$11.6 million [Jackson and Banks 2002:n.p.]) over the life of the mine (PC 1/2/01/2).

Here I provide a partial account of the dispute between PRAMA and PJV as it unfolded within the context of the conjuncture of capitalism and culture that Porgera gold mining inevitably turns upon and the disruptions and eruptions occasioned by that conjuncture. The "green war" of the title refers to these disruptions and eruptions, rooted as they are in a situation-dependent "politics of place." In this usage the word *place* signifies a spatiotemporally grounded site of local–global and/or local–national articulations (Biersack 1999a:81–82; Dirlik 2001; Escobar 2001; Massey 1993; see the introduction), while the phrase *politics of place* (Harcourt, ed., 2002; Moore 1998; Prazniak and Dirlik, eds., 2001) refers to actors' strategies and the power situation as these emerge at specific sites of transcultural articulation (Biersack 2003)—along the Porgera River, for example. The green war this chapter discusses refers to the environmental aspects of the situation along the Porgera River and to the Janus-faced rage that the environmental issue has inspired among certain Porgerans. Lower Porgerans hold the mine accountable, but they also hold accountable their neighbors to the south: Porgerans who, by virtue of their descent line membership and residence within the SML (see map 2), are not only the principal beneficiaries of the mining but own equity in the mine. Some, perhaps most, of these SML landowners are consanguineously or affinally related to their Lower Porgeran victims. Along the Porgera River capitalism participates in and is constrained by a prior field of relations, even as this prior field of relations is inflected and reorganized by capitalism (see Hyndman 1994; Jorgensen 2003; and Kirsch 1997 for a parallel New Guinea case). The conflict the environmental issue has engendered cannot be explained in terms of political economy alone, therefore, but must be accounted for with respect to the conjuncture of political economy, on the one hand, and indigenous sociality and morality, on the other (see Gewertz and Errington 1991). It is to this complexity that my term *green war* points. *Green* evokes the environment but as Porgerans organize and use it—that is, as sociomoral resource. *War*, meanwhile, evokes class war but also tribal warfare, and neotraditional warfare can and does erupt in the mining context.

One further neologism will be important, and that is Escobar's (1999) term *nature regime*.[8] As I understand the term, *nature regime* refers to human–nature (history–biology [ibid.]) articulations viewed as something like Mauss's (1967) "total social phenomenon": at once significant, social, economic, ecological, and always political, and, also like Mauss's total social phenomenon, culturally and historically variable. Unlike the alternative term *mode of production*, *nature regime* lacks domain specificity and suggests multidimensionality. Escobar develops the concept as a contribution to an "antiessentialist" notion of nature, one that acknowledges the sociohistorical production of nature in and through discursive constructions and human activity. Since these vary spatiotemporally, there is not one nature (extradiscursive and external to sociohistorical processes); rather, there are only nature*s*: realms of human–nature articulation that incorporate and themselves impact and constrain that extradiscursive reality to which the term *nature* in the singular refers (and also constructs). Accounts of particular nature regimes and, possibly, their intersection must acknowledge "the biophysical basis" (Escobar 1999a:2) of nature without minimizing the sociohistorical character of nature regimes and the order of determination that operates within them. For all its attention to discourse, culture, and history, Escobar's antiessentialist political ecology is not idealist, therefore, but neither is it reductively materialist. Instead, arguably, it paves the way for pursuing Rappaport's invitation to explore the human condition in all its paradoxes and contradictions (see the introduction).

"After Nature" characterizes two ideal-typical natures that are relevant to this writing, the one capitalist and the other "organic."[9] As Escobar defines it, the capitalist nature regime involves "the progressive incorporation of nature into the twin domains of governmentality ["a quintessentially modern phenomenon by which increasingly vast domains of daily life are appropriated, processed, and transformed by expert knowledge and the administrative apparatuses of the state" (ibid.:6)] and the commodity" (ibid.:7). Capitalist nature posits the nature/culture dichotomy that is so foundational to modernist discourse (see Pálsson, this volume). Moreover, its politics of nature (Robbins, this volume) are amoral—some would say, immoral—premised upon unequal access to resources and the benefits that flow therefrom. In organic nature regimes, however, "nature and society are not separated ontologically" (ibid.) but tend conceptually to interpenetrate and/or fuse (totemism providing a classic instance of the phenomenon [Biersack 1999a]), and its politics of nature are moral (albeit frequently, if not always, sectorally so)—premised upon equal access to resources and the benefits that flow therefrom. Given this contrast between capitalist and organic natures, the term *nature regime* has special importance for the analysis of situations in which capitalist and organic nature regimes interact, as they do in large-scale mining projects outside the North.

I argue that the conflict engendered by the environmental destruction of the Porgera River (the green war of this chapter's title) must be understood with respect to the conjuncture of capitalist nature (in Escobar's sense) with Ipili nature—the nature regime that obtains, that is, in the Porgera and Paiela valleys.[10] I begin with a synopsis of the Ipili nature regime. I go on to sketch a brief history of Porgera alluvial mining from its onset in the late 1940s to roughly 1990 (see also Golub 2001:187–224; Jackson and Banks 2002:33–38), a history that establishes that a tension between local and international (colonial) nature regimes existed almost from the beginning. This tension is traced into the era of hard rock mining and the ensuing campaign to recuperate losses from environmental damage. As O'Connor has pointed out (1998), capitalism suffers from a "second contradiction," for it devours the resources upon which its very profits depend. In the Ipili nature regime, sharing resources ("exchange" broadly construed) is the basis of all sociality. Enemies destroy one another's resources, but friends share them, contributing to one another's material well-being. The conjuncture of capitalism with culture in this one southern valley inevitably pits those who profit from capitalist ventures, but on the condition that they destroy resources, against those whose resources are thus demolished. Given its cannibalization of resources in the pursuit of profits (O'Connor 1998), capitalism will inevitably provoke resistance (Scott 1975). To the extent that the destruction of resources contributes to a deepening rift between those who benefit and those who are victimized, between the haves and the have-nots, capitalism will destabilize those very host communities upon whose goodwill it depends. (In the South more generally, perhaps, capitalism's "second contradiction" [O'Connor 1998] functions within that nexus of nature regimes that capital-intensive resource development creates.) In the final section of the chapter, "The Politics of Place along the Porgera River," I draw conclusions about Porgera's green war, rooted as the war is not just in a global political economy and not just in an indigenous order, but in the tumultuous relationship between the two, as this relationship has been spatiotemporally engaged along the Porgera River.

The Ipili Nature Regime

Even before missionization, the Ipili cosmos turned on a sky–earth axis, one that opposed an extraterrestrial, disembodied god (symbolized by the sun [*nai*] and nowadays called Gote) to mortal human beings (Biersack 1987, 1990,

1995b, 1996a, 1998b, 2001a, 2004b). Divinity lives extraecologically, in a position of transcendence above *(kenga)* in the sky. The sun has no body (Biersack 1990) and consequently is not born, nor does "he" die. Human beings, however, suffer the body's curse, which is its life cycle, and are born and also die (Biersack 1987, 1990, 1995b, 1996a, 1998b, 1999a, 2001a, 2004b). As incarnate subjects, human beings are immanent rather than transcendent, dependent upon the resource base, the earth or ground (*yu*, to which they are cosmically bound. In the Ipili nature regime the human body is the primal human–nature articulation. Nature is thus not distant from people or "outside of history and human context" (Escobar 1999a:1), as it is in Escobar's capitalist nature regime. It is instead as familiar and intimate as the sweet potato that is consumed in the morning and at night.

Sweet potatoes are cultivated in gardens, and inherent in traditional cosmology was the notion of the earth as a host for embodied, skin-and-bone life. Land and water, as locally viewed, were material supports for an equally material species life. Ipili society was, and still largely is, a horticultural society, and the importance of land is self-evident, not only to outsiders but to Ipili speakers themselves. Ipilis richly acknowledge the importance of water as well, in folkloric stories about how waterways originated and were regulated (Biersack 1998b), for example, as well as indirectly in a pervasive discourse concerning bodily growth and decline. The word *ipane*—referring to juice, fat, grease (tree *ipane* [*sia ipane*] or sap, genital *ipane* [*wi ipane*] or semen, breast *ipane* [*andu ipane*] or breast milk, etc.)—contains the word for water (*ipa*) in it. In general, the health and volume of the human body were thought to be dependent upon *ipane* of various sorts. Before missionization, Ipilis employed various kinds of *ipane* (tree sap, dew, mud, breast milk, semen) to produce and cultivate bodies (Biersack 1987, 1998a, 2001a, 2004b; cf. Ballard 1998). More generally, all species of life—plants, humans, and animals—depended upon water, without which the earth would be an infertile wasteland filled with death and the desiccation of death. Before missionization, individual descent lines promoted the fertility of the earth and all that lived on it, including human beings, by feeding pork to the ancestors, who were thought to live in the line's lake. In return for the sacrifice, the ancestors endowed their descendants with an abundance of plant and animal resources, along with healthy and fertile bodies (see Biersack 1999a; Jacka 2001a).

The green values of this nature regime are the anthropocentric and somacentric values of what Ingold (2000) has called an "ecology *of life.*" *Kakasia*, the

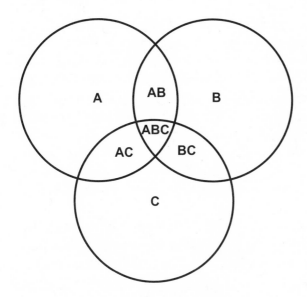

BIERSACK FIGURE 1.
The social relations of
reproduction

vernacular for "green," refers not only to plants but also to bodies of all kinds
and suggests the qualities of life as Ipili speakers conceptualize life: moistness,
freshness, youthfulness, and vitality.[11] It is material *life*, *bodies* that are *kakasia*,
and the word must be interpreted in the context of the centrality of human life
to the local worldview (Biersack 1995b, 1998b, 1999a, 2001a, 2004b). *Green* or
kakasia only indirectly pertains to the environment, for it signifies in the first instance the life, and in particular the *human* life, that the environment sustains.
Ipili environmentalism, in short, is inextricable from Ipili anthropocentrism;
nature, as it is locally constructed, moreover, is inextricable from society (Biersack 1999a; see also Descola 1994; Desola and Pálsson, eds., 1996). I stress this
because it helps explain why Ipili speakers read environmental catastrophes in
sociomoral terms. Damaging the environment jeopardizes human life and is
thus a hostile act.[12]

If the material needs of the human body motivate Ipili environmentalism,
the need to reproduce the human body, given human mortality, supplies the
logic to Ipili social organization, which is best understood as an organization of social reproduction. By a cognatic rule, children are members of all of
the lines of both parents. As such, they create a heritable relationship among
intermarrying lines—in the local idioms, a "road" (*asia*) or "bridge" (*ipa toko*)
among them. They are (in another important local idiom) "in between" (*tom-
bene nga*) paternal and maternal lines. Figure 1 depicts intermarrying lines and

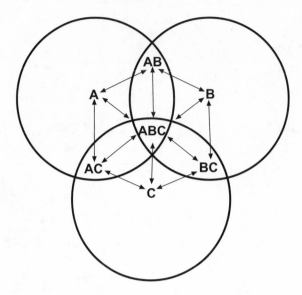

BIERSACK FIGURE 2.
Exchange within the
social relations of
reproduction

the areas of overlap that result from marriage and procreation. Since the configuration is generated by marriage, I refer to such configurations as affinal clusters.

Upon marriage, a woman becomes a "man's wife" (*akali wetene*) of her husband's lines and is obligated to protect and support her husband and his kin as spouse and affine. Similarly, a man who marries in is a "woman's husband" (*wana akalini*) of his wife's lines and is as ethically obligated to them as he is to the paternal and maternal lines of which he is a member. Kin but also kith help one another in the material sense of that word, and the domestic assets of a particular couple are shared with affines no less than with consanguines. Bride-wealth inaugurates an era in which resources (pigs and, nowadays, money, and, as I shall show, garden land and house sites) are shared across the lines that a particular marriage integrates. This flow of assets anticipates the next generation, when the children born to a particular couple will be members of their parents' lines and obligated as members to aid and abet their kin. Because marriage creates ties of mutual aid between people who would otherwise be unobliged, marriage was, and still is, used to pacify lines (Biersack 1991, 1995b, 1996b, 1999b, 2001a, 2001b). Figure 2 depicts the flow of assets from actors located at particular network positions (AB, AC, BC, and ABC) to actors occupying other network locations, flows that cross cognatic descent lines. Actors thus connected include the spouses of the members of particular lines as well as the members themselves. Within affinal clusters, amity—Fortes's famous term for the goodwill of kinship (1970), but in this context describing the ethos of mutual aid among kith and kin alike—ideally prevails.

Along with pigs and, nowadays, money, gardens and house sites circulate within these affinal clusters. A person may inherit gardens and house sites from his or her consanguines and affines, provided that he or she is a member or spouse of a member of the line that owns the estate where the garden or house site is. Additionally, a person may acquire the use of gardens and house sites on estates owned by lines of which the person is neither a member nor the spouse of a member if a relative who is a member or spouse of a member grants usufruct. The operative principle here is the by-now familiar one that kith and kin are obligated to support one another materially. The grantee is called an *epo atene* (if male) or an *epo petene* (if female), terms that can be translated literally as "he (or she) who has come to stay," "he (or she) who has come to reside"— that is, a guest. Host and guest are typically related consanguineously or affinally but through a line or lines other than the corporate line. For example, if an AB owns gardens and house sites on the estate of line A, he or she may grant use rights in one or more of these sites to a B consanguine or affine who has requested them.

One other asset flows in the circuits of figure 2, and that is women. There is a cultural preference to concentrate marriages between lines, such lines being said "to exchange women" (*wanda lawa lawa pi*). Woman exchange is accomplished by marriage sponsors, who encourage particular unions on structural grounds and who ideally contribute to and receive in the distribution of the bridewealth the groom gives to the bride's kin. An ABC person, for example, might sponsor the union of a B or an AB to a C or an AC, on the grounds of strengthening his or her network nodes (BC, AC, or ABC). The children who are born to the sponsored couple as well as the sponsored couple themselves will, from a sociomoral perspective, occupy the same network node, a node that the sponsor himself or herself, along with his or her children, also occupy. In this way, the density of affinal clusters is increased, and these networks, along with the flows they instantiate, become, to a degree, sociocentric. Within both the Porgera and Paiela valleys, adults are aware of which lines "exchange women," and they are also aware of the various network nodes that emerge through this exchange. Since the sublines of particular lines are corporate and since spouses tend to be drawn from proximate rather than distant descent lines, these partially sociocentric networks sprawl spatially, within but also across valleys, creating a distinctive geography of mutual aid.

The purpose of marriage, meanwhile, is sexual reproduction. Bridewealth, the gift of pigs and, nowadays, money that a groom gives to his wife's kin, obligates the bride to bear her husband a "return gift" (*paini*), specifically a child, and the flow of pigs, money, and gardens and house sites that marriage inaugurates, in ongoing exchanges, is designed to support the family as a unit of reproduction. Affinal clusters are clusters of *amity and fertility*. While Fortes's "amity" famously referred to sentiment, amity in the Ipili context is a matter of lending material support to materially needy human beings. Indeed, affinal clusters configure the social relations of reproduction, and it is reproduction in all its materiality and its organization (by means of marriage sponsorship) that Ipili social organization centers upon.

If, now, we inquire into how Ipili speakers meet their physical needs, the answer is in sociomoral ways, through the social relations of reproduction (see figure 1) and the "moral economy" (see figure 2) thereof. The reproductive pair, husband and wife, is also the paradigmatic gardening team, and spouses also typically co-own and husband pigs together. Moreover, access to gardening land is through the social relations of reproduction. Kith and kin are expected to support one another, not in the abstract but in the material sense, providing the wherewithal—the garden, the house site, the pigs, the money, the sexual partner—to live the life of the body, which is a life of the body's cycle and its material need. The social, the moral, and the material are thus integrally bound together within a nature regime that is centered on reproduction and the social relations of reproduction.

Beyond these social relations of reproduction, the sociomoral requirement of mutual aid does not obtain. Those who are not linked through ties of consanguinity or affinity are not obliged to help one another. In fact, they are structural enemies. Ipili morality is thus always sectoral. Within circles of amity and fertility, resources and other assets are moved within a geography of mutual aid. But those who participate in different circles of amity and fertility are strangers and potential enemies. Between circles of amity and fertility, assets (wives, pigs, houses, gardens) may be stolen or plundered, and lives may be taken rather than sustained. Thus, the Ipili social universe is fractured not by the classes of capitalism but by a division, reckoned for each clique, between friend and foe and calibrated sectorally in terms of mutual committedness, material interdependency, and social relatedness.

One other aspect of the Ipili nature regime will be important in this account, and that is the nature of leadership within it. Ipili leaders are "big men" (*akali andane*), achieving rather than inheriting their position of leadership by gathering around them a band of followers. They do so by deploying the key resources of the Ipili nature regime—pigs, land, women—as a "fund of power" (Sahlins 1963) that is used to attract satellites. Affinal clusters are constructed by big men, who lend garden land and house sites and who give women and who contribute to bridewealth to buy such women for the purpose of building up a faction (Biersack 1996b; see Sahlins 1963). Men compete for followers in pursuit of power and prestige. Similarly, men search for leaders and the resources, prestige, and security that leaders can afford. Ipili leaders were also fight leaders, guaranteeing the security of the neighbors they thus attracted— indeed, the security of the neighbor*hood*, that geography of mutual aid their faction building helps construct (see Lawrence 1984). The more substantial the following, the greater the leader's prowess in war, the more secure the group and its resource base. A "politics of nature" (see Robbins, this volume), an environmentalism, inheres in the Ipili political economy. Environmental events, at least those that can be blamed on named actors, will trigger political action, especially a demand for reparations lodged by local leaders in the name of the principle that all losses must be offset by compensatory gains. This principle informs bridewealth and also the "eye for an eye" politics of payback.

What, then, is the Ipili nature regime? Ipili nature (in Escobar's sense) is homo- or anthropocentric rather than ecocentric, placed on a human scale. Viewed cosmically, humanity and nature are two sides of the same coin: mutually implicated in a single, indivisible reality, the earth, the obverse of which is the extraecological (or supernatural) divine sky. By the same token, as in Escobar's organic nature regime, "nature and society are not separated ontologically" (ibid.:7). Rather, nature (like Polanyi's economy) is embedded in society—specifically, in the social relations of reproduction (see figure 1), in and through which the bounty of nature moves. This is the implication of the claim that Ipili social organization is the organization of sexual reproduction or the claim that Ipilis meet their material needs through sociomoral or social organizational means. In this nature regime, environmental dependents meet their needs through social interdependency under a doctrine of mutual aid and responsibility. It follows that human–nature articulations are located in the first instance within the sociomoral realm. Any natural event—the devastation of the environment, say—is also a sociomoral event and will be responded to as such. Because Ipili politics is, among other things, a politics of nature, environmental damage will galvanize political actors in search of the compensation that will set matters right and cement their position of leadership.

The impact of mining depends very much on the way in which mining and the capitalist nature regime it brings with it interact with this nature regime. The green war of the title signifies the conflict occasioned by this interaction, a conflict that can be reduced to neither regime but that must be understood in terms of their articulation within a politics of place that arises out of this articulation. I turn now to the history of mining in the Porgera valley, by way of setting the stage for discussing the present environmental crisis and the fault lines that have emerged with respect to it.

The Alluvial Miners of Porgera and Their Meteoric Rise

From Expatriate to Indigenous Mining

As a center of gold mining, Porgera has acquired a certain national and international prominence. The process began over sixty-five years ago, when two Australians, James Taylor and John Black, entered the area on their famous Hagen-Sepik patrol of 1938–39.[13] The purpose was broadly exploratory: to see parts of New Guinea's interior for the first time and to search for gold (Gammage 1998; Golub 2001:138–48; Jackson and Banks 2002:29). It was in the Porgera valley that Black at long last discovered gold colors "in the Kogai and Kaiya Rivers, in the vicinity of Mungalep" (Ward 1949:13; cf. Gammage 1998:188–89; Golub 2001:144–47; Jackson and Banks 2002:29–30) (see map 2).

There was no exploration or mining during the war years, but in 1947 Bulolo Gold Dredging was granted permission to enter Porgera, spurring rumors of gold (Smalley 1983:sect. 2, pp. 1–2). In March 1948, "several prospectors, on hearing exaggerated reports of the extent of the deposits of alluvial gold, started a minor gold rush" (Ward 1949:13). Jim Taylor, then district officer of the Central Highlands, issued a permit to one Joe Searson (ibid.:sect. 2, p. 2), and Searson and several others entered the area.[14] Results "were disappointing," however, and "most of the prospectors [although not Searson himself] left the area without even pegging claims" (Ward 1949:11; see also Wabag Patrol Report [henceforth, PR] 3, 1948/49). Bulolo Gold Dredging, meanwhile, "declared that there were no important deposits" and abandoned the area (Ward 1949:11). The police post that had been opened at Mungalep at the height of the gold rush in April 1949 was closed as interest fizzled (Wabag PR 6, 1948/49).

The number of expatriates operating in Porgera in the late 1940s and the 1950s was small—no more than seven or eight and rarely, if ever, that many at any one time (Laiagam PR 2, 1958/59). Searson mined "on the southern bank of the Kaiya River about a quarter of a mile west of its junction with Porgera River" (Ward 1949:12).[15] He employed about forty laborers and averaged two ounces of gold a day (Wabag PR 6, 1948/49:5).[16] As of 1959, Searson had left (at least for the time being), but the renowned Taylor, to whom Searson had transferred his claim, was then mining in Porgera (Laiagam PR 2, 1958/59). Porgera soils are notoriously poor, making it difficult to grow food to feed mining crews over the long haul (Wabag PR 3, 1948/49; Wabag PR 2, 1951/52; Simpson interview c. 1950). Taylor shifted the burden of recruiting and feeding laborers to his "tributers," who recruited, fed, and supervised workers, typically their own relatives, in return for 50 percent of the proceeds. Operating from Laiagam (see map 1), the subdistrict office, Taylor supplied the necessary equipment and paid rent on the claim.[17]

Beginning around 1956, two local men, Puluku Poke (referred to as Puruk or Puruku in the patrol reports) and Pawe (a.k.a. Pauwi, Pauwe; d. 2001 [see Golub 2001:211–15]), took it upon themselves to begin mining "in their own interests" (Laiagam PR 1, 1960/61) and "won quantities of gold" that they then sold at Laiagam (Laiagam PR 2, 1959/59).[18] In his short autobiography of 1995, Puluku tells how he started mining:

> I realised . . . that alluvial miners upstream of Kayia [a.k.a. Kaiya] and Pongema Rivers confluences [see map 2] handed all their produce to an Expatriate Prospector by the name of Jim Taylor in exchange for salt, axe, beads and other goods.
>
> I further noted that downstream of the above Rivers Confluence, J. Taylors lease did not extend further than that, so I mobilised my tribesmen and was already involved in alluvial mining.
>
> I advised my relatives from the Mayuni [a.k.a. Maiyuni] and Eno Clans and others that I will not give presents for gold but give them back money for their service. At that time people didn't knew [*sic*] what money was. (Poke 1995:items 9–11)[19]

Sent in May 1960 to investigate "the Native Mining situation," a patrol noted that Puluku's mining had become "a source of very obvious jealousy" (Laiagam PR 4, 1959/60:11). The patrol was "besieged by requests from intending or practicing miners for permission to wash for gold along the PORGERA," predominantly in the vicinity of Puluku's lease (ibid.).[20] Despite the fact that Puluku held a dredging and sluicing lease, six men had started mining on Puluku's lease (ibid.), claiming that "the land which they are mining belongs to them" and that they would "not accept Puruk's right to have sole access to the gold on his lease" (ibid.). The patrol officer was alarmed: "Considering the vehemence with which the deputations presented their views, I would not even be prepared to say that Puruk's life is not in danger" (ibid.). The "native mining situation" had become so unstable that it had "degenerated into a seething mess of intrigue in which there have been threats against the life" of Puluku (ibid.). Teetering "on the brink of outright inter-clan warfare" (Jackson and Banks 2002:35), the situation deteriorated, and Puluku was persuaded to subdivide his lease so that "all clans along the stretch of river in dispute [had] access to the new wealth" (Laiagam PR 1, 1960/61; see also Poke 1995:item 20; see also the account in Golub 2001:231–33).

Porgera was too remote, the overhead too great, the known mineral endowment too meager to sustain small-scale expatriate mining. The colonial administration soon concluded that the area would be "an ideal one for Native miners" instead (Laiagam PR 2, 1958/59), and by the close of the 1950s the administration had refocused its efforts upon the indigenous miners. Mining wardens from the Department of Lands, Surveys and Mines were brought in to offer instruction (Laiagam PR 2, 1960/61), and natural entrepreneurs such as Puluku were flown out of the valley to experience white technology and white enterprise firsthand (Robinson 1960:1–4). As Puluku wrote, "Due to the potential economic significance of the alluvial mining activity, . . . those listed for alluvial leases including myself went to Wabag, then flew to Wau. In Wau, we were trained how to mine alluvial gold using panning dishes and sluice boxes" (Poke 1995:items 21 and 22).

As the altercation between Puluku and those who insisted on sharing his lease with him suggests, interest in mining quickly gained momentum, and indigenous mining would no doubt have mushroomed even without colonial paternalism. As of 1960, an estimated 300 to 350 out of 420 able-bodied men living in the area were working alluvial gold claims, and Porgerans realized an annual income from mining of around seven thousand pounds (Laiagam PR 2, 1960/61). A report stemming from an October 1962 patrol stated that "almost the entire population of the male adults in the Porgera are actively engaged in the highly lucrative industry of gold mining" (Laiagam PR 1, 1962/63:2). Many miners had applied for a lease, and all "were assured of their Claims" (ibid.); the people were "so interested in alluvial mining" that they had foregone disputing (ibid.:1). By mid-May 1964, local miners possessed "bank books with sizeable amounts in them" (ibid.:6). Five years later earnings from alluvial gold mining "by local lease owners, tributors and labourers" was estimated at $35,000 per year (Porgera PR 1, 1969/70), and one Tongope (a.k.a. Tongovi, Tontovi), a *bos-boi* (boss boy) for Taylor, reportedly earned A$2,000 per annum working for Taylor (ibid.). An undated report probably written in the early 1970s estimates the annual income from indigenous alluvial mining to have averaged $10,000 per annum over the previous twenty years or so (Scott n.d.:1).

Alluvial mining continued to flourish in the 1970s, when multinational companies became more active in the area (see note 1), and indigenous entrepreneurs continued to work as either tributers or independent miners. In 1973, Mount Isa Mines Limited (MIM) took over Searson's alluvial leases (Handley 1987:145; Handley and Henry 1990:1717), and it conducted a modest sluicing operation along the Yakatabari Creek (map 2), one that yielded 180,000 grams of gold in the eleven years of its operation (Pacific Agribusiness 1987:vol. 1, p. 7). MIM's 316 tributers brought in an additional 240,000 grams of gold during that period (ibid.) From 1974 to 1981 MIM paid about $577,000 to its tributers (Warrillow 1981:5 [the figure is presumably reported in Australian dollars]; see also Dacol Plant Pty Ltd 1990). An impact study from 1987 prepared for PJV noted that alluvial mining by local villagers was "widespread" in the Alipis, Mungalep, and Yuyan areas, with spotty mining elsewhere (Pacific Agribusiness 1987, vol. 1:7) (see map 2).

Over the years, then, the number of local people engaged in alluvial mining swelled from a handful in the closing years of the 1950s to upward of eight or nine hundred in 1990 (Dacol Plant Pty Ltd 1990; Wangu 1990:1821).[21] Indeed, to this day, alluvial mining is said to be Porgera's "second garden" in the sense of its being a source of cash income (Poke 1995:item 29; see also Sullivan et al. 1992:4). The geographical source of gold may also be referred to as "the mother pig," suggesting, as the epithet second garden suggests, that gold has been assimilated to the world of resources that Ipilis for so long conjured— assimilated too, perhaps, to the sociomorality of the Ipili nature regime.

Alluvial Mining and the Politics of Place

While Puluku's brief autobiography (1995) emphasizes his struggles with expatriates, his more immediate problem was local. Authorized by the colonial government, Puluku's lease nevertheless nearly started a war because it violated the custom of the land. Puluku's opponents were "not prepared to respect" his lease rights because the lease "extended over land belonging to several clans," and Puluku "was winning gold from land that was not traditionally his" (Laiagam PR 1, 1960/61). Moreover, (along with Pawe) Puluku did not have "full customary rights over the land on which their [respective] leases were situated" (Jackson and Banks 2002:36). One patrol report even states that he was from "a local enemy clan" (Laiagam PR 1, 1960/61). Had Puluku been an expatriate, local custom would not have held sway. But in the eyes of Porgerans, the propriety of Puluku's mining was up to them, not the colonial administration, to decide. The emotions aroused were so intense that someone in the landowning line shot one of Puluku's workers with an arrow. As the report stated, "The situation was without doubt fast becoming explosive" (ibid.).

Similar tensions were reported by N. C. Robinson, a senior field assistant in the Division of Mines, Department of Lands, Surveys and Mines, in the Australian colonial administration. In his "Report of Extended Patrol in the Native Mining Area of the Porgera River Western Highlands," dated August to October 1960, Robinson indicated that there was competition among local miners for alluvial rights on the Yakatabari Creek. Robinson indicates that one "Mangabi" (a.k.a. Mangape) had begun mining in the area and that others ("Pauwi [a.k.a. Pauwe, Pawe], Tarin [?], and Egepa [a.k.a. Ekepa]") wished to mine there as well (Robinson 1960:4–5). Robinson speculated in his report on ways to avert future disputes caused by the jealousy inspired by alluvial mining (ibid.:6).

Gold was Porgera's second garden, an earthly resource attached to the estates of various lines and sublines, and a sectoral politics was already in play, lines competing with one another for access to the resource and threatening retaliation to any offender who violated sectoral rights. In these sectoral politics, altercations must be explained in terms of *intersecting* regimes, the one colonial and the other indigenous. By the one, Puluku was in the right. He had, as one patrol report put it, "a legitimate complaint [against those mining on his lease] under S.88 of the Mining Ordinance" (Laiagam PR 4, 1959/69:11). But, by the other, Puluku was woefully in the wrong (see also Robinson's sketchy but interesting ruminations on the relationship between local custom and colonial law [1960:4–6]). From the very beginning of gold mining in the Porgera valley, then, events were *conjuncturally* caused. There would be no gold mining without expatriates and their knowledge and greed, but the conflict engendered by gold mining in all its specificity stemmed from a clash between systems, the one local and the other emanating from outside.

The Fractures of Mining

Uneven Development

Always a mixed blessing, hard rock mining has made some people rich but left other people "relatively deprived" (Biersack 2001a:27–31; Filer 2001:14; Jacka 2001b, 2003; Jackson and Banks 2002:296–98; Nita 2001). In general, it has created invidious distinctions between the major and the minor beneficiaries of mining, on the one hand, and the victims of the mining, on the other. This section explores these sociopolitical fractures.

The benefits of mining are designed to have both general and targeted impacts (see Banks 1997a:chs. 8, 9, 1998:59–61, 1999a; Nita 2001:158–69). The people of the Porgera valley per se, for example, benefit from agreed-upon infrastructural improvements (the creation of new roads and the upgrading of existing ones, the new airstrip at Kairik [see map 2], the hospital, the school, etc.) (Derkeley 1989) and from employment and contractual opportunities created by the mine (see Imbun 2000, 2001). As of the end of 1996, PJV had spent K13 million "on various forms of community infrastructure in the Porgera valley" (Filer 1999:5), and "the PJV had also spent another K20 million on various forms of education and training, much of which was directed towards the population of the Porgera Valley" (ibid.). PJV also undertook infrastructural upgrades elsewhere in Enga Province. According to Nita (2001:160), between 1994 and 1997, PJV spent K33 million on transport and service infrastructure in Porgera as well as in other parts of Enga Province. Other benefits are restricted to those living on land that the mine, in one way or another, uses and for which the mine must therefore make reparations. Royalties and equity shares are earmarked for members of landowning lines and sublines only. In general, lines and sublines that have many hectares of land affected by mining are significantly better off than are lines and sublines with more meager mining-relevant holdings. Table 1 (adapted from Banks 1999b:172, table 5.4) indicates the variation in amount of land lost for mining purposes among the various SML lines and sublines, suggesting that gold mining creates inequalities among and even within SML lines. If, now, we consider the differences between SML locales and locales lying outside the SML, the inequalities are also pronounced. Table 2 (adapted from Banks 1999a:113, table 3.8) suggests the unevenness of development among the SML area (represented in the table by Apalaka), adjacent areas (Anawe, Mungalep), and more distant places such as Tipinini (see map 2), which receives only a modicum of compensation payments, if that, and does

BIERSACK TABLE 1. Differences in percentage of mining-impacted holdings among the various Special Mining Lease (SML) lines and sublines

Lines-sublines	Land Owned in SML	Land within SML Untouched by Mining	
	(Hectares)	(Hectares)	(Percent)
Tiyini-Waingolo	299.0	61.9	20.7
Tiyini-Yangua	186.0	37.0	19.9
Tiyini-Uape	269.0	145.5	54.1
Tiyini-Lakima	89.0	78.4	88.1
Tiyini-Kaimalo	32.0	11.0	34.4
Tiyini-Akira	21.0	21.0	100
Pulumaini-Paramba	56.0	38.0	67.9
Pulumaini-Ambo	257.0	157.3	61.2
Pulumaini-Epeya	21.0	0.0	0
Pulumaini-Yunga	22.0	22.0	100
Anga	2.0	2.0	100
Mamai-Andapo	9.0	9.0	100
Mamai-Kenja	54.0	28.0	51.9
Waiwa	54.0	32.9	60.9
Angalaini-Piko	40.0	35.1	87.8
Angalaini- Mapiandaka	103.0	60.3	58.5
Angalaini-Oyopene	67.0	67.0	100
Tuanda-Yapala	332.0	223.1	67.2
Tuanda-Ulupa	309.0	289.9	93.8
Pakeane-Ringime	6.0	6.0	100

Source: Banks 1999b:172, table 5.4. Data are based on PJV records and reflect the situation as of 1993 (there have been no substantive changes since then).

not receive royalties or equity dividends (see Jacka 2001b, 2003). Apalaka, on the other hand, has received substantial compensation and royalty payments. Meanwhile, Mungalep, which lies just outside the SML (see map 2), received as little compensation in 1992 as Tipinini did, and Mungalep's royalty receipts were negligible (see Biersack 1999b).

Although there are noteworthy discrepancies between the major and the minor beneficiaries of mining (see tables 1 and 2), these differences pale in comparison to the perceived dramatic gulf separating major and minor beneficiaries, on the one hand, from all those who suffer environmental degradation as a result of hard rock mining, on the other hand. This schism is marked geographically by the northern border of the Kaiya Lease for Mining Purposes (LMP) (see map 2), which separates those to the south, who patently benefit from hard rock mining, from those to the north, who not only fail to benefit

BIERSACK TABLE 2. Differences in mining-generated income within the Special Mining Lease (SML) area (compare Apalaka and Anawe) and between the SML and the rest of the Porgera Valley (for example, Mungalep and Tipinini)

	Apalaka	Anawe	Mungalep	Tipinini
Sample Size (Number of Households)	32	24	23	35
Royalties	K30,500	K6,400	K2,048	0
PJV Compensation	K167,500	K12,900	K3,300	K3,050

Source: Adapted from Banks 1999a:113, table 3.8, based on a household survey conducted in 1992.

from hard rock mining but also suffer from it. There are three kinds of environmental damage: "burial of gold-bearing alluvial deposits in the bed and lower banks of the Porgera River" (Sullivan et al. 1992:3; italics removed); the deposit of "waste rock from plant construction activities, and other rock debris" (ibid.), which, among other things, buried the alluvial deposits; and tailings discharge, which reddens the Porgera River. These impacts bridge the Porgera and the Paiela valleys, with the Yuyan-Politika-Bealo region (map 2) appearing to be something of a watershed in terms of the impacts of the tailings and sediment (ibid.:11). This entire region—the Lower Porgera, so-called (see note 6)—suffers from some loss of wildlife and gardens, and many are the allegations that the polluted river has caused illness and even death to a range of species, including human beings. Alluvial losses may not occur beyond the juncture of the Porgera and Silia (a.k.a. Tilia) rivers, although this is not entirely clear (see Newman 1995:6, item 5.1; see overview provided in Jackson and Banks 2002:ch. 17).

Indigenous Perceptions of Environmental Damage

What, then, are the local perceptions of today's environmental degradation? In reporting on local perceptions of the environmental damage, I rely on my own interviews as well as on an indispensable report prepared by a "technical advisory committee" (TAC) that was created in 1995 (see below) to investigate environmental damage along the Porgera River and make a recommendation as to how much compensation was required (TAC 1995).[22] I have also consulted a document presented to the TAC in the course of its investigations, the "Landowners' Submission" of 1995 (PRAMA 1995), which represents the sentiment of certain Lower Porgeran environmental activists.

Local perceptions are unmistakably informed by local cosmology, with its sky–earth axis and its perceptions of human beings as terrestrial, resource-dependent subjects, vulnerable, then, to environmental damage. The seasonal mix of wet and dry as well as the terrestrial combination of water (rivers, lakes, and springs) and dry land—these are understood as being crucial to sustaining human life. With the pollution of the river, a life-sustaining resource has become a life-destroying toxin. The alarm registered in local statements concerning environmental degradation reflects a perceived cosmic threat. The earth and its waterways are the material host for human life, and it is human life itself that is jeopardized.

In his appearance before the TAC, one Kuraro Kimbune expressed himself in a Christian idiom to indicate the material importance of the river and the losses its pollution caused:

> The Porgera River was created and given to us by the Almighty. We use the river for many purposes in our life—wash, drink, water for vegetable gardens etc. Both man and animals used the river water on a day to day basis. . . . we are very scared to use the water again. This is because the tailings from the mine makes [*sic*] the [water] too dirty to drink, the rocks get slippery and people get injured when trying to cross the river, food gardens spoilt and people died. (TAC 1995:25)

One Alungi Keko echoed these same concerns: "Water that sustained life is now polluted, people are affected. I am concerned for my future generation" (ibid.:15). A person who is deeply involved in the reparation effort told me in private conversation,

> We human beings live on water and ground. With this foundation we plant and eat sweet potatoes and vegetables. Having eaten these, we drink good, fresh water. And we wash downstream in the water. We do a great deal of work downstream. Before we drank the water and we cooked food in it. But now the water is contaminated, and we avoid it. The lives of 6,000 people [that is, the entire population of the Lower Porgera] is at stake. These lives are being destroyed. That's why we are fighting about the water and the ground.

A frequent complaint about the river is that it now threatens biodiversity. The river system supports a range of wildlife, but this wildlife has abandoned the area, died, or is now unfit for human consumption. A man I talked to at Yapatep (see map 2) pointed out that there are several important plants (*poke*, *yunangali*, *atipayumi*), snakes, eggs, nuts, wild pigs, and cassowaries that are no longer available at the river's edge because of the pollution. He added that the game that used to come to drink the water have run off because of the chemicals (*kemikal*) in the water. Another person living in the same area told me that the banks along the river, where people had gardened and hunted, had been abandoned for fear of the water and, he said, animals who had drunk the water had subsequently died. On 18 October 1995, at the second meeting of the TAC, Lower Porgeran environmental activists made their case for the extent of riverine damage:

> The Porgera River is the source of drinking water for both domestic and wild animals. Those who continue to drink the water notwithstanding its noxious taste and odour are sickened and their meat rendered unfit for human consumption. The majority of wild animals and birds, however, have left the vicinity because they are unable to drink the water, and local people complain that they are unable either to obtain wild game or catch fish in the river. (PRAMA 1995:13)

Three years before this investigation, many villagers claimed to be "genuinely afraid that this red water is harmful or poisonous," causing sickness in humans and animals alike (Sullivan et al. 1992:5),[23] and it is human as well as animal life that is believed to be at risk. A Porgeran who practices medicine in the Lower Porgera region speculated that the river's surface emitted a steam (he was speaking English) and that this steam could cause malaria.[24] The TAC report and the "Landholders' Submission" given to the TAC during its hearings catalogue many instances of river-related poisoning. For example, two people allegedly "died from eating poisoned animal" (TAC 1995:21); two women allegedly "died after washing in the river" (ibid.); a woman allegedly died after eating contaminated vegetables near the river (ibid.:25); a man allegedly slipped into the river and drowned (ibid.); a man allegedly died after eating food grown near the river (ibid.); a child allegedly drank the water and died (ibid.); a man allegedly died after eating food grown near the river (ibid.). A child also reportedly died in a flood that the rising riverbed, silted with the sediment of the mining operations, had caused, and some people were said to have died from drinking the water (ibid.:20). The medical doctor who attributed an increase in malaria to the Porgera River's steam told me that two women had entered the water and died immediately. He also mentioned a woman who had gone into the Porgera River when she was pregnant and who had then borne a deformed child. Another person told me that "you put your foot into the river and the foot becomes ashen [*pete pene*], and it's impossible to wash it clean. Further down river the water is red. Children get sick from the water, and adults may put their hands in it and then wash their hands, but they can't rinse off the filth." According to the "Landholders' Submission," "There are clear instances of persons suffering illness and death as a direct result of drinking river water" (PRAMA 1995:11), adding that "it is also clear that plants and animals have been harmed by the water pollution" (ibid.).

The redness of the river in particular inspires fear. In 1992, a team of consultants astutely observed that reaction to the pollution of the Porgera River depended largely on its color: "Villagers' or landowners' perceptions of the impact of the mine tailing on the river system are derived almost entirely from the visual impact of the tailing on the system. . . . The red water is considered to be dangerous, as is the red dust which derives from sprayed or windblown droplets of that water" (Sullivan et al. 1992:10–11). Redness evokes blood and in particular menstrual blood. In the local view, as long as menstrual blood remains contained or hidden, it is beneficial. Lying in the womb and bound by semen, menstrual blood is the seed of life. Hidden deep in the forest by women who perform magic over it, menstrual blood can bring health and wealth to husbands. Yet as an effluvium menstrual blood is a killer. In the past special precautions were taken to preclude a man's contact with a menstruating wife and her menstrual flow, and to this day having intercourse with a menstruating woman is considered lethal (see Biersack 1987, 1995b). Menstrual blood was deployed as a poison (*tome*)—dried menstrual blood introduced into a woodpile or someone's food was sure to kill—and some Porgerans have likened the red river to *tome* poison. But the pidgin words *kemikal* ("chemical") and *marasin* ("medicine") appear to have greater currency. Kopi Lapara, from Bealo in the northeast corner of the Paiela valley, for example, decried the impact of the tailings, speaking of the "red water, marasin nogut ["bad medicine"]—animals died, people died after drinking the water"—in his appearance before the TAC (TAC 1995:20). The polluting substance may also be referred to as "shit" (cf. Kirsch 1997:149). Thus, one person told me that "Placer [PJV, the mine] has eaten and shit [into the river], and that's why I'm dying."

Of all substances, putrefying flesh is arguably the most dangerous. Anyone who touches a corpse in the course of mourning or burying it receives a special payment to compensate for the contamination. In 1994, there was an explosion at the mine that claimed the lives of roughly an equal number of nationals and expatriates. The bodies of the deceased were blown to smithereens, a feature of the event that many have mentioned to me. This event continues to haunt those living close to the mine, who imagine that these same bodies disintegrated and fell to earth, where they entered the water supply and garden land. Drinking the water out of the rain tanks in the vicinity of the mine is thus tantamount to imbibing putrefied flesh, and any crops grown in the area would be contaminated as well from the soil (see Banks 1997a:196–99; Putu 1999:8).

The discharge of waste products derived from open pit mining operations has been massive—"far greater than the system has been able to carry, and hence there has been a substantial deposition of sediment in the Lower Porgera river, to a depth of around 1.5m by late 1992" (Banks 1997a:199)—and the buildup only continues (see Jackson and Banks 2002:2). I have heard these waste materials referred to as "garbage" (*kangalamo* in the vernacular; *pipia* in Tok Pisin, an English-based pidgin). A person living in the Paiela valley told me that the company had "cooked" the gold and then dumped the refuse into the river, making the river "garbage laden" (*kangalamo pene, pipia atene*). These idioms suggest food preparation, consumption, and perhaps defecation (*shit* is a recurring metaphor in this discourse). In any case, this person went on to observe, "That's why the water stinks" (cf. Kirsch 1996:663–64). "There has been a significant increase in the incidence of flooding in the Lower Porgera Valley" (Ipara 1994:11). At one point the bridge across the Kaiya River that linked Mungalep with Yuyan (see map 2) and the Upper with the Lower Porgera was washed out (PRAMA 1995:10), and several people were alleged to have drowned. The sediment has also destroyed the vegetation along the shores of the river. According to Kopi Lapara from Bealo (see map 2), "Sediment from the Porgera mine broke gardens, trees, landslide spoil vegetation etc" (TAC 1995:20).

For the alluvial miners of the Lower Porgera, of course, the most devastating impact has been the loss of alluvial gold. The sediment has spilled onto the banks, precluding colluvial mining, and it has buried alluvial deposits, bringing Porgera's alluvial mining industry to a halt. With expanded hard rock mining operations and loss of access to alluvial gold, the Lower Porgera region has been plunged into a recession. Indeed, as early as 1992, Sullivan and her co-consultants reported, "Recent closure of the three tradestores which operated in Yuyan [see map 2] prior to the Porgera mine construction is blamed by villagers on the local lack of income, as the readily available alluvial gold source has been buried" (Sullivan et al. 1992:4).

Lower Porgerans refer to alluvial gold as their "second garden." Gold is not just any garden, but *the* enabling garden, *the* resource when it comes to participating in the new, monied economy and the arenas of prestige it has opened up. "Since 1948 gold has been mined continuously in the area in small amounts by traditional landowners, and sold for cash. . . . The money obtained from the sale of gold was used to pay school fees, and to buy tradestore goods, cars and other items" (Sullivan et al. 1992:4). As Kewando, a resident of Politika (see map 2), put it when we talked, "Before we all got money by mining, and we ate the money. Now, with this red water, we are afraid of it. . . . Some still want the money from the alluvial gold, and they continue to mine. But people fall ill from mining, and we also watch the game die." In the TAC hearings, many speakers "went into details of how the Lower Porgera people depended on alluvial gold as their only source of cash income. . . . Porgera's climate was not good for cash crops like coffee or cardamon" (TAC 1995:3), and Porgerans depended upon its mineral wealth instead.

Idioms identifying gold mining as a "second garden," "mother pig," as a food that is "eaten" assimilate gold mining to horticulture and the terrestrial resource base that hosts human life (Biersack 1999a), and, in keeping with this assimilation, Lower Porgerans now mourn the *death* of their beloved gold. In his testimony before the TAC, Pawe Lembopa, who was among the very first Porgerans to hold a mining lease in the Porgera valley, bemoaned the fact that the sediment had "covered" the alluvial gold, rendering further alluvial mining impossible. "Our alluvial gold is dead" (TAC 1995:25), he said. Despite PJV's assurances to the contrary, this death is considered irreversible by those most affected by it. "Buried men will not be raised. In the same way our alluvial gold that is being buried by PJV will never be mined again," Malingi Ekepa pointed out (ibid.:7). "My children will be poor while Placer's children"—that is, Porgerans benefiting from the mining of alluvial gold and in particular the SML landowners—"will be rich" (ibid.). A Lower Porgeran from Paiela spoke in similar metaphors: "We believe that our Alluvial Gold is dead and can not be dug up again (like a dead person)" (ibid.:21).

The Green War

The environmental degradation caused by hard rock mining must be understood within the wider context of the differential impacts of mining, which pit the interests of the mine as well as those of its principal beneficiaries (see tables 1 and 2, above) against the interests of those who live downstream and who do not benefit appreciably from the mining. This tension must, in turn, be understood against the backdrop of the Ipili nature regime, in which friends and benefactors are distinguished from enemies and malefactors on the basis of who materially benefits and who materially harms whom. Affinal clusters configure not only the social relations of reproduction but, ideally, a geography of mutual aid. Kith and kin should aid and protect one another. This ideal is not always realized, and relatives-turned-enemies will be dismissed as "bad" (*ko*) relatives. Beyond these circles of amity and fertility lie unrelated people, those who are potentially, even actually, enemies. This section chronicles and interprets the Ipili green war in all its complexity, with respect to local–global articulations and conjunctures. Since the State of Papua New Guinea awards mining licenses and is also part owner of PJV, the state is inevitably implicated in these dynamics.

The Porgera River Alluvial Miners Association (PRAMA)

The original agreements (Derkeley 1989) to which the SML landowners, the Enga Provincial Government, the national government, and, at least implicitly, PJV were party made no allowance for environmental compensations in the Lower Porgera. The impact of hard rock mining upon alluvial mining became clear early on, and people downstream from the SML began organizing. A letter that Puluku Poke, one of the original indigenous mining leaseholders in the Porgera valley, along with one Aiyo Anginape, wrote to PJV in 1989 inquiring into the impact of hard rock mining upon the environment appears to have served as a catalyst for action;[25] PJV encouraged the formation of a committee to negotiate the terms of a settlement for environmental damage. A twenty-four-member committee, one member for each of the affected Lower Porgera sublines, was formed under the leadership of Kurubu Ipara and Jonathan Paraia (Ipara 1995; Poke 1995 : item 35). PJV's opening offer was meager. Its final offer, although more generous—K650,000 up front "for the loss of access to the alluvial deposits in the Lower Porgera between the Pongema/Kaiya junction and the Tilia [a.k.a. Silia] junction, a figure which with interest backdated to 1989 came to almost K1 million" (Banks 1997a:203)—remains unacceptable to some Lower Porgerans. This figure, together with the sums agreed upon in compensation for the tailings and waste discharges, comes to about K10 million over the course of the life of the mine. To reach this figure, PJV swept aside the original demands of the landowners. Lower Porgeran landowners initially requested K24 million, K1 million for each affected subline (lowered over time, first to K12 million, then to K4–6 million, and ultimately to K3 million [ibid.:202]). Later they demanded 1 percent of the gross revenue of the mine annually (see discussion of PJV and the state's response in ibid:201–2), a demand that, if met, would have realized an annual revenue of K3 to K4 million for the landowners. PJV's final offer was made in October 1993, and some landowners in the original negotiating committee signed a Heads of Agreement accepting the K10 million package. At the time of the TAC hearings in late 1995, many, if not all, of these stood by this agreement: "They [the negotiators for the landowners] have fought long and hard for six (6) years, to come to this agreement" (TAC 1995:4), and they stood by it "as a matter of business principle" (ibid.; see also ibid.:5).

They did so in the face of an effort mounted by those who perhaps had a greater stake in the alluvial gold and who, in any case, refused to accept PJV's final offer. Puluku Poke was among these. Indeed, he spoke with disdain of the proposed settlement when he addressed the TAC in 1995: "It was small money and if I took it, future generations will complain later" (TAC 1995:7). At the time, Puluku, beginning to show his years, joined forces with a "younger faction" (Newman 1995:4) that held out for a higher sum and that in 1994 coalesced as the Porgera River Alluvial Miners Association. PRAMA's core figure was Opis Papo, a University of Papua New Guinea student with an undergraduate degree in geology (acquired on a PJV scholarship [Banks 1997a:205]), who had conducted one of the studies of alluvial losses (Papo 1992) (see Newman 1995:2–4 for a summary of the various competing assessments and Jackson and Banks 2002:ch. 17 for a discussion of the various estimates). Although Opis was clearly a young man, PRAMA attracted the likes of Puluku himself, along with Pawe Lempoba, as well as Pawe's older and younger sons, Yaliman and John Pawe. PRAMA was formally organized on 16 February 1995, and in the next month it demanded that PJV compensate the alluvial miners K3 million per year (near the annual sum fixed by Opis Papo in his 1992 report) and pay them a total of K12 million for previous years when no compensation was made, beginning immediately (Newman 1995:7).

The gulf between PRAMA and PJV proved to be unbridgeable. Under Papua New Guinea's Water Resources Act of 1982, if landowners and project developers fail to negotiate a compensation package, the minister for environment and conservation may be asked to make a "ministerial determination" (TAC 1995:2). At an impasse with PJV, PRAMA requested such a determination, and Paul Mambei, then-minister for environment and conservation, asked the Water Resources Board to investigate the compensation issue. To undertake this investigation, the Water Resources Board formed the TAC, whose report has already been extensively cited. In January 1996, Mambei made a determination that settled on a compensation package of an estimated K15.2 million over the life of the mine (PC 5/10/96/4).[26]

PJV promptly filed an appeal in the National Court that sought to quash the determination on the grounds that the previous sum had already been agreed to, that PRAMA was not representative of Lower Porgerans, and that the determination "was in excess of the defendant's [the minister for the environment and conservation's] powers under the Water Resources Act" (PC 5/10/96/4). PRAMA, meanwhile, staged a protest march at the Porgera mine site and unsuccessfully sought to deliver a petition to the mine's manager that denounced PJV for its appeal, which, as PRAMA put it, promised to "continue to inflict unwarranted destruction and suffering on innocent people" (PC 5/16/96/13).

A Janus-Faced Rage

So dominant in the early era of indigenous alluvial mining, Puluku Poke has proved to be a vigorous environmental activist in recent years. In 1989, he coauthored the letter to PJV that served as a catalyst for setting up a Lower Porgera negotiating committee. According to his testimony before the TAC, he also urged the formation of PRAMA, or something like it, and it was he who encouraged PRAMA to request a ministerial determination when negotiations between PRAMA and PJV came to a standstill (TAC 1995:7).

In 1995, Puluku shared his thoughts with me on the environmental issue. Mincing no words, he accused PJV of eating "the sweet potato"—the yield of Porgera's "second garden," alluvial mining—and of "defecating and discarding shit." In Puluku's metaphoric language (kokoli), he imagined the company in corporeal terms, with a mouth and an anus. The company "eats" the gold "in front," and it is what is "in front" that the company "thinks about" (nembo ta)—meaning "to attend to," "to safeguard and monitor," "to manage," "to assume responsibility for." But it "discards" the shit "in back," where it assumes no such responsibility. Puluku continued: having erected a wire fence, Placer had put "outside," it had rendered "independent," those very lives it risked: the lives of the Lower Porgerans.

O'Connor (1998) has argued, as noted, that capitalism's "second contradiction" lies in its destruction of the very resources from which its profits stem. Puluku's observations are consistent with O'Connor's, but they refer specifically to Lower Porgerans' resource base—to alluvial gold in particular. Puluku here constructs PJV as a consumer-destroyer of the very resource upon which human existence materially depends: the sweet potato, a metaphor for the alluvial gold of the Lower Porgera. In this, PJV becomes a parasite and thus an enemy, eroding the Lower Porgeran resource base. PJV assumes responsibility "in front," where its hosts, the SML landowners (see map 2), reside, but it defiles those who are "outside," "in back," where PJV is not so beholden and where its policies need not be benign and "green." Instead of sharing what it eats with Lower Porgerans, PJV dumps on Lower Porgerans its noxious, defiling waste products. The eater (PJV) gains, but only at the expense of others, whom PJV destroys. Puluku used these same metaphors in explaining the strategy of the environmentalists, which is to deny PJV its license to mine and with it its liberty to consume and dispose. "The company eats the sweet potato, but we hold it by its neck and keep it from defecating," he said. "'Along what road can I discard this shit?', the company wonders." Puluku's imagery is again telling: the imagery of hand-to-hand (or hand-to-throat) combat. Excluding Lower Porgerans, PJV becomes the enemy of Lower Porgerans. Puluku's simple front-back corporeal scheme—PJV looking out at its own front yard while it craps in its backyard—locates PJV, within Porgeran sectoral politics, "outside," with the other enemies.

For many, the "Porgera Agreements" (Derkeley 1989), which established the conditions under which hard rock mining would proceed, initiated a period of inequality between upstream and downstream Porgerans. These agreements were hammered out in a "forum" process (Banks 1997a:117–22; Filer 1990:97–105; Jackson and Banks 2002:ch. 10) that failed to include Lower Porgera representation, and this exclusion has become a key issue for many Lower Porgerans. Puluku alluded to the exclusion when he addressed the TAC: "PJV started mining . . . in 1989. Signed SML agreement with the SML landowners but it did not notify me on the effects of their operation at the headwaters of the Porgera River" (TAC 1995:7). Yaliman Pawe—an important PRAMA leader and son of Pawe Lembopa, he, along with Puluku, was one of the first Porgerans to be issued a mining lease—summarized the complaint in these terms at one of the TAC hearings: "The 6,000 people of lower Porgera have not had a say or any other part in the SML agreement. There was no agreement—government haven't asked company about the people of lower Porgera. . . . Yet we the Lower Porgera people are the most affected. We have not received any major benefits from the Porgera Gold Mining Project" (TAC 1995:27).

The finger is pointed at PJV in these statements. Yet I have heard others complain about the failure of SML landowners to anticipate the damage to the

Lower Porgera. Ipili is spoken in both the Paiela and the Porgera valleys, and one Paiela man ranted against Tiyinis, a line that has benefited greatly from the hard rock mining (see table 1) because he fervently believed it was the responsibility of the Porgera Tiyinis to alert PJV to the vulnerability of Paiela Tiyinis—and, more generally, of Paielas—to hard rock mining. (Piawe and Bealo [map 2] are considered to be in the Paiela valley, yet they are also reckoned within the Lower Porgera [note 6].) In language reminiscent of Puluku's, he said that Porgera-based Tiyinis have "turned their backs" on Paielas. They told the company (*kampani*) that there were no humans in Paiela that could be affected by the pollution. But they lied. Perhaps a Tiyini or a company man would be killed over this, he speculated. Then he added, rather surprisingly,

> We are not angry with the company—the company is sympathetic [*ondo pene*, a term that is used of all relatives and that suggests David Schneider's "diffuse, enduring solidarity" (1980) or Meyer Fortes's "kinship amity" (1970)]. No, we are angry with Porgerans. They knew full well that Paielas would suffer from the pollution, yet they never informed the company that Paielas were living in the path of the pollution. Those who are in between the two valleys [in the sense of being related to lines in both valleys and thus having relatives in both valleys] know better, yet they lie about the danger to us.

I have heard similar accusations from people living in the Yapatep/Pitika/Politika area (see map 2). One man from this area told me he was angry at both PJV and the SML landowners who had advised the company. He said that the SML landowners had told the company that Lower Porgeran people were "outside men" (*kakita akali*) while the SML landowners were "inside" people—entitled, then, to consideration.

In my conversation with Puluku, the good and bad guys were clearly demarcated along stranger/native, white/black lines. But in the many discussions I have had about mining and pollution with other Lower Porgerans, as well as with those living outside the Lower Porgera region, the word *kampani* ("company") has sometimes been used in a more inclusive sense to signify everyone who has an entrepreneurial stake in hard rock mining, including the SML landowners. Thus, the Paiela man who ranted against Porgera-based Tiyinis referred to all PJV employees and officials, black and white, *as well as to the major beneficiaries of the mining*, as *kampani*, a term, as he used it, of grave opprobrium. Leaders of the main association of SML landowners, the Porgera Landowners Association (PLA or PLOA), were singled out as particularly villainous.

As indicated earlier, exogamous, replicated marriages organize Ipili society into sprawling yet lumpy networks, networks that span districts and even valleys (see figure 1). Such networks comprise interlocking circles of amity and fertility in which the principle of mutual assistance is ideally upheld and assets (pigs, land, women) are shared and secured. If the codifications of mining promote uneven development, Ipili morality dictates sharing and leveling. If mining itself differentially ravages the environment, creating the distinction between an ecologically damaged Lower Porgera and a relatively ecologically intact sml area, mining has polarized upstreamers and downstreamers in social and not just in economic or environmental terms. Upstreamers and downstreamers have become situational enemies, in short. That economic and environmental inequalities have come together is one of the great cruelties of Porgera mining, for it means that tensions have emerged between rich and poor as well as between those whom Lower Porgerans perceive to be relatively environmentally endowed (the sml landowners) and the Lower Porgerans themselves, who are, after all, the relatives of these. The man who denounced the sml landowners for betraying the Lower Porgerans as "outside people" was related to some of the very sml landowners he attacked, making his sense of betrayal all the more acute. He argued that these landowners knew full well the dangers that hard rock mining would present for Lower Porgeran kith and kin. Relatives should take care of one another, "think about" and look after one another's interests, "helping" rather than harming one another; they should treat each other as "insiders" one and all. But—like pjv, which eats "in front" and defecates "behind," where the Lower Porgerans are—these relatives "give their backs" to their kith and kin in the Lower Porgera, visiting upon them the scourge of inadequately regulated mining.

Others, too, have pointed the finger of blame at Upper Porgerans. A Yapatep man began his conversation with me in fall 2000 by denouncing pjv as the enemy. But he soon added that white people were "good" but "outside political men"—men from Laiagam and Hagen, towns to the east—as well as those sml landowners who were growing so rich from the hard rock mining that they could afford many wives and could go to town to spend money on hotels, beer, and prostitutes were the real problem. "The sml landowners get good things, and they throw the stench and shit [that metaphor again!] toward us. These people are greedy, and they only think of themselves and their immediate pleasures, their prostitutes and their beer." He added that it was especially unfair that the sml landowners benefited at the expense of the Lower Porgerans because it was the downstreamers and not the upstreamers who had built the Porgera leg of the Highlands Highway (which terminates in Porgera), and it was the downstreamers and not upstreamers who had built the Porgera airstrip in the 1960s. Those who worked for change in another era are now victimized by it, while those who remained passive in the previous generation now unaccountably reap the harvest of change!

Adding insult to injury is the fact that SML relatives reportedly do not share the proceeds of mining with Lower Porgerans. A prominent PRAMA leader told me, with considerable bitterness, that the members of the seven SML lines (see table 1) are "our enemies." They are "our enemies," he said, because they keep the equity and the royalties for themselves, yet they are negligent in terms of the environment. "That's why when *we* get money, we do not share it with *them*!" The exclusions are systematic when it comes to Paielas, who, by virtue of their residence in the western Ipili-speaking valley (see map 1), are considered ineligible for any of mining's compensations, even if they happen to be Tiyinis, Tuandas, Pulumainis, and so forth, members of the principal landowning lines (see table 1). The elderly Paiela man who had berated Tiyinis, among the greatest beneficiaries of mining, confided, "Everyone is angry with Tiyini and Palata [Placer, the managing company of PJV] because Tiyini does not share its compensation [with Paiela-based Tiyinis], yet everyone suffers from the pollution of the river."

Wherever Lower Porgerans and upstreamers are bonded through descent and affinity (see figure 1), the ethic of resource sharing within a sociomorally benign ecology of life also obtains (see figure 2), and the pollution of the Lower Porgera by relatives living within the SML will inspire moral outrage. Gaining at the expense of Lower Porgerans, the SML landowners have become, transactionally speaking, the enemies of Lower Porgerans. Although PJV also merits this epithet, the animus is reserved for the SML landowners. Where these links are lacking, upstreamer and downstreamer Porgerans confront each other as enemies pure and simple. In either case, the pollution of the lower Porgera River becomes a chapter in the history of the Ipili nature regime, as this nature regime engages with another nature regime, one that remains indifferent to Ipili sociomorality.

Political Has-Beens?

This is a historical, not just an ethnographic account, and the heart of the cruelty of hard rock mining lies in the fact that it follows upon the heels of an era that glamorized and favored Lower Porgerans. The asymmetries of mining so evident today must be read against the backdrop of the entire history of mining in the Porgera valley, a history that has witnessed a critical shift from alluvial to hard rock mining and from downstream to upstream wealth and prestige. The alluvial miners of the past were the first entrepreneurs of Porgera. They were certainly among the first to learn some pidgin, wear clothing, eat rice and tin fish, use pans and sluice boxes, and make and spend money. In 1960, several of them, Puluku Poke included, were transported to Bulolo and Wau in eastern New Guinea to observe the gold operations there, and Taylor's tributers made regular trips to Laiagam (see map 1) to exchange gold for his payment. In addition to being one of the first indigenous miners to hold a lease, Puluku served as an aid post orderly (APO), or doctor, in Wabag (Poke 1995:item 4), became an interpreter at Laiagam Patrol Post (ibid.:item 5; see also note 17 below), was appointed *luluai* (designated leader at a "census point" that the Australian colonial government demarcated), and in 1975, the year that Papua New Guinea achieved independence from Australia, became the first president of the Porgera Local Government Council and was named an interim minister in the Enga Provincial Government (ibid.:item 33). The names of Puluku Poke, Pawe Lembopa (d. 2001 [Golub 2001:213), Tongope (d. 2003), Mangape (d. 1971 [Golub 2001:258–60]) (in the person of Nixon Mangape, former head of the PLA; Nixon has also served on the Landowner Negotiating Committee [LNC] and the Community Issues Committee [CIC] [Banks, e-mail message to Biersack, 5 May 2004]), and Ekepa (d. 1998) (in the person of Tonny Ekepa [a.k.a. Mark Ekepa], president of the PLA) still have considerable salience in the Porgera valley.

As noted, the word *kampani* is sometimes used inclusively to signify those who have strong associations with the gold mine, the SML landowners included, and not just the mine itself. In this, *kampani* sometimes contrasts with *kanaka*. *Kanaka* is a pidgin term that in the colonial era was a pejorative signifier for indigenous peoples. The term is used today by whites and blacks alike to refer to old-timers and rustics, those whom history has rendered obsolete—in the Porgera context, those who are not associated with hard rock mining and its amenities. *Kanaka* means lacking in sophistication and bereft of "good things," desirable worldly goods. In short, *kanaka* suggests someone who, from a developmental perspective, lacks prestige. The rift between *kanaka* or "native in the pejorative sense" and newer-style big men—leaders who are able to communicate and transact with expatriates—began in the 1950s as men such as Puluku emerged as dominant interstitial figures, capable of applying for mining leases, recruiting relatives and others as their own labor force, and finding gold buyers. Puluku in his prime was no *kanaka*; he was a *save* ("knowledgeable"), modern (or, in New Guinea idioms, "new" [*wene* in the vernacular, *nupela* in Tok Pisin]), capable man (see Kulick 1992:ch. 4)—one, moreover, who was astonishingly wealthy by local standards. In an era of hard rock mining—when coastal-quality pidgin, some command of English, and literacy are the hallmarks of capability and when truly wealthy men have Toyotas and expatriate-style houses and travel all over the country, even outside PNG—the alluvial miners of Porgera no longer cut the figure they once did. Moreover, since the type of gold that wealthy overseas companies as well as the State of Papua New Guinea and the officials of Enga Province are interested in is no longer alluvial, the alluvial miners of Porgera have been utterly eclipsed by upstream Porgerans in the interracial "politics of recognition" (Robbins, this volume) they once dominated.

In addition to all the other felt relative deprivations, therefore, Lower Porgerans suffer a loss of power and prestige. Two prominent Porgeran environmental activists, both second-generation alluvial miners, told me that, in the heyday of alluvial mining, the upstream lines had "stayed under," in the sense of being less prominent and less important than, the downstream lines. "Before Hageners, Wabagers, and white men came to us [Lower Porgerans], showering us with money in exchange for our gold. Now everyone flocks to the SML and not to our place." These activists told me they had been encouraged to accept an early PJV offer of compensation for alluvial losses—about half the amount that PJV ultimately settled upon—because the Lower Porgera was marginal in today's mining. They were told that the Lower Porgerans may have a river but they had no mountain—here the reference was to Mount Waruwari (a.k.a. Watokati), the principal source of ore—and were thus "rubbish" (*pipia*)—that is, of no value—in comparison to SML leaders. They were also told that at the feast (of benefits and income) that mining would provide, they would eat as dogs, feeding on the bones rather than the flesh of the pig.

The word *kanaka* also bears something of the burden of the word *bush* (*bus* in Tok Pisin, *siapu* in the vernacular): untamed, unrefined, wild or savage. A Lower Porgeran living at Yapatep told me, "We [Lower Porgeran people] are outside" (*nanima kakita akali*) while the SML landowners are "inside." They are "town men" (*tauni akali*) while we are "bush men" (*siapusia akali*)—that is, *kanaka*. "They disparage us this way, and that makes us angry. Before, when we were able to mine gold, we had money and were able to set up stores and buy cars. Now we can't do this any more; we are *tipiya* ["weak," "rubbish"] whereas the 'town men' are *amango* ["rich"]." Indeed, he said, his kinspeople and affines within the SML looked down on him. Puluku also complained bitterly about his loss of status: "Before I was rich (*amango*). I ate many small pigs. But you [PJV] have killed the pig now [that is, the "mother pig," a metaphor in this context for alluvial gold], and I am weakened. . . . You killed the mother pig and I'm weakened, I tell you. . . . You will diminish my grandchildren as well."

In another era, one that lasted almost forty years, alluvial mining was Porgera's pride and glory. Now, all the glory belongs to the hard rock miners, and the alluvial miners of Porgera "have lost a degree of the centrality that they enjoyed in the pre-mine Porgeran political situation that their proximity to the alluvials of the Kaiya endowed them with" (Banks 1999c:209; see also Banks 1997a:206; Jackson and Banks 2002:252). If nothing else, the Lower Porgera environmental movement establishes an arena in which the alluvial miners can try to step out of the shadow that PJV and the SML landowners now cast and into a spotlight of their own making. Indeed, mining politics continues to be the political arena of choice in the competition for prestige. The winners of the Lagaip-Porgera parliamentary seat in the 1990s campaigned on mining-related platforms. Anton Pakena, the oldest son of the famous Paiela leader Luke Botane, né Pakena (d. 2001), achieved prominence through his opposition to Conzinc Riotinto of Australia, the then-developer of the Mount Kare gold mine just south of the Paiela valley. Opis Papo, who defeated Pakena in 1997, garnered his support, principally in the Porgera valley, as the founding president of PRAMA.

The Politics of Place along the Porgera River

In testimony given before the TAC in October 1995, someone who is prominent in the PLA, the organization that represents the SML landowners, stated that "the amount of compensation paid to PRAMA must not offset the profitability of the Porgera Project. SML Land Owners does [*sic*] not want the Porgera Project to come to a close *just because of a compensation claim by one interest group*" (TAC 1995:10; emphasis added). The aim of the SML landowners, as stipulated in the TAC report of 1995, is to satisfy all interested parties:

> The SML landowners stated, through their representatives, that they are the most affected by the Porgera Project. . . .

They do not want the operation of the Porgera Project to be affected or stopped as a result of the claims put forward by the Lower Porgera River people (PRAMA). SML landowners agree that the Lower Porgera people are affected *but the Porgera Mine must be allowed to operate profitably*. The concerns, by PRAMA, should be solved amicably by the Government so that all parties concerned including PRAMA, SML Landowners, the National Government and the Share-holders of the Porgera Joint Venture [a category that includes the SML landowners], can be satisfied at the end of the day. (TAC 1995:4; emphasis added)

Of course, Lower Porgerans understand full well the position and positioning of the SML landowners. A petition that Lower Porgerans circulated in the context of a march made on Porgera Station on 15 December 1994 stated, "Now we hear that Porgera Joint Venture is trying to expand the mine at the cost of K90 million beginning January 1995. This is a good news for the National Government, the joint venture partners, the Enga Provincial Government *and the* SML *landowners*. Because a bigger operations [*sic*] means more returns for the above parties. But to us the people of Lower Porgera River we will suffer 100 times more than what we suffered for the last four years" (N.A. 1994). In 2003, it was the inequities in development that the new leadership of PRAMA emphasized in conversation with me. "The government and PJV have thrown a lot of 'shit' into our river," one person commented to me, "but PJV has yet to give one business [*bisnis* in Tok Pisin] company to the Lower Porgera. The SML gets development, but not us."

These texts and statements reflect a key aspect of the present situation along the Porgera River: that upstreamers and downstreamers enjoy differential positioning within a capitalist mode of production. But upstreamers and downstreamers confront each other—in some, no doubt many, cases—as relatives and, in any case, as inhabitants of a sociomoral order in which friends and enemies are sorted in terms of the material consequences of their actions. Those who help are ipso facto friends; those who harm are ipso facto enemies. The thorn in the side of at least some Lower Porgerans is not only that the SML landowners are richer, not only that they seem to profit at the expense of the Lower Porgerans, but, and especially, that they are *bad relatives*! Relatives *should* help rather than harm; they *should* share resources rather than privatizing them; they *should* look after one another's material interests. The codifications of mining exclude rather than include, and they do so only on the sufferance of those who are morally obligated to include rather than exclude: the SML landowners. Where downstreamers and upstreamers are not consanguineally or affinally linked, the environmental issue defines them as enemies pure and simple. The Janus-faced rage Porgerans experience today reflects the duality of the SML boundary (see map 2), which functions with respect to both a capitalist *and* an indigenous nature regime.

In 1999, a leader associated with PRAMA said to me as we conversed in his home, "If a pot of food were put down on the floor there, we should all eat from it; yet the food [that is, the proceeds of mining] is not being shared." In a feast, kith and kin gather to share the fruits of the earth, paradigmatically participating in a sociomoral "ecology of life." But Upper Porgerans have "turned their backs" on Lower Porgeran relatives, a manner of speaking that suggests shunning and an abdication of responsibility. Having turned their backs, they have "shat" upon downstreamers, defiling them with the refuse of a feast to which downstreamers were not invited. This recurring image of being shit upon is the obverse of the feast image: cofeasters participate in the same ecology of life, premised as it is on mutual support and the sharing of resources. Those who are covered by the resulting excrement are ipso facto positioned outside that ecology. This Ipili ecology of life is sectoral, a matter of determining who does and who does not participate in the same social relations of reproduction (see figure 1), with its geography of mutual aid (see figure 2). Today, however, relatives are on opposite sides of the SML fence, creating a tension between morality and the "security circle" interests that Ipili social organization creates, on the one hand, and the pecuniary interests that hard rock mining has engendered, on the other—a tension, that is, between an ecology that is embedded in society and an ecology that operates independently of sociomoral considerations. The brother of the man who used the feast image simply dismissed the upstreamers as "our enemies" because they kept the mine equity and the royalties to themselves, failing to share them with their relatives. Tit for tat: "That's why when *we* get money, we do not share it with *them*!"

Today's fractures emerge in a transnational space in which contrasting nature regimes intersect, the volatility of the situation stemming from the fact that political-economic disgruntlements feed, and are fed by, animosities that are *also* culturally inflamed. The real location of the tensions associated with hard rock mining, I would submit, is the complex, conjunctural field that mining creates. On the one hand, local mores foster the reproduction and maintenance of species life within circles of amity and fertility. On the other hand, environmental damage is a by-product of capitalist-cum-state penetration, globalization, and development and the predictable ravages thereof (O'Connor 1998).

Capitalism's bottom line is neither society nor environment but profits.[27] As has been argued (Merchant 1980, among others), capitalism systematically sacrifices the one to the other—all the more so in distant lands, where capitalism's "domination of nature" (ibid.) becomes racialized (Harvey 1996; O'Connor 1998; Smith 1984). Fractures, alliances, and tensions within this field must be understood with respect to the entire history of it, beginning with the discovery of gold at Porgera by white explorers, continuing through the period, first, of expatriate mining and then of indigenous mining, and culminating today in the eclipse of the alluvial heroes of the past by relatives and others whose quest for power and prestige depends upon the arenas of competition that hard rock (rather than alluvial) mining has opened up.

The *kampani/kanaka* contrast encapsulates the complexity of causation in play. *Kampani/kanaka* opposes amoral or immoral capitalists to moral local people, but it also opposes those responsible for the environmental devastation, some of whom are Ipili speakers, to those who suffer from it, all of whom are local. It implies as well the kind of civilized/backward axis that motivated the assumption of "the white man's burden" in this part of the world to begin with and that today also informs rifts among Porgerans, rifts between downstreamers and the upstreamers who look down upon them. The *kampani/kanaka* binary is unstable and context-sensitive, sometimes functioning racially but sometimes differentiating Porgeran from Porgeran. When it distinguishes good from evil Porgerans, *kampani/kanaka* does so in terms of the sectoral sociomorality of the Ipili nature regime. *Kampani* consumes rather than shares; it shits, defiling the resources of those living beyond the SML boundary. The *kampani* that is thus demonized and the *kanaka* who is its victim emerge not through capitalist penetration alone but through the articulations of Ipili culture and foreign interests, operating as these interests do in conjunction with the State of Papua New Guinea and its interests.

The green war emerges out of the complexities engendered by the articulation of two different nature regimes, the one capitalist and the other organic (Escobar 1999a). These complexities are reflected in the very discourse of opposition. Capitalists, SML landowners included, are imagined as parasitic agents engaged in the zero-sum game of appropriating resources they do not own and, instead of reciprocating or compensating, defiling ("shitting upon") those whose material means they have destroyed. While O'Connor (1998) might find in these poetics an implicit recognition of the "second contradiction" of capitalism and Marx might laud Ipili speakers for their moral outrage, they are clearly inspired by the logic of the Ipili nature regime, which not only places nature on a human scale, as the wherewithal of species survival, but embeds nature within sociomoral processes and sectoral geographies of mutual aid. The die was arguably cast with the Porgera Agreements (Derkeley 1989) and the granting of the SML (see map 2), which, taken together, divided a field that was structured in terms of intermarrying lines (see figure 1) and the flow of wealth and resources that the Ipili ecology of life instantiates (see figure 2) into a field that was *also* structured in terms of an opposition between the main beneficiaries of mining and mining's principal victims. In the Ipili nature regime, environmentally dependent subjects are positioned among kith and kin, whose physical well-being they are obligated to promote. This requires a sharing of assets and resources and a protection of these same assets and resources against would-be thieves and marauders—those strangers and unrelated people who are always potentially, if not actually, enemies. In that regime, environmental justice is a parochial rather than a universal right, the right that relatives enjoy vis-à-vis one another. Transgressions of these mores and rights were, and still are, provocation for war. The SML landowners are caught between these two fields. On the one hand, they should be good relatives, but, on the other, it is in their interest to ride the PJV coattails of development, even at the expense of uneven development and (a sectoral) environmental injustice.

The lesson of Porgera is that political ecology can be transnational—attuned to the flow of capital, technology, and ideology (Appadurai 1996), indeed, to the penetration of an alien nature regime—without also being merely political-economic. In the event what is required is a concept that reflects the conjunctural nature of the dynamics of the Porgera environmental issue. The concepts of *place* and *place-based politics* or *politics of place* are crucial to positioning political ecology *after* orthodox political economy and political ecology's first generation (see the introduction), with their narrow focus on capitalism and its history. The politics of place along the Porgera River is a "polyvalent" (Moore 1998:346) one in which "social actors" (Puluku Poke, for example) are situated "within cross-cutting matrices of power" (ibid.) of which Moore (1998) and others (Dirlik 2001; Escobar, Rocheleau, and Kothari 2002; Harcourt and Escobar 2002; Prazniak and Dirlik, eds., 2001) have written. Political ecology's future, I would submit, depends upon its ability to countenance a heterogeneous and untotalized "field" (Roseberry 1998) of causation, a field that sustains more than one ecology (cf. Kirsch 1997:152–53), more than one nature regime. Thinking globalization without totalization and the attendant marginalization of the noncapitalist "rest" is a key task for those who would approach globalization in nonreductionist ways.

Notes

This chapter is based on research I conducted from July 1995 to February 1996 and in fall 1999 and 2000 with funding from the American Philosophical Association, Fulbright, and Wenner-Gren Foundation for Anthropological Research. I gratefully acknowledge this support. In Papua New Guinea, I had wonderful assistance from both Porgerans and Paielas. I would single out, first and foremost, Puluku Poke, who allowed me to read his autobiography and who had several conversations with me about PRAMA and the environmental issue. I am also grateful to Waile Yari, Opis Ipape, Kewando, Pawi, John Tongope Mandi (d. 2003), Yaliman Pawe, John Pawe, and Wangeane Ketene for their assistance. In Porgera, Stephen Hepworth, Jeffrey and Wendy Puge, Sam Adam, Morep Tero, Lewambo, Father Edward Osiecki, Father Andrew Sobon, Father Bogdan Swierczewski, Kauwambo, Koipanda, Peter Takaipa, and Kutubu Ipara have been most generous with their time and hospitality. PJV employees who had provided assistants and insights include Kai Lavu, Kenn Logan, Wass Puluku, Tim Osmundsen, Fritz Robinson, and Mark van Dusen. In Paiela, Luke, Simion, Kasper, Lewambo, and Kauwambo have been particularly helpful in this research. In Port Moresby: Bill Searson, Graham Taylor, the former Porgera mining coordinator, and Malcolm Baibuni, the present Porgera mining coordinator in the Department of Mining, Papua New Guinea Government. My research affiliation was with the National Research Institute, and there I had excellent assistance and intellectual stimulation from Michael Laki and Colin Filer, and I thank both. Jim Robinson provided excellent support in 2003 as I sought a visa for my continuing research. I thank Alex Golub and Glenn Banks for copies of their respective books on Porgera and its mining (Golub 2001; Jackson and Banks 2002). Glenn Banks also gave me a reading of a penultimate draft of the paper, and I am most grateful for his having clarified a number of points for me. Any remaining problems with the text I assume full responsibility for. I also thank Wendy Harcourt for early access to her special issue of *Development*, "Place, Politics and Justice: Women Negotiating Globalization." Thanks also to James Greenberg, Dan Jorgensen, Stuart Kirsch, Alan Rumsey, James Weiner, and the Duke University Press reviewers for their readings of this chapter in its various drafts.

1. From the 1960s until 1984, a series of companies—in chronological order, Bulolo Gold Dredging, Mount Isa Mines (MIM), Anaconda Australia, and Ada Exploration Pty Ltd (a joint venture involving MIM, Rumble Explorations Ltd, and Kimberley Securities Ltd.)—searched for a hard rock source of the alluvial gold. Placer (PNG) Pty acquired the Rumble and Kimberley interest in the hard rock deposit in 1975 (MIM

retaining its interest), and in 1979 Placer entered into a joint venture with MIM and Consolidated Gold Fields of Australia as exploration continued (Handley and Henry 1990:1717).

2. I use the terms *line* and *descent line* rather than *descent group* to avoid the implication that the descendants of any ancestral figure function as a group in the sociological sense of that word. Actors act out of their positionality within networks, not as members of one group or another, an argument I make here at some length. The word *line* is also meant to underscore the cumulative filiative nature of ties between descendants and their ancestors, a point I have made elsewhere (Biersack 1999a, 2001b).

3. Ownership of PJV has indeed been shifting. As of the beginning of the millennium, ownership was divided as follows: 50 percent was owned by Placer (PNG) Pty Ltd (which is 100 percent owned by Placer Dome Asia Pacific), 25 percent by Goldfields Porgera Limited (100 percent owned by Goldfields Limited of Australia), 20 percent by Orogen Minerals Limited (51 percent owned by the State of Papua New Guinea), and 5 percent by Mineral Resources Porgera Pty Ltd (50 percent owned by the State of Papua New Guinea and 50 percent owned by the Enga Provincial Government and by local landowners) (Banks 2001:5). As of May 2004, PJV ownership was divided as follows: 75 percent by Placer Dome, 20 percent by Durban Roodepoort Deep Ltd, a South African mining company, and 5 percent by Mineral Resources Enga (of this 5 percent, 2.5 percent was owned by the Porgera landowners) (Banks to Biersack, 5 May 2004, e-mail message).

4. In October 1997, the underground mine was closed "due to the depletion of mineable ore reserves" (PC 10/17/97; see note 5 on citation style). It was reopened in 2002 and is expected to remain open at least until 2007 (Banks, e-mail message to Biersack, 5 May 2004).

5. In citations of materials in national newspapers, the month, date, and year appear first, followed (where I have the information) with a page reference.

6. A grassroots organization called the Kulini Strickland Landholders Association (PC 6/26/96/14; a.k.a. Kulini Strickland Resource Owners Association [*Independent* 10/25/96/5], and the Strickland-Kulini Landowners Association [Stewart and Strathern 2002:143–44]), which is based well outside the Porgera valley (among the Yokona and Aluni Duna, according to Stewart and Strathern [2002:144]), has been protesting against PJV's environmental impact upon the Lagaip-Strickland area (see PC 6/26/96/14). According to Stewart and Strathern, the association formed as a result of the Strickland turning red due to the discharging of "red oxide-bearing mine tailings" into the Porgera River (Stewart and Strathern 2002:143–44), which runs into the Strickland (see map 1). One of the recurring episodes in Duna *malu* ("'sacred knowledge', 'narrative of origins', or 'genealogy'" [ibid.:20]) and other stories is "pools of water turning red, indicating disruptions of one sort or another among the spirit beings that occupy the water" (ibid.:144). To remedy the situation, "some sort of sacrificial action" (ibid.) was

required. According to the national newspaper *The Independent*, the provocation for the formation of the group was PJV's application for a water use permit allowing it "to dump four times compared to present tailings discharge" (*Independent* 10/25/96/5) into the Strickland River system (see also PC 6/26/96/14). Ruben Yandale, vice chairman of the Kulini Strickland Resource Owners Association, said "Enough is enough. The PJV has been polluting our river for several years now. We don't want it to continue. The government must listen to its people and not give PJV rights to bagarap [destroy] our lives for another 10-years" (*Independent* 10/25/96/5). Responding in part to a petition by Lake Murray and Strickland landowners to the PNG government to have the environmental agreement with PJV reviewed, Herowa Agiwa, then–environment and conservation minister, announced that an independent investigation of the alleged pollution of the Fly River and its tributaries would be undertaken (*The National*, June 23, 1998).

7. The region that is referred to by the term *Lower Porgera* spans the Porgera-Paiela divide (see map 1) and includes locations such as Piawe and Bealo, along with Politika, Pitika, Yapatep, Yuyan, and so on (see map 2). "The Lower Porgera Landowners group is particularly referred to the landowners between Kaiya/Pongema rivers junction to Porgera/Lagaip Rivers Junction" (PRAMA 1995:3) (see maps 1 and 2). The relevant lines include Anga, Pene, Auwakome, Eno, Hewa, Yata, Taiyama, and Pepeyange on the west bank and Kiyo, Bipe, Maiyuni, Yawenakali, Takopa, and Tondopo on the east bank (ibid.:2–3). The Lower Porgera is indeed lower: "By the time it [the Porgera River] joins Lagaip, 25km north of the plant site, the Porgera has fallen nearly 1300m to 910m. The gradient of the Porgera River is therefore 1 in 20, extremely steep, down which slope, on average, flows 15 cubic metres of water (or 15 tonnes) each second" (Jackson and Banks 2002:88–89).

8. While I am sympathetic to the notion that *nature* in all the meanings English speakers assign it may not apply to Melanesian worldviews (Strathern 1980), the significata to which I will refer again and again here—the earth and land, water, the body and its various substances—are sufficiently resonant with the range of meanings that *nature* has for an English speaker that I do not hesitate to use the word here (see the discussion in Robbins, this volume). A key difference between *nature* as English speakers signify it and Ipili concepts is that, in the former, nature is a domain of causes and laws, while the only cause that Ipilis recognize is the cause (or power) of decision making and the human agency it motivates. The events of earth, water, and the body are either explained (animistically) in terms of some kind of agency or they are not explained at all.

9. In typifying capitalist and organic natures, Escobar means to be suggestive rather than definitive, opening the way for particular case studies such as the one offered here.

10. Arguing for the need to examine conjunctures of nature regimes and the dynamics of these conjunctures, my analysis parallels that of Stuart Kirsch in his notion of "colliding ecologies" (Kirsch 1997:152–53). For Kirsch, however, ecology is a matter of subsistence rather than of life and of production rather than reproduction. The orga-

nization of reproduction in the Porgera and Paiela valleys, meanwhile, requires production *for exchange* and not just for subsistence. Similarly, both Kirsch and Hyndman (1994, 2001) have found utility in the Marxist term *mode of production*, identifying the collision between capitalists and indigenous groups with respect to "a struggle between different modes of production . . . between subsistence reproduction for simple reproduction (kinship mode of production) and extended production for private accumulation (capitalist mode of production)" (Hyndman 2001:35). But I draw the contrast differently, with respect to a mode of reproduction focused on fertility, rather than to a mode of production focused on subsistence.

11. Words like *skin* (*umbuaini*) and *bone* (*kulini*) are ubiquitous in local discourse. The bark of a tree is its skin, for example; its pith is its bone. By this logic, plants, like animals and humans, have bodies. Implicit in local discourse is the somacentrism of local thought and philosophy.

12. As total social phenomena, nature regimes are multidimensional and cannot be reduced to a single facet. Working with Escobar's nature regime concept allows me to weigh in on a question that has arisen with respect to environmental issues in the context of New Guinea mining: whether environmental issues ultimately concern, even mask, other issues, such as "community involvement in the decision-making that affects them, their resources, and their environments" (Banks 2002:59) or "control over fundamental questions of community sovereignty" (Ballard and Banks 2003:299; see also Hyndman 2001 and Kirsch 1997). Banks has pointed out that European analysts frequently use the word *environment* Eurocentrically to refer to that which is "external to, and separate from, people's daily lives" (2002:59), thus overlooking the way in which the environment is not "divorced from the rich web of social, economic, and cultural meanings and importance" within local perspectives (ibid.) and, furthermore, "ignoring the cultural, economic, political, and social realities of resource use and control in the areas in which they operate" (ibid.:60–61). Banks's critique is exemplary. But, by the same token, there is little any more to choose between the two sides of the argument, something of which Banks himself seems aware. Working with Escobar's nature regime concept allows us to avoid either pole of the debate and to approach environmentalist discourse, wherever we find it, from a holistic perspective. Among Ipili speakers, the only word for environment is "ground" (*yu*), a word that signifies a cosmic sector, one that is designed to host and sustain human life. Enemy groups have tended, and still tend, to plunder each other's gardens and houses and to kill each other's pigs, women, and men, thinking to pull the cosmic rug out from under each other. Trashing each other in the most comprehensive way, they undermine each other's "economy," "environment," "society," and "polity"—all at once.

13. The Fox twins, Tom and Jack, were the first to pass through the Porgera–Paiela area on an eighty-four-day trek from Mount Hagen possibly to the Strickland River

(Sinclair 1978:217). Although their purpose was to find gold, Tom Fox is reported to have told Dan and Mick Leahy, who were at the time based at Mount Hagen, "We've been clear to the foot of the rainbow . . . and there is no pot of gold anywhere about. We have tried every creek from here to the Dutch border and couldn't raise a colour. It's limestone country mostly, rich soil in the valleys and plenty of natives, all of them full of beans and ready to fight, but there is not enough gold in the lot to fill a tooth!" (ibid.:217) (see also Ballard and Allen 1991; Golub 2001:135–37; and Jackson and Banks 2002:28).

14. At the time, Taylor also issued a permit to one Neptune Blood to enter the area (Smalley 1983:sect. 2, p. 2). Together with Mick and Jim Leahy, John Black, and an expatriate named Ephinstone, these formed the Strickland Inc. Syndicate and entered Porgera (ibid.).

15. A patrol report for 1948–49 places Searson's mining "about 200 yards upstream from the junction of the Kaiya and the Porgera rivers" (Wabag PR 6, 1948/1949). A patrol report from 1949 mentions that Searson was prospecting at Yuyan near the juncture of the Porgera and Kaiya rivers (Wabag PR 1, 1949–50, pp. 7–8). According to Ward's 1949 report, "Gold is found in the Kaiya River below its junction with the Kogai [pronounced Kakai] River, in the Kogai River and in Yagetubali [pronounced Yakotapali] Creek which flows into the Kogai River. No gold has been reported from the Kaiya River . . . west of its junction with the Kogai River and none was found therein when the area was inspected (December, 1948). Only traces of gold have been found in the Kogai River above its junction with Yagetubali Creek. The principal deposit is at Searson's workings on the Kaiya River" (1949:12). Ward goes on to indicate that "two types of gold are present—one with gold/gold + silver ration just over 800, the same as that found in Searson's Workings, and a lower more variable grade of gold with fineness about 700" (ibid.:13).

16. Ward estimated that Searson employed about thirty-five locals to work three alluvial terraces. Searson himself, in an interview with Colin Simpson conducted circa 1950, estimated that he employed "about forty" laborers (a number confirmed in Wabag PR 6, 1948/1949). About half of these forty, according to a patrol report prepared around the same time, came from the vicinity (ibid.), while a later patrol report mentions that Searson's employees included Simbus (a.k.a. Chimbus) (Wabag PR 4, 1950/51). According to a patrol conducted in 1949, Searson employed seventy-eight people, mostly "drawn locally" (Wabag PR 1, 1949–50, pp. 7–8).

17. There appears to have been competition to become Taylor's tributer. A patrol into the Porgera valley in June 1960 found that Pawe had begun mining on Taylor's claim. The gold Pawe had already won had been confiscated by the acting district officer stationed in Wabag, and Pawe was told to work for Taylor as his tributer (Laiagam PR 1, 1960/61). Now that Pawe had been given permission to work on Taylor's lease as his

tributer, the report speculated, others "may consider why they cannot be given the same rights (especially where clan lands are involved) although they have been emphatically" told they have no such rights (ibid.:3).

18. According to a report on a patrol in June–July 1960, Puluku had begun mining three and a half years prior to the report period (Laiagam PR 1, 1960/61). He was soon followed by Pawe. Both are identified as "NMOS" or "native" doctors (Laiagam PR 1, 1960–61). Puluku and Pawe appear to be first mentioned in Laiagam PR 2, 1958/59. Who were these men? In Laiagam PR 2, 1958/59, Pawe is identified as an aid post orderly from Tipinini at the eastern margin of the Porgera valley. In Laiagam PR 1, 1960/61, however, Pawe is said to be an NMO. Puluku, meanwhile, is identified as an "ex-NMO." (Laiagam PR 2, 1958/59). According to Jackson and Banks (2002:35), Puluku Poke "had been taken to Goroka in 1948 by a patrol. He worked there as a cook for several years and during this time visited Kainantu where he saw Papua New Guineans working alluvial gold on their own account. On his return to Porgera around 1953/4 he worked initially as a government interpreter before realising that self-employment was infinitely preferable. He gathered together twenty of his own people and started mining, with picks and crowbars, the lower Porgera River below Yuyan."

19. It was not so easy for Puluku to make good on his promise. He was also accused of stealing the gold from Taylor. The outcome of this—his "first legal battle for alluvial gold," as he calls it in his autobiography (Poke 1995)—was, for one thing, the A$7,000 or so he realized on the eventual sale of the gold he had won. This he distributed to his "workmen, relatives and . . . family members. This was the very first time for these people to feel and see money and they were quite happy" (ibid.:item 17). For another, and more important, he was awarded the lease at the juncture of the Kaiya and Pongema rivers in the Yuyan area (Poke 1995:item 15), a lease he holds to this day.

20. Pawe's lease was "reportedly less rich in alluvial gold" and also lay in a less populated area, making it less coveted than Puluku's lease (Laiagam PR 4, 1959/60:11).

21. Jackson and Bank's (2002:36) numbers are somewhat different:

By late 1960 one Patrol Report estimated that there were 250–300 employed by Porgeran leaseholders in addition to the fifty working with Jim Taylor. The officer calculated that this meant three[-]quarters of the 420 able-bodied men in the area had some part in gold mining. By 1967, Porgerans were producing 735 ounces of gold worth $22,000. Searson, at that time the only white working lease (Taylor's leases being worked by tributors), produced 184 ounces worth $5,800. By 1973, the Porgera patrol officer estimated that gold earnings represented around ten dollars a year for every person in the Porgera area—which gave Porgera the highest per capita income of any part of Enga Province.

In 1979, gold sold in Porgera weighed 12kg . . . and was worth K100,000 (including the value of 3kg silver). This was produced by 67 miners, one of who [*sic*] was Puluku who continued to work the lower Porgera alluvials successfully. In addition, Taylor's tributors recovered over K80,000 worth and Porgera Alluvial Gold Mining (an MIM-owned subsidiary), working the terraces on the Kaiya, had production worth K120,000. Around this time between 1,250 and 2,100 persons were at any one time involved in the valley's alluvial gold industry; according to the 1980 Census at least 211 households (or around 1350 persons) obtained income from mining. In addition to the above, tribute miners—predominantly Porgeran— also took 240kg of gold from MIM alluvial leases between 1973 and 1985.

Talyaga's socioeconomic impact study in 1984 contains the following information about alluvial mining:

> For 15 days in October and November [1984?], we have counted a total of 373 people panning alluvial gold along the Kogai and Kaiya Rivers and their tributaries. On the average, 25 people were working per day. Of these 25 people, over 1/4 were working full time for 6 days a week while less than 1/5 were working for 2 days at the most. On the average, 10 new people were seen working per week and if this pattern is maintained throughout the year, then we estimate that 520 people work here plus 6–8 regular miners, there would be 526–528 people mining alluvial gold around Alipis only. Supposing that a similar number are engaged below Mungalep, Yuyane and Polotika, then we estimate that for this activity there are about 2,112 people. According to the 1980 Census, a total of 211 households were involved in mining alluvial gold. . . . We estimate that 1.056 grammes of gold is produced. . . . through this activity alone, (we estimate that) more than K100,000.00 is entering the local economy. (1984:78)

22. The TAC was formed in 1995 to take up the Porgera compensation issue (TAC 1995:10). Hearings were held with landowners in Kairik, Suyan, Porgera Station, Anawe, Piawe, and Yuyan over a three-day period, from 17 October 1995 to 19 October 1995. Members of the committee were drawn from the Department of Minerals and Petroleum, the Department of Environment and Conservation, the Prime Minister's Officer, and the Department of Enga. One of the speakers at Kairik airstrip was Opis Papo, then the chairman of PRAMA and from 1997 to 2002 the MP for Porgera-Lagaip. The TAC was formed by the Water Resources Board to investigate the environmental damage caused by Porgera mining when the minister for environment and conservation was asked to make a determination. The Water Resources Board formed the TAC (ibid.:2).

23. Banks provides material from Nicole Haley's "When Pigs Fly: Pigs, Pollution and Porgera," a paper given at Australian National University in 1996: " 'The English word "pollution" has entered the local vernacular, with people being told by visiting NGOs that it meant "olsem poison" (the same as poison)'. . . . Poison in the local setting glosses a range of unexplained deaths, sorcery, and witchcraft. As a result people in the area, on hearing that the company is polluting the river, understand that 'the river is deadly and the PJV is killing people'. . . . As a result 'all deaths in the riverine corri-

dor are being attributed to pollution' and 'deaths previously attributed to other causes are being reinterpreted and reconsidered' " (Banks 1997b:4; see also Banks 2002:50–51; Stewart and Strathern 2002:171).

24. For some, the destruction of the river arouses the ancestors, who then inflict disease and death upon their descendants (cf. Stewart and Strathern 2002:171).

25. Puluku Poke himself embodies the intervalley conjuncture that the term *Lower Porgera* signifies. He was born in Bealo on the eastern wall of the Paiela valley (Poke 1995:item 1; see map 2), not in Porgera (although the status of Bealo is ambiguous [see note 7]), and his affiliations include Paiela lines such as Pepeyange and Tondopo as well as Porgerans lines such as Maiyuni and Eno. He also claims Hewa affiliations to the north (see map 1). With respect to the scope of his affiliations, Puluku told me, "I cover all three," Hewa, Paiela, and Porgera; "I see all; I am in the middle [of all]." Puluku's autobiography tells us he was born in Bealo. Bealo is close to Piawe, and Puluku claims Piawe as one of his homes as well. A 1969 patrol report places him at Bealo but also at Politika (Porgera PR 1, 1969/70, p. 5), on the Porgeran side of the Porgera–Paiela divide (see map 2).

26. Interestingly, the difference between PJV's package of K10 million and the ministerial determination of K15.2 million lay in an increase not in compensation for alluvial losses but, rather, in the sum paid for sediment—up from 1 *toae* to 2.5 *toae*s per ton.

27. According to Shearman (2001:178–79), in response to criticism of its environmental track record, PJV has "set itself the goal of becoming the 'Earth's Gold Leader', and a promoter of 'Sustainable mining'. According to Placer 'sustainability means that it adds economic, social and environmental value to society through its activities. In essence, this is the 'triple bottom line' theory in which environmental and social constraints are given equal weighting to the generation of profit" (2001:178–79).

Between Politics and Poetics: Narratives of Dispossession in Sarawak, East Malaysia

J. Peter Brosius

> To defer to a second language . . . is to reorder what one has in mind.
> —Rafael 1988:213

Introduction

On the morning of 5 July 1991, a group of eight individuals from the United States, United Kingdom, Germany, and Australia—most of whom had never met each other until just a few days before—walked onto the grounds of a timber camp at the mouth of the Baram River in Sarawak, East Malaysia, climbed up the booms of several barges and chained themselves there. They hung banners from their perches, played guitars, and ignored the entreaties of officials who asked them to come down. After some eight hours they were brought down by police and arrested. To the great frustration of the authorities, they had hidden their passports and gave as their names locutions such as Chipko Mendes Penan, Stop the Logging, Save the Forests, and Let the Truth Prevail, names that duly appeared on their mug shots taken at Miri police headquarters. When subsequently their identities were established, they were tried, and most were sentenced to sixty days in prison. They were there to protest the destruction of Sarawak's forests by timber companies and the effects of that destruction on a small group of hunter-gatherers, the Penan.

In the past several years my research has focused on events such as this, and on the larger international campaign against logging in Sarawak that precipitated such acts. In a series of interviews with Euro-American environmentalists, Penan resistance to logging was repeatedly cited as an important influence in the growth of the rain forest and indigenous rights movements. Virtually all described the Penan as exemplars of how indigenous peoples can assert control over their own destinies and, in the process, halt the loss of global biodiversity. In short, the Penan became icons of indigenous resistance for environmentalists worldwide. It is a remarkable state of affairs that a small group of forest nomads living in a remote part of Borneo should have become a central focus in a debate that is of global significance. My research has in part focused on how each of the parties involved—the Penan themselves, the Malaysian government, and both Malaysian and Northern NGOs—have constructed the global significance of the Penan and their role in Malaysia's national project of development in distinct ways. My work focuses not merely on explicating the forms of representation that underlie the rhetoric deployed by each of these parties, but on the more complex relationship between representation, discursive production, and political agency. This project is an example of what has recently been termed "multi-sited ethnography"; research has been carried out in Malaysia, North America, Europe, the United Kingdom, Australia, and Japan.

In the present discussion I want to shift my focus back to the Penan. For all of the involvement of international environmental NGOs in the campaign (cf. DeLuca 1999) and for all the celebrities who have spoken out on their behalf, the Penan themselves have been the most eloquent spokespersons on the issue of logging and land rights in Sarawak. In videotaped interviews and published pleas, Penan decry the destruction of the forest and the hardship this has caused them. They speak with moving eloquence of river siltation, the destruction of sago, rattan, and fruit trees, the depletion of game, and the obliteration of graves.

These images and texts, mostly collected, translated, and circulated by Malaysian and Euro-American activists, tell only part of the story. In part this is because most commentaries on the struggle against logging in Sarawak to date—in books, films, action alerts, and postings on the Web—have focused on the most dramatic manifestation of Penan resistance: the erection of blockades. What I wish to address here is the broader context in which these images and texts get made. In particular, I want to examine some of breadth of the forms of rhetoric and practice deployed by Penan in their efforts to assert their claims to land, both "onstage" and "offstage." These texts get produced in a range of settings for a variety of audiences. In some cases Penan are attempting to reach across difference, to convey to various kinds of audiences—government ministers, police, timber company managers, Euro-American environmentalists—their relationship to the landscape, the basis of their land claims, and the rightness of their efforts to resist the incursions of timber companies. Their purpose is to persuade. In other cases they are speaking among themselves, discussing logging in the everyday flow of conversation, rehearsing or recounting the arguments put forth in encounters with others, and offering analyses of particular events.

In considering how Penan frame their struggle against logging, I want to consider not merely the rhetorical elements of these narratives, but also the *forms* they take. Penan present their arguments in any number of forms: letters addressed to government officials, verbal arguments with timber company managers, maps produced with the aid of local activists, videotaped interviews produced by Euro-American documentary filmmakers, and others. What happens when Penan claims are textualized in different ways? How do Penan conceptions of their audience condition the arguments they put forth? In what ways are various expressions of sense or metaphor expressed or elided in various narrative forms?

One of my purposes in attempting this analysis is to provide a minor intervention into how we think about the phenomenon of resistance. The arguments that Penan are putting forth should be viewed not exclusively as acts of resistance but simultaneously as efforts at *engagement*. In making their arguments to loggers, civil servants, environmentalists, and others, Penan are attempting to speak across difference, to *familiarize* themselves, to frame their arguments in ways they hope will be recognizable to outsiders. Recognizing this has important implications for how we think about resistance at a more general level.

At the same time, because their arguments have had little effect, there is a strong element of frustration, indeed desperation, in much of what Penan say. As I will discuss below, the theme of not being heard plays a central role in Penan arguments, and many of their statements constitute an analysis of why logging continues in spite of their efforts to explain to outsiders that it is taking place on lands they claim and creating much hardship for them. What this points to is the need to foreground notions of agency in narratives of landscape and dispossession. The questions of who Penan believe to be responsible for their plight and who they believe is in the best position to help them are as central to this whole domain of discourse as are statements about what is occurring and how it affects their everyday lives. This is as much a poetics of culpability as a poetics of place.

This brings me, then, to the realm of the poetics of landscape and the larger purpose of this chapter, which is to seek links between politics and poetics. In this respect I am much influenced by a volume edited by Charles Zerner entitled *Culture and the Question of Rights* (2003). The concern of these essays is to consider the following questions: "When, under what conditions, do poems and performances become claims to nature? How are these translations and articulations made? Which ones are effective and why? . . . How are performances and culturally distinctive families of imagery refracted in ways that may yield a claim of right?" (ibid.:2). The case studies from Indonesia and Malaysia that make up the volume respond to these questions by placing poetics and performances in contexts of power and contests over rights to land. Such cultural productions, Zerner argues, are as much strategic as they are aesthetic, and they represent attempts at articulation as local communities seek to make "persuasive claims" to a state for whom the local is illegible.

Situating Penan

In interior central Borneo there exist two broad classes of people: longhouse-dwelling Orang Ulu agriculturalists living along the main rivers and hunting-gathering forest nomads such as the Penan living in interior headwaters.[1] The Penan of Sarawak are divided into two distinct populations, Eastern and Western Penan (Needham 1972:177), together numbering some seven thousand individuals. The Eastern Penan inhabit the Baram and Limbang watersheds, while the Western Penan are mostly found in the Balui watershed (map 1).[2] In the late 1950s, 70 to 80 percent of Penan were still nomadic, but they began to settle in increasing numbers during the 1960s. They were encouraged to do so by the Sarawak state government, which provided Penan with incentives to build permanent houses and to learn to farm. By 1970 nearly all Eastern and Western Penan had settled. Today fewer than four hundred Eastern Penan remain fully nomadic, less than 5 percent of the total. Though most Penan are settled, they have not been *resettled*, and they remain on ancestral lands.

In regional perspective, hunter-gatherers such as the Penan have long occupied a specific niche in the economies of central Borneo. They have been a major source of forest products, which are traded to Orang Ulu communities and thence to the coast for consumption or export.[3] More than merely a system for the exchange of commodities, Penan relationships with Orang Ulu communities were tightly knit into the social and ethnic fabric of interior Sarawak.

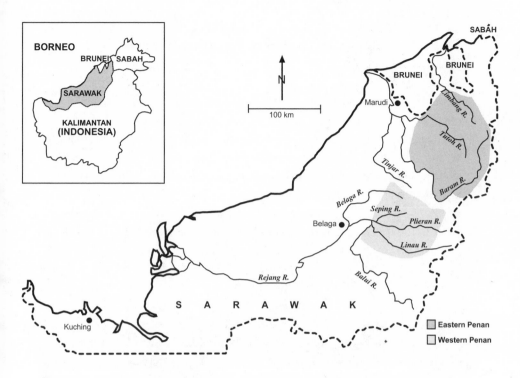

BROSIUS MAP 1. The distribution of Eastern and Western Penan in Sarawak

The presence of a Penan band in an area meant access to forest products and to the income generated by trade in those products. Orang Ulu aristocrats who controlled this trade were proprietary about "their" Penan and jealously guarded their prerogatives to trade with certain groups. Virtually all historical accounts agree that goods were exchanged with Penan at usurious rates and that Penan were continuously in debt to longhouse patrons. This was the situation into which colonial authorities inserted themselves in the late nineteenth century.

Penan and the State: Colonial History and the Project of Development

Sarawak has a rather notable colonial history in that for a century it was controlled by three so-called White Rajahs: James Brooke (1841–68), his nephew Charles Brooke (1868–1917), and Charles's son Vyner Brooke (1917–46).[4] At the advent of Brooke rule in 1841, piracy and headhunting were common-place in Sarawak, and the Brookes' primary concerns were pacification and the establishment of government authority. Through much of their reign the Brookes remained resolutely opposed to the establishment of large-scale commercial enterprises, particularly European-run commercial plantations (Reece 1988), and they maintained a system in which native "welfare" was defined by the preservation of traditional lifeways.[5] It was only in the 1930s that one begins to discern a shift from an ideology of preservation to one of transformation. This trend continued after Sarawak was ceded to the British crown in 1946 and continued with ever-greater vigor after Sarawak joined Malaysia in 1963. In the postcolonial period the concept of development became an increasingly central point of articulation between the government and local populations: in upriver areas the government undertook an accelerated effort to establish schools and dispensaries and to promote health and agricultural development.

Beginning in the early 1970s and continuing ever more earnestly up to the present, a remarkable transformation in the ways in which the development paradigm has been deployed in Sarawak occurs. A discourse of development that is ever more politicized and more grandly visionary emerges, increasingly taken from the realm of the civil service and the discourse of public works and more closely tied to the goals of politicians. A theme that occurs in national-level development/political/civic discourse but that is particularly prominent in Sarawak is the hybridizing imperative that all "communities" (that is, ethnic groups) must strive to take their place in the *mainstream* of Malaysian society. Responding to environmentalist criticisms of the effects of logging on the Penan, for instance, Sarawak Minister of Environment and Public Health James Wong stated that "no one has the ethical right to deprive the Penan of their right to socio-economic development and assimilation into the mainstream of Malaysian society" (Davis and Henley 1990:100). The power of the idea of the mainstream derives not only from the futurity it posits but also from the image of the past it provides. That past, from an official perspective, still exists in the interior. That such a past still exists demands transformative intervention, and development is the single valid form of intervention for bringing those communities into the mainstream and into the present.[6] For development to occur, officials believe, traditional subsistence practices must be abandoned. It is this transformative task that the government has set for itself, and it stands ready with a number of prescriptive measures. Foremost among these is that rural communities must be resettled and their economies transformed.

Taken together, the ideology of development and the associated concept of the mainstream have an imperative force that leaves little latitude for Penan to continue existing within the rain forest. This is evident in any number of official pronouncements about the Penan way of life and the benevolent role the government should play in ameliorating their "plight" as forest dwellers. Sarawak Chief Minister Taib Mahmud, for instance, stated, "That's why we want to slowly settle them and it is our responsibility. We are belted with one philosophy and this is to build an equal society. How can we have an equal society when you allow a small group of people to behave like animals in the jungle? . . . I owe it to the Penans to get them gradually into the mainstream so that they can be like any other Sarawakian" (Siva Kumar 1991:178–79). Penan are spoken of as requiring remedial efforts, and in numerous cases the need to "rehabilitate" them is mentioned. Addressing an audience in Atlanta in 1993, Minister of Primary Industries Lim Keng Yaik stated with reference to the provision of development initiatives for Penan, "We will not apologize, because we will wean, w-e-a-n, not w-i-n, w-e-a-n [them] out of the jungle."

With the exception of nomadic groups, most Penan today have enthusiastically adopted the idea of development and have incorporated it into their notions of the appropriate role of the state in the affairs of local communities. At the same time, they do not always accept some of the government's more consequential development goals, such as commitment to the idea that rural communities should coalesce into larger villages. Any effort to voice reservations about the kinds of development offered to them is dismissed by authorities as irrational conservatism, "confusion," or the product of instigation by external forces, and strategically misinterpreted as opposition to development altogether. Advocates of rain forest conservation and indigenous rights are accused of wishing to deny rural communities their "fundamental right" to development and to relegate those rural communities to the status of museum specimens.

Such discourse points to the often subtle ways in which the master narratives of development and mainstream are strategically deployed by officials to elide the pernicious effects of environmental destruction and the dispossession of indigenous rural communities. Under the guise of inclusiveness, full participation, citizenship, equality, opportunity, and rights and counterpoised to neglect, being left out, or being passed by, the claims of rural communities to land and resources are being extinguished.

The Sarawak Campaign

With the advent of large-scale mechanized logging, which accelerated greatly in the 1970s, the areas covered by primary forest in Sarawak have been reduced drastically, and deforestation continues at a rapid rate. In the 1980s, Sarawak became a major supplier of tropical hardwoods on the international market and experienced one of the highest rates of deforestation in the world. The speed with which logging progressed was remarkable. Though timber companies began to move into the interior only in the late 1970s, by the 1980s they had moved into areas occupied by Penan, and they have now reached the Indonesian border in several places.[7]

Logging has a dramatic effect on the lives of Penan, both nomadic and settled. The most immediate effect of logging is an opening up of the canopy and a phenomenal increase in erosion. As logging roads are bulldozed along rivers and up ridges, massive slides cascade downslope, and rivers become choked with silt. *Eugeissona* palms, which provide Penan with sago, are uprooted by bulldozers and buried by slides. The trees from which Penan collect fruit and blowdart poison are felled. Game disappears, and river siltation kills fish.

For Penan—Eastern and Western, nomadic and settled—logging means hunger. More than this, it completely alters a landscape with which Penan have a deeply historical relationship. What is of as much concern to the Penan as the privation caused by logging is the way in which logging has altered the landscape in which they live. This results not only from the direct action of bulldozers, but also from the process of concealment that occurs as dense secondary vegetation becomes established. Where once the forest floor was relatively open, an impenetrable mass of thorny vines and shrubs becomes established. Recognizable waypoints are transformed, if not obliterated, and movement over the landscape becomes difficult. In this way, the cultural density of that landscape—all the sites with biographical, social, and historical significance— is transfigured. Thus, logging not only undermines the basis of Penan subsistence, but also destroys those places that are iconic of their existence as a society.[8]

Though Eastern and Western Penan are uniformly opposed to logging, the ways in which each of the groups has responded contrast markedly. The Eastern Penan response to logging was to erect and man log rail fence blockades. Before erecting these in 1987, Eastern Penan made numerous efforts to air their grievances to government officials. At last they felt compelled to issue a warning that if their grievances were not addressed, they would take some unspecified action. Finally, having exhausted all attempts at dialogue, they erected blockades in the Baram and Limbang districts on 31 March 1987. The first blockades remained in place for some eight months before being torn down. Blockades continued to spread into other areas occupied by Eastern Penan through the late 1980s and early 1990s, and a new series of blockades was erected just recently. When blockades are erected, Eastern Penan from distant groups flock to the blockade sites to lend support, and these sites have sometimes been occupied by several hundred people at a time. Inevitably the blockades have been broken up and those present arrested. What is most striking about the blockades is the degree to which they have been characterized by a sense of unity among bands of people who have no history of unified political action. The Western Penan response to logging stands in marked contrast. Until very recently they have not responded with blockades. What has most marked the Western Penan response to logging has been cooperation with timber companies. The form this cooperation has taken is a willingness to negotiate compensation packages and to work for companies. To the degree that they have undertaken acts of resistance, they have done so primarily to press for higher compensation.[9]

In an examination of this contrast in Penan responses to logging, it is important that this contrast not be overstated. Many Eastern Penan have recently negotiated compensation packages with timber companies, and increasing numbers have begun to work for them. This has led to some tension between groups of Eastern Penan, particularly between members of settled communities who are working for companies and nomadic groups on whose lands they are working. Likewise, there have been several incidents in which Western Penan have resisted timber companies in various ways. Clearly, patterns of resistance and acquiescence continue to evolve.[10]

It was as a result of the blockades of 1987, when images of blockades began to circulate transnationally, that a concerted international campaign began to be waged on behalf of the Penan. Summarizing the history of the Sarawak campaign is no easy matter, given the many sites at which it has been carried on, the multiplicity of actors involved, and the ways in which the issue itself has been transformed through time.[11] Indeed, to call it a campaign is a great oversimplification, and I refer to it as such only as a matter of convenience.

The history of the Sarawak campaign can be written as one of increasing and then decreasing momentum. The early part of the campaign focused on the civil disobedience of the Penan—blockades, arrests, and trials—as well as on the local efforts of the Malaysian environmental organization Sahabat Alam Malaysia (SAM, Friends of the Earth-Malaysia) to support the Penan struggle. SAM became instrumental not only in the worldwide Sarawak campaign, but also in supporting Penan at the local level. SAM representatives helped Penan draft letters in an attempt to establish land claims, provided lawyers, and contributed material support at blockade sites.

The early part of the campaign also focused on the charismatic figure of the Swiss environmentalist Bruno Manser. Manser took up residence with a band of nomadic Eastern Penan in 1984 and remained among them for six and a half years. It was Manser who was most responsible for bringing the situation of the Penan to world attention. Starting in 1985, he began writing to a number of environmental organizations, describing in vivid terms the plight of the Penan. Filmmakers and environmentalists soon began to seek him out in the forest. At the same time Manser was working to make the situation of the Eastern Penan known outside of Sarawak, he was engaged in organizing the normally retiring population to resist.[12] Manser traveled extensively throughout the Baram and Limbang districts, organizing large meetings that were attended by representatives of numerous communities. Along with SAM, Manser provided Penan the opportunity to internationalize their cause.[13] As the international Sarawak campaign accelerated, numerous individual environmentalists attempted to visit Eastern Penan in order to document their plight.

Much of the rhetoric of the Sarawak campaign at this time centered around the imperative to save the Penan. The threat facing the Penan was constructed by environmentalists according to what might be termed the *Fern Gully* allegory, after the animated film. The image presented was of pristine indigenous innocents living a timeless existence in the depths of the rain forest, as bulldozers churned toward them, devouring everything in their path. Such an image had the effect of producing a sense of great urgency: little time remained, and it was imperative that the bulldozers be stopped.

In the face of a threat represented in such harsh terms, the campaign gained wide support among Northern environmentalists. As the momentum of the campaign grew, extensive media coverage served to raise the profile of the Penan even further.[14] As the campaign became increasingly internationalized in the late 1980s, there was a sustained series of direct actions and other campaign activities in the United States, United Kingdom, Japan, Australia, and Europe, which served to keep a focus on the situation in Sarawak. Numerous public figures supported the cause of indigenous rights in Sarawak. In 1989, members of the Grateful Dead testified before the U.S. Congress on behalf of the Penan. Al Gore held two press conferences with Manser and Penan and wrote about the Penan struggle in *Earth in the Balance* (Gore 1992:283–84).

The Malaysian government responded vigorously to this campaign. At the local level, there was outright repression: the arrest of several hundred Penan at blockade sites, the employment of gangsters to provide extralegal security on timber concession lands, and the harassment or arrest of members of Malaysian environmental organizations. Along with such explicitly repressive measures, government officials dismissed Penan blockades as the product of foreign instigators. Through the rhetoric of instigation, Penan were portrayed as being confused: deluded objects of pity to whom only sympathy was due. They insisted that Penan should be given the opportunity to enter the mainstream of Malaysian society by bringing them the fruits of development. Malaysia also initiated an extremely effective rhetorical offensive against Northern environmentalists. Advocates of rain forest conservation and indigenous rights were accused of wishing to relegate Penan to the status of museum specimens. Malaysian officials claimed that environmentalists were a front for Northern softwood interests, and they persistently linked Northern environmental activism to the legacy of colonialism. They made compelling counterarguments about the linkages between North and South, asking why the North should impose standards of sustainability for logging in tropical forests when no such efforts are made in their own countries, and they insisted on the link between forest destruction in the South and consumption in the North. Such arguments and efforts were highly effective in blunting the moral/political force of Northern environmentalist rhetoric. The overall effect was that the debate over logging in Sarawak shifted from a focus on forest destruction and the rights of indigenous communities to an issue of sustainable forest management. The discursive contours of the debate were shifted away from the moral/political domain toward the domain of governmentality and environmental management (see Brosius 1999a). By the early 1990s the passion that had maintained the momentum around this issue began to dissipate.

Contextualizing Penan Narratives

Penan put forth their arguments about logging and land claims to many different types of audience, and the form and content of their arguments have much to do with their assumptions about whom they are speaking to. Penan assumptions about whom they are addressing, who opposes them, who supports them, and what is possible are refracted through a particular set of historical experiences. Eastern and Western Penan have very different analyses of their situation and thus make something very different of particular actors. Understanding contemporary forms of Penan engagement and resistance thus requires some attention to the historical perspective through which Eastern and Western Penan view contemporary affairs.

Both Eastern and Western Penan historical narratives are framed with reference to three main periods: (1) the distant past, before the establishment of colonial rule; (2) the colonial period, including both the Brooke period and British period, often conflated because there was little change in the way Penan were administered; and (3) the post-1963 period, when Sarawak joined Malaysia, an era recognized by Penan as being marked by Malay rule. Because Eastern and Western Penan experienced the colonial period in different ways, however, they have divergent interpretations of the significance of this common tripartite historical scheme and its implications for their struggle against logging.

From reading historical documents one is able to discern, throughout the Brooke and British periods, a strong strain of what might be termed Penan exceptionalism. Alone among indigenous interior communities in not practicing headhunting and conspicuously timid in their relations with outsiders, Penan were viewed as an inoffensive people apart, always reclusive and in need of special protection, both from Iban headhunting raids and from exploitation by Orang Ulu communities. From their earliest encounters with Penan, Brooke regime officials in both the Baram and Belaga districts voiced concern about how Penan were exploited and expressed a desire to protect them.

In spite of this, Brooke officials responded differently in the Baram and Belaga districts. Officials in the Baram District established strict regulations about contact and trade with Penan, and district reports reveal a constant effort to enforce these rules. Government-supervised trade meetings established in 1906 were held at several mutually agreed upon places in the Baram District three or four times a year. Trade was not the only point of the meetings. Government officials collected taxes, provided medical services, and held dialogue sessions. The last such meeting was held in 1976 (Langub 1984:12). The involvement of colonial officials in the lives of Western Penan in the Belaga District was very different. Regular trade meetings were never institutionalized, and Penan in the Belaga were visited much less frequently than those in the Baram. This contrast is reflected today in Penan recollections of the colonial period. Eastern Penan in the Baram District today recall trade meetings with evident nostalgia. They describe the messages of reassurance given to them by colonial officers: that the government would look after them and protect them and that their lands were reserved for them alone. For Eastern Penan, accounts of trade meetings are the embodiment of the colonial era. In contrast, Western Penan accounts of their infrequent meetings with colonial authorities lack the deep sense of nostalgia so evident in Eastern Penan accounts.

Eastern Penan narratives about contemporary political conditions continually hark back to the colonial period. In contrast to the colonial government, they say, the contemporary government "does not know how to hold us." For this reason, Eastern Penan have today turned toward a belief in the imminent return of colonialism. They are intent on insisting on the illegitimacy of contemporary Malay rule and on the legitimacy of colonial rule, based on precedence and historical depth.[15] It was *orang putih*, they state, who governed them in ancestral times. Malays, by contrast, are mere newcomers. In this way Eastern Penan have historicized the logging issue, maintaining a historical dichotomy that opposes an idealized life in the colonial past with their present condition. In the Eastern Penan view, during the colonial period, government authorities behaved in a manner that was appropriate to their role. They not only left Penan alone, but made sure that others did as well. The current government, by contrast, has abandoned its ordained role as protector and instead become a willing agent of dispossession.

It is into this environment of colonial nostalgia, violated trust, and transgression that contemporary environmentalists have stepped. The nostalgia Eastern Penan feel for the colonial period has been transformed into a tangible sense of hope. Many Eastern Penan see their only salvation in a return to colonialism, manifested in the person of the queen. As noted, after the international Penan campaign began to accelerate, numerous environmentalists visited Eastern Penan in order to document their plight. Because foreign environmentalists have expressed a desire to stop the incursion of timber companies, Eastern Penan see them as acting in a way that is consistent with the behavior of former colonial authorities. Foreign environmentalists who have surreptitiously visited them are thus the embodiment of the colonial past and are seen as the vanguard of its return.[16] When Eastern Penan describe their present situation to Northern environmentalists, they believe they are talking to individuals who have the power to put an end to both Malay hegemony and logging, and they declare that they will be steadfast in waiting for the queen.[17]

The Poetics of Dispossession

Whether they are actively engaged in explicit acts of resistance or not, the topic of logging is one that consumes Penan, a matter they discuss endlessly. Recent events have become a part of Penan oral history, and the stories Penan tell about such events are remarkable for their detail. Their narratives recount confrontations between themselves and state authorities or company representatives: police, judges, government ministers, camp managers, and others. They recount the arguments put forth by themselves and others: why they decided to blockade, why they should not be blamed for those blockades, and whom they believe to be ultimately responsible.

Any effort to understand Penan narratives of dispossession must begin with a recognition of the variety of forms they take. Such narratives, and the forms of action they prescribe, exist on a continuum of directness and obliqueness: from the concrete to the aesthetic, from references to subsistence to references to sound and sense. At times, Penan are making direct claims: they speak of boundaries and of the need to prohibit the entry of outsiders onto their lands. At other times Penan speak movingly about the qualities of the forest and their life within it. They speak of those less tangible qualities: the sounds and smells of the forest, coolness and heat, sunlight, vegetation, and mud. The words and images they employ are contrastive and tinged with nostalgia: what the forest was like before logging and after. Rather than forming two distinct zones of discourse, these must be viewed as refractions of the same conversation about the making of claims to land.

In the following I examine the range of discursive forms that characterize the Penan response to logging. These include (1) livelihoods, (2) lost places, (3) narratives of belonging, (4) contrast and separation, (5) sounds, colors, textures, (6) metaphor and analogy, (7) boundaries, borders, and blockades, (8) maps, letters, declarations, and (9) narratives of agency.

Livelihoods

For Penan, the destruction caused by logging is no distant abstraction but something that directly affects their lives and livelihoods. Many of the concerns expressed by Penan refer to the everyday effects of logging and the substantive hardships it creates for them. Significantly, when Eastern Penan describe the effects of logging, they do not employ the term generally used to denote the temporary depletion of an area caused by their own foraging activities (*siat*). Rather, when speaking of the effects of logging, Penan refer to the land being "broken" (*tasa'*).

Penan accounts of the impact of logging describe a litany of specific effects: (1) that sago and fruit trees are bulldozed; (2) that the rivers are muddy, making it difficult to find clean drinking water; (3) that river siltation kills fish; (4) that game has disappeared because of the noise of logging activities, because the trees that provide forage for pigs and other types of game are felled, and because loggers bring in shotguns; (5) that they suffer from new kinds of illness; and (6) that rattan is destroyed, making it impossible to participate in the cash economy.

Eugeissona sago characteristically grows in dispersed groves located on steep slopes or along ridges, precisely where logging roads tend to be located. As a result, wherever they occur, timber operations destroy a large percentage of the *Eugeissona*. What bulldozers themselves don't actually destroy, landslides from road building do.[18]

The siltation that occurs from logging is another topic of frequent discussion. Western Penan living along the Seping River decry the fact that it is now almost completely silted in as the result of logging. What were previously sand or gravel banks are now covered with mud, and the banks of the river are littered with discarded boards and zinc roofing. Penan there say that the ubiquitous patches of diesel fuel that foul the river cause a painful skin condition.

With regard to hunting, Penan state that animals, disturbed by the noise and activity of heavy machinery, become extremely wary (*ka'an lajam* [E. Penan]). Furthermore, hunting methods that work well in primary forest do not work in the dense secondary growth (*repo'*) that results from logging. Penan in logged areas say that before logging it was easy to shoot game with a blowpipe "both high in the trees and near to the ground." Today, however, whatever game is encountered is at too great a distance and, because of the thinner canopy, is better able to detect hunters. Game that is near the ground is impossible to see or to reach because of the thorny, dense mat of secondary growth that covers the ground. Likewise, when hunting with dogs, Penan find it impossible to pursue game through such growth. Finally, Penan complain that timber workers with shotguns hunt out all the game. Indeed, in areas that are being actively logged, the sound of shotgun blasts is ubiquitous, and game becomes increasingly scarce.

Lost Places

Though to all appearances a wilderness, the Penan landscape is instead one that is imbued with cultural significance, full of places that for one reason or another have meaning to Penan. Some of these places are physically marked, others are marked only in the domain of memory. Some have direct relevance to subsistence, many others do not. Rather than being sacred in some abstract sense, the places have a significance that is often biographical and highly personal: the place where one was nearly bit by a pig, a former camp where fruit was plentiful, a tree that bears marks made by a now-deceased favorite niece (see Brosius 2001). When traveling in the forest with Penan, one hears a continuous commentary on meaningful places and the events that occurred there. Such locations are highly evocative of past shared experiences with the living and the dead.

Even when not visibly marked such places are, as noted, the foundation of Penan claims to land. One of the most common types of place Penan point to in narratives of place are the sites of former camps (*lamin*). It is with reference to former *lamin* sites that Penan primarily place events sequentially and map them onto the landscape. More than this, reference to former *lamin* evokes bittersweet feelings of loss for an unrecoverable past shared with loved ones. Of even greater consequence for Penan are the burial sites of kin. It is the location of burials in particular watersheds that Penan cite as justifying their right to exploit those watersheds. Given the nomadic basis of Penan society, burial sites are widely scattered and inconspicuous at best. Even when their precise location is no longer known, the memory of graves as being located in specific watersheds persists for generations.

With the advent of logging, many such places have been either obliterated or made unrecognizable by bulldozers, and this is profoundly disturbing to Penan. On one occasion, while I was hiking along an as yet undisturbed ridge with a group of nomadic Eastern Penan, we came to an unusual high spot that was covered with a low, grassy fern and devoid of saplings. One of the men said that this place was the former *lamin* of the group's ancestors (*tepun sehau*) from long ago and that they did not want to see the place destroyed. How many times had their ancestors made *lamin* here, he asked, yet with one single pass of a bulldozer it is destroyed. On another occasion an elderly woman was looking across a deep valley to the opposite ridge. She commented to me that when she saw that ridge, she felt great longing (*tawai*) because that was where the *lamin* of her family and ancestors had been built, and it would soon be destroyed. When one travels with Penan along logging roads or in the back of logging trucks, moving across the landscape in a way very different from how they used to, one hears a continuous commentary on place, as Penan try to pick out places originally known to them in their undisturbed state, but now both transformed and seen from a completely new vantage point. Penan constantly lament the destruction of these places by the activities of logging companies.

The thing that Penan lament most of all is the destruction of graves, a matter voiced with particular frequency by nomadic Eastern Penan. These nomadic groups almost always construct their camps on ridges and bury their dead there as well: precisely where logging roads are constructed. Eastern Penan graves thus fall directly in the path of bulldozers. The headman of one nomadic group recounted to me how the graves of thirty-one of his closest kin—a spouse, parents, grandparents, siblings, children, and others, all of whom he had known well—were destroyed by bulldozers. Another man described how the graves of his mother and father had already been destroyed, and he lamented that the grave of one of his beloved deceased grandchildren would soon also be destroyed. On another occasion, a young woman borrowed my tape recorder to make a tape to send to her father, who lived on the opposite side of the Tutoh River. The greater part of her message was taken up with a warning that the grave of her brother, near where we were camped, was about to be bulldozed. She indicated that they had already placed markers around the grave as an indication not to destroy it, but, she added, "How many times have we talked to them?" What is most upsetting to Penan is that even when they attempt to inform timber companies about the location of graves, the information is often ignored. On numerous occasions I have witnessed Penan tell loggers about graves in the vicinity and have heard of numerous cases in which those efforts are ignored. Most often, when graves are destroyed, the company refuses to provide compensation, citing a lack of any evidence of the presence of a grave. Indeed, Penan are often simply told that they are lying.

Finally, Penan point to any number of other minor markers of place in describing their claims to land. One nomadic Penan headman described to me what he planned to say to the manager of the local timber company: "If I talk to the manager, this is what I want to ask." Then, pointing across the valley, he said, "On that ridge over there is a hole in a tree where my father collected honey from *nyiwan* [a type of bee]. It is still there. Where are the marks made by your father?"

Narratives of Belonging

In asserting their rights to land, Penan speak not only in terms of specific places in the landscape, but of a more general sense of belonging or of their land having been bestowed upon them by a higher power. Often such statements are made in the context of discussions about timber companies' suggestions that they should simply move elsewhere. In some cases, Penan state that they are unaccustomed (*be' malai* [E. Penan]) to living elsewhere. In other instances, Penan speak in terms of inheritance—that they live where they do because their ancestors lived there—and they point to the graves of those ancestors as proof. One Eastern Penan headman described how the people from the timber company were continually urging him to move elsewhere. In describing these exchanges, he asserted that moving was impossible because here in the Tepen River valley were the sago groves and fruit trees of his parents and grandparents. In a final rhetorical flourish, he declared that he would only move once— when he goes to heaven.

The theme of divine sanction for their land claims is one that is heard often among Penan. On one occasion, a nomadic Eastern Penan man was recounting a conversation he had had a few days before with a group of loggers. The loggers asserted that this land did not belong to Penan, that it had already been divided up between companies, and that the manager had maps to prove this. Those who were listening responded with a series of interjections. An elderly woman responded by saying, "The land is given to us by God, Jesus, Allah; not by [Chief Minister] Taib Mahmud." She added that this land and all the things it contains—sago, rattan, fruit, game—were created by God. On another occasion a nomadic Penan headman asserted that the land was divided by God, lest people bother each other. He then went on to provide an example: "When the rivers flood, even huge logs wash downriver. How many times has this happened? How many logs have washed downriver? But the fish are always here; they always return to us. That is because God has provided for us, has given us this portion of land."

Contrast and Separation

In their efforts to convey their concerns about logging to others, one of the most common tropes Penan employ is that of contrast: the lives of coastal peoples and the lives of Penan, how government treated them long ago and how it treats them now, what the forest is like before logging and after logging, and so forth.

Among the most salient contrasts characterizing the Penan worldview is the distinction between the realm of forest and headwaters they inhabit and the "realm below" (*daleh ra'*) or "realm downriver" (*daleh bai*). Penan speak of the forest as a familiar, comfortable place—cool, clean, and undisturbed. The realm below, in contrast, is seen as a threatening and dangerous place, miserably hot and defiled by human and animal waste. In speaking about their own lives, Penan describe how they prefer to "mix with the trees" (*pekelet ngan kayo*). One man spoke of how they live their lives "on the mountains, on the ridges, in mossy forest, in the headwaters of the rivers" (*tong pegi, tong tokong, tong payah, tong iut ba*). This they contrast with life "in the open" (*tong nawa*), in the sunlight (*tong pete*). Even settled Penan reflect this attitude. As one settled Eastern Penan headman described to me, "We Penan aren't accustomed to living in secondary growth" (*Be' ami Penan malai murip lem repo'*). A nomadic Penan, responding to the urgings of an elderly Kayan man to persuade him to settle, said that to live in a longhouse would be to live like chickens in a cage.

The contrast Penan make between the lives of those downriver and the lives of Penan plays on the idea of separation: that just as Penan do not interfere in the lives of downriver people, so they should not bother Penan. Such rhetoric is deployed in reference both to logging and to the efforts of government officials to persuade Penan to settle. As Penan see it, upriver and downriver are separate orders of existence: they believe they have respected others' lives by leaving them alone and believe that others should respect them in return. If downriver people stayed in their place, according to one Penan headman, they would not be at fault (*be' salah*). But they refuse to do so, and this makes their presence a transgression. Penan express this view in less direct terms as well. One evening an argus pheasant (*kuai*) began calling from a ridge nearby. The headman of the nomadic group I was staying with commented on this, saying that *kuai* called in this way when they have found fruit and want to tell other *kuai* about it. He then said that downriver people are accustomed to hearing the calls of carabao, goats, chickens, pigs, and other domestic animals, while

Penan hear the calls of *kuai* and other forest birds: *metui*, *belengang*, *lukap*, *bi'ui*, and *pegem*. These, he said, are the sounds they are familiar with and fond of, sounds that make them feel longing for the land, sounds that belong here. The sounds of domestic animals, on the other hand, belong downriver, as do those who keep them.

This theme of difference and separation is expressed in other ways as well. One nomadic Eastern Penan headman stated that Penan life is based on eating sago, not bread and sardines. He said that when government ministers eat chicken or sardines, Penan don't offer to help them: "We don't ask if they want to eat *ußud* [pig] or anything else." In other words, he did not see why they insist on always trying to get Penan to change their way of life, trying to get them to adopt a new diet. Penan are satisfied to leave them to their own wants, and they should be satisfied to let Penan follow their own wants. On another occasion, a group of Penan were expressing their discontentment with how their complaints were consistently ignored or dismissed. One woman, playing on an inversion of the idea of difference, began to joke about what she would do if the chief minister came to visit them. The moment he stepped out of his helicopter, she would walk up to him, shake his hand, and, as a gesture of welcome, give him a bottle of diesel fuel to drink, telling him it was the only clear liquid around. Then, she said, they would put a loincloth on him, give him a blowpipe, darts, machete, and all the things Penan view as necessary to survive in the forest, and let him live as a Penan so he could see what it is like to live their life. Teach him all we know, she said. No, another man disagreed; let him figure things out for himself. She, meanwhile, said she would switch places with him, going to town, having money, drinking coffee in coffee shops, sleeping, and going to coffee shops again.

Eastern Penan extend this conception of appropriate locations/identities to the realm of government as well and attach it to a historical dichotomy that contrasts colonial and postcolonial governments. Remarks about their current situation are constantly contrastive in this regard. On several occasions I was told that *orang putih* were like real fathers to them, whereas the present Malay government was like a stepfather. Often people said they did not want to take the medicines given to them by Malays, but that they wanted medicines from *orang putih*. Before, Eastern Penan say, it was easy to get shotguns; today it is impossible. *Orang putih*, they say, were happy to sit with and eat with them; Malays refuse to do so. Eastern Penan portray colonial officers as predictable and trustworthy, people who abided by their word. The present government, by contrast, is portrayed as duplicitous. During the colonial period, according to one Penan, the Forest Department protected trees and "used laws" (*pakai udang udang*), whereas the present Forest Department is interested only in cutting trees. The point of this pervasive Eastern Penan contrast is that they believe the colonial government respected them and the integrity of the lands they occupied, while the current government does not. As one nomadic Penan man said, they never had to raise blockades against *orang putih* but only against Malays.

Finally, the rhetoric of contrast is often applied to their lives before and after logging. According to one Eastern Penan, today they must travel far to procure food (*pita urip ju*, lit. "search for life far away"). He continued by saying that before they "followed the sago" (*kißu ußud*); today, on the other hand, they must follow the shoots of rattan (*kißu saßi*). I will consider other such contrasts in the following discussion.

Sounds, Colors, Textures

When Penan talk about logging, they focus not only on the tangible effects, but on the intangible and aesthetic as well. Among the most poignant expressions of concern about logging are those that refer to sound. Aside from the buzzing and clicking of insects, the sound of wind, and the calls of birds, the forest is a relatively quiet place. Penan value this quietness, especially nomadic Eastern Penan, who construct their *lamin* on ridges. One of the primary reasons they do so is so that they can hear when others call out to them. In the steep mountains of the upper Tutoh, sound travels far, bouncing off ridges and traveling miles up the valleys. Today, these ridges and valleys reverberate with the sounds of logging: the rumble of bulldozers, the whining of chainsaws, and the concussion of falling trees. Sitting in the camps of nomadic Penan, one can hear the continuous distant rumble of logging trucks upshifting and downshifting along the steep mountain roads. Penan continually exclaim at the sounds of logging: *Tulow!* (Crazy!), *Matai!* (Death!). On one occasion, as I was resting with a group of Penan on a ridge, we listened as bulldozers cleared a road, a process accompanied by the sharp cracks of trees breaking and the concussion of large trees falling to the forest floor. At last, hearing a tree fall, an elderly widow exclaimed, "*Ineh! Ha' patai!*" (There! The sound of death!).

With such sounds continually assaulting their senses, Penan speak with great nostalgia for the soundscape that characterized the forest before logging. As one Penan man put it, all the game was now gone, and he "missed the voice of the argus pheasant, missed the voice of the langur, missed the sounds of pigs," and his "head hurt, [his] brain hurt from the sounds of bulldozers, the sounds of chainsaws."

Associated with the rhetoric of sounds is, again, the theme of contrast and separation: that it is appropriate to hear some sounds in the forest and appropriate to hear other things downriver. One man stated that in the forest it was good to hear the call of the argus pheasant but not the crowing of chickens owned by loggers; it was good to hear the creaking of trees but not the whining of chainsaws. In statements about the appropriateness of separation, Eastern Penan state that they do not interfere in the lives of downriver people and do not bring their sounds to them; likewise it is inappropriate that downriver people should bring *their* sounds to the forest.

Among the most tangible manifestations of logging is the opening of enumerable roads and bulldozer tracks, and these are the subject of frequent commentary by Penan. Here color and texture are most often commented upon. Penan contrast the unmarked category *tanah* ("earth/land/forest") with the red earth (*tanah bala*) characteristic of logging roads. With the high rainfall characteristic of central Borneo, these soils often become supersaturated and, as noted, the detritus from road building often spills hundreds of feet downslope from where roads are built. Both large landslides (*besale' ja'au*) and small landslips of viscous mud are common: Penan refer to the latter as "dissolved/melted earth" (*tanah munyai*). They decry the way such soils are transported quickly into the rivers following any substantial rainfall, choking those rivers with mud. Occasionally, Penan express their concerns with a sort of gallows humor. Penan who live adjacent to the now-muddy Ubung River have a running joke about how lucky they are because they have an endless supply of Milo, a chocolate drink mix. In the town of Marudi, they say, one must buy Milo; in the Ubung River, it flows freely.

Metaphor and Analogy

Among Penan, one of the personal qualities most highly valued is the ability to speak with rhetorical flair. The mark of an effective leader is an ability to persuade through elegance of expression. In prayers, songs, and everyday utterances, Penan delight in the play of clever indirection through metaphor and analogy. The Eastern and Western Penan dialects are rich in terms intended to avoid reference to death, illness, or misfortune as well as to health and well-being, on the theory that such subjects are likely to attract the attention of malevolent spirits. Whether in the context of everyday conversations, sly asides, mocking references, impassioned speeches, or heated exchanges, Penan seek to convey meaning through metaphor and analogy. This is reflected in the arguments Penan make about logging.

As noted, in speaking to loggers, civil servants, environmentalists, and others, Penan attempt to speak across difference and to familiarize themselves, and here the turn to metaphor and analogy comes into play. For example, a common rhetorical strategy among Penan is to compare the forest to things that they know outsiders are familiar with: banks, shops, houses, rice fields. On one occasion Penan explained to me that for them, the forest was like their rice field: "How would it be if someone drove through your rice field with a bulldozer; don't you think you would have the right to be upset. How is it that the government cannot see this?" This person asked how the chief minister would feel if a group of Penan drove a bulldozer through the middle of *his* house. One Penan explained patiently to me that the forest was like their office: "Civil servants go to the office every day, and that is how they make their living. And then they get paid. We Penan, we go to the forest every day: the forest is our office. But our money is not there waiting for us. We must get things in the forest to make our living."

Penan metaphorize the instruments, the effects, and the agents of logging. Concerning the instruments of logging, Penan commentary on bulldozers (*lipan*, literally centipede) is especially prevalent. On one occasion when I was traveling through a timber camp with a group of Penan, we stopped to look at bulldozers parked nearby. In disgust, one man referred to them as *sitan tokong* (ridge devils). On another occasion a nomadic Penan headman complained to me that Penan were now under assualt. However, he explained, they were being killed not by guns or bombs but by *lipan*. Like weapons, he added, *lipan* are aimed right at them.

Another set of metaphors and analogies is intended to describe the effects of logging—the hunger, hardship, and heat that befall Penan as a result of logging. Penan often refer to logging as an epidemic (*penyakit*). They frequently comment directly on the destitution they have experienced, but they express this in indirect ways as well. One young man explained to me that before logging, their feet were covered with *lengurep*, a type of small fly. He went on to describe how *lengurep* are attracted to the dried pig blood that often covers their calves and feet when they are carrying a pig they have killed while hunting. In other words, with the arrival of logging, all the pigs are gone and *lengurep* are therefore not attracted to them. Another Penan man said he has tried to explain to civil servants that the effects of logging are the same as if the timber companies had cut their chests and stomachs open, taking out their lungs, stomach, and intestines, that logging destroys their ability to eat and to breath.

The heat and desiccation resulting from logging are also frequently mentioned. One nomadic Penan explained to me that once their land is logged, theirs will be a life of doing nothing but sitting under *gogong*, a large-leafed tree that grows along logging roads and is associated with bright sunlight, heat, and dust—for Penan, an image of utter desolation. Another Penan living in a heavily logged area said that with logging, they were now like fish living in hot water. On one occasion, I was complaining about a headache and joked that it was caused by poison given to me by loggers. One man responded by saying it was caused by sunlight (*pété*), and then he added slyly that sunlight was indeed the poison given to them by the loggers who fell the forest.

Finally, Penan direct many of their comments at those who they believe are responsible for creating hardship. One nomadic Penan compared timber companies to hornbills feeding on the fruits of a *nonok* (*Ficus sp.*) tree. Hornbills, he said, consume all the good fruit and let only rotten fruit fall to the ground. Once they have finished off the fruit, they fly away, leaving nothing behind. On another occasion, a Western Penan man was comparing the behavior of companies to the act of butchering a pig. Among Penan, sharing is a central value, and this applies especially to meat brought back from hunting trips, which is shared evenly among households. As this man put it, the behavior of the company is reprehensible because they insist on taking all the land themselves, leaving only the smallest fragments to Penan. This, he said, was as if, in dividing up a pig, the company took all the meat and left a single hair and a sliver of the toenail to Penan.

Boundaries, Borders, and Blockades

Another prominent discursive element in Penan narratives of dispossession is that of boundaries and borders. Indeed, much of their response to logging, whether in the form of blockades or in their not-infrequent arguments with company officials, can be seen as an extended discourse of boundaries and their violation.

In making their arguments about boundaries, Penan cite colonial practices as historical precedent. In the Tutoh River area, Penan put particular stock in signs erected by the Forest Department in the late 1930s. These signs, only a few of which still exist, indicated that significant portions of the Tutoh and Baram watersheds were "Protected Forest." Such Protected Forests, which existed in several parts of Sarawak, were established in large part to prevent expansionistic Iban swidden farmers from moving into particular areas, in this case the Tutoh and Baram watersheds. Penan throughout the region describe how these signs were erected along ridges by a colonial officer they call Tuen Nubun and say they regarded them as an indication that the government was dividing up one portion of the land for Penan (*tulat tanah Penan*). As Penan recall, colonial agents reassured them that nobody would move into their areas or otherwise bother them. Now, however, timber companies pass through this border (*pajao sempadan*) with no regard for Penan claims. Indeed, Penan claim that timber companies are purposely targeting these signs, burying them with bulldozers, so as to erase any sign that this land was ever set aside for Penan. As one nomadic Penan expressed it, these are the *real* sign from the government; company people make their maps duplicitously from high above (a point to which I will return).

The blockades for which Eastern Penan has become so well known are an extension of the discourse of boundaries and borders. Blockading extends far beyond the erecting of major blockades along main roads. Throughout the forest, Penan have erected myriad small markers, fences, and minor blockades intended to indicate to loggers that they should proceed no further. Often sharpened sticks and poisoned darts are placed facing down-ridge as a threat to loggers (in spite of the fact that Penan have never followed through on such threats). Among nomadic Penan in particular, the primary strategy is one of boundary defense. Throughout the area between the Magoh and Tutoh rivers, nomadic groups are playing a game of cat and mouse with loggers, setting up their camps just inside the zone where logging operations are occurring in order to keep an eye on the progress of bulldozers and trying to anticipate where they will go next and to dissuade them from progressing any further.

All such efforts are directed at maintaining at least some areas as undisturbed forest—what Penan refer to, using Malay terms, as *pulau* (islands) or *tanah simpan* (saved land). These *pulau* are of various sizes, from just a few hectares to many square kilometers. Recognizing that logging has continued despite their blockades, Penan see the effort to preserve *pulau* as a last-ditch effort to save whatever they can of the remaining forest in their immediate areas. Some *pulau* are established as a result of negotiations with companies, but these tend to be small, intended primarily to assure a supply of clean water to settled communities, and company managers consistently urge Penan not to ask for too much.

The government has also weighed in on the saving of portions of forest by alternately proposing and then disavowing or ignoring the establishment of Penan Biosphere Reserves. Penan have become active participants in this discussion: indeed, their efforts to maintain *pulau* are in part intended to indicate to the officials where they want to see reserves established. In the early 1990s, there was discussion within the government of establishing a series of specific reserves in the Adang, Magoh, and Melana river areas—some sixty-five thousand hectares in all. These were officially announced, and maps were circulated. The Sarawak State Government declared the Melana Forest Reserve to be a Biosphere Reserve set aside in perpetuity for the Penan. All the nomadic groups in the Tutoh area are aware of this declaration but have stated unequivocally that they will not move there. They recognize that the Melana area has already been logged (by one of the most notoriously abusive companies, no less) and say it would at best be no different from where they are now. The proposed Adang and Magoh Biosphere Reserves are presently being logged: indeed, in the Magoh area (between the Magoh and Tutoh rivers), logging is proceeding at a rapid pace, and only a small portion of it remains undisturbed. The proposed Pulong Tau National Park has repeatedly been diminished in size by the granting of timber concessions, and roads have been pushed into this area as well.

From one perspective, logging can also be viewed as a set of boundary-making practices. Timber operations are organized in terms of coupes (areas licensed to a company that can be harvested for one year) and blocks (smaller harvesting units, mapped out by companies as part of their harvesting plan and marked by survey crews). Throughout those areas that are just inside the frontier of areas being logged, one encounters trees marked with numbers and splotches of paint (*ritit*) indicating block boundaries. To logging companies, the grid they lay over the landscape is a numbered one of coupes and blocks. With the exception of a few of the larger rivers, place-names are irrelevant. One strategy of Penan resistance to logging is the attempt to erase those boundary markers. Wherever one finds *ritit* in the forest, one is also likely to see some attempt by Penan to remove them, usually by cutting the bark off trees on which they occur. Penan who have encountered survey crews have also confiscated block maps by force.

Part of the discourse of boundaries and borders is a discourse on their vio-

lation. Penan speak frequently of timber companies or the government disregarding (*lebuau*) or opposing/violating (*ngelawan*) the boundaries they establish or transgressing boundaries so as to bother (*ngasao*) them. In describing
how others disregard the boundaries they claim, Penan frequently invoke the
idea of laws (*udang*). On the top of a small ridge blockade in the vicinity of the
Puak River, a group of nomadic Penan placed a leaf in which was put a handful
of dirt said to represent the land in which ancestors were buried. As the headman of this community explained, should the company cut the post on which it
sat and the leaf full of earth fall to the ground, it would be seen as a declaration
that the company had "violated Penan laws" (*ngelawan udang Penan*).

In many cases, the rhetorics and practices associated with boundary making
have precipitated dispute not only with the government and loggers, but also
with Orang Ulu communities and other Penan. In central Borneo boundary disputes between adjacent agricultural communities are the norm, and
such disputes may persist for decades. With compensation agreements and employment opportunities at stake, logging has only served to exacerbate such
disputes.

Boundary disputes between Orang Ulu and Penan have become particularly acute in recent years; indeed, nearly every settled Penan community in
the Baram District is involved in a dispute with its neighbors. In part the conflicts stem from Orang Ulu communities' resentment of Penan efforts to stop
logging by establishing blockades. But they are also a product of the fact that
many Penan occupy lands that were granted to them by Orang Ulu communities when they settled, at a time when having Penan in the vicinity of one's
longhouse represented a form of wealth and the lands given to Penan were
mostly unused. Now that Penan are claiming large tracts of land and com-
promising longhouse compensation agreements with timber companies, many
Orang Ulu communities are telling Penan they must leave. Always a marginalized community, settled Penan are in an especially disadvantaged position in
their disputes with Orang Ulu communities.

Equally significant, the advent of logging has exacerbated disputes among
both nomadic and settled Penan over boundary claims. One nomadic group,
for instance, began to encroach on lands that had been occupied by another
nomadic group for several generations. When the other group protested, the
headman of the encroaching group said mockingly that the other headman
was "unimportant" (*be' guna*) and that, if he wanted a *pulau*, it should be no
bigger than from his hut to where he goes to defecate. He subsequently trav-

eled to Marudi and asked representatives of Sahabat Alam Malaysia to draw him a map asserting his claims to land, which he then presented to the District Office. On this map he claimed a large swath of land, including much of the area that the other group occupied, areas he had traveled to only briefly; he did not even know the correct river names. This precipitated a series of hostile exchanges between the two Penan groups involved.

More serious have been disputes between Penan that occur when those from one Penan community enter the lands of another to do survey work for timber companies. With their skills in the forest, Penan are in demand to serve on survey crews. Nomadic Penan who have steadfastly refused employment with timber companies consider Penan surveyors from other communities to be absolute traitors. On one occasion a group of nomadic Penan were commenting on the fact that Penan from other communities had been seen leading survey crews. One man responded angrily, "If I see Penan surveyors, I'll shoot them with my blowpipe—no discussion." On another occasion, a group of visiting Penan were telling those from another group how they had encountered Penan from a settled group surveying their area. Everyone expressed disgust at this. One man said if he had been there he would have led them away and burned their paint. Another added, "Not just their paint! I would take their knives, their supplies, their roof tarps, and everything else!" Sometime later this individual sent out a photocopied map of the Magoh River and its tributaries, accompanied by a letter prepared by representatives from Sahabat Alam Malaysia and intended for distribution to other Penan groups. While one portion of the letter was written in Malay and intended for managers, another portion was written in Penan. It was a strong warning to Penan from other groups not to enter their area to do survey work:

> I, Saya Ikan Megut, prohibit survey work, kayu garu work, prohibit fishing, prohibit any work in our land. I say this to those Penan at Lg. Siang (Tama Baun), Moyong (Ba A'eh), T.K. Gadong (Lg. Kawa), T.K. Baran (Lg. Balau), Lg. Sebayang (Bajah). I prohibit you (you who are corrupt with the company) making difficulty for me in Ba Magoh. All of you people from those groups who don't agree, don't work here anymore. All of you who oppose what I say, I promise you will just die. No negotiation because you oppose what we say. You simply cannot oppose what I am saying here.

Such disputes also occur between communities of settled Penan. This, as noted, is particularly prevalent among Western Penan. These disputes are associated not only with conflicting claims over land, but also with regard to employment. Western Penan have repeatedly attempted to persuade companies to deny employment to individuals from other communities, arguing that only members of their own community have a right to employment within the areas to which they lay claim. In 1992, Western Penan from one community came upon an empty forest camp being used by a survey crew that included members of another Western Penan community. Upon finding this camp, they slashed all the tins of rice, biscuits, and other supplies.

Maps, Letters, Declarations

In asserting claims to land, arguing for the establishment of *pulau*, attempting to demarcate borders, and contesting the claims of timber companies, Penan make use of several forms of inscription. The two most significant are maps and letters or declarations. Penan see that loggers bring in maps, show them official letters, and try to compel them to sign documents, and that all of these serve to validate company claims to Penan lands. Penan recognize that these are the single most effective way to assert their claims in a way that is meaningful to outsiders. As a result, Penan have repeatedly sought to produce such maps, letters, and declarations or to have others produce them on their behalf. Penan often bring out maps when discussing logging, and District Office files are full of maps and letters from Penan communities.

Such maps are often accompanied by statements or declarations, sometimes handwritten but often typed by representatives of Sahabat Alam Malaysia, sometimes in Penan, other times in Bahasa Malaysia, and almost always signed with the thumbprints of Penan headmen. Such documents, intended for either the District Office or timber companies, usually request that land be set aside. They cite the Penan need for food and the products the land provides and often assert the historicity of their relation to a given piece of land. A 1988 letter prepared by the members of a settled Penan community illustrates such documents. This letter, written in somewhat rudimentary Malay, reads as follows: "These are all the names of previous headmen or Penghulu that have died. Because these are our ancestors, we know that this is our land. Many of these graves in the hills above deteriorated even before we came down to make longhouses. These are all the names of the hills and mountains where we lived before." This is followed by several brief lists: a list of mountains in the Baram and Patah river watersheds; another list of mountains in the Tutoh and Apoh river watersheds; a list of former Penan headmen in the Baram and Patah rivers; a list of former Penan headmen in the Tutoh and Apoh rivers; a list of the "names of government" including *laja king*, *laja kuwin* (queen), *laja beruk* (Brooke), and several Baram district officers from the turn of the century; and a list of native officers from before World War Two. The man who showed me these lists stated that they were prepared for the company, because company officials so often say that Penan are lying about their land claims. In showing me this letter, he stated that whenever they present such things to the government or companies, they just wait: there is never any answer.

At the same time they are asserting their own claims to land, Penan deny the validity of maps produced by others. One nomadic headman, referring obliquely to map-making practices, described timber companies as "stealing [land] from open places" (*nekau jin sawang*)—that is, from the outside. Another member of his group, asserting the validity of the "Protected Forest" signs erected in the 1930s, stated that, in contrast to the Brooke government, contemporary government maps are nothing but a lie because they are made from high above. That is, the government flies over, makes their maps, and gives them to timber company survey crews. All they see is the crude physical shape of the land. The fact that the government makes these maps from a distance is seen by Penan as an indication of duplicity. They don't go to Penan to negotiate, and when Penan go to try to find them, they can never be found and are trying to avoid Penan. On one occasion, the headman of one nomadic Penan group was telling the members of another group how they should deal with timber companies. Don't go to them, he said; make them come to you. Make sure to write down their names, so they can't give you the runaround later and say they don't know whom you talked to. And make sure they bring maps—which they try to hide in their offices. Without maps, any negotiation is an exercise in futility, he said. As if to stress how one must proceed in the most legalistic way when dealing with timber companies, he then pulled out a slip of paper on which was written, "I met with Penan, 18/8/93," followed by the names of the manager and his foreman.

Penan contrast the way companies make maps from a distance with the way they themselves do: by walking through and over every valley and ridge, by filling the place with names, and by sustaining themselves on resources that have been passed down for generations. As one nomadic Penan man sarcastically said he would ask loggers, "If this is your land, why do you always ask us the names of rivers? Do you know the names of places? You and your people are always asking—what is the name of this river?, what is the name of that river? If you don't know these, you don't belong here."

Narratives of Agency: Responsibility and Respect

The Penan response to logging is a product not only of the tangible effects of environmental degradation, but also of the way they perceive themselves to have been treated by those with an interest in its continuation: camp managers, police, politicians, and others. Any analysis of Penan land-claim narratives must therefore take into account how Penan subject those they believe are responsible for it to criticism. Both Eastern and Western Penan feel they are looked down upon, ignored, and treated unjustly. In short, Penan are responding not only to logging as an activity that directly affects their lives, but also to the *agents* of logging.

Penan hold two parties responsible for the present situation: logging companies and the government. In fact, they often conflate these, assuming either that they are a single entity or that logging companies are working under direct instructions from the government. As evidence of this, Penan cite the fact that when they have blockaded logging roads, it is police who come to dismantle their blockades. Penan assume that most government officials are acting as agents of logging companies for purely personal gain. To the extent they recognize the distinction between the government and logging companies, Penan believe the government does not listen to them and supports only logging companies because it looks down on them. While I was with the Penan, I repeatedly heard statements such as "When they look into our eyes, they see the eyes of a monkey, the eyes of a dog," "They think we have tails," and "They look at us like they look at dog shit." As one woman commented, government officials think Penan just "sit around in the headwaters."

Many Penan, especially the remaining nomadic groups, do not know exactly what the government is. At one point during a discussion with several Penan, I used the phrase *"perinta Sarawak"* (Sarawak government), after which one man asked another what I meant. Another man answered him by saying, "Taib Mahmud." That is to say, nomadic Penan sum up the Sarawak State Government in the person of the chief minister. One nomadic Penan asked me, "Where is the actual person of the government [*usa perit*], Taib Mahmud? They [loggers] only show us letters that they say are sent to them by the government. They come by helicopter. But the government itself is never visible." For these groups, the distinction between the political domain and the civil service is unclear, as is the distinction between the state and federal governments.

Penan view both the government and timber companies as insensitive at best, but more often as duplicitous and vindictive. Penan believe that timber companies have no regard for them and wish only to harrass them. The term Penan use to characterize the behavior of companies more than any other perhaps is *ngasao* ("bother, harass") — that is, they see themselves as being harassed for no reason and owing to no fault of their own. One woman compared the behavior of logging companies to the presence of Iban forest collecting parties early in the century, groups that not uncommonly took heads when they could get away with it. It is not only the logging itself by which Penan feel harassed: timber workers are continually seeking out Penan settlements, looking for young women, and timber companies hire gangsters to intimidate them. Nomadic groups believe that government efforts to persuade them to settle are nothing more than a crude ploy to remove them from the forest so that it may be logged without interference. In areas where blockades have occurred, Penan express fear that because the government is displeased with them, it has sent *penyamun* out to get them. *Penyamun* are people who use stealth to take heads or steal blood, particularly from women and children. Company managers, frustrated by Penan demands, threaten Penan that they will be arrested. One company manager threatened nomadic Penan that if they interfered with his work, they would be arrested, taken downriver, thrown in jail, and die. Companies often ignore Penan warnings as to the locations of graves, assuring Penan that they will not bulldoze places where graves occur, and then doing so as soon as Penan are not paying attention. Penan characterize government officials and company representatives as people who "don't know how to pity" or "don't know how to think." They recognize that their efforts to explain their situation have had little effect, and they find it inconceivable that their concerns are so completely disregarded.

When Eastern Penan discuss why they erect blockades, they provide many reasons. But one theme arises more than any other: Penan say they blockade because "the government does not hear what we say." Both Eastern and Western Penan repeatedly described the government and companies as being deaf. One man said that companies come to his place with their ears blocked and their eyes closed, and that no matter how much they talk to the companies or what they say, it does no good. Another man said that even if his mouth opened all the way down to his chest and clear down to his feet, company people would still not hear what he said. He said that talking to company people is like talking to a cartoon: they look at you and never respond. Penan say that companies don't want to hear their complaint and that government officials are not any help. In every Penan community Penan recount with frustration their efforts to meet with timber camp managers: how they travel great distances only to find that the manager has gone to town for the day or is otherwise unavailable. Penan are often treated with visible contempt by timber company representatives. When they try to tell company people about the existence of graves, they are scolded and told they are lying and that they shouldn't interfere with logging. As Eastern Penan describe it, they blockade because they believe this is their only recourse: they declare that they do it as a last resort, and then only to the extent necessary to be heard.

Company and government officials do not listen to them, Penan assert, because they do not respect (*mengadet*) them, and they interpret this as a form of insult. The notion of respect or regard (*mengadet*) has wide currency in Penan social discourse, whether in talking about relations among those within a community or about relations with those outside a community. Significantly, the stem of the term *mengadet* is the word *adet* (*adat*). Discussions of the concept of *adat* are widespread in the ethnographic and historical literature on insular Southeast Asia (von Benda-Beckmann and Strijbosch 1986; Holleman 1981; Hooker 1978a, 1978b). Numerous discussions have considered the multiple meanings of the concept of *adat*—as custom, tradition, and the like—or examined the degree to which the interpretation of *adat* as law is a colonial product.

As Penan employ the concept of *adet*, it indeed conveys a sense of custom or tradition: for instance, Western Penan often contrast true '*ade*' *(adet lan*; alternatively *adet sao*, or old *adet)* with more recent cultural innovations, which they see as less genuinely Penan. But this far from exhausts the semantic dimensions of the term. One of the most important contexts in which the term *adet* is used is in highlighting particularity and contrast along dimensions of both ethnicity and community: Penan *adet* versus Kayan *adet* or the *adet* of one's own community versus that of other Penan communities. An important dimension of meaning of the Penan concept of *adet* is that it is learned. Children are often excused for actions that would be severely criticized if they were adults on the grounds that they simply "do not know *adet*" (*iyeng mejam adet* or *mujen adet* [W. Penan]; *Be' mejam adet* [E. Penan]). While not knowing *adet* is acceptable for children, it is entirely unacceptable for adults.

This points to another dimension of the meaning of the term *adet* among Penan: it is employed as an evaluative device. The language of judgment for Penan is almost entirely framed in terms of *adet*. The *adet* of an individual or community is evaluated in terms of its intrinsic goodness or badness; those who are perceived as good are characterized as *dian adet* (good *adet*), while those who are perceived as bad are characterized as *saat adet* (bad *adet*). To be characterized as an adult lacking in *adet* (*kurang adet*, *iyeng pun adet* [W. Penan], *be' puun adet* [E. Penan]) or not knowing *adet* is one of the strongest forms of condemnation.

To turn to the relation between *adet* and respect, the concept of *adet* is frequently linked to matters of feeling. This linkage is often made in the context of characteristically reduplicative evaluative statements, such as when Penan might say of a person that they "do not know *adet*, do not know feelings." As such, breaches of *adet* are seen to reflect a lack of regard of one person or community for others. To conform to *adet*, therefore, is to show regard for, to respect the feelings of others. This is often manifested in matters such as the proper (or affectionate) use of personal names, kinship terms, or death-names. The point I wish to stress here is the centrality of the notion of respect or regard in Penan social discourse generally and, in the present case, in statements about their relations with logging companies and the government. Penan attribute the unwillingness of these agents to listen to them to a simple lack of respect. Western Penan in particular view this unwillingness to listen as a direct insult.

Penan construct the issue of blockading not only in terms of disrespect and insult, but also in terms of fault (*tißeh* [W. Penan], *salah* [E. and W. Penan]). Fault, they assert, lies with those who bother them rather than staying in their own places downriver. In statements about their response to logging, Penan go to great lengths to avoid any implication of fault on their side. As Penan describe it, all they are trying to do is "search for food, search for life" (*pita kinan, pita urip*), just wanting to be left alone. When they attempt to negotiate with the government or companies, they then sit back and wait for some result; repeatedly they talk again and wait again. They describe themselves as being patient, slow to anger, and unwilling to act foolishly or precipitously.[19] As one woman put it, once they have spoken to the government, they wait patiently "in front of the government, not behind." Only when they lose patience with waiting—when they are "fed up with talking" (*sarah pani* [E. and W. Penan])— do they blockade. In their view, because they first wait patiently and make numerous attempts at dialogue, they are entirely without fault in the matter of blockades: they are driven to it by the inaction of the government. Such statements about their patience serve as a way of definitively assigning fault—exonerating themselves from blame and laying the blame squarely at the feet of companies and the government. Any action they might then take can no longer be considered their fault, they assert: they have acted in good faith and done all they can. In their attempts to place fault on those other than themselves, Penan are employing principles that are a feature of traditional moral discourse and ethnojurisprudence, principles that are employed in divorce proceedings and in other instances of dispute adjudication.

Penan describe their disagreement with the government and logging companies in terms of the ability to answer (*sap* [W. Penan], *jawap* [E. Penan]). In any kind of dispute among Penan, the *answer* has a kind of climactic quality. It is considered a good quality to wait patiently through multiple accusations, letting one's opponent criticize or attack one again and again. The answer, at last, is a definitive moment, an unambiguous statement of the rightness of one's own case. The party at fault, Penan assert, cannot answer. If they do, they "do not know how to feel shame." In speaking about their reasons for blockading, Penan represent their actions as a kind of answer: the act itself, in their moral evaluation, is a statement of the rightness of their cause.

Discussion

The present discussion is a work in progress, and I would like to draw on the material I have provided here to address, tentatively, a series of issues I believe those engaged in the documentation of similar struggles might wish to consider.

The first matter concerns the issue of resistance. More to the point, I am interested in the question of how recent theoretical trends have shaped the perception of indigenous and other mobilizations treated in scholarly accounts, and how this has caused us to misread what we are observing. Resistance, of course, is a topic about which much has been written in recent decades by scholars across a range of disciplines.[20] The theorizing of domination has consistently been framed as being manifested in contests in which there are agents who exercise power/hegemony and agents who resist. What the present analysis points to is a recognition of the fact that much of what we have come to designate resistance in our analyses may be something quite different. What we may in fact be observing are efforts at engagement/articulation: efforts born of frustration and desperation, to be sure, but efforts at engagement all the same (Zerner 2003). As noted, in making their arguments to loggers, civil servants, environmentalists, and others, Penan are attempting to speak across difference, to familiarize themselves, to frame their arguments in ways they hope will be recognizable to outsiders. This is what lies behind Penan arguments linking the forest to a supermarket or a bank and linking the act of driving a bulldozer through the forest to driving it through the house of the chief minister: such arguments are meant to appeal to what Penan presume is a shared sense of justice and respect. Penan are forever looking for just the right analogy, as if the problems confronting them are the result of people simply not understanding the situation they are facing. Even those most visible icons of Penan resistance, blockades, can be viewed as something more than acts of defiance against the state. They are erected, Penan state, in an effort to get the government to listen to them. To be sure, not all Penan responses to the incursion of timber companies—small ridge blockades festooned with poisoned darts, for instance—can be viewed as attempts at engagement. A good deal of what we observe in the Penan response to logging can also be seen as reflecting Scott's distinction between public transcripts and hidden transcripts (Scott 1990). Nevertheless, much of the Penan response to logging might be assessed as something other than resistance, and this in itself should compel us to invoke the notion of resistance a bit more cautiously.

The second matter I wish to address concerns the need to foreground notions of agency in narratives of landscape and dispossession. In recent years we have observed a florescence of scholarship focused on conceptions of landscape and "senses of place."[21] This important literature has alerted us to the rich variety of narrative forms through which societies inscribe and express their presence in the landscape. This literature has been of considerable influence as I have struggled to understand and explicate Penan conceptions of landscape. It would be a mistake, however, to accept uncritically all Penan statements about the forest and its destruction as reflective of some fixed Penan conception of landscape.[22] Rather, I believe we need to make an effort to discern how Penan conceptions of their audience condition the arguments they put forth. The question I posed earlier is apropos here: in what ways are various expressions of sense or metaphor expressed or elided in various narrative forms intended for different audiences? Penan recognize that the claims they are making in narratives of belonging are mostly illegible to outsiders, but the discursive forms they deploy in the effort to make those claims legible shift according to their perception of the audience they are addressing. As noted, this is as much a poetics of culpability as a poetics of place. An additional issue centers around the question of whether mobilizations themselves have an influence on those discourses of belonging that brought them into being. As the Sarawak campaign gathered momentum and Penan began to come into ever more frequent contact with agents who themselves were responding to Penan claims — Northern environmentalists, government ministers, police, and others — how did Penan incorporate the responses of these agents into their claims in new ways? I have not adequately addressed this question in the present discussion, but it is an issue that would seem to deserve further consideration.

Third, I want to address the matter of translation. In speaking of translation, I prefer a more expansive definition, one that extends beyond the notion of formal translation of a written or spoken text. Indeed, one could argue that acts of translation can occur between those speaking the same language, as when Penan enter into discussions with officials through the medium of Malay. I regard translation as any effort to reach across difference and to make one('s) view known to another who is presumed to be unfamiliar with it.

While neither traditional hermeneutic concerns nor Heideggerian questions about the incommensurability of translation have quite disappeared, in recent years they have been upstaged by a whole set of questions about the relationship between translation and power. Indeed, the entire sweep of work running from *Orientalism* (Said 1978) and postcolonial scholarship to the "crisis of representation" (Marcus and Fischer 1986) and "the problem of speaking for others" (Alcoff 1991) intersects with questions of translation at numerous points and in numerous ways. It is impossible today to speak about translation without addressing a whole range of questions: Who is translating for whom? What is the nature of the relationship(s) between speaker/writer, translator, and audience, and what does this have to do with what gets translated? What silences are imposed with different forms of translation produced by different agents? What are the implications of the fact that translations now move through seamless transnational networks of circulation?

What is clear is that it is no longer enough to assume that there is such a thing as the single best translation of a text and that the act of translation is more problematic than ever. Taking seriously the kinds of questions posed here demands that we acknowledge that there is a politics of translation, that there is no privileged position from which one may produce a translation, and that in our own engagements with various texts we must be alert to the conditions under which translation occurs.

In the case of the Sarawak campaign, many kinds of agents have been engaged in the production of translations. Certainly, as I have shown, Penan themselves are engaged in a constant effort at reaching across difference and making themselves known to others. But for the sake of discussion I want to focus briefly on recent analyses of Northern environmental and indigenous rights discourse. In recent years a considerable number of scholarly analyses of activist movements have been published, and in these analyses the critique of essentialist discourse has been a prominent theme. This approach has characterized my own work. In an article published in *Human Ecology* (Brosius 1997a), I examined how Northern environmentalists constructed Penan land rights claims in terms of an appeal to essentialized notions of indigenous wisdom and the sacred. Such imputed qualities, I argued, when imposed over indigenous landscapes and ecologies and incorporated into a broader circulation of campaign images, may in fact distort their significance to indigenous communities.

If we accept the arguments that there is no privileged position from which to produce a translation and that there is no such thing as a single best translation, it requires that we place academic projects of translation, the present chapter included, on the same playing field as other projects of translation: as subject to our own politics and practices and as worthy of interrogation as any other such project. This is unsettling: how do we respond to the suggestion that, despite our efforts at developing scholarly competence, our translations are just as contingent and problematic as other translations? While I do not wish to end this discussion on a note of reflexive hand wringing, I do think it useful to leave this as a question for discussion rather than to attempt a definitive answer. It does seem to me, however, that there is a place for an enterprise focused on elucidating the conditions under which translations, our own and others', get made, that focuses on the micropolitics of translation as well as on the macropolitics of circulation and reception. For instance, one question that any treatment of the Sarawak campaign must address is the way in which Malaysian political culture shapes the reception of Penan narratives, whether those narratives come directly from Penan or whether they first circulate through activist networks. The official view of Penan is that of a people who wander aimlessly through the forest in search of food, living a hand-to-mouth existence, a people without history and without a sense of place, utterly

outside the "space of citizenship" (Painter and Philo 1995). To Malaysian officials, their way of life is little more than a form of vagrancy in which would-be
subjects are able to evade the gaze of the state. Forests and those living within
them are a terrain for creating a "national biography" (Anderson 1983): objects
to be brought back into history, to be transformed and made "legible" (Scott
1998) through development and through the production of a thoroughly modernist landscape. The only way Penan can be heard, the only discourse audible
to the state, is that of development, or rather a certain form of development:
a hypermodern vision in which dispossession is cast as opportunity. As Brennan argues in a recent analysis of the cold war encounter between capitalism
and communism, in the encounter between Penan and the state "there are no
grounds even for persuasion" (Brennan, forthcoming).

Finally, I would like to suggest that attention to the politics of translation
can provide a productive link between academic and activist projects. We have
reached a point at which it is critical to develop a successor project to academic
critiques of activist discourses. The effort to elucidate the contexts, politics,
and practices of translation in the context of environmental/indigenous rights
mobilizations such as I have described here provides just such an opportunity,
even if the precise outlines of that effort are at present still unclear.

Notes

1. See King 1993 and Rousseau 1990 for overviews of the societies of Borneo. In
Sarawak the term *Orang Ulu* is used to designate groups such as Kayan, Kenyah, Kela-
bit, Berawan, Kajang, and other central Bornean ethnic groups, not including Iban. In
many contexts Penan are classified as Orang Ulu, but for present purposes I use this
term to refer only to stratified, longhouse-dwelling agriculturalists.

2. Though in broad outline the forest adaptations of Eastern and Western Penan are
very similar, and though they speak mutually intelligible subdialects of the same language, there are significant differences between these two groups with regard to subsistence technology, settlement patterns, social organization, and the tenor of social
relationships. In Sarawak there are also several small, scattered groups of long-settled
Penan with close linguistic affinities to Eastern and Western Penan. For more information on Penan in Sarawak, see Arnold 1958; Brosius 1986, 1988, 1991a, 1992a, 1992b,
1993a, 1993b, 1995a, 1995b, 1995–96, 1997a, 1997b, 1999a, 1999b, 2001; Harrisson 1949;
Huehne 1959; Kedit 1978, 1982; Langub 1972a, 1972b, 1974, 1975, 1984, 1989, 1990;
Needham 1954a, 1954b, 1954c, 1965, 1972; Nicolaisen 1976a, 1976b, 1978; Urquhart 1951.

3. The type of products collected has varied through time. Camphor, *jelutong* (a type

of latex), *damar* (a resin), and rhinoceros horn were important trade products at various times in the past. Both in the past and at present the Penan have been known for the fine woven rattan mats and baskets they produce. In exchange for these products, Penan have received metal, cloth, salt, and tobacco.

4. See Baring-Gould and Bampfylde 1909; Irwin 1955; Payne 1960; Porritt 1997; Pringle 1970; Reece 1982; Runciman 1960; Tarling 1971, 1982.

5. This conservative attitude was perpetuated both by a self-interested concern that a European commercial class in Sarawak might challenge Brooke authority and by a belief that such enterprises were antithetical to the interests of indigenous communities (Reece 1988:32).

6. The idea of development in Sarawak is valorized—indeed, hypervalorized—into a totalizing discourse aimed at producing a thoroughly modernist landscape. One senior official described this landscape in the following terms:

> I can see a state that is peaceful and harmonious where the people live in love, joy, prosperity and happiness. It is a beautiful land where there are excellent and thoughtfully planned roads, lights, power, water supply, communication lines, schools, clinics, and hospitals reaching the rakyat in all parts of Sarawak.
>
> The landscape is a beautiful scenery of smartly irrigated land covered by high yielding crops contributing to high income and a dignified standard of living especially to our rural lot. (Effendi Norwawi 1993:27)

7. Today the pace of logging has diminished, as timber stands are much depleted and as companies from Sarawak have moved to Papua New Guinea, Surinam, Guyana, and elsewhere. See World Rainforest Movement and Forests Monitor, Ltd, 1998.

8. Sarawak state law does not recognize Penan principles of land tenure. In contrast to the longhouse communities of Kayan, Kenyah, and other ethnic groups, even settled Penan generally lack the prerequisites for the legal recognition of land claims. According to Sarawak land law, communities can only claim land that they cultivated before 1958. The majority of Penan settled after that. Thus, their claims to land are without legal basis. Nomadic groups are in an even more difficult position with respect to land claims. Burials are one basis for the recognition of Native Customary Rights land in longhouse communities. Because Penan graves are scattered and are visible for only a few years, the government does not recognize them as having any legal significance.

9. Another characteristic of the Western Penan response to logging has been a distinct lack of unity among communities. In fact, as logging has entered the areas claimed by various communities, Western Penan have devoted as much attention to undermining each other's claims as they have to responding to the incursions of logging companies. The reasons for such antagonism vary, but they are often associated with conflicting claims over certain plots of land for which communities are demanding compensation. Among many Western Penan communities there are long-standing disputes over rights to land. Even before the advent of logging, such disputes were a central feature of West-

ern Penan intercommunity relations. The entrance of logging companies has only exacerbated an already existing situation.

10. See Brosius 1997b.

11. I provide a more detailed history of the Sarawak campaign in Brosius 1999a. Also see Colchester 1989; Hong 1987; INSAN 1989; and Sesser 1991 for information on the situation of indigenous communities in Sarawak. The focus on Penan in this campaign occurred in spite of the insistence of Malaysian environmentalists and others that this was an issue that involved indigenous peoples in Sarawak as a whole, rather than just the Penan. One focus of my research is to try to understand why so much of the imagery of the international campaign was focused on the Penan.

12. Despite being the object of a massive manhunt by government authorities between 1985 and 1990, Manser was never successfully apprehended, largely because the Penan uniformly denied any knowledge of his existence. Recently, Manser disappeared while returning illegally to Sarawak, and his fate is presently unknown.

13. See Manser 1996.

14. In the United States, the Sarawak situation received coverage on *NBC Evening News*, National Public Radio, CNN, and *Primetime Live* as well as in *Newsweek*, *Time*, *The New Yorker*, *The Wall Street Journal*, and *Rolling Stone* (for example, see Linden 1991 and Sesser 1991). The BBC and *National Geographic* both produced documentaries on the Penan. The Australian film *Blowpipes and Bulldozers* and the Swedish film *Tong Tana* both reached large audiences and received wide acclaim. Meanwhile, Penan were awarded the Reebok Human Rights Award and the Sierra Club–sponsored Chico Mendez Award, and the SAM activist Harrison Ngau was awarded the Goldman Prize for his work against logging in Sarawak.

15. In speaking of "Malay rule," I must stress that I am referring to the Penan conception of government. The Sarawak State government in particular is conspicuously multiethnic.

16. Among Eastern Penan today there are any number of expressions of this hope for a return to colonialism. Among the most common are declarations of how they feel when seeing foreign visitors. On one occasion, while speaking to a group of Eastern Penan, one man commented wistfully, "When we think of you [*orang putih*], we think of our mothers and fathers." Another expression of Eastern Penan hope for a return to colonial rule is direct questions about when *orang putih* can return. One woman asked me, "When you leave, when are *orang putih* coming back? We will just stay here and wait." One of the most tangible Eastern Penan expressions of the expectation of return to colonial rule is that they consistently refer to Westerners as *perita* ("government"), a borrowing of the Iban/Sarawak Malay term *perintah*, or use the terms *orang putih* and *perita* as synonyms.

17. For Western Penan, logging is an issue that is negotiated entirely with reference to the present, with contemporary government authorities. Western Penan talk about

the colonial past does not have nearly the same resonance as it does among Eastern Penan, and they express little in the way of colonial nostalgia. It is also significant that Western Penan have only rarely been visited by environmentalists.

18. The processing of sago requires clean water. In watersheds affected by logging, clean water is almost impossible to find. Thus, even when the sago in a particular area has not been destroyed, it is nonetheless impossible to process because of the scarcity of clean water.

19. Both Eastern and Western Penan use the expression "long feelings" (*kebi kenin* [E. Penan]; *buat konep* [W. Penan]) to express such patience. The opposite, a negative quality, is to have "short feelings" (*suti kenin* [E. Penan]; *suta' konep* [W. Penan]) to express such patience.

20. Comaroff 1985; Foucault 1978; Ong 1987; Scott 1985, 1990.

21. Basso 1984; Feld 1982; Hirsch and O'Hanlon 1995; Myers 1991; Povinellii 1993; Rosaldo 1980; Roseman 1991; Weiner 1991; Zerner 2003.

22. On this point see Kumar 1997:212.

Between Nature and Culture

Rappaport's Rose: Structure, Agency, and Historical Contingency in Ecological Anthropology

J. Stephen Lansing, John Schoenfelder, and Vernon Scarborough

"By isolating man from the rest of creation and defining too narrowly the boundaries separating him from other living beings," writes Claude Lévi-Strauss, "the Western humanism inherited from antiquity and the Renaissance has deprived him of a bulwark" (Lévi-Strauss 1985:23). Roy Rappaport often echoed a similar theme: "I predict revitalization of the ecosystem concept because it seems to accord with a general public's commonsense experience of a world beset by multiplying and interrelated environmental disorders, most of which it can attribute to humanity itself" (1990:69). Such remarks were seldom well received; Lévi-Strauss complains that he was "often reproached for being antihumanist,"[1] and it is possible to read Rappaport's intellectual trajectory as one long struggle to reconcile his scientific methods with his humanist aims. How is it possible to situate human subjects in the environments they occupy and shape without paying the theoretical price of turning them into objects and anthropology into mere calorie counting? Can ecosystems include human subjects? If not, as Rappaport famously inquired, "How shall we understand a rose?" (1990:68).

This problem is ours to cope with, if we (as social scientists) intend to make any serious forays into ecology. We cannot wait for a new or expanded ecology to solve it for us because the problem of agency, or conscious design, only appears when we introduce thinking and laboring subjects into an ecosystem. Even *Annales* historians such as Fernand Braudel, who explicitly recognized the formative power of the "structures of the *longue durée*" on human life, treat historical actors as passive objects shaped by ponderous environmental constraints. Similarly, Rappaport and other anthropologists who adopted the methods of systems ecology were forced to treat humans purely as objects, as sources and sinks of energy flows.² To date, the only serious attempt to address both the subjective and objective aspects of the encounter of humans with nature is Marx's philosophical anthropology. Marx proposed a solution to what we might call the problem of the rose: "natural" phenomena that cannot be explained without reference to human agency. More important, Marx provided a framework with which to understand how humanized nature— objects like roses, with intentional design—might in turn actively shape the world of human subjects. But these aspects of Marxist theory have been largely neglected by social theorists, who until quite recently were content to leave nature to the natural scientists.

As Marx recognized, the introduction of the human subject into a material ecology poses the problem of agency, the efficacy of human intention, in a way that references time or, more specifically, history. Ordinarily, when anthropologists consider the human subject their focus is on their informants, the people they actually encounter in fieldwork. Most theoretical discussions of agency, therefore, are addressed to the phenomenology of this encounter, an approach that is attentive to issues pertaining to individual subjects. But cultivated roses, or for that matter radioactive by-products, are not the intentional creations of a single mind. They are, instead, products of the engagement of many minds with material objects, over historical time. Thus, a Balinese landscape of terraced fields and aqueducts is both a material reality and a social creation. This is what we take Marx to have meant by "humanized nature." The presence of human subjects distinguishes it from "external nature" (*sinnliche Aussenwelt*), a material reality that bears no trace of human labor or conscious design. Marx observes that "external nature" exists today "nowhere except perhaps on a few Australian coral islands" (Marx 1927 I, 3:44). Thus, for the social theorist what counts is "humanized nature," which is brought into being by human society. Anthony Giddens puts it well: "In Marx, nature appears as the medium of the realization of human social development. Marx emphasizes that social development must be examined in terms of an active interplay between human beings and their material environment" (1981:59).³

What arguments does Marx develop to support this conclusion? "It is as clear as noon-day," he begins, "that man, by his industry, changes the forms of materials furnished by Nature, in such a way as to make them useful to him" (Marx 1961:71). The resulting "humanized nature" has both an objective and a subjective meaning. Objectively, humanized nature is technology or the engineered landscape; it is the world we inherit from our predecessors, modified by their purposive labor. Born into a landscape of terraced fields and irrigation works, a Balinese farmer inherits a functioning *techne*, a technology that both defines and constrains the possibilities for his own engagement with the material world. Clearly, this techne as an objective, material reality bears the traces of purposive design; it also provides a tangible record of changes in a society's relationship to the material world. Techne also has a subjective meaning for Marx, signifying the process by which it came into being. Techne exists because society exists; it signifies not merely the immediately preceding generation from whom it is inherited, but also the entire historical process that brought it into being.[4] But techne is not only an (inherited) technology: it also establishes the material conditions for work and so for one's engagement with other members of society. The "material exchange between man and nature" is a "perpetual necessity"; it happens in real historical time and simultaneously shapes the material world and the human subject (Marx 1967:47). Ultimately, it brings forth the "social subject," the consciousness of self as part of a social whole. This argument is neatly summarized by Jürgen Habermas:

> Only in its process of production does the species first posit itself as a social subject. Production, that activity which Marx apostrophizes as continuous sensuous labor and production, gives rise simultaneously to the specific formations of nature with which the social subject finds itself confronted, and the forces of production that put the subject in a position to transform historically given nature in its turn, thereby forming its own identity. (1971:39)

Techne both constrains and empowers the social actor—constrains because it defines our productive engagement with the material world, empowers because it stimulates the consciousness of self as a social being that is a prerequisite for *praxis*, which is Marx's term for salient agency. Because human nature is constituted by this process, "history is the true natural history of man" (Marx and Engels 1927 I[3]:162). Thus did Marx "turn old Hegel on his head" and relocate the growth of historical self-awareness from philosophy to the labor process; as Marx put it, "The much-renowned 'unity of man with nature' has always existed in industry" (Marx and Engels 1965:43).

The weak link in this argument is the presumption that humanized nature must invariably signify Marx's own concept of "society" as a historical subject. The individual laborer's experience of his tools, his associates, and the tasks at hand is assumed to lead inexorably to the grand Marxian metanarrative of "the world-historical self-formative process of mankind" (Habermas 1971:39). But for this to be the case, each human subject would have to follow a chain of signifiers leading from the immediate and the particular to the most abstract: society, history, and freedom as universal categories. In other words, the experience of labor is supposed to lead inexorably to an awareness of oneself as a historical subject, in the Marxian sense. If we have learned anything from the comparative anthropological study of cognitive systems, it is that such abstractions are universals only as they appear within the context of post-Kantian Western philosophy. Paradoxically, it also robs individual subjects of agency, since the path of historical development is laid down in advance as the growth of the Marxian-Hegelian concept of freedom.

So, is humanized nature a meaningful category if we relinquish the assumption that it points inexorably to the Marxian metanarrative? We suggest that, at a minimum, it is a reasonable starting place for the study of ecosystems that include human subjects. Marx was correct: nature "taken abstractly, for itself—nature, fixed in isolation from man—is *nothing* for man" (1961 [1844]:169). What is most valuable in the concept of humanized nature is the insistence that the symbolic associations pointing back from the object world to the human subject are real and fundamental to our experience of material reality. Thus, a thousand-year-old Balinese rice terrace, or *sawah*, is at once an object with its own biophysical properties and the congealed labor of thirty generations, rich with symbolic meaning—a site where the living generation collectively encounters the natural world largely, but not entirely, transformed into a techne by their predecessors. All this may be true, even though the experience of working together in such a site does not compel the farmers mentally to recapitulate *The Phenomenology of Mind*.

From this perspective, the salience of human agency in the material world becomes apparent. Humanized nature appears as the product of a temporal process in which individual actors engage in purposeful modification of their environments; large red roses are at once herbaceous plants and objectifications of a cultural aesthetic.

The Problem of Agency

Marx's concept of humanized nature provides a conceptual framework that enables us to introduce concepts of subjectivity, meaning, and history to the analysis of ecosystems that have been shaped by human labor. Humanized nature appears as the outcome of a historical process in which social actors intelligently modify their environments. But this presents a problem as a research strategy, if we wish to make use of the tools and methods of ecological analysis as they have been developed in the natural sciences. The difficulty is that ecology is built on mathematical foundations that leave no space for intelligent agency. Although two quite different mathematical approaches are used in modern ecology, neither is compatible with a concept of active human agency. Systems ecology constructs models consisting of coupled linear differential equations to predict changes in flows of nutrients and energy. The focus is on an entire system of relationships that determines patterns of change and growth. Behavioral ecology, by contrast, focuses on the individual; its conceptual foundation is the mathematical theory of natural selection. Despite these differences, both systems and behavioral ecology use ordinary differential equations to predict patterns of change: rates of growth in the case of systems theory and the distribution of fitness measures within populations in the case of behavioral ecology. For this reason, both are fully deterministic and leave no room for salient agency.

One way out of this difficulty is exemplified by the research we describe in this chapter. We adopt the analytical framework of nonlinear dynamics, a relatively new branch of mathematics that can be used to study the interactions of populations of heterogeneous agents. In nonlinear systems, effects are not additive: the solution to two equations will not be equal to the solution to the sum of these equations.[5] The detailed behavior of most nonlinear systems cannot be predicted but may be explored and characterized through simulation. In principle, nonlinear dynamics enable us to examine the effects of intelligent agents interacting with one another within environments that include both living and nonliving components. It is also possible to include linear systems within this analytic framework, so that we have full access to the tools of systems and behavioral ecology. If large-scale patterns emerge, they will do so as a result of a historical process of interactions among agents, which will gradually change the characteristics of the ecosystem itself. Thus nonlinear dynamic models provide a possible mathematical foundation for the study of humanized nature.

Adopting a nonlinear dynamical viewpoint places us in somewhat the same position as the social and natural scientists of the late nineteenth century, who grappled with the causal implications of the new science of statistics. For as with statistics, while the behavior of individual agents may appear to be entirely unpredictable, the behavior of large numbers of individuals may turn out to fall into simple patterns, the issue that troubled Nietzsche. This creates a kind of paradox: free will at the level of the individual can lead to emergent patterns of order at the level of the group. A century ago, this paradox was a major scientific and philosophical issue for such scholars as Charles S. Peirce, Francis Galton, Ludwig Boltzman, and James Clerk Maxwell. Clerk Maxwell, who borrowed Quetelet's social statistics to reformulate the laws of motion probabilistically, became obsessed with this question. Invoking the poetry of Tennyson to describe the movement of molecules, Maxwell observed that chance interactions could generate higher-order patterns. Maxwell developed this reasoning into an argument against determinism, in which physical laws would appear as the outcome of statistical tendencies: the actual behavior of molecules or atoms could arise from the aggregates of "multitudes of causes each of which is by no means uniform with the others" (1890, vol. II:53). As Maxwell came to see it, "chance" may not be measurement error but, rather, intrinsic to such interactions (as physicists were later to prove). In a similar way, the interactions of human agents pursuing different strategies and behaving, in a word, indeterministically may generate patterns of emergent order. Structure in the cultural or historical sense may be an emergent property—more than the sum of its parts. The processes by which structures can emerge from the interaction of autonomous or semiautonomous agents is a central problem for nonlinear dynamics; here we will describe a search for such patterns. We invoke Maxwell's argument to head off the objection that mathematical models of human subjects must necessarily rob them of agency. On the contrary, both chance at the level of the individual and contingency at the level of history are fundamental to this approach. Here the search for Braudel's "structures of the long run" begins with the individual.

Structure from Agency

> The explanation of the amazingly high standard of rice cultivation in Bali is to be found in Montesquieu's conclusion that "the yield of the soil depends less on its richness than on the degree of freedom enjoyed by those who till it."
> —F. A. Liefrinck, a senior Dutch colonial administrator in Bali, circa 1887

To illustrate this argument, we describe the results of a series of investigations into the role of agency in the development of the "engineered landscape" of irrigated rice terraces in Bali. The concept of humanized nature that constitutes the foundation of this analysis results in a research strategy in which we are compelled to tack back and forth between ecosystemic processes and human intentions. We aim to show that this seeming eclecticism is a productive way to explore the question of how agency can generate structure as a historical process. Later sections will add a temporal dimension to our argument, through an analysis of recent archaeological research.

Bali is a volcanic island located just south of the equator in the Indonesian archipelago, in the region of tropical monsoons. Each year, several hundred inches of rain fall on most of the island. To the observer looking down from the summit of a volcano toward the seacoast, the effects of this rainfall on Bali's fertile soils are apparent in the dense tropical forests. Until about a thousand years ago, when the Balinese developed irrigation technology, these forests covered most of the island. But today they survive only at high elevations and in the western third of the island, which lacks suitable conditions for irrigation and is mostly uninhabited.

The vast majority of Balinese live in a south-facing natural amphitheater created by the curving chain of volcanoes that form the geological backbone of the island. The dimensions are small: from the eastern border of the Balinese rice-bowl to the western is about fifty miles, and from the uppermost rice terraces to the sea is never more than twenty-five miles. This landscape is constantly being rearranged by volcanic eruptions, which deposit large quantities of ash over whole districts while burying others under lava flows. There are about eighty rivers in the southern ricebowl, and most of them have sliced channels fifty to two hundred feet below the surface of the surrounding landscape. Within this region—the southern ricebowl of Bali—for more than a thousand years generations of farmers have gradually transformed the landscape, clearing forests, digging irrigation canals, and terracing hillsides to enable themselves and their descendants to grow irrigated rice. As the rice terraces expanded and the population grew, villages were probably forced to migrate from the valleys to the hillsides, eventually moving all the way up to the ridge-tops, where the irrigation canals could not reach. Today most villages are strung almost end to end along the flanks of the volcanoes. The rest of the landscape is almost entirely given over to the rice terraces.

The rice terraces are managed by hundreds of local farmer associations called *subak*. The membership of each subak generally consists of all of the farmers who obtain irrigation water from a common tertiary irrigation source, most often a canal. Subak members meet regularly to manage their irrigation system, decide on cropping schedules, and organize annual cycles of agricultural rituals in their fields. These rituals appear to have a performative effect, timing the actual sequences of agricultural labor in the fields. In the 1970s, Clifford Geertz proposed an elegant model suggesting that the timing of the ceremonies of the rice cult is "symbolically linked to cultivation in a way that locks the pace of that cultivation into a firm, explicit rhythm." For example, the "water-opening ceremony" held in certain temples actually schedules the beginning of the irrigation schedule, just as the harvest ceremonies mark its end. The rituals of the rice cult thus provide a means for the farmers to time the flow of water and the phases of agricultural labor. In Bali, Geertz wrote, "a complex ecological order was both reflected in and shaped by an equally complex ritual order, which at once grew out of it and was imposed upon it" (1980:82). This argument was soon criticized by another anthropologist, Mark Hobart, who argued that the actual sequence of rituals is often badly synchronized with what is happening in the fields. Hobart criticized Geertz for creating an idealized picture of the match between rituals and rice growth and suggested that the real picture was far more complex. In effect, Hobart argued that Geertz's model of ritual-as-template neglected the real agency of individual farmers (Lansing 1987).

Our research began with an attempt to resolve this dispute. Lansing's first fieldwork (1971, 1974–76) happened to coincide with a period of dramatic changes in Balinese agriculture, changes which posed the question of agency in practical as well as theoretical terms. The 1970s marked the introduction of the Green Revolution to Bali, in the form of technology "packets," including new high-yielding rice varieties, commercial fertilizers and pesticides, and a system of credit designed to encourage the farmers to purchase these "inputs." From the perspective of the foreign consultants charged with promoting the Green Revolution, the ritual calendar of the agricultural temples seemed to pose an obstacle to increasing rice production, because it allowed for only two harvests of slow-growing native Balinese rice per year. Water temple rituals amounted to a template for subsistence agriculture, which would have to be abandoned as a practical guide for scheduling cropping cycles, in favor of more frequent plantings. This would create a need for more irrigation water, which could be met by a new $55 million irrigation development project.

The expert view was perfectly rational, based on a Braudelian view of the farming system as a historical accretion of rites and practices that enabled the farmers to exploit their landscape in a traditional way. But the Green Revolution in Bali soon led to "chaos in the water scheduling system" and "an explosion of pests and diseases." Through participant observation, Lansing learned that the farmers see the water temples as places to meet and debate the advantages of different cropping schedules, providing a flexible framework for groups of farmers to sustain complex patterns of cropping cycles that are responsive to environmental conditions. These decisions appeared to be based on a sophisticated understanding of the ecology of wet rice.[6] But the Asian Development Bank, which took a leading role in the Green Revolution in Bali, was reluctant to concede that the water temples could still play a constructive role in boosting rice production (Project Performance Audit Report 1988:47).

A second phase of this project began in 1986 with an attempt to decide this issue. James N. Kremer, a systems ecologist, and Lansing developed an ecological simulation model to evaluate the effect of the water temples on the productivity of the rice terraces. Since one of the most important features of water temples, according to the farmers, is the ties they sustain with other temples, in order to capture their role it was necessary to study networks of temples along a river, not just individual water temples. The model we developed encompassed nearly two hundred subaks along two adjacent rivers in central Bali. It was designed to simulate the flow of water and the growth of rice and rice pests in each of these subaks over the period of a year. Using this spatially detailed model of rivers and subaks, we could also simulate the effects of varying scales of social cooperation in the selection of cropping patterns.

A cropping pattern is a plan that determines which crops will be planted and when. For example, a typical cropping plan might be "plant *cicih* rice during the week of 20 February and *mansur* rice the week of 10 August." Once this has been decided, the irrigation schedules can be fixed. Rice terraces need a lot of water at the start of a cultivation cycle: the fields must be flooded and an artificial pond created. Later, the water level can be slowly reduced until the fields are dry at harvest time. Because the subaks are generally very close together, the timing of the cropping patterns of upstream subaks affects the amount of irrigation left over for downstream subaks.

Cropping patterns also influence the population dynamics of rice pests, including rats, insects, and insect-borne diseases. If all of the fields in a sufficiently large area are harvested at the same time and subsequently flooded, rice pests are deprived of their habitat. If no alternative hosts are available, the pest population will drop (Aryawan et al. 1993). The need to minimize losses from pests is a strong motivation for farmers to cooperate with their neighbors in synchronous planting schedules, even though this forces everyone to plant exactly the same crops and may lead to water and labor bottlenecks.

Choosing the best cropping pattern involves finding the scale of spatial synchronization that optimizes the trade-off between water shortages (caused by too many synchronized subaks experiencing peak irrigation demand at the same time) versus pest damage (caused by too little synchronization of cropping patterns). When a subak selects its cropping pattern, it actively modifies ecological conditions for its neighbors (pest populations and irrigation water flows). Given the hundreds of subaks distributed in many branches along a typical river, there is an enormous number of possible cropping schedules.

Comparisons of model predictions with real data on irrigation flows, harvest yields, and the population dynamics of rice pests showed that the temple networks achieved near-optimal rice harvests by minimizing water shortages and the dispersal of rice pests. This result led us to speculate on the role of agency, of human intentionality, in the water temple system. How do the water temples get it right? To see how complex and unlikely the solution is, consider the following illustration.

Imagine a jigsaw puzzle of a watershed with one hundred subaks, where each color signifies a cropping plan for the year: yellow might mean "plant a particular rice variety the week of 15 February and a different rice variety the week of 20 July." Groups of subaks up and down the river choose this plan, while others choose different plans, symbolized by different colors. The result is a patchwork of colors covering the whole watershed. A vast number of different-sized and different-colored patches is possible, but nearly all of them would lead to acute water shortages and pest outbreaks. For example, if everyone followed the yellow plan, pests would be minimized by a fallow period extending over the whole watershed. But water shortages would be disastrous because all fields would experience peak irrigation demand at the same time. Yet our computer simulations showed that the subaks somehow find their way to near-optimal solutions to this complex problem of optimization. How could dozens of local plans add up to a watershed-level solution to the problem of avoiding water shortages? Our point is that the subaks do not consciously attempt to create an optimal pattern of staggered cropping schedules for a whole watershed. Nonetheless, such patterns occur and are probably typical. Management at the local level, by many small groups of neighboring subaks, leads to region-wide solutions. But how? Where was the salient agency in such a decentralized system?

Nonlinearity and Trajectories of Change

First Chaos came into being, but next Gaia.
—Hesiod, *Theogony*, 116–17

In the absence of a central authority with the ability to calculate and impose an optimal cropping pattern for an entire watershed, it must be the case that the subaks somehow find their way to a global solution, even though each subak is only trying to find the optimal cropping pattern for its own immediate neighborhood. We needed a simple model that could predict whether any given pair of subaks would benefit by deciding to synchronize their cropping pattern. There should be two players in each interaction: an upstream subak, which by virtue of its location controls water flow, and a downstream subak, which needs some of this water. To simplify the problem, let's assume that these players can adopt one of two possible cropping patterns, A and B (for example, A could mean planting on 1 January and 1 May, while B could mean planting on 1 February and 1 June). Further, assume that the water supply is adequate for both subaks if they stagger their cropping pattern, but if both plant at the same time, the downstream subak will experience water stress, and its harvests will be somewhat reduced. Finally, assume that pest damage will be higher if plantings are staggered (because the pests can migrate from one field to the next) and lower if plantings are synchronized. Let p ($0 < p < 1$) represent the damage caused by pests, and w ($0 < w < 1$) represent the damage caused by water shortage. Given these assumptions, the payoff matrix is as in figure 1, where U and D designate the actions of the upstream and downstream subaks, respectively.

In figure 1 the first number is the payoff (harvest) for the upstream subak, and the second is the harvest for the downstream subak. Thus, if both subaks plant on the same schedule (either A or B), the harvest for the upstream subak is 1, but it is 1-w for the downstream subak because of insufficient irrigation water. If the two subaks choose different schedules (U choosing A and D choosing B, or vice versa), then each subak achieves a harvest of 1-p. We can immediately draw several conclusions about the payoffs for alternative strategies. The upstream subaks don't care about water stress (they are never affected by w), but their downstream neighbors do. (This is the well-known "tail-ender" problem, common to most irrigation systems: the farmers at the tail end of an irrigation system are at the mercy of their neighbors upstream, who control the irrigation flow.) But the upstream subaks do care about pest damage,

	D_A	D_B
U_A	1, 1-w	1-p, 1-p
U_B	1-p, 1-p	1, 1-w

LANSING ET AL. FIGURE I.
Payoffs for the game

since pests, unlike water, are quite capable of moving upstream. So a strategy of synchronized cropping patterns to control pests will always produce higher yields for the upstream subaks. When p > w, the downstream subak will also achieve higher yields by synchronizing. Note that if they do so the aggregate harvest is higher (that is, mean harvests for both subaks go up). If w > p, adding more pests to the fields actually increases the aggregate harvest for the two subaks since it encourages cooperation. But if the farmers aren't worried about pests, the upstream subak has little incentive to give up some of its water in a synchronized cropping plan with its downstream neighbor.

How well does this simple model capture the actual basis for decision making by the farmers? In the summer of 1998, with the help of Balinese colleagues, we undertook an extensive survey of farmers in ten subaks located in the Tegallalang district of south-central Bali. In each of the ten subaks, we chose a random sample of fifteen farmers. Of these fifteen, five were from the upstream region of their subak, five were more from the middle of the subak, and the last five were from the downstream end of the subak. In order to test the predictions of the simple two-player game outlined above, we asked, "Which problem is worse, damage from pests or irrigation water shortages?" The results, shown in figure 2, show that upstream farmers worry more about pests while downstream farmers are more concerned with water shortages.

Based on these perceptions, behavior in accordance with the model may be predicted. In general, the downstreamers should prefer greater offsets in irrigation schedules and be willing to accept higher losses from pests as a result, up to p > w. The upstreamers, meanwhile, should be willing to give up some of their water to enable the downstreamers to synchronize their irrigation schedule. Both, then, benefit from a coordinated fallow period and consequently fewer pests. Put another way, the presence of pests in the ecosystem gives the downstream farmers a lever with which to persuade their upstream neighbors to give them the water they need to avoid shortages. For this reason, the upstream farmers have a reason to help maintain a well-functioning and equitable irrigation system that extends below their own fields.

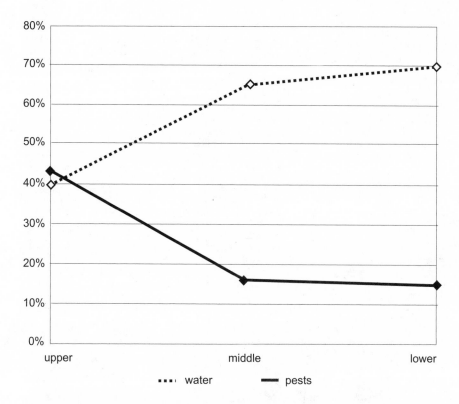

LANSING ET AL. FIGURE 2. Which is worse, pests or water shortages? Aggregate responses to this question by location of fields (n = 149)

The same dynamics can occur at the next level up. Not only individual farmers but whole subaks must decide whether or not to cooperate. In our sample, six of the ten subaks are located in upstream/downstream pairs, where the downstream subak obtains most of its water from its upstream neighbor. Thus, it was also possible to compare the aggregate response of all the farmers in each subak to the response of their neighbors. Figure 3 shows this result.

In figure 3 also, the upstream farmers are more concerned with potential damage from pests than from water shortages, and so have a motive to co-operate with downstream neighbors. By adjusting their own irrigation flows to help achieve w < p for their downstream neighbors, the upstream subaks have the power to promote a solution that is beneficial to everyone. In the real world, losses from pest outbreaks can quickly approach 100 percent after a few seasons of unsynchronized cropping schedules. By contrast, reducing one's

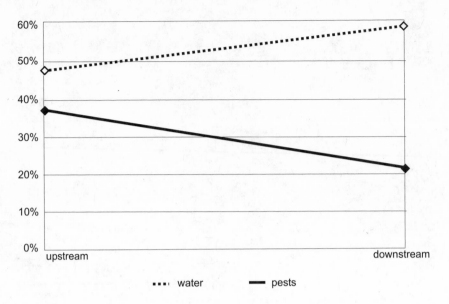

LANSING ET AL. FIGURE 3. Which is worse, pests or water shortages? Aggregate responses to this question given by farmers in three upstream *subaks* and three downstream *subaks* (n = 90)

irrigation flow by 5 or 10 percent (or using one's labor to reduce seepage losses in an irrigation system and so improve its efficiency) imposes lesser costs on the farmers, unless water is very scarce indeed.

These results are also supported by our videotaped records of monthly meetings in which elected representatives of all ten subaks (plus four others not included in the survey) discuss matters of mutual interest. The willingness of upstream subaks to synchronize cropping patterns seems to be strongly related to the perceived threat of pest invasions. It is important to note that which subaks synchronize cropping plans with their neighbors varies from year to year. An increased threat of pest damage, such as has occurred recently in several cycles of pest infestations (brown planthoppers; rice tungro virus) quickly leads to larger sychronized groups, while a year of light rains encourages greater fragmentation. Thus, we appear to have a decent working understanding of the trade-offs involved when subaks decide whether or not to synchronize cropping patterns with their neighbors. But how do the decisions made by interacting pairs of subaks lead to regionwide cropping patterns that apparently optimize conditions for everyone?

To answer this question we need to shift our attention from the interaction of pairs of autonomous agents (the upstream and downstream subaks in the two-player game) to the entire dynamic system—in this case, all of the subaks in a watershed. Intuitively, this is reasonable since the actual flow of water in the rivers and irrigation systems will depend on the cropping schedules set by all the subaks, not just pairs of subaks. We can speculate that the patterns of cooperation (synchronization of cropping patterns) among the subaks could be the outcome of a historical process in which the subaks sought to find the best balance between water sharing and pest control. Using real data on the location, size, and field conditions of 172 subaks in the watershed of the Oos and Petanu rivers in southern Bali, we modeled changes in the flow of irrigation water and the growth of rice and pests as subaks chose whether to cooperate with their neighbors. Here each subak behaves as an "adaptive agent" that seeks to improve its harvest by imitating the cropping pattern of more successful neighbors: "As a new year begins, each of the 172 subaks in the model begins to plant rice or vegetables. At the end of the year, harvest yields are calculated for each subak. Subsequently, each subak checks to see whether any of its closest neighbors got higher yields. If so, the target subak copies the cropping pattern of its (best) neighbor. The model then simulates another year of growth, tabulates yields, and continues to run until each subak has reached its local optimum" (Lansing and Kremer 1993:212).

The simulation begins with a random distribution of cropping patterns (figure 4). After a year the subaks in the model begin to aggregate into patches following identical cropping patterns, which helps to reduce pest losses. As time goes on, these patches grow until they overshoot and cause water stress. Yields fluctuate but gradually rise. The program ends when the model generates a distribution of cropping patterns that optimizes both pest control and water sharing (figure 5). The close relationship between this pattern as calculated in the model (see figure 5) and the actual pattern of synchronized planting units (figure 6) is apparent. In the model, as patterns of coordination resembling the water temple networks emerge, both the mean harvest yield and the highest yield increase while variance in yield across subaks declines (figure 7). Subsequent runs showed that if the environment was perturbed dramatically by decreasing the rainfall or increasing the virulence of pests, a few subaks change their cropping patterns, and within a few years a new equilibrium is achieved (ibid.:215–16).

The model accurately predicts the broad patterns of spatial cooperation.

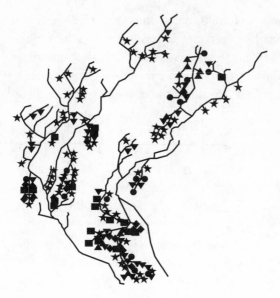

LANSING ET AL.
FIGURE 4. Initial conditions
for a simulation model of
irrigation flows and rice and
pest growth for 172 *subaks*.
Differences in cropping
patterns are indicated by
differences in symbols; *subaks*
with the same symbols have
identical cropping patterns

LANSING ET AL.
FIGURE 5. Model cropping
patterns after eleven years

LANSING ET AL.
FIGURE 6. Historic
cropping patterns

Harvest yields (tons rice per hectare per year)

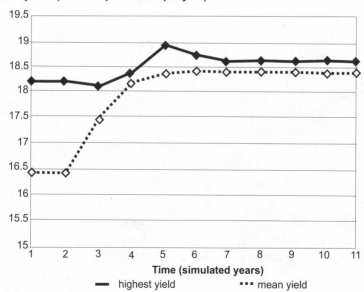

LANSING ET AL. FIGURE 7. Increase in harvest yields in the Bali model. Variance in yields also declines as yields converge toward the (rising) mean

Interestingly, the model also predicts that variance in harvest yields will decline while average yields increase. This also appears to be empirically accurate: in the areas of Bali where synchronous planting is the norm, there is very little variation in harvest yields. In the region where we conducted the survey described above, variance in yields from test plots seldom exceeds 5 percent. This suggests an explanation for the stability of these patterns of cooperation. In game theory, a Nash equilibrium is a state in which each player can do no better by changing her strategy given the strategies of the other players (Nash 1950). Such an equilibrium is more stable than a nonequilibrium state, in which strategies and players continue to compete. Evolutionary game theorists observe that if a game includes evolutionary dynamics, then a Nash equilibrium is also an evolutionarily stable strategy, or ESS (Maynard Smith 1982). Once the players have found an ESS, the system becomes stable. In Bali, it appears that patterns of cooperation among subaks are ancient and very stable; this is easier to understand if we imagine that all of the farmers over large areas obtain harvest yields that are indistinguishable from their neighbors'.

In the latest phase of the research, our attention has accordingly shifted to these local patterns of interaction. In 1996, we began a multiyear study of subaks, water temples, and rice terraces in the region of Sebatu, central Bali. Here, fifteen subaks make up the congregation of a regional water temple, the Masceti temple Pamos Apuh. We wondered whether the "structures of the long run" were to be found at this level: perhaps these fifteen subaks discovered centuries ago that they could best manage their rice terraces at this level. In that case, the ritual cycles that encompass the Masceti temple and the temples of each subak might have become an objectified "structure"—a kind of template defining the relationship of the farmers to the landscape and each other. But, once again, the template vanished on closer inspection. It did not take long to discover that the relations between subaks, the rituals of the temples, and even the irrigated landscape itself are all in a constant state of flux. The closer we looked, the more the balance tilted away from an objectified structure toward a model of active agency. What appears as structure seems increasingly to be the aggregate effect of agency, an ongoing compromise between competing interests.

Archaeological Time Supplies the Canvas

> Still mankind ever since its first emergence has been continually
> experimenting not only in controlling external nature, but also in organizing
> that control co-operatively. The results of these experiments are embodied
> on the one hand in the archaeological record—the concrete relics and
> monuments of the past—and on the other hand in documents transmitted
> orally, pictorially or best of all in writing. History should be the scientific
> study of all these sources.
> —V. Gordon Childe 1953:3

In the summer of 1997, we began an archaeological investigation of a water temple and nearby rice terraces, which we selected as a candidate for one of the oldest such complexes in Bali. Our aim was to explore the historical development of the rice terraces, irrigation systems, temples, and subaks in this region. How stable were the patterns of this "humanized landscape"? Quite to our astonishment, we found that the rice terraces immediately downstream of the water temple appear to be in a constant state of flux—reengineered on a time scale of decades, not centuries. Through mapping, soil coring, and interviews, we discovered that our tiny study area contained several defunct irrigation tunnels and that at least parts of the modern rice terraces are constructed upon several meters of sediment deposited as a result of earlier dam-building efforts. Facts of landscape seem at first glance to constrain irrigation system organization, but, on closer inspection, it appears that these "facts" are themselves to a significant degree results of purposive human action. The landscape bears the marks of past negotiations and is today constructed in such a way as to allow, or even facilitate, further negotiations in the future. The area most closely examined was not a complete subak, nor was it the entirety of the irrigation system watered from the spring. Nonetheless, the microregional processes we observed at this site demonstrate a point that also holds true for larger areas: water rights and even the physical canal systems linking the subaks were constantly renegotiated, and this continues today.

The site investigated was Pura Gunung Kawi Sebatu, which lies in a small valley between the village (*desa adat*) of Pujung Kaja and the village of Sebatu (figure 8). The focal point of this functioning Balinese temple is a springhead that provides water for offerings and for both sacred and secular bathing. The central portion of the temple is maintained by Sebatu, but this is flanked by two connected subtemples: one to the west, which honors a separate springhead sacred to Pujung Kaja, and one to the east, which is one of the "clan

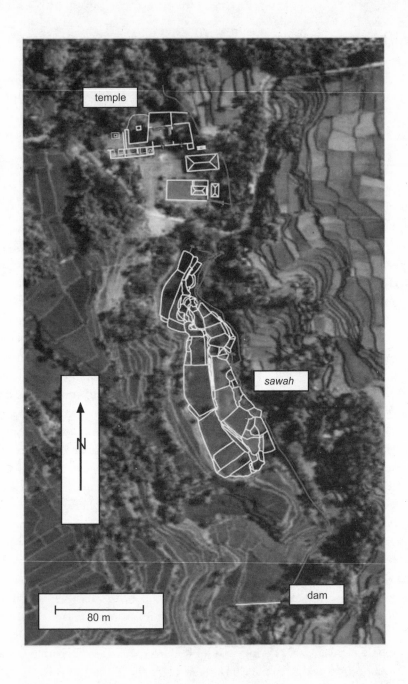

LANSING ET AL. FIGURE 8. Pura Gunung Kawi Sebatu, the adjoining mapped *sawah* area, and immediate surroundings

temples" for the Pasek lineage. A "total station" was used to produce a detailed map covering the temple and a 0.89-hectare area of *sawah*, or rice terrace, in a small valley immediately downstream from the temple spring. At eighteen locales within this zone, a JMC Environmentalist's Subsurface Probe was used to extract soil cores, to depths ranging from 1 to 5 meters as local conditions allowed. Sedimentological, pollen, and phytolith analyses were performed on several of these cores, and a number of AMS radiocarbon samples were processed for dating purposes (see Scarborough, Lansing, and Schoenfelder 1999).[7] While some of these technical analyses proved inconclusive, the evidence as a whole indicates a great deal of dynamism in the landscape.

Most of the water that issues from the spring eventually waters the sawah area that comprises Subak Dlod Blungbang (map 1). Before it gets there, however, it goes through a series of splits and merges that illustrate the considerable complexity of Balinese irrigation systems. Each of the two springs (Sebatu and the much smaller Pujung Kaja) feeds into a separate set of associated bathing pools. Two draining channels serve the bathing areas; the western one commingles the waters of the two springs before flowing south and disappearing into a small tunnel (tunnel A hereafter) under a road causeway built around 1960. The eastern drain, which feeds a large, ornamental reflecting pool, is completely subterranean; it is unclear whether this latter drain contains mixed waters or is purely fed from the Sebatu source. A stream flows past the temple on its east side, and the greater flow from the channel issuing from the reflecting pool joins this smaller water before entering a second tunnel (B) under the causeway.

South of the causeway, we mapped what is locally referred to as a *babakan* — a small area of sawah situated in a valley bottom (map 2). These fields draw from the spring's water before the bulk of that water begins the four-kilometer journey to the fields of Subak Dlod Blungbang. The western tunnel (A) under the causeway apparently forks before emerging; there are thus three tunnel mouths on the south side of the causeway (A1, A2, and B). The westernmost tunnel mouth (A1) feeds immediately into the highest of the mapped sawah terraces, at an elevation 5 meters below that of the main springhead. This is the sole source of water for about 71 percent of the babakan. Because A1 receives at least a sizable portion of its water from the holy spring maintained by the village of Pujung Kaja, the babakan is considered to be socially linked to Subak Pujung to the degree that it is associated with any larger subak at all. The remainder of the mapped sawah receives water from B, the easternmost tunnel.

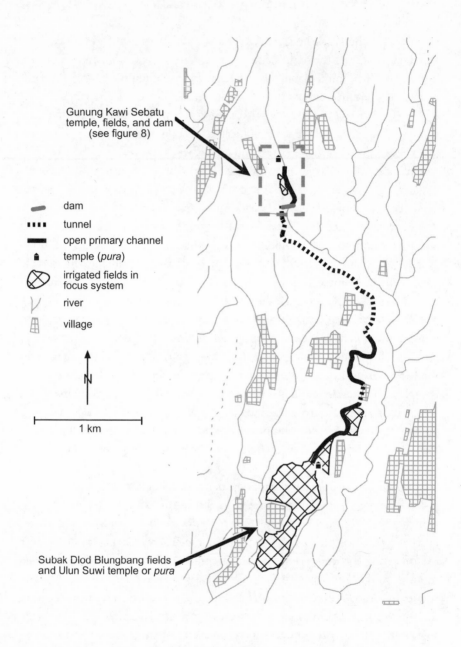

Gunung Kawi Sebatu
temple, fields, and dam
(see figure 8)

dam
tunnel
open primary channel
temple (*pura*)
irrigated fields in
focus system
river
village

N

1 km

Subak Dlod Blungbang fields
and Ulun Suwi temple or *pura*

LANSING ET AL. MAP 1. The irrigation system bearing water from Pura Gunung
Kawi Sebatu to Subak Dlod Blungbang

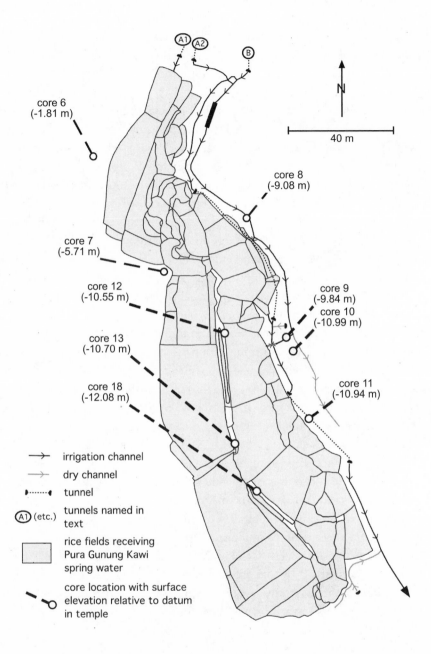

core 6
(-1.81 m)

core 8
(-9.08 m)

core 7
(-5.71 m)

core 12
(-10.55 m)

core 9
(-9.84 m)

core 10
(-10.99 m)

core 13
(-10.70 m)

core 18
(-12.08 m)

core 11
(-10.94 m)

N

40 m

→ irrigation channel

⇢ dry channel

⬤┈┈┈◖ tunnel

Ⓐ① (etc.) tunnels named in text

▢ rice fields receiving Pura Gunung Kawi spring water

━ ○ core location with surface elevation relative to datum in temple

LANSING ET AL. MAP 2. Terrace locations, channel courses, and soil coring locations in a small area of valley-bottom *sawah* lying immediately south of Pura Gunung Kawi Sebatu and receiving irrigation water from that temple's springs

This connects to a small channel which hugs the cliff that forms the eastern edge of the valley at this point. The flow from this channel enters the fields via a bamboo conduit that crosses the deep slot through which runs the channel described in the next paragraph.[8] Here, on a very small scale, is the first example of the fluidity and flexibility of the Balinese irrigated landscape. At the point at which the water is diverted toward the bamboo conduit, a dry channel continues toward the south. Though it is not clear where it was intended to lead, this watercourse (including several meters of pipe used to span a side ravine) had clearly seen use in recent years or months at the time we observed it, and it stands ready to be called back into use in the future.

Long before this, however—in fact, just a few meters after it emerges from the tunnel under the causeway—a large portion of the water from B spills down a short slope to join the water emerging from A2. The channel thus formed has by far the greatest flow, and flows directly to the Dlod Blungbang area without contributing to the irrigation of the babakan we studied. As it skirts the eastern margin of the mapped sawah (a journey of only 213 meters), it twice passes through tunnels. Remarkably, even in this short stretch we can detect multiple instances of reengineering. Approximately halfway down the length of the babakan, the mouths of one or possibly two disused tunnels adjoin the gorgelike, three-meter-plus-deep slot through which the channel runs. The overgrowth in the area is such that it cannot be easily ascertained whether the abandoned tunnel or tunnels originally served to contribute water or to draw it away, but it is at least clear that there has been some design change at this point. Farther south, another dry tunnel mouth is visible in the shallow ravine that causes and marks the southern end of the spring-watered babakan; in this case, the higher elevation relative to the main channel makes clear that this tunnel once contributed to the flow, but it seems it no longer does so.

The small valley bottom in which our fields and channels lie is nowhere wider than 64 meters east to west (see map 1). It is flanked by the sawah of Subak Pujung to the west and by that of Subak Sebatu to the east. Both of these field areas belong to the 329-hectare area irrigated by channels from the Sebatu dam, over six kilometers to the north. Except for narrow terraces stepping down the hillsides, these paddies are well above ours, and both sides of the valley are extremely steep—at one measured point, the western slope rises 15 meters over a horizontal distance of only 30.8 meters, making this a 49 percent grade. Since it is at the low point of the valley, the main channel from the spring at Pura Gunung Kawi Sebatu is situated so as to supplement its flow with run-off from the mapped babakan and from both hillsides. The channel holds this privileged position from the temple grounds to the southern tip of the babakan and maintains it until, after another 170 meters of generally southward travel, it reaches the diversionary dam (weir) maintained by Subak Dlod Blungbang. At this point, the water of the spring no longer continues to follow anything resembling a natural watercourse and embarks on a journey through tunnels (at least five of note—the longest being at least 1.5 kilometers—plus numerous shorter bores) alternating with stretches of hillside-hugging open canal. At the far end, it passes Pura Ulun Suwi Dlod Blungbang and is spread, by numerous branching channels, among the 31 hectares of sawah maintained by the members of that subak (Subak Dlod Blungbang 1990).

An inscription at the existing dam gives a date of 22 May 1969, but locals have assured us that the dam is older than that; the date may refer to such improvements to the earthen structure as the addition of concrete reinforcement and a spillway for excess flow. Local informants also told us there had once been a pond associated with the dam. Today, the area immediately upstream from the dam is planted in rice, and the general ground level is almost as high as the top of the dam. From this evidence, a significant amount of siltation is plainly indicated.

The rapidity of landscape change also seems to have manifested itself in fairly frequent relocation of the dam; the distances involved were not great, but the investment required for these reengineering efforts would have been substantial. A local tunnel engineer informed us that an earthen dam once spanned the mapped sawah area, somewhere in the vicinity of a line drawn through the location of core 11 west to core 13. No surface evidence today directly confirms his claim, but the first of the abandoned tunnels discussed above may have related to this dam. Given the depth of our coring operations within the center of the paddy fields—core 12 descended to a 5-meter depth, for example—it is likely that much of the matrix defining the rich planting surfaces was derived by capturing the clays and silts behind such man-made dams.[9] Yet another defunct dam, perhaps of an earlier date, lies under the road causeway but is apparent in an eroded cross section at its eastern end. When it was brought to his attention, the head of the Masceti Pamos Apuh subak network (the *pekasih subak gde*) avowed knowledge of this structure.

We achieved only limited success from our efforts to acquire chronometric dates from our soil cores. Of eight radiocarbon samples submitted, only two possessed isotope ratios that indicated they originated before the begin-

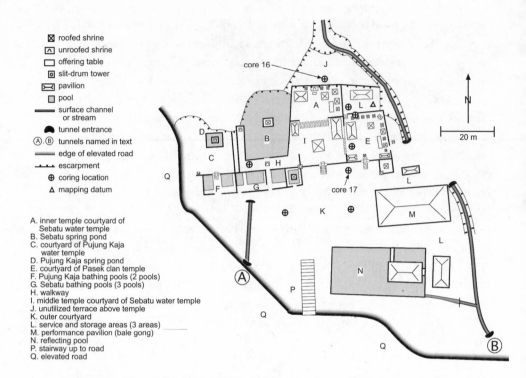

LANSING ET AL. MAP 3. Pura Gunung Kawi Sebatu spring temple, showing structures, ponds, channels, soil coring locations, and other features

ning of the twentieth century. Many coring locations were quite damp, and this no doubt contributed greatly to the vertical movement of carbon; rapid soil deposition, as discussed above, may also have been a factor in some cases. The oldest date, 17620 ±50 BP, comes from the basal reaches (295 centimeters below surface) of core 17, in the outer courtyard of the temple. No interpretable pollen or phytoliths were retrieved from this context, but the date appears to be associated with swamplike peat sediments.

The other notable date was retrieved from core 16, which descended from a currently unutilized terrace surface north of the temple, 5.62 meters above the courtyard surface where core 17 was taken (map 3). If accepted, this 450 ±50 BP determination (from 275 centimeters below ground level) indicates that nearly 3 meters of soil was deposited at this location during the past five hundred years.[10] During this period, this area above the water temple appears to have been covered with periodic episodes of alluvial or colluvial depositions inter-laminated with burning events, believed to be of human origin. Core 16 also yielded the best phytolith record, which also suggests a dynamic environment (Kealhofer 1999). From bottom (4.50 meters) to top, the general impression is of a palm-dominated forest, with human management suggested by the fre-quency of potential economic species (banana, for example). The central sec-tion of the core had lower phytolith abundance than the top or the bottom, indicative of more rapid sediment deposition or a change in the chemical con-tent of the deposited materials; this same section also had a lowered level of species diversity. The top meter had the highest proportion of grass phyto-liths, about 20 percent (still lower than typically found in agricultural contexts, but twice the level found in deeper levels), and the only rice phytoliths were recovered from this context (60–65 centimenters below the surface).

A single phytolith sample was analyzed from core 14, in the same courtyard as core 17 and with a surface elevation only 15 centimeters higher. This sample, from 60 to 63 centimeters below the surface, had a grass phytolith percentage similar to that found in the top meter of core 16 and can likewise be interpreted as suggestive of nearby rice cultivation. The best pollen evidence comes from this context, and our pollen analyst characterizes the assemblage from the top meter of this core as indicative of an open grass/sedge wetland environment, with some disturbed forest in the region (Haberle 1998a, 1998b). It is not un-reasonable to speculate that the wetlands were already present when the 17620 ±50 BP carbon was deposited nearby. While rice cultivation would not have begun until well after this date, such swampy areas adjacent to springs may have been among the first adopted by rice farmers; unfortunately, the pollen samples from the lower reaches of this core were too degraded to allow us to use these data to confirm fully either the age of the natural ecosystem or the antiquity of the human adaptation to it.

In the course of our investigations at Pura Gunung Kawi Sebatu, we also learned about the irrigation system's current potentials for change and about ongoing negotiations that take advantage of these potentials. Subak Dlod Blungbang is not part of the congregation of any overarching masceti temple, but each year it affirms its relationship with Pura Gunung Kawi by bringing lavish *suwinih* (offerings) to the main festival (*odalan*) at the temple. Since the main spring contained inside the temple, or *pura*, is controlled by Sebatu, the suwinih, which includes cash, benefits Sebatu. Currently, Dlod Blungbang does not offer any suwinih to Subak Pujung, though the latter owns the smaller of the two springs at the temple site. Another subak, Cebok, has a weir on the "Gunung Kawi stream," downstream from the Dlod Blungbang weir. Since Dlod Blungbang takes all the water from the spring at their weir, Cebok captures only the small flow from seepage (called *tiyisan* or *tirisan*) that collects in the ravine. Cebok does not offer suwinih to Gunung Kawi because it is thought that the water they capture at their weir would otherwise belong to the Manuaba subaks farther to the south, since it would flow down and be captured at the Manuaba weir. So Cebok offers suwinih at the masceti temple of Manuaba subaks, called Pura Griya Sakti Manuaba.

Several years ago Cebok made a well-received proposal to Pujung, to take their portion of the Gunung Kawi water and in return to begin to offer suwinih at the shrine at the Pujung spring. There are two ways Cebok could take this water: they could build a new irrigation system starting at the Pujung spring, or they could measure the flow coming out of the spring at Pujung shrine and request that that amount be released at the Dlod Blungbang weir; then it would flow down and be captured at the Cebok weir. In that case, Cebok would stop or reduce their suwinih contributions to Manuaba and instead offer suwinih to Pujung. What will become of this plan is not yet decided; if this were to happen it would, of course, make Dlod Blungbang unhappy, and they have not yet been officially approached about this plan. But Lansing is videotaping the meetings of the *subak gde* and has engaged a couple of Balinese researchers who will continue to follow this story.[11]

The expansion of agriculture across the landscape of Bali seems to have followed what Scarborough (1993) has described as an "accretive growth model." Overall, environmental modification was the result of a multitude of small changes rather than the product of huge earth-moving enterprises and massive labor projects, such as those found in the great hearths of arid- and semiarid-zone civilizations. From the interaction between a dissected "natural" landscape and numerous local development decisions emerged a rich web of small channels and small terraced areas, a landscape that could smoothly absorb further modifications as its inhabitants continued to negotiate local balances between faction and faction and between the inertia of structure and the will to improve.[12] Just as the social institution of water temple meetings provides a flexible framework for water distribution and timing decisions to respond to environmental conditions, the net of interconnecting waterways provides a flexible framework for the physical delivery of the water needed to carry out these decisions.

With their constellations of numerous small shrines (over thirty at Pura Gunung Kawi) arrayed in multiple courtyards, Balinese temples can likewise be described as growing by accretion. If the proposed diversion of Pujung water to Cebok comes to pass, for example, the attendant shift in relations between social groups will quite likely be accompanied by changes or additions to the plan of the temple we studied. Both temples and engineered landscapes are the congealed labor of generations of contributors who have each added to the complexity of the whole. In both cases, each contribution is limited by that which came before and affects the future trajectory of actions (both uses and revisions). Numerous small-scale "materializations" of social realities (DeMarrais et al. 1996), such as the continuous small-scale adjustments to earthworks and waterworks, generate a landscape that reflects, allows, and even facilitates the ever-evolving compromises that result from active agency. And on Bali, these things are inextricably linked: when the techne of irrigation systems and agricultural practices shifts, the techne of temples and rituals changes as well.

From Congealed Mind to Objective Reality

> Society is a human product. Society is an objective reality. Man is a social product.
> —Peter Berger and Thomas Luckmann 1967

On a timescale of hours and days, human agency is apparent to an anthropologist observing the farmers of Sebatu as they carry out their daily routines in the terraces or at the water temples. Their choices seem quite constrained, since both rice and rice rituals have their own fixed schedules. But in monthly meetings of the subaks, there is a strong sense of salient agency: concerns are voiced, plans are made, decisions taken.

The constraints that limit the scope of these choices largely derive from the objective reality that the farmers inhabit, an engineered landscape of terraces, irrigation systems, and water temples.[13] On a timescale of the everyday, this world seems fixed and permanent. But on an archaeological timescale, this reality is seen to evolve in response to human agency; indeed, there is virtually nothing present in the world of the farmers that is not the product of the labor of past generations. The key question we have addressed in this chapter is the relationship between the agency of individual subjects (social life as observed by the ethnographer) and the agency of generations of farmers that brings into being the "structures of the *longue durée*."

The question of the relationship between the intelligent agency of social actors—society as a human product—and society as an objective reality that constrains agency is central to any social theory. Yet most anthropological theories land on one side or the other of this dichotomy. Only in the Marxian tradition do social actors appear as both subjects and objects, struggling to make sense of historical change in worlds they share with others and which they attempt to comprehend. Like Marx, we hope to understand history by trying to glimpse the dialectic of structure and agency "on the wing." But as noted in the introduction, we part company with Marx on the question of determinism. Marx believed he saw the unfolding of the dialectic of a world-historical Spirit in the formation and development of class consciousness. Complexity theorists sometimes ask, "What would happen if we reran the tape (of history)?"[14] Marx's answer is clear: history has but a single plot. Our crystal ball is cloudier; we doubt that any historical trajectory is entirely fixed.

Our analysis could be viewed as a test of the third part of Berger's and Luckmann's syllogism: "Man is a social product." Structure is the historical product of agency. So stated, this is no more than a truism. But in this chapter we have tried to provide a detailed empirical account of the ways in which the social world evolves in response to the choices made by individuals. As we noted in the introduction, there is a parallel between the perspective adopted here and the development of statistical thinking a century ago, in that both approaches aim to reveal historical patterns in the behavior of groups. But the nonlinear dynamical models we employ are unlike statistics in that they forefront agency, historical process, and indeterminism. Indeed, the methods we use here were originally developed to study chaos and will not impose a pattern where none exists. For this reason, to interpret our analysis as functionalist would be to misconstrue it. Our formal models treat farmers as agents in adaptive nonlinear networks. An essential element of such networks is that they do not act simply in terms of stimulus and response. Instead, they anticipate. Agents build models of their worlds and act on the basis of predictions generated by these models. Such anticipative models do not need to be explicit, coherent, comprehensive, or even mutually consistent. Attempts at adaptation can fail. But they can also succeed, in the sense that patterns of organization may emerge that are greater than the sum of their parts and allow the network as a whole to acquire adaptive value. In our farming simulations, the ability of agents to manipulate cropping patterns has effects on the local environment that encourage the formation of local networks that are strikingly similar in their structure and function to water temple networks.

We conclude from this that no global controller is needed to sustain these networks; instead, temple networks can emerge through a process of self-organization. Once they appear, the world inhabited by the farmers undergoes a fundamental change. The temple networks themselves become an important part of the adaptive landscape — an "objective reality," a structure. In this way, our toy simulations illustrate the process by which agency yields structures that in turn influence future historical developments.

Turning from our simulations to the terraces, temples, and subaks themselves, we are struck by the sheer brilliance of the technical and social innovations the farmers have created to control their environment by controlling the flow of water. The irrigation systems do much more than bring water to the fields: they deliver mineral nutrients leached from the volcanic rock; create a habitat for nitrogen-fixing bacteria, and effectively control the diffusion of rice pests. But for these effects to occur, thousands of farmers must make skillful use of the subak and water temple institutions inherited from their predecessors. Temples, tunnels, and terraces are all, like Rappaport's rose, the product of intentionality: congealed mind as well as labor.

Notes

1. Lévi-Strauss, interview with John-Marie Benoist, quoted in Lilla 1994:43.

2. Similar problems beset anthropologists who adopt the methods of behavioral ecology: what is the relationship between predictions of the fitness payoffs for behavioral strategies and the subjective reality of social actors? Answers to this question cannot appear from within the horizons of behavioral ecology itself and so require an expanded analytic framework. The methodological framework proposed in this paper is compatible with both systems ecology and behavioral ecology, as will become evident in the discussion.

3. William H. Shaw makes the same point in *Marx's Theory of History*: "The development of the productive forces through history tells the story of man's evolving dialectical intercourse with nature" (1978:152).

4. Here we paraphrase Marx's and Engels's critique of the objective materialism of Feuerbach, who "does not see how the sensuous world around him is, not a thing given from eternity, remaining ever the same, but the product of industry and of the direct state of society; and, indeed, in the sense that it is an historical product, the result of

the activity of a whole succession of generations, each standing on the shoulders of the preceding one" (1965:57).

5. A lineal differential equation $F(x,y,y^1, \ldots, y^n) = 0$ is linear if F is a linear function of the variables $y, y^1, \ldots y^n$, meaning that all of the variables appear to the first power only. Cf. Strogatz (1994).

6. One farmer asked Lansing about the nationality of a foreign consultant. Learning that the man was English, the farmer asked how long the English had been growing paddy rice.

7. James Nicholas at the University of Cincinnati is responsible for accessing the sedimentology, while Simon Haberle at the Australian National University generously provided his time in evaluating two of the cores for ancient pollen. Lisa Kaelhofer of the College of William and Mary examined and interpreted phytolith assemblages from two cores. Chronometric dating was conducted by Beta Analytic Inc.

8. The area watered by B is concentrated to the east and southeast of the narrow strip of unirrigated land from which cores 12 and 13 were taken. Twenty-one percent (0.18 hectares) of our 0.89-hectare study area draws water solely from B; the remaining 8 percent is irrigated with a mix of AI and B waters. The "mixed water" area includes the extreme southeast corner of the babakan, which, at 6.9 meters below the point at which AI water enters the sawah, is the lowest of the terraces.

9. The lowest meter of core 12 was too wet to process. Cores 13 and 18 probably would have descended to a comparable depth if time and mechanical difficulties had not interceded.

10. A second AMS date was retrieved from core 16 at 342 cm. BSD, yielding a date early in the twentieth century, one believed intrusive. This is not taken as indicative of gross soil missing, since clear patterning is visible in the phytolith and sedimentology records. An event affecting matrices deposited to this depth within living memory would have been conveyed to us by the temple functionaries.

11. Another example of the potential for renegotiation inherent in the landscape involves the small stream that flows past the east side of Pura Gunung Kawi, joining the outflow from the reflecting pool. This stream is said to flow with considerable volume once a decade or so, when it receives exceptional overflow from weirs yet further upstream. Should all interested parties agree, this situation could be turned into a reliable source of additional water for the Dlod Blungbank weir. The *pekasih subak gde* considered this a case worth pointing out, but we know of no plans for such reengineering.

12. The overall topography of the South Balinese landscape, with its gently sloping plain sliced by hundreds of deep gorges, is no doubt in part a result of human-induced erosion. A tragic reminder of these forces occurred on 8 January 1999, when forty people lost their lives in a landslide that occurred during irrigation channel repair work in a

village only two kilometers northeast of Sebatu. Even if we ignore the dry fields, rice terraces, canals, roads, and villages, this landscape is still "humanized nature."

13. Exogenous forces like prices, taxes, and the weather are, of course, also present.

14. This question may have been first posed by Stephen Jay Gould; it is the theme of the Santa Fe Institute Bulletin for winter 1999 (vol. 14, no. 1).

Works Cited

Abu-Lughod, Janet. 1997. "Going Beyond Global Babble." In *Culture, Globalization and the World System*, ed. Anthony King, 131–38. Minneapolis: University of Minnesota Press.

Acheson, J. M., and J. A. Wilson. 1996. "Order Out of Chaos: The Case for Parametric Fisheries Management." *American Anthropologist* 98:579–94.

Alcoff, Linda. 1991. "The Problem of Speaking for Others." *Critical Inquiry* 20:5–32.

Althusser, Louis. 1977. *Lenin and Philosophy (and Other Essays)*. London: New Left Books.

Alvarez, Robert R., Jr. 1994. "La Maroma: Chile, Credit, and Chance: An Ethnographic Case of Global Finance and Middlemen Entrepreneurs." Manuscript.

Alvarez López, Juan. 1988. "El medio ambiente en el desarrollo económico de la frontera norte de México." *Cuadernos de economía* (Tijuana, Baja California, Mexico); ser. 3, no. 5. Tijuana, B.C., Mexico: Universidad Autónoma de Baja California, Facultad de Economía.

Alvarez, Sonia E., Evelina Dagnino, and Arturo Escobar, eds. 1998a. *Cultures of Politics/Politics of Cultures: Re-visioning Latin American Social Movements*. Boulder: Westview Press.

———. 1998b. "Preface and Acknowledgments." In *Cultures of Politics/Politics of Cultures: Re-visioning Latin American Social Movements*, ed. S. Alvarez, E. Dagnino, and A. Escobar, xi–xiii. Boulder: Westview Press.

———. 1998c. "Introduction: The Cultural and the Political in Latin American Social Movements." In *Cultures of Politics/Politics of Cultures: Re-visioning Latin American Social Movements*, ed. S. Alvarez, E. Dagnino, and A. Escobar, 1–29. Boulder: Westview Press.

Anderson, Benedict. 1983. *Imagined Communities: Reflections on the Origin and Spread of Nationalism*. London: Verso.

Anderson, David G., and Eeva Berglund, eds. 2003. *Ethnographies of Conservation: Environmentalism and the Distribution of Privilege*. New York: Berghahn Books.

Anonymous. 1964. *Commercial Fisheries Review* 26(11): 98–102.

Appadurai, Arjun. 1990. "Disjuncture and Difference in the Global Economy." *Public Culture* 2(2):1–24.

———. 1991. "Global Ethnoscapes: Notes and Queries for a Transnational Anthropology." In *Recapturing Anthropology*, ed. Richard G. Fox, 191–210. Santa Fe: School of American Research Press.

———. 1996. *Modernity at Large: Cultural Dimensions of Globalization*. Minneapolis: University of Minnesota Press.

———. 2001. "Grassroots Globalization and the Research Imagination." In *Globalization*, ed. A. Appadurai, 1–21. Durham: Duke University Press.

Arendt, Hannah. 1998 (1958). *The Human Condition*. Chicago: University of Chicago Press.

Arnold, Guy. 1958. "Nomadic Penan of the Upper Rejang (Plieran), Sarawak." *Journal of the Malayan Branch of the Royal Asiatic Society* 31(Pt. 1)(181):40–82.

Arthur, Chris. 1985. "Personality and the Dialectic of Labour and Property—Locke, Hegel, Marx." In *Radical Philosophy Reader*, ed. R. Edgley and R. Osborne, 43–68. London: Verso.

Asad, Talal. 1975. *Anthropology and the Colonial Encounter*. Ithaca: Cornell University Press.

Asian Development Bank. 1988. *Project Performance Audit Report, Bali Irrigation Project in Indonesia*. PE-241 L-352-INO. Manila: Asian Development Bank, Post Evaluation Office.

Aubert, V. 1959. "Chance in Social Affairs." *Inquiry* 2:1–24.

Ayryawan, I. G. N., I. N. Widiarta, Y. Suzuki, and F. Nakasuji. 1993. "Life Table Analysis of the Green Rice Leafhopper, Nephotettix Virescans (Distant), an Efficient Vector of Rice Tungro Disease in Asynchronous Rice Fields in Indonesia." *Research in Population Ecology* 35:31–43.

Bahl, Vinay, and Arif Dirlik, eds. 2000. "Introduction." In *History after the Three Worlds: Post-Eurocentric Historiographies*. Lanham, Md.: Rowman and Littlefield.

Balée, William, ed. 1998. "Introduction." *Advances in Historical Ecology*. New York: Columbia University Press.

Ballard, Chris. 1997. "It's the Land, Stupid! The Moral Economy of Resource Ownership in Papua New Guinea." In *The Governance of Common Property in the Pacific Region*, ed. P. Larmour, 47–65. Canberra: National Centre for Development Studies and Resource Management Asia-Pacific.

———. 1998. "The Sun by Night: Huli Moral Topography and Myths of a Time of Darkness." In *Fluid Ontologies: Myth, Ritual and Philosophy in the Highlands of Papua*

New Guinea, ed. L. R. Goldman and C. Ballard, 67–85. Westport, Conn.: Bergin and Garvey.

Ballard, Chris, and Bryant Allen. 1991. " 'Inclined to be Cheekey': Huli Responses to First Contact." Paper presented at the conference "New Perspectives on the Papua New Guinea Highlands: An Interdisciplinary Conference on the Huli, Duna, and Ipili Peoples," organized by A. Biersack, Canberra, August 16–18, 1991, Australian National University.

Ballard, Chris, and Glenn Banks. 2003. "Resource Wars: The Anthropology of Mining." *Annual Review of Anthropology* 32:287–313.

Banks, Glenn. 1997a. "Mountain of Desire: Mining Company and Indigenous Community at the Porgera Gold Mine, Papua New Guinea." Ph.D. thesis, Department of Human Geography, Research School of Pacific and Asian Studies, Australian National University.

———. 1997b. "Mountain of Desire, Rivers of Controversy: A Post-Colonial Geography of Pollution." Paper given at the second joint Institute of Australian Geographers, New Zealand Geographical Society Conference, Hobart, Tasmania, January 1997.

———. 1998. "Compensation for Communities Affected by Mining and Oil Developments in Melanesia." *Malaysian Journal of Tropical Geography* 29(1):53–67.

———. 1999a. "The Economic Impact of the Mine." In *Dilemmas of Development: The Social and Economic Impact of the Porgera Gold Mind, 1989–1994*, ed. C. Filer, 88–127. Canberra: Asia Pacific Press and Research School of Pacific and Asian Studies, Australian National University.

———. 1999b. "Gardens and *Wantoks*." In *Dilemmas of Development: The Social and Economic Impact of the Porgera Gold Mine, 1989–1994*, ed. C. Filer, 160–90. Canberra: Asia Pacific Press and Research School of Pacific and Asian Studies, Australian National University.

———. 1999c. "The Next Round of Relocation." In *Dilemmas of Development: The Social and Economic Impact of the Porgera Gold Mine, 1989–1994*, ed. C. Filer, 191–221. Canberra: Asia Pacific Press and Research School of Pacific and Asian Studies, Australian National University.

———. 2002. "Mining and the Environment in Melanesia: Contemporary Debates Reviewed." *The Contemporary Pacific* 14(1):39–67.

Banuri, Tariq. 1993. "The Landscape of Diplomatic Conflicts." In *Global Ecology: A New Arena of Political Conflict*, ed. Wolfgang Sachs, 49–67. London: Zed Books.

Barber, Benjamin. 1995. *Jihad vs. McWorld*. New York: Ballantine.

Baring-Gould, S., and C. A. Bampfylde. 1909. *A History of Sarawak under its Two White Rajahs*. London: Henry Sotheran.

Barlow, Kathleen. 2001. "Working Mothers and the Work of Culture in a Papua New Guinea Society." *Ethos* 29(1):78–107.

Barrera Guevara, J. C. 1992. "The Conservation of Totoaba macdonaldi (Gilbert) (Pisces Sciaenidae) in the Gulf of California, Mexico." *Journal of Fish Biology* 37 (Suppl A):201–02.

Basch, Linda, Nina Glick Schiller, and Cristina Szanton Blanc. 1994. *Nations Unbound.* Langhorne, Penn.: Gordon and Breach.

Basso, Keith. 1984. "Stalking with Stories: Names, Places and Moral Narratives among the Western Apache." In *Text, Play, and Story: The Construction and Reconstruction of Self and Society,* ed. E. Bruner, 19–55. Washington: American Ethnological Society.

Bateson, Gregory. 1936. *Naven.* Stanford: Stanford University Press.

———. 1958. *Naven.* 2nd. ed. Stanford: Stanford University Press.

———. 1972. *Steps to an Ecology of Mind.* New York: Ballantine Books.

Bateson, Mary Catherine. 1984. *With a Daughter's Eye: A Memoir of Margaret Mead and Gregory Bateson.* New York: Washington Square Press.

Battaglia, Debbora. 1994. "Retaining Reality: Some Practical Problems with Objects as Property." *Man* (n.s.) 29(4):631–44.

Baudrillard, Jean. 1975. *The Mirror of Production.* Translated by Mark Poster. St. Louis: Telos Press.

Belk, Russell. 1983. "Worldly Possessions: Issues and Criticisms." *Advances in Consumer Research* 10:514–19.

Benavides, Margarita. 1992. "Asháninka Self-Defence in the Central Forest Region." IWGIA Newsletter 2/92, April–June, pp. 36–45. IWGIA, Copenhagen.

———. 1993. "Los Asháninka, víctimas de la violencia y la guerra." *Ideele* 59–50 (December 1993): 116–18. Lima.

von Benda-Beckmann, Keebet, and Fons Strijbosch, eds. 1986. *Anthropology of Law in the Netherlands: Essays on Legal Pluralism. Verhandlingen van het Koninklijk Instituut voor Taal-, Land-, en Volkenkunde* 116. Dordrecht, Netherlands: Foris Publications.

Benhabib, Seyla. 1984. "Obligation, Contract and Exchange: On the Significance of Hegel's Abstract Right." In *The State and Civil Society: Studies in Hegel's Political Philosophy,* ed. Z. A. Pelczynski, 159–303. Cambridge: Cambridge University Press.

Bennett, John. 1976. *The Ecological Transition.* New York: Pergamon Press.

Benton, Ted. 1989. "Marxism and Natural Limits: An Ecological Critique and Reconstruction." *New Left Review* 178:51–86.

———. 1991. "Biology and Social Science: Why the Return of the Repressed Should Be Given a (Cautious) Welcome." *Sociology* 25(1):1–29.

Berglund, Eeva. 1997. "Clear-Cut Madness in Russian Karelia." *The Ecologist* 27(6):237–41.

———. 1998. *Knowing Nature, Knowing Science: An Ethnography of Local Environmental Activism.* Cambridge: White Horse Press.

———. 2001. "Facts, Beliefs and Biases: Perspectives on Forest Conservation in Finland." *Journal of Environmental Planning and Management* 44, part 6, 833–49.

Berglund, Eeva, and David G. Anderson. 2003. "Introduction: Towards an Ethnography of Ecological Underprivilege." In *Ethnographies of Conservation: Environmentalism and the Distribution of Privilege*, ed. D. Anderson and E. Berglund, 1–15. New York: Berghahn Books.

Bergmann, Frithjof. 1975. "On the Inadequacies of Functionalism." *Michigan Discussions in Anthropology* 1:2–23.

Berlin, Brent, Dennis Breedlove, and Peter Raven. 1974. *Principles of Tzeltal Plant Classification: An Introduction to the Botanical Ethnography of a Mayan-Speaking People of the Highland Chiapas*. New York: Academic Press.

Berry, Erick. 1972. *The Land and People of Finland*, revised edition. Philadelphia: J. B. Lippincott.

Biddick, Kathleen. 1990. "People and Things: Power in Early English Development." *Comparative Studies in Society and History* 32(1):3–23.

Biersack, Aletta. 1987. "Moonlight: Negative Images of Transcendence in Paiela Pollution." *Oceania* 57:178–94.

———. 1990. "Histories in the Making: Paiela and Historical Anthropology." *History and Anthropology* 5:63–85.

———. 1995a. "The Huli, Duna, and Ipili Peoples Yesterday and Today." Introduction to *Papuan Borderlands: Huli, Duna, and Ipili Perspectives on the Papua New Guinea Highlands*, ed. A. Biersack, 1–54. Ann Arbor: University of Michigan Press.

———. 1995b. "Heterosexual Meanings." In *Papuan Borderlands: Huli, Duna, and Ipili Perspectives on the Papua New Guinea Highlands*, ed. A. Biersack, 231–63. Ann Arbor: University of Michigan Press.

———. 1996a. "Word Made Flesh: Religion, the Economy, and the Body in the Papua New Guinea Highlands." *History of Religions* 36:85–111.

———. 1996b. "'Making Kinship': Marriage, Warfare, and Networks among Paielas." In *Works in Progress*, ed. H. Levine and A. Ploeg, 19–42. Franfurt am Main: Peter Lang.

———. 1996c. "The Human Condition and Its Transformations: Nature and Society in the Paiela World." Paper given at the annual meeting of the American Anthropological Association.

———. 1998a. "Sacrifice and Regeneration among Ipilis: The View from Tipinini." In *Fluid Ontologies: Myth, Ritual, and Philosophy in the Highlands of Papua New Guinea*, ed. L. Goldman and C. Ballard, 43–66. Westport, Conn.: Greenwood Press.

———. 1998b. "Horticulture and Hierarchy: The Youthful Beautification of the Body in the Paiela and Porgera Valleys." In *Adolescence in Pacific Island Societies*, ed. G. Herdt and S. Leavitt, 71–91. Pittsburgh: University of Pittsburgh Press.

———. 1999a. "The Mount Kare Python and His Gold: Totemism and Ecology in the New Guinea Highlands." In "Ecologies for Tomorrow: Reading Rappaport Today," ed. A. Biersack, a "contemporary issues forum," *American Anthropologist* 101:68–87.

Biersack, Aletta. 1999b. "Porgera—Whence and Whither?" In *Dilemmas of Development: The Social and Economic Impact of the Porgera Gold Mine, 1989–1994*, ed. C. Filer, 260–79. Canberra: National Research Institute and Asia Pacific Press.

———. 1999c. "Introduction: From the 'New Ecology' to the New Ecologies." In "Ecologies for Tomorrow: Reading Rappaport Today," ed. A. Biersack, a "contemporary issues forum." *American Anthropologist* 101(1):5–18.

———. 2001a. "Reproducing Inequality: The Gender Politics of Male Cults in Melanesia and Amazonia." In *Gender in Amazonia and Melanesia: An Exploration of the Comparative Method*, ed. T. Gregor and D. Tuzin, 69–90. Berkeley: University of California Press.

———. 2001b. "Dynamics of Porgera Gold Mining: Culture, Capital, and the State." In *Mining in Papua New Guinea: Analysis and Policy Implications*, ed. B. Y. Imbun and P. A. McGavin, 25–44. Waigani, NCD: University of Papua New Guinea Press.

———. 2003. "Introduction to the panel 'Political Ecology and the Politics of Place'." Annual meeting of the American Anthropological Association, November 22, 2003, Chicago.

———. 2004a. "Grassroots Globalization: Joint-Venture Capitalism at Mt. Kare." Paper given at the annual meeting of the Association of Social Anthropologists of Oceania, Salem, Massachusetts, February 25, 2004.

———. 2004b. "The Bachelors and Their Spirit Wife." In *The Unseen Characters: Women in Men's Rituals in New Guinea*, ed. P. Bonnemère, 203–45. Philadelphia: University of Pennsylvania Press.

———. 2004c. "Political Ecology and the Politics of Place." *Anthropology News* (February 2004), 33.

Bird-David, Nurit. 1990. "The Giving Environment: Another Perspective on the Economic System of Gatherer-Hunters." *Current Anthropology* 31(2):189–96.

———. 1992. "Beyond the Original Affluent Society: A Culturalist Reformulation." *Current Anthropology* 33(1):25–47.

———. 1993. "Tribal Metaphorizations of Human–Nature Relatedness: A Comparative Analysis." In *Environmentalism: The View from Anthropology*, ed. K. Milton, 112–25. London: Routledge.

Blaikie, Piers. 1985. *The Political Economy of Soil Erosion in Developing Countries*. London: Longman.

———. 1999. "A Review of Political Ecology: Issues, Epistemology and Analytic Narratives." *Zeitschrift fur Wirtschaftsgeographie* 43(nos. 3–4):131–47.

Blaikie, Piers, and Harold Brookfield, eds. 1987a. "Introduction." *Land Degradation and Society*. London: Methuen.

———. 1987b. "Defining and Debating the Problem." In *Land Degradation and Society*, ed. P. Blaikie and H. Brookfield, 1–26. London: Methuen.

————. 1987c. "Retropect and Prospect." In *Land Degradation and Society*, ed. P. Blaikie and H. Brookfield, 239–50. London: Methuen.

Bloch, Maurice. 1986. *From Blessing to Violence*. Cambridge: Cambridge University Press.

————. 1997. "Ideology." In *Encyclopedia of Social and Cultural Anthropology*, 293–94. London: Routledge.

Blühdorn, Ingolfur. 2000. *Post-Ecologist Politics: Social Theory and the Abdication of the Ecologist Paradigm*. London: Routledge.

Bodley, John H. 1975. *Victims of Progress*. Menlo Park, N. J.: Cummings.

Bourdieu, Pierre. 1977. *Outline of a Theory of Practice*. Cambridge: Cambridge University Press.

————. 1990. *The Logic of Practice*. Translated by R. Nice. Cambridge: Polity Press.

Braudel, Fernand. 1972/73 [1966]. *The Mediterranean and the Mediterranean World in the Age of Philip II*. Translated by Siân Reynolds. 2 vols. New York: Harper and Row.

————. 1986 [1979]. *The Perspective of the World: Civilization and Capital, 15th–18th Century*, vol. 3. Translated by Siân Roberts. New York: Harper and Row.

Braun, Bruce, and Noel Castree, eds. 1998. *Remaking Reality: Nature at the Millennium*. London: Routledge.

Braun, Bruce, and Joel Wainwright. 2001. "Nature, Poststructuralism, and Politics." In *Social Nature: Theory, Practice, and Politics*, ed. Noel Castree and Bruce Braun, 41–63. Malden, Mass.: Blackwell.

Brennan, Timothy. 2001. "The Cuts of Language: The East/West of North/South." *Public Culture*. Special Issue:39–63.

Brosius, J. Peter. 1986. "River, Forest and Mountain: The Penan Gang Landscape." *Sarawak Museum Journal* 36(57)(n.s.):173–84.

————. 1988. "A Separate Reality: Comments on Hoffman's *The Punan: Hunters and Gatherers of Borneo*." *Borneo Research Bulletin* 20(2):81–106.

————. 1991a. "Foraging in Tropical Rainforests: The Case of the Penan of Sarawak, East Malaysia (Borneo)." *Human Ecology* 19(2):123–50.

————. 1991b. "Thrice-Told Tales: A Review of *The Nightbird Sings: Chants and Songs of Sarawak Dayaks*." *Borneo Research Bulletin* 22(2):241–67.

————. 1992a. "The Axiological Presence of Death: Penan Geng Death-Names." Ph.D. diss., University of Michigan.

————. 1992b. "Perspectives on Penan Development in Sarawak." *Sarawak Gazette* 119(1519):5–22.

————. 1993a. "Contrasting Subsistence Ecologies of Eastern and Western Penan Foragers (Sarawak, East Malaysia)." In *Food and Nutrition in the Tropical Forest: Biocultural Interactions and Applications to Development*, ed. C. M. Hladik et al., 515–22. Paris: UNESCO, Parthenon Man and the Biosphere Series.

Brosius, J. Peter. 1993b. "Penan of Sarawak." In *State of the Peoples: A Global Human Rights Report on Societies in Danger*, ed. Marc S. Miller, 142–43. Boston: Beacon Press (for Cultural Survival, Inc.).

———. 1995a. "Bornean Forest Trade in Historical and Regional Perspective: The Case of Penan Hunter-Gatherers of Sarawak." In *Society and Non-Timber Products in Tropical Asia*, ed. J. Fox, 13–26. East-West Center Occasional Papers: Environmental Series no. 19.

———. 1995b. "Signifying Bereavement: Form and Context in the Analysis of Penan Death-Names." *Oceania*, 66(2):119–46.

———. 1995–96. "Father Dead, Mother Dead: Bereavement and Fictive Death in Penan Geng Society." *Omega: Journal of Death and Dying* 32(3):197–226.

———. 1997a. "Endangered Forest, Endangered People: Environmentalist Representations of Indigenous Knowledge." *Human Ecology* 25(1):47–69.

———. 1997b. "Prior Transcripts, Divergent Paths: Resistance and Acquiescence to Logging in Sarawak, East Malaysia." *Comparative Studies in Society and History* 39(3):468–510.

———. 1999a. "Green Dots, Pink Hearts: Displacing Politics from the Malaysian Rainforest." In "Ecologies for Tomorrow: Reading Rappaport Today," a "contemporary issues forum," ed. A. Biersack. *American Anthropologist* 101(1):36–57.

———. 1999b. "Locations and Representations: Writing in the Political Present in Sarawak, East Malaysia." In special issue of *Identities: Global Studies in Culture and Power* 6(2–3) entitled "Ethnographic Presence: Environmentalism, Indigenous Rights and Transnational Cultural Critique," ed. J. Peter Brosius.

———. 1999c. "Analyses and Interventions: Anthropological Engagements with Environmentalism." *Current Anthropology* 40(3): 277–309.

———. 2000. "Endangered Forest, Endangered People: Environmentalist Representations of Indigenous Knowledge." In *Indigenous Environmental Knowledge and Its Transformations: Critical Anthropological Perspectives*, ed. R. Ellen, P. Parkes, and A. Bicker, 293–318. Australia: Harwood Academic Publishers.

———. 2001a. "Local Knowledges, Global Claims: On the Significance of Indigenous Ecologies in Sarawak, East Malaysia." In *Indigenous Traditions and Ecology*, ed. J. Grim, 125–57. Cambridge, Mass.: Harvard University Press and the Center for the Study of World Religions, Harvard University.

———. 2001b. "The Politics of Ethnographic Presence: Sites and Topologies in the Study of Transnational Movements." In *New Directions in Anthropology and Environment: Intersections*, ed. C. Crumley, with E. van Deventer and J. Fletcher, 150–76. Walnut Creek, Calif.: Altamira Press.

———. 2003. "Voices for the Borneo Rain Forest: Writing the History of an Environmental Campaign." In *Nature in the Global South: Environmental Projects in South and*

Southeast Asia, ed. Paul Greenough and Anna Lowenhaupt Tsing, 319–46. Durham: Duke University Press.

Brown, Michael F., and Eduardo Fernández. 1991. *War of Shadows: The Struggle for Utopia in the Peruvian Amazon*. Berkeley: University of California Press.

Bryant, Raymond L. 1992. "Political Ecology: An Emerging Research Agenda in Third World Studies." *Political Geography* 11:12–36.

———. 1998. "Power, Knowledge and Political Ecology in the Third World: A Review." *Progress in Physical Geography* 21(1):79–94.

———. 2001. "Political Ecology: A Critical Agenda for Change?" In *Social Nature: Theory, Practice, and Politics*, ed. N. Castree and B. Braun, 151–69. Malden, Mass.: Blackwell.

Bryant, Raymond L., and S. Bailey. 1997. *Third World Political Ecology*. London: Routledge.

Bunker, Stephen G. 1985. *Underdeveloping the Amazon: Extraction, Unequal Exchange, and the Failure of the Modern State*. Urbana: University of Illinois Press.

Burningham, Kate, and Geoff Cooper. 1999. "Being Constructive: Social Constructionism and the Environment." *Sociology* 33(2):297–316.

Burridge, Kenelm. 1960. *Mambu: A Study of Melanesian Cargo Movements and Their Social and Ideological Background*. New York: Harper and Row.

Burton, John. 1997. "Principles of Compensation in the Mining Industry." In *Compensation for Resource Development in Papua New Guinea*, ed. S. Toft, 116–36. Law Reform Commission of Papua New Guinea, monograph no. 6.

Carney, Judith A. 1996. "Converting the Wetlands, Engendering the Environment: The Intersection of Gender with Agrarian Change in Gambia." In *Liberation Ecologies: Environment, Development, Social Movements*, ed. R. Peet and M. Watts, 165–87. London: Routledge.

Carrier, James G. 1998. "Property and Social Relations in Melanesian Anthropology." In *Property Relations: Renewing the Anthropological Tradition*, ed. C. M. Hann, 85–103. Cambridge: Cambridge University Press.

Carrier, James G., and Josiah Heyman. 1997. "Consumption and Political Economy." *Journal of the Royal Anthropological Institute* 3(2):355–73.

Casey, Edward S. 1996. "How to Get from Space to Place in a Fairly Short Stretch of Time: Phenomenological Prolegomena." In *Senses of Place*, ed. S. Feld and K. Basso, 13–52. Santa Fe: School of American Research Press.

Castree, Noel. 1995. "The Nature of Produced Nature: Materiality and Knowledge Construction in Marxism." *Antipode* 27(1):12–48.

Castree, Noel, and Bruce Braun. 1998. "The Construction of Nature and the Nature of Construction: Analytical and Political Tools for Building Survivable Futures." In *Remaking Reality: Nature at the Millenium*, ed. B. Braun and N. Castree, 3–42. London: Routledge.

Castree, Noel, and Bruce Braun. 2000. "The Production of Nature." In *A Companion to Economic Geography*, ed. E. Sheppard and T. Barnes, 275–89. Oxford: Blackwell.

Castree, Noel, and Bruce Braun, eds. 2001. *Social Nature: Theory, Practice, and Politics*. Malden, Mass.: Blackwell.

Castree, Noel, and Tom Macmillan. 2001. "Actor-Networks and the Reimagination of Nature." In *Social Nature: Theory, Practice, and Politics*, ed. N. Castree and B. Braun, 208–24. Malden, Mass.: Blackwell.

Castro Arenas, M. 1973. *La Rebelión de Juan Santos*. Lima: Editorial Millas Batres.

Chávez, Ernesto A., and Daniel Lluch. 1971. "Estado actual de la pesca de camarón en el noroeste de México." *Revista de la Sociedad Mexicana de Historia Natural* 32:141–56.

Chayanov, A. V. 1966. *The Theory of the Peasant Economy*. Homewood, Ill.: Richard Irwin.

Childe, V. Gordon. 1953. *What Is History?* New York: Henry Schuman.

Clark, Jeffrey. 1993. "Gold, Sex, and Pollution: Male Illness and Myth at Mt. Kare, Papua New Guinea." *American Ethnologist* 20:742–57.

———. 1995. "Highlands of History: Images of Deviance and Desire." In *Papuan Borderlands: Huli, Duna, and Ipili Perspectives on the Papua New Guinea Highlands*, ed. A. Biersack, 379–400. Ann Arbor: University of Michigan Press.

Clifford, James. 1992. "Traveling Cultures." In *Cultural Studies*, ed. L. Grossberg, C. Nelson, and P. Treichler, 17–51. Cambridge, Mass.: Harvard University Press.

———. 1997a. *Routes: Travel and Translation in the Late Twentieth Century*. Cambridge, Mass.: Harvard University Press.

———. 1997b. "Spatial Practices: Fieldwork, Travel, and the Disciplining of Anthropology." In *Routes: Travel and Translation in the Late Twentieth Century*, 52–91. Cambridge, Mass.: Harvard University Press.

Clifford, James, and George E. Marcus, eds. 1986. *Writing Culture: The Poetics and Politics of Ethnography*. Berkeley: University of California Press.

Cohen, I. Bernard. 1994. *Interactions: Some Contacts between the Natural Sciences and the Social Sciences*. Cambridge: MIT.

Cohn, N. 1981. *En Pos del Milenio: Revolucionarios milenaristas y anarquistas místicos de la Edad Media*. Madrid: Editorial Alianza Universidad.

Colchester, M. 1989. *Pirates, Squatters and Poachers: The Political Ecology of Dispossession of the Native Peoples of Sarawak*. London: Survival International.

Comaroff, Jean. 1985. *Body of Power, Spirit of Resistance: The Culture and History of a South African People*. Chicago: University of Chicago Press.

Comaroff, Jean, and John Comaroff. 1991. *Of Revelation and Revolution*. Volume 1: *Christianity, Colonialism, and Consciousness in South Africa*. Chicago: University of Chicago Press.

Conklin, B. 1997. "Body Paint, Feathers, and VCRs: Aesthetics and Authenticity in Amazonian Activism." *American Ethnologist* 24(4):711–37.

Conklin, Harold C. 1954. "The Relation of Hanuno'o Culture to the Plant World." Ph.D. diss., Yale University. Ann Arbor: University Microfilms.

———. 1975/1957. *Hanuno'o Agriculture: A Report on an Integral System of Shifting Cultivation in the Philippines*. Northford, Conn.: Elliot's Books. (Originally published by the Food and Agriculture Organization, Rome.)

———. 1980. *Ethnographic Atlas of Ifugao: A Study of Environment, Culture, and Society in Northern Luzon*. New Haven: Yale University Press.

Craig, J. A. 1926. "A New Fishery in Mexico." *California Fish Game* 12(4):166–69.

Croll, E., and David Parkin, eds. 1992. *Bush Base, Forest Farm: Culture, Environment and Development*. London: Routledge.

Cronon, William, ed. 1996. *Uncommon Ground: Rethinking the Human Place in Nature*. New York: W. W. Norton.

Crumley, Carol L., ed. 1994. *Historical Ecology: Cultural Knowledge and Changing Landscapes*. Santa Fe: SAR Press.

———. 2001. *New Directions in Anthropology and Environment: Intersections*. Walnut Creek, Calif.: Altamira Press, Rowan and Littlefield.

CSIRO. 1996. "Review of Riverine Impacts: Porgera Joint Venture." ACT, Australia: CSIRO Environmental Projects Office.

Dacol Plant Pty Ltd. 1990. "IPGD Gold Project Environmentall Plan." Volume B. Prepared for Ipili-Porgera Gold Dredging Joint Venture, July 16, 1990, report no. DP8925A; office of the Porgera Mining Coordinator, Department of Mining, PNG Government, Konedobu.

Davis, J. 1992. "The Anthropology of Suffering." *Journal of Refugee Studies* 5(2):149–61.

Davis, Shelton H. 1977. *Victims of the Miracle: Development and the Indians of Brazil*. Cambridge: Cambridge University Press.

Davis, Wade, and Thom Henley. 1990. *Penan: Voice for the Borneo Rainforest*. Vancouver: Western Canada Wilderness Committee.

Deacon, Margaret. 1997. *Scientists and the Sea 1650–1900: A Study of Marine Science*. Aldershot, Hampshire: Ashgate.

DeLuca, Kevin. 1999. *Image Politics: The New Rhetoric of Environmental Activism*. New York: Guilford Press.

DeMarrais, Elizabeth, Luis Jaime Castillo, and Timothy Earle. 1996. "Ideology, Materialization, and Power Strategies." *Current Anthropology* 37:15–31.

Demeritt, David. 1998. "Science, Social Constructivism, and Nature." In *Remaking Reality: Nature at the Millennium*, ed. B. Braun and N. Castree, 173–93. New York: Routledge.

———. 2001. "Being Constructive about Nature." In *Social Nature: Theory, Practice, and Politics*, ed. N. Castree and B. Braun, 22–40. Malden, Mass.: Blackwell.

Denevan, William, and M. S. Chrostowski. 1970. *The Biogeography of a Savanna Landscape: The Gran Pajonal of Eastern Peru*. Montreal: McGill University.

Denevan, William, and Christine Padoch, eds. 1988. *Swidden-Fallow Agroforestry in the Peruvian Amazon*. Advances in Economic Botany, no. 5. New York: New York Botanical Gardens.

Derkley, H., ed. 1989. "The Porgera Agreements (Annotated)." Enga Province: Legal Services Unit, Office of the Secretary, Department of Enga. Typescript.

Derrida, Jacques. 1978. *Writing and Difference*. Translated by A. Bass. Chicago: University of Chicago Press.

Descola, Philippe. 1994. *In the Society of Nature: A Native Ecology of Amazonia*. Translated by Nora Scott. Cambridge: Cambridge University Press.

Descola, Philippe, and Gíslí Pálsson, eds. 1996. *Nature and Society: Anthropological Perspectives*. London: Routledge.

Diamond, Jared. 1990. "Bach, God and the Jungle." *Natural History* 12(90):22–27.

Dickens, P. 1996. *Reconstructing Nature: Alienation, Emancipation and the Division of Labour*. London: Routledge.

Dirlik, Arif. 1996. "The Global in the Local." In *Global-Local: Cultural Production and the Transnational Imaginary*, ed. Rob Wilson and Wimal Dissanayake, 21–45. Durham: Duke University Press.

———. 2001. "Place-Based Imagination: Globalism and the Politics of Place." In *Places and Politics in an Age of Globalization*, ed. R. Prazniak and A. Dirlik, 15–51. Lanham, Md.: Rowman and Littlefield.

Dirlik, Arif, Vinay Bahl, and Peter Gran, eds. 2000. *History after the Three Worlds: Post-Eurocentric Historiographies*. Lanham, Md.: Rowman and Littlefield.

Dirlik, Arif, and Roxann Prazniak. 2001. "Introduction: Cultural Identity and the Politics of Place." In *Places and Politics in an Age of Globalization*, ed. R. Prazniak and A. Dirlik, 3–13. Lanham, Md.: Rowman and Littlefield.

Dove, Michael R. 1982. "The Myth of the 'Communal' Longhouse in Rural Development." In *Too Rapid Rural Development*, ed. C. MacAndrews and L. S. Chin, 14–78. Athens: Ohio University Press.

———. 1983a. "Forest Preference in Swidden Agriculture." *Tropical Ecology* 24(1):122–42.

———. 1983b. "Theories of Swidden Agriculture and the Political Economy of Ignorance." *Agroforestry Systems* 1:85–99.

———. 1984. "The Chayanov Slope in a Swidden Economy." In *Chayanov, Peasants, and Economic Anthropology*, ed. P. E. Durrenberger, 97–132. New York: Academic Press.

———. 1985a. "The Agroecological Mythology of the Javanese and the Political-Economy of Indonesia." *Indonesia* 39:1–36.

———. 1985b. *Swidden Agriculture in Indonesia: The Subsistence Strategies of the Kalimantan Kantu'*. Berlin: Mouton.

———. 1988. "The Ecology of Intoxication Among the Kantu' of West Kalimantan." In

The Real and the Imagined Role of Culture in Development: Case Studies from Indonesia, ed. M. R. Dove, 139–82. Honolulu: University of Hawaii Press.

———. 1993a. "Smallholder Rubber and Swidden Agriculture in Borneo: A Sustainable Adaptation to the Ecology and Economy of the Tropical Forest." *Economic Botany* 47(2):136–47.

———. 1993b. "Uncertainty, Humility and Adaptation to the Tropical Forest: The Agricultural Augury of the Kantu'." *Ethnology* 40(2):145–67.

———. 1994. "The Transition from Native Forest Rubbers to *Hevea Brasiliensis* (EU-PHORBIACEAE) Among Tribal Smallholders in Borneo." *Economic Botany* 48(4):382–96.

———. 1996a. "Process versus Product in Kantu' Augury: A Traditional Knowledge System's Solution to the Problem of Knowing." In *Redefining Nature: Ecology, Culture, Domestication*, ed. K. Fukui and R. F. Ellen, 557–96. Oxford: Berg.

———. 1996b. "Rice-Eating Rubber and People-Eating Governments: Peasant versus State Critiques of Rubber Development in Colonial Indonesia." *Ethnohistory* 43(1):33–63.

———. 1997. "Political Ecology of Pepper in the 'Hikayat Bandjar': The Historiography of Commodity Production in a Bornean Kingdom." In *Paper Landscapes: Explorations in the Environmental History of Indonesia*, ed. P. Boomgaard, F. Colombijn, and D. Henley, 341–77. Verhandelingen 178. Leiden: Koninklijk Instituut voor Taal-, Land- en Volkenkunde.

———. 1998. "Living Rubber, Dead Land, and Persisting Systems in Borneo: Indigenous Representations of Sustainability." *Bijdragen tot de taal-, land- en volkenkunde* 154(1):20–54.

———. 1999a. "The Agronomy of Memory and the Memory of Agronomy: Ritual Conservation of Archaic Cultigens in Contemporary Farming Systems." In *Ethnoecology: Situated Knowledge/Located Lives*, ed. V. Nazarea, 45–70. Tucson: University of Arizona Press.

———. 1999b. "Forest Augury in Borneo: Indigenous Environmental Knowledge—About the Limits to Knowledge of the Environment." In *Cultural and Spiritual Values of Biodiversity*, ed. D. Posey, 376–80. London: Intermediate Technology Publications, for UNEP.

———. 2001. "Interdisciplinary Borrowing in Environmental Anthropology and the Critique of Modern Science." In *New Directions in Anthropology and Environment: Intersections*, ed. C. Crumley, with A. van Deventer and J. Fletcher, 90–110. Lanham, Md.: Altamira Press.

Dove, Michael R., and D. M. Kammen. 1997. "The Epistemology of Sustainable Resource Use: Managing Forest Products, Swiddens, and High-Yielding Variety Crops." With D. M. Kammen. *Human Organization* 56(1):91–101.

Dow, James. 1981. "The Image of Limited Production: Envy and the Domestic Mode of Production in Peasant Society." *Human Organization* 40:360–64.

Durkheim, Émile. 1964 [1933]. *The Division of Labor in Society*. Translated by George Simpson (Original: *De la division du travail social* [Paris, Félix Alcan]). New York: Free Press.

———. 1984 (1893). *The Division of Labor in Society*. Translated by W. D. Halls. New York: Free Press.

Dwyer, Peter D., and Monica Minnegal. 1999. "The Transformation of Use-Rights: A Comparison of Two Papua New Guinean Socieites." *Journal of Anthropological Research* 55(3):361–83.

Ebihara, May M., Carol A. Mortland, and Judy Ledgerwood, eds. 1994. *Cambodian Culture Since 1975: Homeland and Exile*. Ithaca: Cornell University Press.

Echols, John M., and Hassan Shadily. 1992. *Kamus Indonesia-Inggeris: An Indonesian-English Dictionary*. 3d edition. Jakarta: P. T. Gramedia.

Eckersley, Robyn. 1992. *Environmentalism and Political Theory: Toward an Ecocentric Approach*. Albany: State University of New York Press.

Effendi Norwawi, Datuk. 1993. "A Vision of Sarawak as a Model State." *Backbench* 8, August 1993:27.

Ellen, Roy. 1996. "Introduction." In *Redefining Nature: Ecology, Culture and Domestication*, ed. R. Ellen and K. Fukui. Oxford: Berg.

Ellen, Roy, Peter Parkes, and Alan Bicker, eds. 2000. *Indigenous Environmental Knowledge and Its Transformations: Critical Anthropological Perspectives*. Australia: Harwood Academic Publishers.

Engel, J. Ronald. 1989. "The Symbolic and Ethical Dimension of the Biosphere Reserve Concept." In *Proceedings of the Symposium on Biosphere Reserves, Fourth World Wilderness Congress, Estes Park, Colorado, Sept. 11–18, 1987*, ed. William P. Gregg, Jr., Stanley L. Krugman, and James D. Wood Jr., 21–32. Atlanta: National Park Service, Science Publications Office.

Equihua Ballesteros, Serafin. 1983. "El puerto de San Felipe." In *Panorama histórico de Baja California*, ed. David Piera Ramirez, 507–15. Mexico City: Centro de Investigaciones Historicas, Universidad Nacional Autónoma-Unversidad Autónoma de Baja California.

Erikson, Kai. 1976. *Everything in Its Path*. New York: Simon and Schuster.

Escobar, Arturo. 1992. "Culture, Economics, and Politics in Latin American Social Movements Theory and Research." In *The Making of Social Movements in Latin America: Identity, Strategy, and Democracy*, ed. A. Escobar and S. Alvarez, 62–85. Boulder: Westview Press.

———. 1995a. *Encountering Development: The Making and Unmaking of the Third World*. Princeton: Princeton University Press.

———. 1995b. "Imagining a Post-Development Era?" In *Power of Development*, ed. J. Crush, 211–27. London: Routledge.

———. 1996. "Constructing Nature: Elements for a Poststructural Political Ecology." In *Liberation Ecologies: Environment, Development, Social Movements*, ed. R. Peet and M. Watts, 46–68. London: Routledge.

———. 1997. "Cultural Politics and Biological Diversity: State, Capital, and Social Movements in the Pacific Coast of Colombia." In *Between Resistance and Revolution: Cultural Politics and Social Protest*, ed. R. Fox and O. Starn, 40–64. New Brunswick: Rutgers University Press.

———. 1999a. "After Nature: Steps to an Antiessentialist Political Ecology." *Current Anthropology* 40:1–30.

———. 1999b. Comment on Brosius' "Analyses and Interventions: Anthropological Engagements with Environmentalism." *Current Anthropology* 40(3):291–93.

———. 2001. "Culture Sits in Places: Reflections on Globalism and Subaltern Strategies of Localization." *Political Geography* 20:139–74.

Escobar, Arturo, and Sonia E. Alvarez, eds. 1992. *The Making of Social Movements in Latin America: Identity, Strategy, and Democracy*. Boulder: Westview Press.

Escobar, Arturo, Dianne Rocheleau, and Smitu Kothari. 2002. "Environmental Social Movements and the Politics of Place." In "Place, Politics and Justice: Women Negotiating Globalization," ed. W. Harcourt. Special issue. *Development* 45(1):28–36.

Fabian, Johannes. 1983. *Time and the Other: How Anthropology Makes Its Object*. New York: Columbia University Press.

Fairhead, James, and Melissa Leach. 1996. *Misreading the African Landscape: Society and Ecology in a Forest-Savanna Mosaic*. Cambridge: Cambridge University Press.

Featherstone, Mike. 1993. "Global and Local Cultures." In *Mapping the Futures: Local Cultures, Global Change*, ed. J. Bird, B. Curtis, T. Putnam, G. Robertson, and L. Tickner, 169–87. London: Routledge.

Feld, Steven. 1982. *Sound and Sentiment: Birds, Weeping, Poetics, and Song in Kaluli Expression*. Philadelphia: University of Pennsylvania Press.

Feld, Steven, and Keith Basso, eds. 1996. *Senses of Place*. Santa Fe: School of American Research Press.

Ferguson, James. 1990. *The Anti-Politics Machine: "Development," Depoliticization, and Bureaucratic Power in Lesotho*. Cambridge: Cambridge University Press.

———. 2000. *Expectations of Modernity: Myths and Meanings of Urban Life on the Zambian Copperbelt*. Berkeley: University of California Press.

Ferguson, James, and Akhil Gupta. 2002. "Spatializing States: Toward an Ethnography of Neoliberal Governmentality." *American Ethnologist* 29(4):981–1002.

Filer, Colin. 1990. "The Bougainville Rebellion, the Mining Industry and the Process of Social Disintegration in Papua New Guinea." In *The Bougainville Crisis*, ed. R. J. May and Matthew Spriggs, 73–112. Bathurst: Crawford House Press.

———. 1999. "Introduction." In *Dilemmas of Development: The Social and Economic Impact of the Porgera Gold Mine 1989–1994*, ed. C. Filer, 1–18. Canberra: Asia Pacific Press and Research School of Pacific and Asian Studies, Australian National University.

———. 2001. "Between a Rock and a Hard Place: Mining Projects, 'Indigenous Communities', and Melanesian States." In *Mining in Papua New Guinea: Analysis and Policy Implications*, ed. B. Y. Imbun and P. A. McGavin, 7–23. Waigani, NCD: University of Papua New Guinea Press.

Finnish Forest Industries. 1994. "Renewable, Recyclable, Responsible." Promotional brochure. Helsinki: Finnish Forest Industries Federation.

Fortes, Meyer. 1970. *Kinship and the Social Order*. Chicago: Aldine.

Foster, John Bellamy. 2000. *Marx's Ecology: Materialism and Nature*. New York: Monthly Review Press.

Foucault, Michel. 1973. *The Birth of the Clinic: An Archaeology of Medical Perception*. Translated by A. M. Sheridan. London: Tavistock.

———. 1978. *The History of Sexuality*. Volume 1. New York: Random House.

———. 1982. "Afterword: The Subject and Power." In *Michel Foucault: Beyond Structuralism and Hermeneutics*, ed. Hubert L. Dreyfus and Paul Rabinow, 208–26. Chicago: University of Chicago Press.

Fox, James J. 2000. "The Impact of the 1997–98 El Niño on Indonesia." In *El Niño—History and Crisis*, ed. Richard H. Grove and John Chappell, 171–90. Cambridge: White Horse Press.

Fox, Richard G, and Orin Starn, eds. 1997. "Introduction." In *Between Resistance and Revolution: Cultural Politics and Social Protest*, 1–16. New Brunswick: Rutgers University Press.

Frank, Andre Gunder. 1969a. *Capitalism and Underdevelopment in Latin America: Historical Studies of Chile and Brazil*. New York: Monthly Review Press.

———. 1969b. *Latin America: Underdevelopment or Revolution*. New York: Monthly Review Press.

———. 1978. *World Accumulation, 1492–1789*. New York: Monthly Review Press.

Franklin, Sarah. 1995. "Science as Culture, Cultures of Science." *Annual Review of Anthropology* 24:163–84.

———. 1996. "Making Transparencies: Seeing through the Science Wars." In *Science Wars*, ed. A. Ross, 151–67. Durham: Duke University Press.

Fraser, Nancy. 1997. *Justice Interruptus: Critical Reflections on the "Postsocialist" Condition*. London: Routledge.

———. 1999. "Introduction." In *Dilemmas of Development: The Social and Economic Impact of the Porgera Gold Mine 1989–1994*, ed. C. Filer, 1–18. Canberra: Asia Pacific Press and Research School of Pacific and Asian Studies, Australian National University.

Freeman, J. D. 1960. "Iban Augury." In *The Birds of Borneo*, ed. B. E. Smythies, 73–98. Edinburgh: Oliver and Boyd.

————. 1970. *Report on the Iban*. London School of Economics Monographs on Social Anthropology no. 41. New York: Humanities Press.

Friedman, Jonathan. 1974. "Marxism, Structuralism and Vulgar Materialism." *Man* (n.s.) 9:444–69.

————. 1975. "Tribes, States, and Transformations." In *Marxist Analyses and Social Anthropology*, ed. M. Bloch, 161–202. London: Malaby.

————. 1979. "Hegelian Ecology: Between Rousseau and the World Spirit." In *Social and Ecological Systems*, ed. P. C. Burnham and R. Ellen, 253–70. A.S.A. Monograph no. 18. London: Academic Press.

————. 1994. *Cultural Identity and Global Process*. London: Sage.

FSIS (Forest Statistics Information Service) Statistical Yearbook of Forestry 1995. Helsinki: Finnish Forest Research Institute/METLA.

Fujimura, Joan. 1992. "Crafting Science: Standardized Packages, Boundary Objects, and 'Translation'." In *Science as Practice and Culture*, ed. Andrew Pickering, 168–211. Chicago: University of Chicago Press.

Gammage, Bill. 1998. *The Sky Travellers: Journeys in New Guinea 1939–1939*. Melbourne: Melbourne University Press.

Gaonkar, Dilip Parameschwar, ed. 2001. *Alternative Modernities*. Durham: Duke University Press.

García Hierro, Pedro, Søren Hvalkof, and Andrew Gray. 1998. *Liberation through Land Rights in the Peruvian Amazon*, ed. A. Parellada and S. Hvalkof. IWGIA Document no. 80. Copenhagen: IWGIA.

Gare, Arran E. 1995. *Postmodernism and the Environmental Crisis*. London: Routledge.

Gates, Henry Louis, Jr., ed. 1985. *"Race," Writing, and Difference*. Chicago: University of Chicago Press.

Gatti, Luis Maria, and Graciela Alcala. 1985. *La Vida en un Lance: Los Pescadores de México*. Mexico City: Museo Nacional de Culturas Populares, Dirección General de Culturas Populares, SEP Cultura: Secretaría de Pesca.

Geertz, Clifford. 1973. *The Interpretation of Cultures*. New York: Basic Books.

————. 1980. *Negara*. Princeton: Princeton University Press.

Gellert, Paul. 1998. "A Brief History and Analysis of Indonesia's Forest Fire Crisis." *Indonesia* 65:63–85.

Gewertz, Deborah, and Frederick Errington. 1991. *Twisted Histories, Alternate Contexts*. Cambridge: Cambridge University Press.

Geyer, Michael, and Charles Bright. 1995. "World History in a Global Age." *American Historical Review* (October 1995):1034–60.

Ghai, Yash P., Robin Luckham, and Francis G. Snyder. 1987. *The Political Economy of Law: A Third World Reader*. New York: Oxford University Press.

Gibson-Graham, J. K. 1995. "Waiting for the Revolution, or How to Smash Capitalism While Working at Home in Your Spare Time." In *Marxism in the Postmodern*

Age: Confronting the New World Order, ed. A. Callari, S. Cullenberg, and C. Biewener, 188–97. New York: Guilford Press.

———. 1996/97. "Querying Globalization." *Rethinking Marxism* 9(1):1–27.

Gibson-Graham, J. K., Stephen Resnick, and Richard Wolff. 2001. "Toward a Poststructuralist Political Economy." Introduction to *Re/Presenting Class: Essays in Postmodern Marxism*, ed. J. K. Gibson-Graham, S. Resnick, and R. Wolf, 1–22. Durham: Duke University Press.

Giddens, Anthony. 1981. *A Contemporary Critique of Historical Materialism*. Berkeley: University of California Press.

Godelier, Maurice. 1984. *The Mental and the Material: Thought, Economy and Society*. Bristol: Verso.

———. 1986. *The Making of Great Men*. Cambridge: Cambridge University Press.

Goldammer, J. G. 1990. "The Impact of Drought and Forest Fires on Tropical Lowland Rain Forest of East Kalimantan." In *Fire in the Tropical Biota: Ecosystem Processes and Global Challenges*, ed. J. G. Goldammer, 11–31. Berlin: Springer-Verlag.

Goldman, Stanford. 1960. "Further Consideration of Cybernetic Aspects of Homeostasis." In *Self-Organizing Systems*, ed. M. Yovits and S. Cameron, 108–21. New York: Pergamon Press.

Golub, Alex. 2001. *Gold Positive: A Short History of Porgera 1930–1997*. A Porgera Development Authority Monograph. Porgera: Porgera Development Authority.

Gomes, E. H. 1911. *Seventeen Years Among the Sea Dyaks of Borneo: A Record of Intimate Association with the Natives of the Bornean Jungles*. London: Seeley.

Goodman, Alan H., and Thomas L. Leatherman. 1998. "Traversing the Chasm between Biology and Culture: An Introduction." In *Building a New Biocultural Synthesis: Political-Economic Perspectives on Human Biology*, ed. A. Goodman and T. Leatherman, 3–41. Ann Arbor: University of Michigan Press.

Gore, Al. 1992. *Earth in the Balance: Ecology and the Human Spirit*. New York: Plume/Penguin.

Gould, David M. 1996. "Mexico's Crisis: Looking Back to Assess the Future." In *Changing Structure of Mexico: Political, Social, and Economic Perspectives*, ed. Laura Randall, 15–39. New York: M. E. Sharpe.

Greenberg, James B. 1998. "The Tragedy of Commoditization: Political Ecology of the Colorado River Delta's Destruction." *Research in Economic Anthropology* 19:133–52.

Greenberg, James B., and Thomas K. Park. 1994. "Political Ecology." *Journal of Political Ecology* 1:1–12.

Greenough, Paul, and Anna Lowenhaupt Tsing. 2003. "Introduction." *Nature in the Global South: Environmental Projects in South and Southeast Asia*, ed. P. Greenough and A. Tsing, 1–23. Durham: Duke University Press.

———, eds. 2003. *Nature in the Global South: Environmental Projects in South and Southeast Asia*. Durham: Duke University Press.

Greider, William. 1997. *One World, Ready or Not*. New York: Simon and Schuster.

Grey, Andrew. 1997. "Peru. Freedom and Territory: Slavery in the Peruvian Amazon, Enslaved Peoples in the 1990s." In *Indigenous Peoples, Debt Bondage and Human Rights*, 183–215. Anti-Slavery International and IWGIA Document no. 83. Copenhagen: IWGIA.

———. 1998. "Demarcating Development: Titling Indigenous Communities in Peru." In *Liberation through Land Rights in the Peruvian Amazon*, ed. A. Parellada and S. Hvalkof, 163–216. IWGIA Document no. 80. Copenhagen: IWGIA.

Grey, Andrew, and Søren Hvalkof. 1990. "Indigenous Land Titling in the Peruvian Amazon." In *IWGIA Yearbook 1989*, 230–43. Copenhagen: IWGIA.

Grim, John, ed. 2001. *Indigenous Traditions and Ecology: The Interbeing of Cosmology and Community*. Cambridge, Mass.: Harvard University Press.

Grimshaw, Jean. 1986. *Philosophy and Feminist Thinking*. Minneapolis: University of Minnesota Press.

Gross, Daniel, George Eiten, Nancy Flowers, Francisca Leoi, Madeline Ritter, and Dennis Werner. 1979. "Ecology and Acculturation among Native Peoples of Central Brazil." *Science* 206(30):1043–50.

Gross, Paul R., and Norman Levitt. 1994. *Higher Superstition: The Academic Left and Its Quarrels with Science*. Baltimore: Johns Hopkins University Press.

Grundmann, Reiner. 1991. *Marxism and Ecology*. Oxford: Clarendon Press.

Guadarrama, Roco. 1985. "Los Proyectos Colonizadores." In *Historia General de Sonora: Historia Contemporánea de Sonora 1929–1984*, volume 5, ed. Gerardo Conejo Murrieta, 167–71. Hermosillo, Sonora: Gobierno del Estado de Sonora.

Guarnizo, Luis Eduardo, and Michael Peter Smith. 1998. "The Locations of Transnationalism." In *Transnationalism from Below*, ed. M. Smith and L. Guarnizo, 3–34. Comparative Urban and Community Research. New Brunswick: Transaction.

Gudeman, Stephen. 1992. "Remodeling the House of Economics: Culture and Innovation." *American Ethnologist* 19(1):141–54.

Gupta, Akhil. 1998. *Postcolonial Developments: Agriculture in the Making of Modern India*. Durham: Duke University Press.

Gupta, Akhil, and James Ferguson. 1997a. "After 'Peoples and Cultures'." In *Culture, Power, Place: Explorations in Critical Anthropology*, ed. A. Gupta and J. Ferguson, 1–29. Durham: Duke University Press.

———. 1997b. "Beyond 'Culture': Space, Identity, and the Politics of Difference." In *Culture, Power, Place: Explorations in Critical Anthropology*, ed. A. Gupta and J. Ferguson, 33–51. Durham: Duke University Press.

———. 1997c. "Discipline and Practice: 'The Field' as Site, Method, and Location in Anthropology." In *Anthropological Locations: Boundaries and Grounds of a Field Science*, ed. A. Gupta and J. Ferguson, 1–46. Berkeley: University of California Press.

Haberle, Simon. 1998a. "Report on the Gunung Kawi Sebatu Pollen Samples: Core 16 and 14." Unpublished report in files of Vernon L. Scarborough.

——. 1998b. "Second Report on the Gunung Kawi Sebatu Pollen Samples: Core 14 and 17." Unpublished report in files of Vernon L. Scarborough.

Habermas, Jürgen. 1971. *Knowledge and Human Interests.* Translated by Jeremy Shapiro. London: Heinemann Educational Books.

Haddock, Bruce. 1994. "Hegel's Critique of the Theory of Social Contract." In *The Social Contract from Hobbes to Rawls*, ed. D. Boucher and P. Kelly, 147–63. London: Routledge.

Hajer, Maarten A. 1995. *The Politics of Environmental Discourse: Ecological Modernization and the Policy Process.* Oxford: Clarendon Press.

Hall, Stuart. 1997a. "Introduction: Spaces of Culture, Spaces of Knowledge." In *Culture, Globalization and the World-System: Contemporary Conditions for the Representation of Identity*, ed. Anthony D. King, 19–39. Minneapolis: University of Minnesota Press.

——. 1997b. "The Work of Representation." In *Representation: Cultural Representations and Signifying Practices*, ed. S. Hall, 13–74. London: Sage Publications.

Handley, G. A. 1987. "Exploration of the Porgera Gold Deposit." In *Pacific Rim Congress 87*, 145–49. Parkville, Victoria: Australasian Institute of Mining and Metallurgy.

Handley, G. A., and D. D. Henry. 1990. "Porgera Gold Deposit." In *Geology of the Mineral Deposits of Australia and Papua New Guinea*, ed. F. E Hughes, 1717–24. Melbourne: Australasian Institute of Mining and Metallurgy.

Hann, C. M. 1998. "Introduction: The Embeddedness of Property." *In Property Relations: Renewing the Anthropological Tradition*, ed. C. M. Hann, 1–47. Cambridge: Cambridge University Press.

Hanna, Susan, Carl Folke, and Karl-Goran Maler. 1996. "Property Rights and the Natural Environment." In *Rights to Nature: Ecological, Economic, Cultural, and Political Principles of Institutions for the Environment*, ed. S. Hanna, C. Folke, and K.-G. Maler, 1–10. Washington: Island Press.

Hannerz, Ulf. 1989. "Notes on the Global Ecumene." *Public Culture* 1(2):66–75.

Hannigan, John A. 1995. *Environmental Sociology: A Social Constructionist Approach.* London: Routledge.

Hansen, Art. 1994. "The Illusion of Local Sustainability and Self-Sufficiency: Famine in a Border Area of Northwestern Zambia." *Human Organization* 5(1):11–20.

Haraway, Donna. 1989. *Primate Visions: Gender, Race and Nature in the World of Modern Science.* New York: Routledge.

——. 1991. *Simians, Cyborgs, and Women: The Reinvention of Nature.* London: Free Association Books.

——. 1997. *Modest_Witness@Second_Millennium: FemaleMan_Meets_OncoMouse Feminism and Technoscience.* London: Routledge.

Harcourt, Wendy, ed. 2002. "Place, Politics and Justice: Women Negotiating Globalization." Special Issue, *Development* 45(1):7–14.

Harcourt, Wendy, and Arturo Escobar. 2002. "Women and the Politics of Place." In "Place, Politics and Justice: Women Negotiating Globalization," ed. W. Harcourt. Special issue. *Development* 45(1):7–14.

Hardin, G. 1968. "The Tragedy of the Commons." *Science* 162:1243–48.

Harrison, Robert P. 1992. *Forests: The Shadow of Civilization*. Chicago: University of Chicago Press.

Harrisson, Tom. 1949. "Notes on Some Nomadic Punans." *Sarawak Museum Journal* 5(1)(n.s.):130–46.

———. 1960. "Men and Birds in Borneo." In *The Birds of Borneo*, ed. B. E. Smythies, 20–61. Edinburgh: Oliver and Boyd.

Harvey, David. 1974. "Population, Resources and the Ideology of Science." *Economic Geography* 50:256–77.

———. 1989. *The Condition of Postmodernity*. Oxford: Basil Blackwell.

———. 1993. "From Space to Place and Back Again: Reflections on the Condition of Postmodernity." In *Mapping the Futures: Local Cultures, Global Change*, ed. J. Bird, B. Curtis, T. Putnam, G. Robertson, and L. Tickner, 3–29. London: Routledge.

———. 1996. *Justice, Nature and the Geography of Difference*. Cambridge, Mass.: Blackwell.

Harwell, Emily. 2000a. "The Unnatural History of Culture: Ethnicity, Tradition and Territorial Conflicts in West Kalimantan, Indonesia, 1800–1997." Ph.D. diss., Yale University.

———. 2000b. "Remote Sensibilities: Discourses of Technology and the Making of Indonesia's Natural Disaster." *Development and Change* 31:307–40.

Hecht, Susanna B. 1985. "Environment, Development and Politics: Capital Accumulation and the Livestock Sector in Eastern Amazonia. *World Development* 13(6):663–84.

Hecht, Susanna B., Richard B. Nordgaard, and Giogio Possio. 1988. "The Economics of Cattle Ranching in Eastern Amazonia." *Interciencia* 13(5):233–39.

Hegel, Georg Wilhelm Friedrich. 1942. *Hegel's Philosophy of Right*. Translated by T. M. Knox. Oxford: Oxford University Press.

Helgason, Arnar S., and Gísli Pálsson. 1997. "Contested Commodities: The Moral Landscape of Modernist Regimes." *Journal of the Royal Anthropological Institute* (incorporating *Man*) 3(3):451–71.

———. 1998. "Cash for Quotas: Disputes over the Legitimacy of an Economic Model of Fishing in Iceland." In *Virtualism: A New Political Economy*, ed. J. Carrier and D. Miller, 117–34. Oxford: Berg.

Henry, D. D., and G. A. Handley. 1987. "Report on Small Scale Mining." Appendix 8 of TAC 1995. Prepared for Porgera Joint Venture. Department of Mining, Papua New Guinea Government.

Herzfeld, Michael. 2001. *Anthropology: Theoretical Practice in Culture and Society*. London: Blackwell.

Hewitt, K., ed. 1983. *Interpretations of Calamity, from the Viewpoint of Human Ecology*. Boston: Allen and Unwin.

Heyman, Josiah. 1994. "The Mexico–United States Border in Anthropology: A Critique and Reformulation." *Journal of Political Ecology* 1:43–65.

Heyman, Josiah. 1997. "Imports and Standards of Justice on the Mexico-United States Border." In *The Allure of the Foreign*, ed. Benjamin Orlove, 151–83. Ann Arbor: University of Michigan Press.

Hirsch, Eric, and Michael O'Hanlon, eds. 1995. *The Anthropology of Landscape: Perspectives on Place and Space*. Oxford: Clarendon Press.

Holbrook, Morris. 1991. *The Semiotics of Consumption: Interpreting Symbolic Consumer Behavior in Popular Culture and Works of Art*. Berlin: Mouton de Gruyter.

Holleman, J. F., ed. 1981. *Van Vollenhoven on Indonesian Adat Law*. Koninklijk Instituut voor Taal-, Land-, en Volkenkunde Translation Series 20. The Hague: Martinus Nijhoff.

Holling, C. S. 1978. "Myths of Ecological Stability: Resilience and the Problem of Failure." In *Studies on Crisis Management*, ed. C. F. Smart, C. F. Stanbury, and W. T. Stanbury, 97–109. Toronto: Institute for Research on Public Policy.

———. 1994. "Simplifying the Complex: The Paradigms of Ecological Function and Structure." *Futures* 26(6):598–609.

Holling, C. S., P. Taylor, and M. Thompson. 1991. "From Newton's Sleep to Blake's Fourfold Vision: Why the Climax Community and the Rational Bureaucracy Are Not the Ends of the Ecological and Social-Cultural Roads." *Annals of the Earth* 9(3):19–21.

Hong, E. 1987. *Natives of Sarawak: Survival in Borneo's Vanishing Forests*. Pulau Pinang: Institut Masyarakat.

Honneth, Axel. 1996. *The Struggle for Recognition: The Moral Grammar of Social Conflicts*. Translated by Joel Anderson. Cambridge: MIT.

Hooker, M. B. 1978a. *Adat Law in Modern Indonesia*. Kuala Lumpur: Oxford University Press.

———. 1978b. *A Concise Legal History of South-East Asia*. Oxford: Clarendon Press.

Hornborg, Alf. 1999. Comment on Brosius' "Analyses and Interventions: Anthropological Engagements with Environmentalism." *Current Anthropology* 40(3):294.

Horowitz, Daniel. 1988. *The Morality of Spending*. Baltimore: Johns Hopkins University Press.

Huehne, W. H. 1959. "A Doctor Among 'Nomadic' Punans." *Sarawak Museum Journal* 9(13–14)(n.s.):195–202.

Hunt, Robert C. 1998. "Properties of Property: Conceptual Issues." In *Property in Economic Context*, ed. R. C. Hunt and A. Gilman, 7–27. Lanham, Md.: University Press of America.

Hurst, Philip. 1990. *Rainforest Politics: Ecological Destruction in South-East Asia*. London: Zed Books.

Hvalkof, Søren. 1986. "El Drama Actual del Gran Pajonal. Primera parte: Recursos, Historia, Población y Producción Ashéninka." In *Amazonia Indígena, Boletín de Análisis* 6(12). Lima: Copal.

———. 1987. "El Drama Actual del Gran Pajonal. Segunda parte: Colonización y Violencia." In *Amazonia Indígena, Boletín de Análisis* 7(13). Lima: Copal.

———. 1989. "The Nature of Development: Native and Settlers' Views in Gran Pajonal, Peruvian Amazon." *Folk* 31:125–50. Copenhagen: Danish Ethnographic Society.

———. 1994. "The Asháninka Disaster and Struggle—The Forgotten War in the Peruvian Amazon." *Indigenous Affairs* no. 2/94. Copenhagen: IWGIA.

———. 1997. "From Curaca to President . . . Indigenous Leadership in Peruvian Amazon: The Ashéninka Case." Paper presented at the session "Contemporary Indigenous Leadership in the Amazon." American Anthropological Association annual meeting, Washington, D.C., November 19–23.

———. 1998. "From Slavery to Democracy: The Indigenous Process of Upper Ucayali and Gran Pajonal." In *Liberation through Land Rights in the Peruvian Amazon*, ed. A. Parellada and S. Hvalkof, 83–162. IWGIA Document no. 90. Copenhagen: IWGIA.

———. 2002. "Beyond Indigenous Land Titling: Democratizing Civil Society in the Peruvian Amazon." In *Space, Place and Nation: Neoliberalism in the Americas*, ed. J. Chase, 87–118. Bloomfield, Conn.: Kumarian Press.

Hvalkof, Søren, and Arturo Escobar. 1998. "Nature, Political Ecology and Social Practice: Toward an Academic and Political Agenda." In *Building a New Biocultural Synthesis: Political-Economic Perspectives on Human Biology*, ed. A. H. Goodman and T. L. Leatherman, 425–50. Ann Arbor: University of Michigan Press.

Hyndman, David. 1994. *Ancestral Rainforests and the Mountain of Gold: Indigenous Peoples and Mining in New Guinea*. Boulder: Westview Press.

———. 2001. "Academic Responsibilities and Representation of the Ok Tedi Crisis in Postcolonial Papua New Guinea." *The Contemporary Pacific* 13/1:33–54.

Illich, Ivan. 1977. *Toward a History of Needs*. New York: Pantheon.

Imbun, Benedict. 2000. "Mining Workers or 'Opportunist' Tribesmen?: A Tribal Workforce in a Papua New Guinea Mine." *Oceania* 71:129–49.

———. 2001. "Human Resource Management in Papua New Guinea Mining: Evidence from Porgera." In *Mining in Papua New Guinea: Analysis and Policy Implications*, ed. B. Y. Imbun and P. A. McGavin, 95–112. Waigani, NCD: University of Papua New Guinea Press.

Ingold, Tim. 1991. "Foreword." In *Coastal Economies, Cultural Accounts: Human Ecology and Icelandic Discourse*, by Gísli Pálsson, vii–x. Manchester: University of Manchester Press.

———. 1993. "Globes and Spheres: The Topology of Environmentalism." In *Environmentalism: The View from Anthropology*, ed. K. Milton, 31–42. London: Routledge.

———. 1995. "Building, Dwelling, Living: How Animals and People Make Themselves at Home in the World." In *Shifting Contexts: Transformations in Anthropological Knowledge*, ed. M. Strathern, 57–80. London: Routledge.

———. 2000. *The Perception of the Environment: Essays in Livelihood and Dwelling and Skill*. London: Routledge.

INSAN (Institute for Social Analysis). 1989. *Logging against the Natives of Sarawak*. Petaling Jaya: INSAN.

Instituto Nacional de Estadística, Geografía e Informática. 1990. *Estadísticas Históricas de México*. Volume 1: *Aguacalientes, Ags*. Mexico City: Instituto Nacional de Estadística, Geografía, e Informática.

Ipara, Kurubu. 1994. "Lower Porgera Land Investigation Report." Prepared for Porgera Joint Venture.

———. 1995. "Brief History of Negotiations." In "Minutes of meeting on the environment and alluvial gold compensation (lower Porgera)," March 2, 1995. File SLO 1/6/2J, Project Coordination Unit, PDA files.

Irwin, A., and B. Wynne, eds. 1996. *Misunderstanding Science: The Public Reconstruction of Science and Technology*. Cambridge: Cambridge University Press.

Irwin, Graham. 1955. *Nineteenth-Century Borneo: A Study in Diplomatic Rivalry*. Singapore: Donald Moore Books.

Jacka, Jerry. 2001a. "Coca-Cola and *Kolo*: Land, Ancestors, and Development." *Anthropology Today* 17:3–8.

———. 2001b. "On the Outside Looking In: Attitudes and Responses of Non-Landowners towards Mining at Porgera." In *Mining in Papua New Guinea: Analysis and Policy Implications*, ed. B. Y. Imbun and P. A. McGavin, 45–62. Waigani, NCD: University of Papua New Guinea Press.

———. 2003. "God, Gold, and the Ground: Place-Based Political Ecology in a New Guinea Borderland." Ph.D. thesis, University of Oregon.

Jackson, J. 1995. "Culture, Genuine and Spurious: The Politics of Indianness in the Vaupés, Colombia." *American Ethnologist* 22(1):3–27.

Jackson, Peter. 2002. "Consumption in a Globalizing World." In *Geographies of Global Change*, ed. R. J. Johnston, P. J. Taylor, and M. J. Watts, 283–95. Oxford: Basil Blackwell.

Jackson, Richard. 1997. "Cheques and Balances: Compensation and Mining in Papua New Guinea." In *Compensation for Resource Development in Papua New Guinea*, ed.

S. Toft, 105–15. Law Reform Commission of Papua New Guinea, Monograph no. 6. Canberra: Australian National University.

Jackson, Richard, and Glenn Banks. 2002. *In Search of the Serpent's Skin: The Story of the Porgera Gold Project*. Port Moresby: Placer Niugini Limited.

Jameson, Fredric. 1984. "Postmodernism, or the Cultural Logic of Late Capitalism." *New Left Review* 146:53–92.

Jay, Martin. 1973. *The Dialectical Imagination: A History of the Frankfurt School and the Institute of Social Research, 1923–59*. Boston: Little, Brown.

Jensen, E. 1974. *The Iban and Their Religion*. Oxford Monographs on Social Anthropology. Englewood Cliffs, N.J.: Oxford University Press.

Jorgensen, Dan. 1997. "Who and What Is a Landowner? Mythology and Marking the Ground in a Papua New Guinea Mining Project." *Anthropological Forum* 7(4):599–627.

———. 1998. "Whose Nature? Invading Bush Spirits, Travelling Ancestors and Mining in Telefolmin." *Social Analysis* 42(3):100–116.

———. 1999. "Generic Tradition, Legibility and the Politics of Identity in a Papua New Guinea Mining Project." Paper presented at the Annual Meeting of the American Anthropological Society.

———. 2003. "Mining and Its Cultural Consequences in Papua New Guinea: A Brief History from Telefolmin." Paper given at the workshop "Mining Frontiers: Social Conflicts, Property Relations and Cultural Change in Emerging Boom Regions," organized by G. Schlee, T. Grätz, and Katja Werthmann, Max-Planck-Institut, Halle, Germany, June 16–18, 2003.

Kalland, Arne, and Gerard Persoon, eds. 1998. *Environmental Movements in Asia*. Richmond, Surrey: Curzon.

———. 1998. "An Anthropological Perspective on Environmental Movements." In *Environmental Movements in Asia*, ed. A. Kalland and G. Persoon, 1–43. Richmond, Surrey: Curzon.

Karjalainen, Harri, et al. 1993. "Finland and Forest—A Success Story?" Bulletin of Finnish nongovernmental organizations on the Ministerial Conference on the Protection of Forests in Europe, Helsinki, June 16–17, 1993. Helsinki: World Wildlife Fund, Finland.

Kealhofer, Lisa. 1999. "Preliminary Phytolith Report: Core 16, Sebatu, Bali." Unpublished report in files of the authors.

Kearney, Michael. 1995. "The Local and the Global: The Anthropology of Globalization and Transnationalism." *Annual Review of Anthropology* 24:547–65.

Kedit, Peter M. 1978. *Gunong Mulu Report: A Human-Ecological Survey of Nomadic/Settled Penan within the Gunong Mulu National Park Area, Fourth/Fifth Division, Sarawak*. Sarawak Museum Field Report Series no. 1. Kuching: Sarawak Museum.

Kedit, Peter M. 1982. "An Ecological Survey of the Penan." *Sarawak Museum Journal*, Special Issue no. 2, 30(51)(n.s.):225–79.

Kelly, Raymond C. 1968. "Demographic Pressure and Descent Group Structure in the New Guinea Highlands." *Oceania* 39:36–63.

Kennedy, Danny. 1996. "Ok Tedi All Over Again: Placer and the Porgera Gold Mine." *Multinational Monitor*, March 1996, 22–24.

Kennedy, Paul. 1993. *Preparing for the Twenty-First Century*. New York: Harper Collins.

King, Victor T. 1977. "Unity, Formalism and Structure: Comments on Iban Augury and Related Problems." *Bijdragen tot de taal-, land- en volkenkunde* 133(1):63–87.

———. 1993. *The Peoples of Borneo*. Oxford: Blackwell.

———. 1996. "Environmental Change in Malaysian Borneo: Fire, Drought and Rain." In *Environmental Change in South-East Asia: People, Politics and Sustainable Development*, ed. Michael J. G. Parnwell and Raymond L. Bryant, 165–89. London: Routledge.

Kirsch, Patrick V. 1997. "Introduction." In *Historical Ecology in the Pacific Islands: Prehistoric Environmental and Landscape Change*, ed. P. Kirsch and T. Hunt, 1–21. New Haven: Yale University Press.

Kirsch, Stuart. 1996. "Return to Ok Tedi." *Meanjin* 55(4):657–66.

———. 1997. "Indigenous Response to Environmental Impact along the Ok Tedi." In *Compensation for Resource Development in Papua New Guinea*, ed. S. Toft, 143–55. Monograph no. 6, Law Reform Commission of Papua New Guinea. Boroko: Law Reform Commission.

Knapen, Han. 1997. "Epidemics, Droughts, and Other Uncertainties on Southeast Borneo during the Eighteenth and Nineteenth Centuries." In *Paper Landscapes: Explorations in the Environmental History of Indonesia*, ed. P. Boomgaard, F. Colombijn, and D. Henley, 121–52. Verhandelingen 178. Leiden: Koninklijk Instituut voor Taal-, Land- en Volkenkunde.

Knauft, Bruce M. 2002. *Exchanging the Past: A Rainforest World of Before and After*. Chicago: University of Chicago Press.

———. n.d. "Complicated Subjects in Melanesian Modernities." In *Interrogating Individuals: Crossing Discourses of Subjectivity in the Western Pacific*, ed. K. Sykes. Manuscript under review.

Kottak, Conrad. 1980. *The Past in the Present: History, Ecology, and Cultural Variation in Highland Madagascar*. Ann Arbor: University of Michigan Press.

———. 1999. "The New Ecological Anthropology." In "Ecologies for Tomorrow: Reading Rappaport Today," ed. A. Biersack, a "contemporary issues forum." *American Anthropologist* 101(1):23–35.

Kottak, Conrad, and Elizabeth Colson. 1994. "Multilevel Linkages: Longitudinal and Comparative Studies." In *Assessing Cultural Anthropology*, ed. Robert Borofsky, 396–412. New York: McGraw-Hill.

Krüggeler, Thomas. 1997. "Changing Consumption Patterns and Everyday Life in Two Peruvian Regions: Food, Dress, and Housing in the Central and Southern Highlands (1820–1920)." In *The Allure of the Foreign*, ed. Benjamin Orlove, 31–66. Ann Arbor: University of Michigan Press.

Kulick, Donald. 1992. *Language Shift and Cultural Reproduction*. Cambridge: Cambridge University Press.

Kumar, Amitava. 1997. "Translating Resistance." In *Articulating the Global and the Local: Globalization and Cultural Studies*, ed. A. Cvetkovich and D. Kellner, 207–25. Boulder: Westview Press.

Laaksonen, P., and S. L. Mettomäki, eds. 1994. *Metsä ja metsänviljaa*, Kalevalaseuran vuosikirja 73. Helsinki: Suomalaisen Kirjallisuuden Seura (SKS).

Laclau, Henri, and Chantal Mouffe. 1987. "Post-Marxism without Apologies." *New Left Review* 166:79–106.

Laitakari, Erkki. 1961. "A Century of Finnish State Forestry, 1859–1959." *Silva Fennica*, no.112, offprint. Helsinki.

Lakoff, George, and Mark Johnson. 1980. *Metaphors We Live By*. Chicago: University of Chicago Press.

Langub, Jayl. 1972a. "Adaptation to a Settled Life by the Punans of the Belaga Subdistrict." *Sarawak Gazette* 98(1371):83–86.

———. 1972b. "Structure and Progress in the Punan Community of Belaga Subdistrict." *Sarawak Gazette* 98(1378):219–21.

———. 1974. "Background Report on Potential for Agricultural and Social Extension Service in the Penan Community of Belaga District." *Sarawak Gazette* 100(1395):93–96.

———. 1975. "Distribution of Penan and Punan in the Belaga District." *Borneo Research Bulletin* 7(2):45–48.

———. 1984. "Tamu: Barter Trade between Penan and Their Neighbors." *Sarawak Gazette* 110(1485):11–15.

———. 1989. "Some Aspects of Life of the Penan." *Sarawak Museum Journal*, Special Issue no. 4, Pt. III, 40(61)(n.s.):169–84.

———. 1990. "A Journey through the Nomadic Penan Country." *Sarawak Gazette* 117(1514):5–27.

Lansing, J. Stephen. 1987. "Balinese Water Temples and the Management of Irrigation." *American Anthropologist* 89(2):326–41.

———. 1991. *Priests and Programmers: Technologies of Power in the Engineered Landscape of Bali*. Princeton: Princeton University Press.

Lansing, J. Stephen, and James N. Kremer. 1993. "Emergent Properties of Balinese Water Temple Networks: Coadaptation on a Rugged Fitness Landscape." In *Artificial Life III*, ed. C. G. Langton. Reading, Mass.: Addison-Wesley.

Latour, Bruno. 1987. *Science in Action*. Cambridge, Mass.: Harvard University Press.

Latour, Bruno. 1993. *We Have Never Been Modern*. Translated by Catherine Porter. Cambridge, Mass.: Harvard University Press.

———. 1999. "On Recalling ANT." In *Actor Network Theory and After*, eds. J. Law and J. Hassard, 15–25. Oxford: Blackwell.

Lattas, Andrew. 1993. "Essentialism, Memory and Resistance: Aboriginality and the Politics of Authenticity." *Oceania* 63(3):240–67.

Lave, Jean. 1988. *Cognition in Practice: Mind, Mathematics and Culture in Everyday Life*. Cambridge: Cambridge University Press.

Law, John, and John Hassard, eds. 1999. *Actor Network Theory and After*. Oxford: Blackwell and Sociological Review.

Lawrence, Peter. 1984. *The Garia: An Ethnography of a Traditional Cosmic System in Papua New Guinea*. Melbourne: Oxford University Press.

Lea, David. 1997. *Melanesian Land Tenure in a Contemporary and Philosophical Context*. Lanham, Md.: University Press of America.

Leach, Melissa, and Robin Mearns, eds. 1996. *The Lie of the Land: Challenging Received Wisdom on the African Environment*. London: International African Institute.

Lees, Susan H., and Daniel G. Bates. 1990. "The Ecology of Cumulative Change." In *Ecosystem Ecology in Biology and Anthropology: A Critical Assessment*, ed. Emilio Moran, 247–78. Ann Arbor: University of Michigan Press.

Lefebvre, Henri. 1991. *The Production of Space*. Oxford: Oxford University Press.

Lehnertz, Jay F. 1972. "Juan Santos, Primitive Rebel on the Campa Frontier (1742–52)." In *Actas del XXXIX Congreso Internacional de Americanistas*. Volume 4. Lima.

Lehtinen, Ari Aukusti. 1991. "Northern Natures: A Study of the Forest Question Emerging within the Timber-line Conflict in Finland." *Fennia* 169(1):57–169.

———. 2001. "Globalization and the Finnish Forest Sector: On the Internationalization of Forest Industrial Operations." *Fennia* 179(2):57–169.

Leighton, Mark, and Nengah Wirawan. 1986. "Catastrophic Drought and Fire in Borneo Associated with the 1982–1983 El Niño Southern Oscillation Event." In *Tropical Rainforests and the World Atmosphere*, ed. Gilian T. Prance, 75–102. Washington: American Association for the Advancement of Science.

Lenoir, Timothy. 1997. *Instituting Science: The Cultural Production of Scientific Disciplines*. Stanford: Stanford University Press.

Lewellen, Ted. 1978. *Peasants in Transition: The Changing Economy of the Peruvian Aymara: A General Systems Approach*. Boulder: Westview Press.

Lévi-Strauss, Claude. 1966. *The Savage Mind*. Chicago: University of Chicago Press.

———. 1985. *The View from Afar*. Translated by Joachim Neugroschel and Phoebe Hoss. New York: Basic Books.

Liefrinck, F. A. 1969. "Rice Cultivation in Northern Bali." In *Bali: Further Studies in Life, Thought and Ritual*, ed. J. L. Swellengrebel, 3–73. The Hague: Van Hoeve.

Lilla, Mark, ed. 1994. *New French Thought: Political Philosophy*. Princeton: Princeton University Press.

Linden, Eugene. 1991. "Lost Tribes, Lost Knowledge." *Time*, September 23, 1991, 138(12):46–56.

Little, Paul. 1998. "Beyond Sovereignty and Autonomy: Political Ecology Research and Contemporary Amazonian Territorial Struggles." Paper presented at the session "Political Ecology and Action Research in Forest Communities," Fourteenth ICAES, July 26–August 1, College of William and Mary, Williamsburg, Virginia.

Little, Peter D., and Michael M. Horowitz. 1987. "Introduction: Social Science Perspectives on Land, Ecology, and Development." In *Lands at Risk in the Third World: Local-Level Perspectives*, ed. P. Little, M. Horowitz, and A. Nyerges, 1–16. Boulder: Westview Press.

Low, Setha M., and Denise Lawrence-Zúñiga, eds. 2003. *The Anthropology of Space and Place: Locating Culture*. Malden, Mass.: Blackwell.

Lower Porgera Landowners. 1995. "The Lower Porgera Compensation Dispute: The Landholders' Submission." Department of Mining, Papua New Guinea Government.

Loyaza, Francisco A. 1942 (1742–55). *Juan Santos, el invencible*. Lima: Editorial D. Miranda.

Ludwig, D., R. Hilborn, and C. Walters. 1993. "Uncertainty, Resource Exploitation, and Conservation: Lessons from History." *Science* 260 (April 2):17–36.

MacCormack, Carol, and Marilyn Strathern, eds. 1980. *Nature, Culture and Gender*. Cambridge: Cambridge University Press.

Malkki, Liisa H. 1997a. "News and Culture: Transitory Phenomena and the Fieldwork Tradition." In *Anthropological Locations: Boundaries and Grounds of a Field Science*, ed. A. Gupta and J. Ferguson, 86–101. Berkeley: University of California Press.

———. 1997b. "National Geographic: The Rooting of Peoples and the Territorialization of National Identity among Scholars and Refugees." In *Culture, Power, Place: Explorations in Critical Anthropology*, ed. A. Gupta and J. Ferguson, 52–74. Durham: Duke University Press.

Mann, Michael. 1993. *The Sources of Social Power*. Volume 2: *The Rise of Classes and Nation-States, 1760–1914*. Cambridge: Cambridge University Press.

Manser, Bruno. 1996. *Voices from the Rainforest: Testimonies of a Threatened People*. Basel and Petaling Jaya (Malaysia): Bruno Manser Foundation and INSAN (Institute of Social Analysis).

Marcus, George E. 1995. "Ethnography of/in the World System: The Emergence of Multi-Sited Ethnography." *Annual Review of Anthropology* 24:95–117.

Marcus, George E., and Michael Fischer. 1986. *Anthropology as Cultural Critique: An Experimental Moment in the Human Sciences*. Chicago: University of Chicago Press.

Margalef, Ramon. 1968. *Perspectives in Ecological Theory*. Chicago: University of Chicago Press.

Marx, Karl. 1977 [1867]. *Capital*. Volume 1. New York: Vintage Books.

———. 1967 [1867]. *Capital*. Volume 1. New York: International Publishers.

———. 1961 [1844]. *Economic and Philosophical Manuscripts of 1844*. Moscow: Foreign Languages Publishing House.

Marx, Karl, and Fredrick Engels. 1947 [1845–46]. *The German Ideology*. New York: International Publishers.

———. 1977 [1845–46]. "The German Ideology." In *Karl Marx: Selected Writings*, ed. David McLellan, 159–91. Oxford: Oxford University Press.

———. 2000. "The German Ideology." Excerpted in *Anthropological Theory: An Introductory History*, ed. R. McGee and R. Warms, 53–66. 2d edition. Mountain View, Calif.: Mayfield.

———. 1927. *Historisch-Kritische Gesamtausgabe*. Berlin and Frankfurt am Mein: Marx-Engels Instituts.

Massey, Doreen. 1993. "Power-Geometry and a Progressive Sense of Place." In *Mapping the Futures: Local Cultures, Global Change*, ed. J. Bird, B. Curtis, T. Putnam, G. Robertson, and L. Tickner, 59–69. London: Routledge.

Maxwell, J. C. 1890. *Scientific Papers*, 2 vols., ed. W. D. Niven. Cambridge: Cambridge University Press.

Mayer, Judith. 1996. "Impacts of the East Kalimantan Forest Fires of 1982–1983 on Village Life, Forest Use, and Land Use." In *Borneo in Transition: People, Forests, Conservation, and Development*, ed. C. Padoch and N. Peluso, 187–218. Kuala Lumpur: Oxford University Press.

Maynard Smith, John. 1982. *Evolution and the Theory of Games*. Cambridge: Cambridge University Press.

McCay, Bonnie J. 1998. *Oyster Wars and the Public Trust: Property, Law, and Ecology in New Jersey History*. Tucson: University of Arizona Press.

McCay, Bonnie J., and James M. Acheson, eds. 1987. *The Question of the Commons: The Culture and Ecology of Communal Resources*. Tucson: University of Arizona Press.

McCracken, Grant. 1988. *Culture and Consumption: New Approaches to the Symbolic Character of Consumer Goods and Activities*. Bloomington: Indiana University Press.

McGoodwin, James R. 1979. "The Decline of Mexico's Pacific Inshore Fisheries." *Oceanus* 22(2):51–59.

———. 1987. "Mexico's Conflictual Inshore Pacific Fisheries: Problems Analysis and Policy Recommendations." *Human Organization* 46(3):221–32.

———. 1990. *Crisis in the World's Fisheries: People, Problems, and Policies*. Stanford: Stanford University Press.

McGuire, Thomas R., and James B. Greenberg, eds. 1993. "Maritime Community and Biosphere Reserve: Crisis and Response in the Upper Gulf of California." Occasional

Paper Number 2. Tucson, Arizona: Bureau of Applied Research in Anthropology, University of Arizona.

Mead, William R. 1968. *Finland*. London: Ernest Benn.

Meade, Adalberto Walther. 1986. *El Distrito Norte de Baja California*. Mexicali, B.C.: Universidad Autónoma de Baja California.

Melucci, Alberto. 1998. "Third World or Planetary Conflict?" In *Cultures of Politics/ Politics of Cultures: Re-visioning Latin American Social Movements*, ed. S. Alvarez, E. Dagnino, and A. Escobar, 422–36. Boulder: Westview Press.

Mercado, S. P., and S. Leanos-G. 1976. "Fish Resources in the Gulf of California." *Natural Resources Journal* 16(3):515–34.

Merchant, Carolyn. 1980. *The Death of Nature: Women, Ecology and the Scientific Revolution*. New York: Harper and Row.

Messer, Ellen, and Michael Lambek, eds. 2001. *Ecology and the Sacred: Engaging the Anthropology of Roy A. Rappaport*. Ann Arbor: University of Michigan Press.

Metcalf, Peter. 1976. "Birds and Deities in Borneo." *Bijdragen tot de taal-, land- en volkenkunde* 132(1):96–123.

Metraux, Alfred. 1942. "A Quechua Messiah in Eastern Peru." *American Anthropologist* 44:721–25.

Michelsen, Karl-Erik. 1995. *History of Forest Research in Finland, Part I: The Unknown Forest*. Helsinki: Finnish Forest Research Institute.

Mikkeli, Heikki. 1992. "Metsäturkki ja sen jurot parturit: Näkemyksiä metsäluonnon ja kansansluonteen suhteesta 1800–1900 luvulla." *Historiallinen Aikakauskirja* 90:200–215.

Miller, Daniel. 1990. "Fashion and Ontology in Trinidad." *Culture and History* 7:49–78.

———. 1995a. "Consumption and Commodities." *Annual Review of Anthropology* 24:141–61.

———, ed. 1995b. *Acknowledging Consumption*. London: Routledge.

———. 1997. *Capitalism: An Ethnographic Approach*. Oxford: Berg.

Milton, Kay. 1996. *Environmentalism and Cultural Theory: Exploring the Role of Anthropology in Environmental Discourse*. London: Routledge.

Mineral Policy Institute (MPI). 1995. "The Porgera File: Adding to Australia's Legacy of Destruction; A Report on the Environmental and Social Impacts of the Porgera Mine, Papua New Guinea." Sydney: MPI.

Mintz, Sidney. 1985. *Sweetness and Power: The Place of Sugar in Modern History*. New York: Penguin.

Mitchell, Timothy. 1988. *Colonising Egypt*. Cambridge: Cambridge University Press.

Mittelman, James, ed. 1997. *Globalization: Critical Reflections*. Boulder: Lynne Reinner.

Moberg, Mark. 1991. "Marketing Policy and the Loss of Food Self-Sufficiency in Rural Belize." *Human Organization* 50(1):16–25.

Moberg, Mark. 1992. *Citrus, Strategy, and Class: The Politics of Development in Southern Belize*. Iowa City: University of Iowa Press.

Moctezuma-Hernández, Patricia, and Juan Alvarez-López. 1989. "Estructura y funcionamiento de la industria pesquera." In *La pesca en Baja California*, ed. Mario Siri Chiesa and Patricia Moctezuma-Hernández, 145–64. Mexicali, B.C.: Universidad Autónoma de Baja California.

Moore, Donald S. 1998. "Subaltern Struggles and the Politics of Place: Remapping Resistance in Zimbabwe's Eastern Highlands." *Cultural Anthropology* 13(3):344–81.

Moore, Donald S., Anand Pandian, and Jake Kosek. 2003. "Introduction: The Cultural Politics of Race and Nature: Terrains of Power and Practice." In *Race, Nature, and the Politics of Difference*, ed. D. Moore, J. Kosek, and A. Pandian, 1–70. Durham: Duke University Press.

Moore, Donald S., Jake Kosek, and Anand Pandian, eds. 2003. *Race, Nature, and the Politics of Difference*. Durham: Duke University Press.

Moran, Emilio F., ed. 1990. *The Ecosystem Approach in Anthropology: From Concept to Practice*. Ann Arbor: University of Michigan Press.

Morley, David, and Kevin Robins. 1995. *Spaces of Identity: Global Media, Electronic Landscapes, and Cultural Boundaries*. London: Routledge.

Munk Christiansen, Peter, ed. 1996. *Governing the Environment: Politics, Policy and Organization in the Nordic Countries*. Copenhagen: Nordic Council of Ministers.

Munn, Nancy D. "Gawan Kula: Spatiotemporal Control and the Symbolism of Influence." In *The Kula: New Perspectives on Massim Exchange*, eds. J. Leach and E. Leach, 277–308. Cambridge: Cambridge University Press.

———. 1986. *The Fame of Gawa: A Symbolic Study of Value Transformation in a Massim (Papua New Guinea) Society*. New York: Cambridge University Press. 1st paperback printing, Durham: Duke University Press, 1992.

Myers, Fred. 1991. *Pintupi Country, Pintupi Self: Sentiment, Place, and Politics among Western Desert Aborigines*. Berkeley: University of California Press.

N.A. 1994. "A Petition from the Lower Porgera River People to Porgera Joint Venture on the 15th Day of December 1994." In file 3–1–6 ("Porgera Alluvial Mining Compensation EPPOR"), in the office of the Porgera mining coordinator, Porgera District Administration, Porgera Station.

Nader, Laura. 1997. "The Phantom Factor: Impact of the Cold War on Anthropology." In *The Cold War and the University: Toward an Intellectual History of the Postwar Years*, ed. Noam Chomsky et al., 107–46. New York: New Press.

Nash, John. 1950. "The Bargaining Problem." *Econometrica* 18:155–62.

National Research Council. 1997. *Environmentally Significant Consumption: Committee on Human Dimensions of Global Change*. National Research Council. Washington: National Academy Press.

Nazarea, Virginia D., ed. 1999. *Ethnoecology: Situated Knowledge/Located Lives*. Tucson: University of Arizona Press.

Needham, Rodney. 1954a. "A Penan Mourning Usage." *Bijdragen tot de Taal-, Land- en Volkenkunde* 110:263–67.

———. 1954b. "Penan and Punan." *Journal of the Malayan Branch, Royal Asiatic Society* 27(1):73–83.

———. 1954c. "Reference to the Dead among the Penan." *Man* 54:10.

———. 1954d. "The System of Teknonyms and Death-Names of the Penan." *Southwestern Journal of Anthropology* 10:416–31.

———. 1965. "Death-Names and Solidarity in Penan Society." *Bijdragen tot de Taal-, Land- en Volkenkunde* 121:58–76.

———. 1972. "Punan-Penan." In *Ethnic Groups of Insular Southeast Asia*. Volume 1: *Indonesia, Andaman Islands, and Madagascar*, ed. Frank M. Lebar, 176–80. New Haven: Human Relations Area Files Press.

Nelson, Hank. 1976. *Black, White and Gold: Goldmining in Papua New Guinea 1978–1930*. Canberra: Australian National University.

Netting, Robert McC. 1965. "A Trial Model of Cultural Ecology." *Anthropological Quarterly* 38:81–96.

———. 1969. "Ecosystems in Process: A Comparative Study of Change in Two West African Societies." In *Ecological Essays: Proceedings of the Conference on Cultural Ecology*, ed. David Damas, 102–12. National Museum of Canada Bulletin no. 230. Ottawa: National Museum of Canada.

———. 1981. *Balancing on an Alp: Ecological Change and Continuity in a Swiss Mountain Community*. Cambridge: Cambridge University Press.

———. 1993. *Smallholders, Householders: Farm Families and the Ecology of Intensive, Sustainable Agriculture*. Stanford: Stanford University Press.

Newman, C. J. 1995. Letter to the Secretary of Mining and Petroleum and the Technical Advisory Committee, Water Resources Board, October 27, 1995. In "Porgera Alluvial Compensation Report," by C. Newman and E. Piawi, in "Submission by the Department of Mining & Petroleum." DMP files.

Nicholls, Neville. 1993. "ENSO, Drought and Flooding Rain in South-East Asia." In *South-East Asia's Environmental Future: The Search for Sustainability*, ed. H. Brookfield and Y. Byron, 154–75. Tokyo and Kuala Lumpur: United Nations University Press and Oxford University Press.

Nicolaisen, Johannes. 1976a. "The Penan of Sarawak: Further Notes on the Neo-Evolutionary Concept of Hunters." *Folk* 18:205–36.

———. 1976b. "The Penan of the Seventh Division of Sarawak: Past, Present and Future." *Sarawak Museum Journal* 24(45)(n.s.):35–61.

———. 1978. "Penan Death-Names." *Sarawak Museum Journal* 26(47)(n.s.):29–41.

Nietschmann, Bernard. 1973. *Between Land and Water: The Subsistence Ecology of the Miskito Indians, Eastern Nicaragua*. New York: Seminar Press.

Nita, Albert K. 2001. "New Power Structures and Environmental Management: Evidence from Porgera Gold Mine." In *Mining in Papua New Guinea: Analysis and Policy Implications*, ed. B. Y. Imbun and P. A. McGavin, 157–72. Waigani, NCD: University of Papua New Guinea Press.

Nyerges, A. Endre, and Glen Martin Green. 2000. "The Ethnography of Landscape: GIS and Remote Sensing in the Study of Forest Change in West African Guinea Savanna." *American Anthropologist* 102(2):271–89.

O'Connor, James. 1998. *Natural Causes: Essays in Ecological Marxism*. New York: Guilford Press.

Odling-Smee, F. J. 1994. "Niche Construction, Evolution and Culture." In *Encyclopedia of Anthropology*, ed. T. Ingold. London: Routledge.

Odum, Eugene P. 1971. *Fundamentals of Ecology*. 3d ed. Philadelphia: Saunders College Publishing.

OECD. 1997a. *Economic Globalization and the Environment*. Paris: Organization for Economic Cooperation and Development.

———. 1997b. *Sustainable Consumption and Production*. Paris: Organization for Economic Cooperation and Development.

Oliver-Smith, Anthony, and Susanna M. Hoffman. 1999. *The Angry Earth: Disasters in Anthropological Perspective*. London: Routledge.

ONERN. 1968. Inventario, Evaluación e Integración de los Recursos Naturales de la Zona del Rio Tambo–Gran Pajonal. Lima: ONERN, Republica del Peru.

Ong, Aihwa. 1987. *Spirits of Resistance and Capitalist Discipline: Factory Women in Malaysia*. Albany: State University of New York Press.

———. 1999. *Flexible Citizenship: The Cultural Logics of Transnationality*. Durham: Duke University Press.

Orlove, Benjamin S., John C. H. Chiang, and Mark A. Cane. 2000. "Forecasting Andean Rainfall and Crop Yield from the Influence of El Niño on Pleiades Visibility." *Nature* 403:68–71.

Ortner, Sherry B. 1974. "Is Female to Male as Nature Is to Culture?" In *Woman, Culture and Society*, ed. M. Rosaldo and L. Lamphere, 67–88. Palo Alto: Stanford University Press.

———. 1984. "Theory in Anthropology Since the Sixties." *Comparative Studies in Society and History* 26:126–66.

———. 1996a. "Resistance and the Problem of Ethnographic Refusal." In *The Historic Turn in the Human Sciences*, ed. T. McDonald, 281–304. Ann Arbor: University of Michigan Press.

———. 1996b. "So, Is Female to Male as Nature Is to Culture?" In *Making Gender: The Politics and Erotics of Culture*, 173–80. Boston: Beacon Press.

Paasi, Anssi. 1996. *Territories, Boundaries and Consciousness: The Changing Geographies of the Finnish–Russian Border*. New York: John Wiley and Sons.

Pacific Agribusiness. 1987. "Social and Economic Impact Study—Porgera Gold Mine." 2 vols. Melbourne.

Painter, Joe, and Chris Philo. 1995. "Spaces of Citizenship: An Introduction." *Political Geography* 14(2):107–20.

Palo, Matti, and Eeva Hellström, eds. 1993. *Metsäpolitiikka Valinkauhassa—yleiskatsaus*. Helsinki: Finnish Forest Research Institute/METLA.

Pálsson, Gísli. 1994. "Enskilment at Sea." *Man* 29(4):901–27.

———. 1998. "The Birth of the Aquarium: The Political Ecology of Icelandic Fishing." In *The Politics of Fishing*, ed. T. Gray, 209–27. London: Macmillan.

Pálsson, Gísli, and Kristin E. Harðardóttir. 2002. "For Whom the Cell Tolls: Debates in Biomedicine." *Current Anthropology* 43 (2):271–301.

Papo, Opis J. 1992. "A Report on the Porgera River Alluvial Goldfield Prepared for Porgera Development Authority," November 1992.

Paré, Luisa. 1986 [1975]. "Caciquismo y Estructura de Poder en la Sierra Norte de Puebla." In *Caciquismo y poder político en el México rural*, ed. Roger Bartra, 31–61. 8th edition. Mexico City: Siglo Veintiuno.

———. 1990. "The Challenges of Rural Democratization in Mexico." *Journal of Development Studies* 26(4):79–97.

Parpart, Jane L. 1993. "Who Is the 'Other'? A Postmodern Feminist Critique of Women and Development Theory." *Development and Change* 24:439–64.

Payne, Robert. 1960. *The White Rajahs of Sarawak*. New York: Funk and Wagnalls.

Peet, Richard, and Michael J. Watts. 1993. "Introduction: Development Theory and Environment in an Age of Market Triumphalism." *Economic Geography* 69:227–53.

———. 1996. "Liberation Ecology: Development, Sustainability, and Environment in an Age of Market Triumphalism." Introduction to *Liberation Ecologies: Environment, Development, Social Movements*, ed. R. Peet and M. Watts, 1–45. London: Routledge.

———, eds. 1996. *Liberation Ecologies: Environment, Development, Social Movements*. London: Routledge.

Peluso, Nancy Lee. 1992. *Rich Forests, Poor People: Resource Control and Resistance in Java*. Berkeley: University of California Press.

Peluso, Nancy Lee, and Michael Watts. 2001. "Violent Environments." In *Violent Environments*, ed. N. Peluso and M. Watts, 3–38. Ithaca: Cornell University Press.

Pemberton, John. 1994. *On the Subject of "Java."* Ithaca: Cornell University Press.

Plant, Roger, and Søren Hvalkof. 2001. "Land Titling and Indigenous Peoples." Technical Paper Series. Inter-American Development Bank. Sustainable Development Department, Indigenous Peoples and Community Development Unit. SDS/IND, August, Washington, D.C.

Poke, Puluku. 1995. "A Brief History of Puluku Poke, Paramount Chief of Lower Porgera." Typescript.

Polanyi, Karl. 1944. *The Great Transformation*. Boston: Beacon Press.

Porgera Joint Venture (PJV). 1996. "Porgera and the Environment: The Porgera Joint Venture's Response to the Mineral Policy Institute's Document 'The Porgera File'." Sydney: Placer Pacific Limited.

Porgera River Alluvial Miners Association (PRAMA). 1995. "The Lower Porgera Compensation Dispute: The Landholders' Submission." In the files of the Porgera Mining Coordinator, Department of Mining, PNG Government. NCD, Papua New Guinea.

Porritt, Vernon L. 1997. *British Colonial Rule in Sarawak, 1946–1963*. Oxford: Oxford University Press.

Povinelli, Elizabeth. 1993. *Labor's Lot: The Power, History and Culture of Aboriginal Action*. Chicago: University of Chicago Press.

Prazniak, Roxann. 2000. "Is World History Possible? An Inquiry." In *History after the Three Worlds: Post-Eurocentric Historiographies*, eds. Arif Dirlik, Vinay Bahl, and Peter Gran, 221–40. Lanham, Md.: Rowman and Littlefield.

Prazniak, Roxann, and Arif Dirlik, eds. 2001. *Places and Politics in an Age of Globalization*. Lanham, Md.: Rowman and Littlefield.

Pringle, Robert. 1970. *Rajahs and Rebels: The Ibans of Sarawak under Brooke Rule, 1841–1941*. Ithaca: Cornell University Press.

Puntenney, P. 1995. "Solving the Environmental Equation: An Engaging Anthropology." In *Global Ecosystems: Creating Options through Anthropological Perspectives*, ed. Pamela Puntenney, 4–18. NAPA Bulletin 15. Washington: American Anthropological Association.

Putu, Benedict. 1999. "Life in Porgera: The Environmental Issue." Manuscript in the hands of its author.

Quesada, Alejandro. 1952. *La pesca*. Mexico City: Fondo de Cultura Económica.

Radcliffe-Brown, A. R. 1952. *Structure and Function in Primitive Society: Essays and Addresses*. New York: Free Press.

Raffles, Hugh. 1999. "'Local Theory': Nature and the Making of an Amazonian Place." *Cultural Anthropology* 14(3):323–60.

——. 2002. *In Amazonia: A Natural History*. Princeton: Princeton University Press.

Ramírez, Jose Carlos, and Roco Guadarrama. 1985. "La Agricultura Comercial." In *Historia General de Sonora. Historia Contemporánea de Sonora 1929–1984*, volume 5, ed. Gerardo Conejo Murrieta, 175–86. Hermosillo: Gobierno del Estado de Sonora.

Rappaport, Roy A. 1968. *Pigs for the Ancestors: Ritual in the Ecology of a New Guinea People*. New Haven: Yale University Press.

——. 1978. "Maladaptation in Social Systems." In *Evolution of Social Systems*, ed. J. Friedman and M. Rowland, 49–71. London: Duckworth.

——. 1979. *Ecology, Meaning, and Religion*. Richmond, Calif.: North Atlantic Books.

―――. 1984. *Pigs for the Ancestors: Ritual in the Ecology of a New Guinea People*. New, enlarged edition. New Haven: Yale University Press.

―――. 1990. "Ecosystems, Populations, and People." In *The Ecosystem Approach in Anthropology: From Concept to Practice*, ed. Emilio Moran, 41–72. Ann Arbor: University of Michigan Press.

―――. 1993. "The Anthropology of Trouble." Distinguished Lecture in General Anthropology. *American Anthropologist* 95(2):295–303.

―――. 1994a. "Disorders of Our Own: A Conclusion." In *Diagnosing America: Anthropology and Public Engagement*, ed. S. Forman, 235–94. Ann Arbor: University of Michigan Press.

―――. 1994b. "Humanity's Evolution and Anthropology's Future." In *Assessing Cultural Anthropology*, ed. Robert Borofsky, pp. 153–67. New York: McGraw-Hill.

―――. 1995. "Foreword." In *Global Ecosystems: Creating Options through Anthropological Perspectives*, ed. Pamela J. Puntenney, 1. NAPA Bulletin 15. Washington: National Association for the Practice of Anthropology, American Anthropological Association.

―――. 1999. *Ritual and Religion in the Making of Humanity*. Cambridge: Cambridge University Press.

Redclift, Michael. 1996. *Wasted: Counting the Costs of Global Consumption*. London: Earthscan Publications.

Reece, R. H. W. 1982. *The Name of Brooke: The End of White Rajah Rule in Sarawak*. Oxford: Oxford University Press.

Renard-Casevitz, France-Marie. 1980. "Contrast between Amerindian and Colonist Land Use in the Southern Peruvian Amazon (Machiguenga Area)." In *Land, People and Planning in Contemporary Amazonia*, ed. F. Barbira-Scazzocchio, 249–55. Cambridge: Cambridge University Centre of Latin American Studies.

Richards, Anthony. 1972. "Iban Augury." *Sarawak Museum Journal* 20:63–81.

―――. 1981. *An Iban-English Dictionary*. Oxford: Clarendon.

Ritchie, James. 1994. *Bruno Manser: The Inside Story*. Singapore: Summer Times.

Robbins, Joel. 1994. "Equality as a Value: Ideology in Dumont, Melanesia and the West." *Social Analysis* 36:21–70.

―――. 1995. "Dispossessing the Spirits: Christian Transformations of Desire and Ecology among the Urapmin of Papua New Guinea." *Ethnology* 34(3):211–24.

―――. 1996. "Between Apology and Compensation: Equivalent Exchange as Ritual Reconciliation among the Urapmin of Papua New Guinea." Paper presented at the annual meeting of the Association of Social Anthropologists of Oceania.

―――. 1999. " 'This Is Our Money': Modernism, Regionalism, and Dual Currencies in Urapmin." In *Money and Modernity: State and Local Currencies in Contemporary Melanesia*, ed. J. Robbins and D. Akin, 82–102. Pittsburgh: University of Pittsburgh Press.

―――. 2003. "Properties of Nature, Properties of Culture: Possession, Recognition, and the Substance of Politics in a Papua New Guinea Society." *Suomen Antropologi* 28(1):9–28.

———. n.d. "Welcome to Big Bush Urapmin: Environment, Development and the Construction of Poverty in a Papua New Guinea Society." Manuscript.

Robinson, N. C. 1960. "Report of Extended Patrol in the Native Mining Area of the Porgera River Western Highlands, August–October, 1960." National Archives of Papua New Guinea, Waigani, NCD, Papua New Guinea.

Rocheleau, Dianne, Mohamud Jama, and Betty Wamalwa-Muragori. 1995. "Gender, Ecology, and Agroforestry: Science and Survival in Kathama." In *Gender, Environment and Development in Kenya: Perspectives from the Grassroots*, eds. B. Thomas-Slayter and D. Rocheleau, 47–74. Boulder: Lynn Rienner.

Rocheleau, Dianne, Barbara Thomas-Slayter, and Esther Wangari. 1996. "Gender and Environment: A Feminist Political Ecology Perspective." In *Feminist Political Ecology: Global Issues and Local Experiences*, ed. D. Rocheleau, B. Thomas-Slayter, and E. Wangari, 3–23. London: Routledge.

———, eds. 1996. *Feminist Political Ecology: Global Issues and Local Experiences*. London: Routledge.

Rolston, Holmes III. 1997. "Nature for Real: Is Nature a Social Construct?" In *The Philosophy of the Environment*, ed. T. Chappell, 38–64. Edinburgh: Edinburgh University Press.

Root, Deborah. 1996. *Cannibal Culture*. Boulder: Westview Press.

Rosaldo, Renato. 1980. *Ilongot Headhunting, 1883–1974: A Study in Society and History*. Stanford: Stanford University Press.

———. 1993/1989. *Culture and Truth: The Remaking of Social Analysis*. Boston: Beacon Press.

Roseberry, William. 1996. "The Unbearable Lightness of Anthropology." *Radical History Review* 65:5–25.

———. 1998. "Political Economy and Social Fields." In *Building a New Biocultural Synthesis: Political-Economic Perspectives on Human Biology*, ed. A. Goodman and T. Leatherman, 75–91. Ann Arbor: University of Michigan Press.

Roseman, Marina. 1991. *Healing Sounds of the Malaysian Rainforest: Temiar Music and Medicine*. Berkeley: University of California Press.

Rousseau, Jérôme. 1990. *Central Borneo: Ethnic Identity and Social Life in a Stratified Society*. Oxford: Clarendon Press.

Rumsey, Alan, and James Weiner, eds. 2001. *Emplaced Myths*. Honolulu: University of Hawaii Press.

Runciman, Steven. 1960. *The White Rajahs: A History of Sarawak from 1841 to 1946*. Cambridge: Cambridge University Press.

Russell, Philip. 1977. *Mexico in Transition*. Austin: Colorado River Press.

Ryan, Peter. 1991. *Black Bonanza: A Landslide of Gold*. South Yara, Victoria: Hyland House.

Sahlins, Marshall. 1963. "Poor Man, Rich Man, Big Man, Chief." *Comparative Studies in Society and History* 5:285–303.

———. 1972. *Stone Age Economics*. Chicago: Aldine.

———. 1976. *Culture and Practical Reason*. Chicago: University of Chicago Press.

———. 1981. *Historical Metaphors and Mythical Realities: Structure in the Early History of the Sandwich Island Kingdom*. ASAO monographs no. 1. Ann Arbor: University of Michigan Press.

———. 1985. *Islands of History*. Chicago: University of Chicago Press.

———. 1992. "The Economics of Develop-man in the Pacific." *Res* 21:3–25.

———. 2000. *Culture in Practice*. New York: Zone Books.

Said, Edward. 1978. *Orientalism*. New York: Pantheon.

Sala, Fray Gabriel A. P. 1897. "Apuntes de Viaje de R.P. Fray Gabriel Sala, exploración de los rios Pichis, Pachitea y Alto Ucayali, y de la Región del Gran Pajonal." In *Coleccion de Leyes, decretos, resoluciones y otros documentos oficiales referentes al Departamento de Loreto Lima*, ed. Carlos Larrabure y Correa. Imprenta de "la Opinión Nacional." 18 volumes, 1905–9.

Salafsky, N. 1994. "Drought in the Rain Forest: Effects of the 1991 El Niño-Southern Oscillation Event on a Rural Economy in West Kalimantan, Indonesia." *Climatic Change* 27:373–96.

Sandin, B. 1980. *Iban Adat and Augury*. Penang: Universiti Sains Malaysia.

Santos-Granero, Fernando. 1987. "Epidemias y sublevaciones en el desarrollo demográfico de las misiones Amuesha del Cerro de la Sal, siglo XVIII." *Histórica* 11(1). Lima: Pontificia Universidad Católica del Perú.

———. 1992. *Etnohistoria de la Alta Amazonía. Del siglo XV al XVIII*. Quito: Editorial Abya-Yala.

Scarborough, Vernon L. 1993. "Water Management in the Southern Maya Lowlands: An Accretive Model for the Engineered Landscape." In *Economic Aspects of Water Management in the Prehistoric New World*, ed. Vernon L. Scarborough and B. Isaac, 17–69. *Research in Economic Anthropology*, Supplement 7. Greenwich,Conn.

Scarborough, Vernon L., J. Stephen Lansing, and John Schoenfelder. 1999. "Water Management and Landscape Transformation in an Ancient Balinese Context." *Research in Economic Anthropology*, 20:299–330.

Schackt, Jon. 1986. "One God—Two Temples." Occasional Publications in Social Anthropology, Number 13. Oslo: University of Olso.

Schäfer, Manfred. 1988. "Ayompari, Amigos und die Peitsche: Die Verflechtung der Ökonomische Tauschbeziehungen der Ashéninka in der Gesellschaft des Gran Pajonal/Ostperu." Doctoral dissertation, Ludwig-Maximilians-Universtät zu München. Amorbach: Selbstverlag.

Scheper-Hughes, Nancy. 1995. "The Primacy of the Ethical: Propositions for a Militant Anthropology." *Current Anthropology* 36(3):409–40.

Schmidt, A. 1971. *The Concept of Nature in Marx*. London: New Left Books.

Schmink, Marianne, and Charles H. Wood. 1987. "The 'Political Ecology' of Amazonia." In *Lands at Risk in the Third World*, ed. Paul E. Little, Michael M. Horowitz, and Endre Nyerges, 38–57. Boulder: Westview Press.

Schneider, David. 1980. *American Kinship: A Cultural Account*. 2d edition. Chicago: University of Chicago Press.

Schroeder, Jeanne L. 1998. *The Vestal and the Fasces: Hegel, Lacan, Property, and the Feminine*. Berkeley: University of California Press.

Schroeder, Richard A. 1993. "Shady Practice: Gender and the Political Ecology of Resource Stabilization in Gambian Garden/Orchards." *Economic Geography* 69(4):349–48.

———. 1999. *Shady Practices: Agroforestry and Gender Politics in the Gambia*. Berkeley: University of California Press.

Schroeder, Richard A., and Krisnawati Suryanata. 1996. "Gender and Class Power in Agroforestry Systems." In *Liberation Ecologies: Environment, Development, Social Movements*, ed. R. Peet and M. Watts, 188–204. London: Routledge.

Scitovsky, T. 1992. *The Joyless Economy*. New York: Oxford University Press.

Scoones, I. 1999. "New Ecology and the Social Sciences: What Prospects for a Fruitful Engagement?" In *Annual Review of Anthropology* 28:479–507. Palo Alto: Annual Reviews.

Scott, Geoffrey A. J. 1979. *Grassland Development in the Gran Pajonal of Eastern Peru: A Study of Soil-Vegetation Nutrient Systems*. Hawaii Monographs in Geography, University of Hawai, Honolulu.

Scott, James. 1985. *Weapons of the Weak: Everyday Forms of Peasant Resistance*. New Haven: Yale University Press.

———. 1990. *Domination and the Arts of Resistance: Hidden Transcripts*. New Haven: Yale University Press.

———. 1998. *Seeing Like a State: How Certain Schemes to Improve the Human Condition Have Failed*. New Haven: Yale University Press.

Scott, L. n.d. Patrol report by reporting officer L. Scott for Porgera Station, Western Highlands District, Lagaip Subdistrict, Porgera Census Division (estimated date: early 1970s).

Secretaría de Medio Ambiente, Recursos Naturales, y Pesca. 1995. *Anuario Estadístico de Pesca*. Mexico City: Mexican Government.

SEMARNP: http://www.semarnp.gob.mx/sspesca/anuario95.htm. 6/13/99. 1996. Anuario Estadístico de Pesca. Mexican Government: SEMARNP: http://www.semarnp.gob.mx/sspesca/anuario96.htm. 6/13/99. 1997. Anuario Estadístico de Pesca. Mexi-

can Government: SEMARNP. http://www.semarnp.gob.mx/sspesca/anua97/anua97
.htm. 6/13/99.

Sen, Amartya. 1995. "Food, Economics, and Entitlements." In *The Political Economy of
Hunger: Selected Essays*, ed. Jean Drèze et al., 50–68. Oxford: Clarendon.

Sesser, Stan. 1991. "Logging the Rain Forest." *The New Yorker*, May 17, 1991, 42–67.

Shaw, William H. 1978. *Marx's Theory of History*. Palo Alto: Stanford University Press.

Shearman, Phil. 2001. "Giving Away Another River: An Analysis of the Impacts of
the Porgera Mine on the Strickland River System." In *Mining in Papua New Guinea:
Analysis and Policy Implications*, ed. B. Y. Imbun and P. A. McGavin, 173–90. Waigani,
NCD: University of Papua New Guinea Press.

Siep, Ludwig. 1996. "The Struggle for Recognition: Hegel's Dispute with Hobbes in
the Jena Writings." In *Hegel's Dialectic of Desire and Recognition*, ed. J. O'Neill, 273–88.
Albany: State University of New York Press.

Sillitoe, Paul. 1986. "Property Ownership in the New Guinea Highlands." *Research in
Melanesia* 10:1–11.

Simpson, Colin. n.d. (ca. 1950). Interview with Joe Searson. Supplied to the author
by William Searson. Handwritten transcription from taped materials collected in
Sydney, April 1950.

Sinclair, James. 1978. *Wings of Gold: How the Aeroplane Developed New Guinea*. Sydney:
Pacific Publications.

Siva Kumar, G. 1991. *Taib: A Vision of Sarawak*. Kuching: Jacamar.

Smalley, Ian F. 1983. "Porgera Genealogical Survey, vol. 2: Angalaini, Mamai, Pakien,
Pianda, Pulumaini." Prepared for Porgera Joint Venture.

Smith, Michael Peter. 2001. *Transnational Urbanism: Locating Globalization*. Malden,
Mass.: Blackwell.

Smith, Neil. 1984. *Uneven Development: Nature, Capital and the Production of Space*. London: Basil Blackwell.

———. 1992. "Contours of a Spatialized Politics: Homeless Vehicles and the Production of Geographical Scale." *Social Text* 33:54–81.

Smith, Neil, and Phil O'Keefe. 1996. "Geography, Marx and the Concept of Nature."
In *Human Geography: An Essential Anthology*, ed. John Agnew, David N. Livingtone,
and Alisdair Rogers, 282–95. London: Blackwell.

Söderqvist, Thomas. 1986. *The Ecologists: From Merry Naturalists to Saviours of the Nation. A Sociologically Informed Narrative Survey of the Ecologization of Sweden, 1895–1975*.
Stockholm: Almqvist and Wiksell International.

Sokal, Alan, and Jean Brichmont. 1998. *Fashionable Nonsense: Postmodern Intellectuals'
Abuse of Science*. New York: Picador.

Solway, J. 1994. "Drought as 'Revelatory Crisis': An Exploration of Shifting Entitlements and Hierarchies in the Kalahari, Botswana." *Development and Change*
25(3):471–98.

Soper, Kate. 1995. *The Problem of Nature*. Oxford: Blackwell.

Spencer, Jonathan. 1997. "Post-Colonialism and the Political Imagination." *Journal of the Royal Anthropological Institute* 3(1):1–19.

Starn, Orin. 1992. "'I Dreamed of Foxes and Hawks': Reflections on Peasant Protest, New Social Movements and the *Rondas Campesinas* of Northern Peru." In *The Making of Social Movements in Latin America*, ed. A. Escobar and S. Alvarez, 89–111. Boulder: Westview Press.

Staski, Edward, and Richard Wilk. 1985. "La cultura material de areas marginales y gente pobre: Un caso del distrito de Toledo, Belice." *Revista Mexicana de estudios antropológicos* 31:155–62.

Steins, Nathalie A. 2001. "New Directions in Natural Resource Management: The Offer of Actor-Network Theory." *IDS Bulletin* 32(4):18–25.

Stewart, Pamela J., and Andrew Strathern. 2002. *Remaking the World: Myth, Mining, and Ritual Change among the Duna of Papua New Guinea*. Washington: Smithsonian Institution Press.

Strathern, Marilyn. 1972. *Women in Between: Female Roles in a Male World, Mount Hagen, New Guinea*. London: Seminar Press.

———. 1980. "No Nature, No Culture: The Hagen Case." In *Nature, Culture and Gender*, ed. C. MacCormack and M. Strathern, 174–222. Cambridge: Cambridge University Press.

———. 1988. *The Gender of the Gift: Problems with Women and Problems with Society in Melanesia*. Berkeley: University of California Press.

———. 1990. "Negative Strategies in Melanesia." In *Localizing Strategies: Regional Traditions of Ethnographic Writing*, ed. R. Fardon, 204–16. Edinburgh: Scottish Academic Press.

———. 1992. *After Nature: English Kinship in the Late Twentieth Century*. Cambridge: Cambridge University Press.

———. 1998. "Divisions of Interest and Languages of Ownership." In *Property Relations: Renewing the Anthropological Tradition*, ed. C. M. Hann, 214–32. Cambridge: Cambridge University Press.

Strogatz, Steven H. 1994. *Nonlinear Dynamics and Chaos*. New York: Addison-Wesley.

Sturgeon, N. 1997. *Ecofeminist Natures: Race, Gender, Feminist Theory, and Political Action*. London: Routledge.

Subak Dlod Blungbang. 1990. *Eka Ilikita: Monografi Subak Dlod Blungbang*. Tegallalang.

Sullivan, M. E., J. Galowa, S. Iddings, and R. Kimbu. 1992. "Porgera Environmental Impacts and Compensation." Prepared for Porgera Joint Venture.

Talyaga, Kundapen. 1984. "Porgera Gold Mine: Socio-Economic Impact Study, Interim Report." Volume 2. *The Porgera District and the Mine Development*. Prepared for the National Planning Office.

Tarling, Nicholas. 1971. *Britain, the Brookes and Brunei*. Oxford: Oxford University Press.

———. 1982. *The Burden, the Risk, and the Glory: A Biography of Sir James Brooke*. Oxford: Oxford University Press.

Taussig, Michael. 1980. *The Devil and Commodity Fetishism*. Chapel Hill: University of North Carolina Press.

Taylor, Charles. 1994. *Multiculturalism: Examining the Politics of Recognition*. Princeton: Princeton University Press.

Technical Advisory Committee (TAC). 1995. "Lower Porgera River Compensation Claim Assessment Hearing by Members of the Government's Technical Advisory Committee (TAC)." Available in Graham Taylor's office.

Thomas, Nicholas. 1991. *Entangled Objects: Exchange, Material Culture, and Colonialism in the Pacific*. Cambridge, Mass.: Harvard University Press.

———. 1994. *Colonialism's Culture: Anthropology, Travel and Government*. Cambridge: Polity Press, in conjunction with Blackwell.

Thomas-Slayter, Barbara, and Dianne Rocheleau. 1995. "Gender, Resources, and Local Institutions: New Identities for Kenya's Rural Women." In *Gender, Environment and Development in Kenya: Perspectives from the Grassroots*, eds. B. Thomas-Slayter and D. Rocheleau, 7–22. Boulder: Lynn Rienner.

———, eds. 1995. *Gender, Environment and Development in Kenya: Perspectives from the Grassroots*. Boulder: Lynn Rienner.

Thompson, E. P. 1966. *The Making of the English Working Class*. New York: Vintage Books.

Tibesar. 1952. "San Antonio de Eneno: A Mission in the Peruvian Montaña." *Primitive Man* 25(1–2):23–39.

Timmerman, Peter. 1996. "Breathing Room: Negotiations on Climate Change." In *Earthly Goods: Environmental Change and Social Justice*, ed. Fen Hampson and Judith Reppy, 221–44. Ithaca: Cornell University Press.

Toledo Maya Cultural Council and the Toledo Alcaldes Association. 1997. *Maya Atlas*. Berkeley: North Atlantic Books.

Touraine, Alain. 1988. *Return of the Actor: Social Theory in Postindustrial Society*. Minneapolis: University of Minnesota Press.

Tsing, Anna Lowenhaupt. 1993. *In the Realm of the Diamond Queen: Marginality in an Out-of-the-Way Place*. Princeton: Princeton University Press.

———. 2000. "The Global Situation." *Cultural Anthropology* 15(3):327–60.

———. 2001a. "Inside the Economy of Appearances." *Public Culture* 12(1):115–44.

———. 2001b. "Nature in the Making." In *New Directions in Anthropology and the Environment*, ed. C. Crumley, with A. van Deventer and J. Fletcher, 3–23. Lanham, Md.: Altamira Press.

Turner, Terrence. 1993a. "From Cosmology to Ideology: Resistance, Adaptation and Social Consciousness Among the Kayapo." In *Cosmology, Values and Inter-Ethnic Contact in South America*, ed. T. Turner, 1–13. South American Indian Studies no. 2, Bennington College, Bennington, Vt.

———. 1993b. "The Role of Indigenous Peoples in the Environmental Crisis: The Example of the Kayapo of the Brazilian Amazon." *Perspectives in Biology and Medicine* 36(3):526–45.

———. 2003. "Class Projects, Social Consciousness, and the Contradictions of 'Globalization.'" In *Violence, the State and Globalization*, ed. Jonathan Friedman, 35–66. New York: Altamira.

Urquhart, Ian A. N. 1950. "More Pleasures and Tribulations in the Ulu." *Sarawak Gazette* 76(1112):278–80, 76(1113):303–7.

———. 1951. "Some Notes on Jungle Punans in Kapit District." *Sarawak Museum Journal* 5(13)(n.s.):495–533.

———. 1956. "Excerpts from Administrative Officers' Reports for the First-Half of 1956: Fourth Division (Baram District Report)." *Sarawak Gazette* 82(1185):292–94.

———. 1957. "Some Kenyah/Pennan Relationships." *Sarawak Museum Journal* 8(10)(n.s.):113–16.

———. 1959. "Nomadic Punans and Pennans." In *The Peoples of Sarawak*, ed. T. Harrisson, 73–83. Kuching: Sarawak Museum.

Vail, John. 1995. "All That Glitters: The Mt. Kare Gold Rush and Its Aftermath." In *Papuan Borderlands: Huli, Duna, and Ipili Perspectives on the Papua New Guinea Highlands*, ed. A. Biersack, 343–74. Ann Arbor: University of Michigan Press.

Valeri, Valerio. 1990. "Both Nature and Culture: Reflections on Menstrual and Parturitional Taboos in Huaulu (Seram)." In *Power and Difference: Gender in Island Southeast Asia*, ed. J. M. Atkinson and S. Errington, 235–72. Stanford: Stanford University Press.

Väliverronen, Esa. 1996. *Ympäristöuhkan anatomia: tiede, mediat ja metsän sairaskertomus*. Tampere, Finland: Vastapaino.

Varese, Stefano. 1973. *La Sal de Los Cerros: Una Aproximación al Mundo Campa*. Lima: Retablo de Papel.

Various Patrol Reports. Read at the National Archives, NCD, Papua New Guinea.

Vasquez-Leon, Marcela. 1993. "The Political Organization of Fishing." In *Maritime Community and Biosphere Reserve: Crisis and Response in the Upper Gulf of California*, ed. Thomas R. McGuire and James B. Greenberg, 27–44. Tucson: Occasional Paper no. 2, Bureau of Applied Research in Anthropology.

Vasquez-Leon, Marcela, Thomas R. McGuire, and Hernan Aubert. 1993. "Suggestions for a Sustainable Fishery." In *Maritime Community and Biosphere Reserve: Crisis and Response in the Upper Gulf of California*, ed. Thomas R. McGuire and James B. Greenberg, 118–34. Tucson: Occasional Paper no. 2, Bureau of Applied Research in Anthropology.

Vayda, Andrew P., and Bonnie J. McCay. 1975. "New Directions in Ecology and Ecological Anthropology." *Annual Reviews in Anthropology* 5:293–306.

Vayda, Andrew P., and B. B. Walters. 1999. "Against Political Ecology." *Human Ecology* 27(1):167–79.

Veber, Hanne M. 1991. "Schools for the Ashéninka: Ethno-Development in the Making." Paper presented to 47th International Congress of Americanists, New Orleans, July 7–11.

———. 1998. "The Salt of the Montaña: Interpreting Indigenous Activism in the Rain Forest." *Cultural Anthropology* 13(3): 382–413.

———. 2001. "Arawakan Messianism: 'Black Hole' in Western Amazonian Ethnography?" Manuscript. Danish Institute for Advanced Studies in the Humanities.

———. 2003. "Asháninka Messianism: The Production of a 'Black Hole' in Western Amazonian Ethnography." *Current Anthropology* 44(2):183–211.

Wagner, Roy. 1977. "Analogic Kinship: A Daribi Example." *American Ethnologist* 4(4):623–42.

Ward, H. J. 1949. "Geological Reconnaissance of the Country Between Mount Hagen and Mongureba, Central Highlands District, Mandated Territory of Papua New Guinea." Photocopy of typescript supplied to author by William Searson.

Wallerstein, Immanuel. 1974. *The Modern World System I: Capitalist Agriculture and the Origins of the European World-Economy in the Sixteenth Century*. New York: Academic Press.

Warrilow. 1981. Report on a visit to Porgera filed with the Assistant Secretary (Major Projects), Department of Minerals and Energy, PNG Government. In the possession of the author.

Watson, James B. 1969. "Review: 'Pigs for the Ancestors: Ritual in the Ecology of a New Guinea People'." *American Anthropologist* 71:527–29.

Watson, James, ed. 1997. *Golden Arches East: McDonalds in East Asia*. Stanford: Stanford University Press.

Watts, Michael J. 1983a. "On the Poverty of Theory: Natural Hazards Research in Context." In *Interpretations of Calamity from the Viewpoint of Human Ecology*, ed. K. Hewitt, 231–62. Boston: Allen and Unwin.

———. 1983b. *Silent Violence: Food, Famine and Peasantry in Northern Nigeria*. Berkeley: University of California Press.

———. 1983c. "The Political Economy of Climatic Hazards: A Village Perspective on Drought and Peasant Economy in a Semi-Arid Region of West Africa." *Cahiers d'Études Africaines* 89–90, 23(1–2):37–72.

———. 1998. "Nature as Artifice and Artifact." In *Remaking Reality: Nature at the Millennium*, ed. B. Braun and N. Castree, 243–68. London: Routledge.

———. 2000. "Political Ecology." In *A Companion to Economic Geography*, ed. E. Sheppard and T. Barnes, 257–74. Oxford: Blackwell.

Watts, M. J., and H. G. Bohle. 1993. "Hunger, Famine and the Space of Vulnerability." *GeoJournal* 30(2):117–25.

Weiner, Annette B. 1992. *Inalienable Possessions: The Paradox of Keeping-While-Giving*. Berkeley: University of California Press.

Weiner, James. 1991. *The Empty Place: Poetry, Space, and Being among the Foi of Papua New Guinea*. Bloomington: Indiana University Press.

White, Leslie A. 1949/1969. *The Science of Culture: A Study of Man and Civilization*. New York: Farrar, Straus and Giroux.

Wilk, Richard. 1983. "Little House in the Jungle: The Causes of Variation in House Size Among Modern Kekchi Maya." *Journal of Anthropological Archaeology* 2(2):99–116.

———. 1987. "The Search for Tradition in Southern Belize: A Personal Narrative." *America Indigena* 47(2):77–95.

———. 1989. "Houses as Consumer Goods: Social Processes and Allocation Decisions." In *The Social Economy of Consumption*, ed. Ben Orlove and Henry Rutz, 373–406. Lanham, Md.: University Press of America.

———. 1991. *Household Ecology: Economic Change and Domestic Life Among the Kekchi Maya of Belize*. Tucson: University of Arizona Press, and DeKalb: Northern Illinois University Press.

———. 1993. "Consumer Goods as Dialogue about Development: Colonial Time and Television Time in Belize." In *Consumption and Identity*, ed. J. Friedman, 97–118. Chur, Switzerland: Harwood Academic.

———. 1994. "Colonial Time and TV Time." *Visual Anthropology Review* 10(1):94–102.

———. 1995. "Learning to Be Local in Belize: Global Systems of Common Difference." In *Worlds Apart: Modernity Through the Prism of the Local*, ed. D. Miller, 110–33. London: Routledge.

———. 1996. *Economies and Cultures: Foundations of Economic Anthropology*. Boulder: Westview Press.

———. 1997. "Emerging Linkages in the World System and the Challenge to Economic Anthropology." In *Economic Analysis Beyond the Local System*, ed. Richard Blanton, Peter Peregrine, Deborah Winslow, and Thomas Hall, 97–108. Monographs in Economic Anthropology, no. 13. Lanham, Md.: University Press of America.

———. 1998. "Emulation, Imitation, and Global Consumerism." *Organization and Environment* 11(3):314–33.

Wilkinson, R. J. 1959. *A Malay-English Dictionary*. 2 vols. London: Macmillan.

Wilson, H. Clyde. 1969. "Review: 'Pigs for the Ancestors: Ritual in the Ecology of a New Guinea People.'" *Journal of Asian Studies* 28(3):658–59.

Wilson, Rob. 2000. *Reimagining the American Pacific: From* South Pacific *to Bamboo Ridge and Beyond*. Durham: Duke University Press.

Wilson, Rob, and Wimal Dissanayake, eds. 1996. *Global-Local: Cultural Production and the Transnational Imaginary*. Durham: Duke University Press.

Wolf, Eric R. 1972. "Ownership and Political Ecology." *Anthropological Quarterly* 45:201–5.

———. 1982. *Europe and the People without History*. Berkeley: University of California Press.

———. 1990. "Facing Power." *American Anthropologist* 92(3):586–96.

———. 1996. "Global Perspectives in Anthropology: Problems and Prospects." In *The Cultural Dimensions of Global Change: An Anthropological Approach*, ed. Lourdes Arizpe, 31–43. Vendôme, France: UNESCO.

———. 1999a. *Envisioning Power: Ideologies of Dominance and Crisis*. Berkeley: University of California Press.

———. 1999b. "Cognizing 'Cognized Models'." In "Ecologies for Tomorrow: Reading Rappaport Today," ed. A. Biersack, a "contemporary issues forum." *American Anthropologist* 101(1):19–22.

Wolff, Janet. 1997. "The Global and the Specific: Reconciling Conflicting Theories of Culture." In *Culture, Globalization and the World System*, ed. Anthony King, 161–73. Minneapolis: University of Minnesota Press.

World Rainforest Movement and Forests Monitor, Ltd. 1998. *High Stakes. The Need to Control Transnational Logging Companies: A Malaysian Case Study*. Montevideo, Uruguay: World Rainforest Movement; Ely, U.K.: Forests Monitor, Ltd.

World Rainforest Movement and Sahabat Alam Malaysia. 1990. *The Battle for Sarawak's Forests*. 2d edition. Penang: World Rainforest Movement and Sahabat Alam Malaysia.

Worsley, Peter. 1968. *The Trumpet Shall Sound: A Study of "Cargo" Cults in Melanesia*. New York: Schocken.

Worster, Donald. 1990. "The Ecology of Order and Chaos." *Environmental History Review* 14:1–18.

———. 1995. "Nature and the Disorder of History." In *Reinventing Nature: Responses to Postmodern Deconstruction*, ed. Michael E. Soule and Gary Lease, 65–85. Washington: Island Press.

Wynne, Brian. 1996. "May the Sheep Safely Graze? A Reflexive View of the Expert-Lay Knowledge Divide." In *Risk, Environment and Modernity: Towards a New Ecology*, ed. S. Lash et al., 27–43. London: Thousand Oaks; New Delhi: Sage.

Wynne-Edwards, V. C. 1965. "Self-Regulating Systems in Populations of Animals." *Science* 147:1543–47.

Zarzar, Alonso. 1989. "Apo Capac Huayno Jesus Sacramento." *Mito, utopía y milenarismo en el pensamiento de Juan Santos Atahualpa*. Lima: CAAAP.

Zerner, Charles. 1994. "Through a Green Lens: The Construction of Customary Environmental Law and Community in Indonesia's Maluku Islands." *Law and Society Review* 28(5):1079–1122.

———, ed. 2003. *Culture and the Question of Rights*. Durham: Duke University Press.

Zimmerman, Michael E. 1994. *Contesting Earth's Future: Radical Ecology and Postmodernity*. Berkeley: University of California Press.

Contributors

Eeva Berglund received her doctorate in anthropology from Cambridge University and currently writes for academic and nonacademic audiences on environmentalism, technoscience, and identity politics. She is the author of *Knowing Nature, Knowing Science* (1998), *Ethnographies of Conservation: Environmentalism and the Distribution of Privilege* (coedited with David G. Anderson [2003)].

Aletta Biersack is professor of anthropology at the University of Oregon. She is the editor of *Ecologies for Tomorrow* (1999), *Papuan Borderlands* (1995), and *Clio in Oceania* (1991).

J. Peter Brosius is associate professor, Department of Anthropology, and director of the Conservation and Community Lab at the University of Georgia. He is the author of *After Duwagan? Deforestation, Succession, and Adaptation in Upland Luzon, Philippines* (1990).

Michael R. Dove is the Margaret K. Musser Professor of Social Ecology and professor of anthropology at Yale University. He has carried out research in West Kalimantan, Indonesia, in Central Java, and in Pakistan on human use of tropical forests and grasslands, the political dimensions of natural disaster and resource degradation, indigenous environmental knowledge, and contemporary and historical environmental relations.

James B. Greenberg is Senior Research Anthropologist in the Bureau of Applied Research in Anthropology at the University of Arizona. He is the author of *Santiago's Sword: Chatino Peasant Religion and Economics* (1981), *Blood Ties: Life and Violence in Rural Mexico* (1989), and he is coeditor of the *Journal of Political Ecology*.

Søren Hvalkof is an anthropologist who is currently a senior consultant at the Nordic Agency for Development and Ecology. He is the coauthor of *Liberation Through Land Rights in the Peruvian Amazon* (2002) and *Land Titling and Indigenous Peoples* (2002).

J. Stephen Lansing is professor of anthropology at the University of Arizona and Research Professor at the Santa Fe Institute. He is the author of *Evil in the Morning of the World: Phenomenological Approaches to a Balinese Community* (1974), *The Three Worlds of Bali* (1983), *Priests and Programmers: Technologies of Power in the Engineered Landscape of Bali* (1991), and *The Balinese* (1994).

Gíslí Pálsson is professor of anthropology at the University of Iceland. Among his books are *Nature and Society: Anthropological Perspectives* (1996, coedited with Philippe Descola) and *The Textual Life of Savants: Ethnography, Iceland and the Linguistic Turn* (1995).

Joel Robbins is associate professor of anthropology at the University of California, San Diego. He is the author of *Becoming Sinners: Christianity and Moral Torment in a Papua New Guinea Society* (2003) and coeditor of the *Journal of Anthropological Theory*.

Vernon L. Scarborough is professor of anthropology at the University of Cincinnati. His current research includes studies of water management in Belize and Guatemala; he has also worked in the Argolid, Greece, and in Bali, Indonesia.

John W. Schoenfelder is research associate of the Cotsen Institute of Archaeology at the University of California, Los Angeles. His research has explored the development of states and coexisting institutions in Bali and in Hawaii.

Richard Wilk is professor of anthropology and gender studies at Indiana University. He is the author of *Economies and Culture: Foundations of Economic Anthropology* (1996), *Household Ecology: Economic Change and Domestic Life Among the Kekchi Maya in Belize* (1991), and *The Anthropology of Media*, coedited with Kelly Askew (2002).

Index

Library of Congress Cataloging-in-Publication Data
Reimagining political ecology / edited by Aletta Biersack and
James B. Greenberg.
p. cm. — (New ecologies for the twenty-first century)
Includes bibliographical references and index.
ISBN-13: 978-0-8223-3685-3 (cloth : alk. paper)
ISBN-10: 0-8223-3685-5 (cloth : alk. paper)
ISBN-13: 978-0-8223-3672-3 (pbk. : alk. paper)
ISBN-10: 0-8223-3672-3 (pbk. : alk. paper)
1. Political ecology. 2. Human ecology. I. Biersack, Aletta.
II. Greenberg, James B. III. Series.
JA75.8.R43 2006
304.2—dc22   2006011045